Gilbert William Child

Church And State Under the Tudors

Gilbert William Child

Church And State Under the Tudors

ISBN/EAN: 9783337004606

Printed in Europe, USA, Canada, Australia, Japan

Cover: Foto ©ninafisch / pixelio.de

More available books at **www.hansebooks.com**

CHURCH AND STATE

UNDER THE TUDORS

PRINTED BY
SPOTTISWOODE AND CO., NEW-STREET SQUARE
LONDON

CHURCH AND STATE

UNDER THE TUDORS

BY

GILBERT W. CHILD, M.A.

EXETER COLLEGE, OXFORD

'*Look unto the rock whence ye are hewn, and to the hole of the pit whence ye are digged*'—Isaiah li. 1

LONDON
LONGMANS, GREEN, AND CO.
AND NEW YORK: 15 EAST 16th STREET
1890.

PREFACE

A NEW book on a subject on which so much has been already written may seem to call for an apology. I think, however, that there are several reasons why such a book may be acceptable.

A very large amount of new material for the history of the sixteenth century has been brought to light in recent years by the publication of State papers, ambassadors' letters, and other original documents which were formerly but little known. Much of this, it is true, has been worked up into many volumes by learned and able writers, to whom I am greatly indebted; but of these, some are works read almost exclusively by students *ex professo*, and many others, from the extent of ground which they have to cover, are too voluminous for ordinary readers: some, too, are written with so strong a party bias as to mislead rather than guide those who consult them.

Again, any one whose reading has not been confined to recent works on English Church history, can hardly help remarking that the change of view in the new, as compared with the older, books, is often so great that it is scarcely an exaggeration to say that, in the popular delineations of the subject, the lights and shadows seem almost to have changed places within the memory of living men. In such a state of things, it is not easy to believe that the last word has yet been spoken, and it becomes interesting to inquire which of these diverse presentations accords best with the facts.

The relations of Church and State form one very important and interesting branch of Church history, and it is to the purpose of illustrating this single portion of the subject that the following pages are devoted; where I may seem to have strayed into others, it has been with the purpose of throwing light upon this. For the ordinary facts of the history I have had recourse to recent and accredited historians—to Hallam, Bishop Stubbs, Mr. Froude, Mr. Green, and others. The Introductory Sketch is taken mainly from Bishop Stubbs and Dr. Hook. But for the main portion of the work I have gone, wherever possible, to original sources; by which I mean, not necessarily matter never published before, but the speeches, letters, and deeds of the actors in the events narrated, or of their coadjutors and contemporaries.

The Notes in Appendix I. consist mainly of extracts from contemporary documents in support or illustration of statements made in the text; and I have added also an Appendix of some of the more important Statutes of the period, in order that my readers may be able to judge to some extent, by the veritable Acts of the State, how far it did or did not occupy the position which I have ventured to assign to it. This I have felt it necessary, from considerations of space, to compress more than I could have wished. It remains for me to express my thanks to those from whom I have received encouragement or help, and especially to the officials of the State Paper Office, to whom I fear I must have been sometimes troublesome, but who have been invariably most kind and helpful; and, among them, particularly to the late Mr. Selby, whose loss is so widely felt. Above all, I must thank my old friend, the Rev. C. W. Boase, Fellow and Librarian of Exeter College, who has most kindly helped me throughout, and supplied me with many illustrations out of his stores of historical learning; and also the Rector and Fellows of the College, who have allowed me the unrestricted use of their valuable library.

CONTENTS

CHAPTER I

INTRODUCTION

	DATE	PAGE
Object of the Book—The Relations between Church and State	—	1
In Saxon Times	—	2
Courts, and Law administered by them	—	3
The Church older than the State—Consequent Foreign Origin of Church Law	—	4
Norman Conquest	—	5
Develops still further the Foreign Elements	—	6
Effect of the Character of the Kings—Rivalry between Church and State	—	8
Unity of the Western Church until the Reformation	—	9
Its Independent Position depended on its Unity	—	10

CHAPTER II

INTRODUCTION (*continued*)

Historical Sketch from Henry II. to Henry VIII

	PAGE
Increase of Power of the Church—Four Parties in the State, viz., the King, the Baronage, and the Church, and, subsequently, the People	13
Tendencies to Divisions in the Church—Held in check by the Papal Authority	15
Sources of the Power of the Clergy	16

	DATE	PAGE
Ideal of the Papacy	—	17
Development of its Power	—	18
The Church in England—the Daughter of the Church of Rome	—	19
Papal Power in England—Not less than elsewhere, but greater	—	20
Depression of the Papacy after Boniface VIII.—Anti-papal Legislation of the Plantagenets and subsequent Kings coincident with it	—	21
Papal Power considerable throughout it—Illustrations of this	—	22
Reign of Richard II. (Wycliffe)	—	29
Statute of Præmunire	1393	30
Reign of Henry IV.	—	31
He hangs an Archbishop, and is not censured	1405	32
Council of Pisa	1409	33
Reign of Henry V.—Council of Constance—Election of Martin V.—Revival of the Papacy—Its Effect in England	1414 1417	34 34
Dean Hook's Theory	—	36
Church in England Papal throughout	—	37
The Anti-papal Legislation	—	38
The Relation of the English Clergy to the Papacy and the Crown respectively	—	39
The Papal Power in France and elsewhere—Social and Moral Influence of the Clergy	—	40

CHAPTER III

REIGN OF HENRY VIII

	DATE	PAGE
Characteristics of the Tudor Times—General Ferment of Ideas	—	44
Conditions under which Henry VIII.'s Statesmen worked	—	45
Peculiarities of the Reformation in England—Thomas Cromwell	—	46
What he learnt from Wolsey	—	48
His Aims	—	49
The Præmunire—Its Effect on the Clergy and the Laity respectively	—	50
Character of Henry VIII.	—	51
King-worship in the Sixteenth Century	—	53
Low Moral Standard of the Time	—	54
Position of the Church at the Accession of Henry VIII.	—	55

CHAPTER IV

REIGN OF HENRY VIII (*continued*)

	DATE	PAGE
Murder of Hun	1513	58
Case argued before the King—Henry's Speech on the Occasion	—	59
Unpopularity of the Clergy—Henry's Divorce affords the immediate Occasion of the Breach with Rome . . .	—	60
Primâ facie Henry was right	—	61
Different Views of the Papal Dispensation	—	62
Character of Clement VII.—How Henry became a Reformer	—	63
Rise of the Divorce Question—Parliament	1529	64
Its important Acts—Henry's Proclamation	1530	65
Submission of the Clergy	1531	65
Important Acts—Limiting the Privilege of the Clergy . .	1532	66
Petition of Convocation against the Annates—Complaint of the Commons against the Clergy	1532	66
Petition of the Clergy against recent Acts—Surrender of Convocation	—	67
Comments of Chapuys on the Work of the Session . . .	—	68
Bishop Stubbs's account of the Mediæval Theory of Church and State	—	69
Henry, Pope of England—Protest and Death of Archbishop Warham—Parliament not always submissive . . .	—	70
Statute of Appeals . . . . April 5th,	1533	71
Convocation pronounces Katherine's Marriage null . .	—	71
Coronation of Anne Boleyn, June 1st—Date of her Marriage .	—	72
Act for the Submission of the Clergy—Act against Payment of Annates—Act against Payment of Peter's Pence, &c.—The Supremacy Act	1534	73
Convocation Petitions for a Translation of Scripture—The Archbishop changes his Title	—	74
Act for the Oath to the Succession—Attainder of Fisher and More—Act of Supremacy	—	75
Made Henry Pope	—	77
Cromwell becomes Vicegerent—Fisher and More beheaded—Paul III. excommunicates Henry—First Visitation of the Monasteries	1535	78
Act for Review of Ecclesiastical Laws—Act for Dissolving Smaller Religious Houses—Dissolution of Parliament of 1529—New Parliament and Convocation—Fall of Anne Boleyn	—	78

	DATE	PAGE
Cromwell takes his seat as Vicar-General	1536	79
First Articles of Religion—Parliament dissolved . . .		80
Cromwell's Injunctions		80
Act of Proclamations—Act for making Bishops by Letters Patent—Dissolution of the Abbeys—Act of Six Articles .	1539	80
History of this Act	—	81
The Part taken in it by Convocation	—	83
Bonner takes out a Commission from the King . . .	—	84
Act for the Dissolution of the Marriage with Ann of Cleves—Act concerning Christ's Religion—Execution of Cromwell—Henry marries Catherine Howard	1540	85
Proclamation for a Bible in every Church	1541	86
Omission of the Pope's Name from Service-Books—Attainder of Catherine Howard and Lady Rochford	1542	86
Bill for Bishops' Chancellors to marry—History of this Measure	—	87
Publication of the King's Book—Reformation of Service-Books—An Act for the Advancement of True Religion . .	1543	88
Modification of the Six Articles—Act for Review of Ecclesiastical Laws renewed—Publication of the King's Primer—	1544 1545	89 90
Heresy Act disappears in the Commons (Note) . . .	—	90
Colleges and Chantries, &c., delivered up to the King—Married Doctors of Law (Chancellors) to exercise Jurisdiction—Attainder of Duke of Norfolk and Lord Surrey—Death of Henry VIII.	—	90

CHAPTER V

REIGN OF HENRY VIII.—SUMMARY

Separation from Rome complete in Henry's Reign—The Five Acts which accomplished it	—	91
Paul III.'s Excommunication completes it on the opposite side—Changes in Doctrine and Ritual slight, but not non-existent—Not such as to satisfy the Protestants . .	—	92
Church in England entirely revolutionised—Henry's Anglican *via media*—Marillac's Estimate of the Result . . .	—	93
Judgment of it by the Roman and Protestant Parties . .	—	94
Value of these Judgments—Archbishop Bramhall's Judgment	—	95
Small Share of Convocation in Henry's Legislation . .	—	96
It disclaims all Share in it up to 1532 inclusive—Its Share in the Legislation of 1534	—	9

	DATE	PAGE
Subsequently presided over by Cromwell, and entirely helpless	—	98
The Reasons of this	—	100
The Clergy had many Enemies—Their only Ally was the Pope—He was worse than none—Character of Clement VII.—Complete Subservience of Convocation	—	101

CHAPTER VI

REIGN OF EDWARD VI

	DATE	PAGE
Cromwell's System of Government—Depended upon a constant Alliance between King and Parliament	—	103
Henry himself felt this on certain Occasions—But least in the Government of the Church	—	104
Condition of Parties at Henry's Death	—	105
The Fall of the Howards—Left the Reactionary Party without Leaders	—	107
Moderate Man helpless in Revolutionary Times	—	108
Importance of Religious Questions throughout Europe—Lord Hertford and Sir William Paget overcome the Reactionary Party—Identification of the Progressive Party with the Protestants	—	109
Reaction of the last Years of Henry's Reign had embittered both Parties	—	110
Bishops take out Commissions—Issue of Edward VI.'s Injunctions and of the Book of Homilies—A Royal Visitation announced—Bonner and Gardiner sent to the Fleet	1547	111
Meeting of Parliament (November)—Revolutionary Measures—Repeal of the Act of Proclamations	—	112
Convocation—Its Petitions—Issue of the first English Prayer Book—Its Significance	1549	114
Different Views of the Intentions of those who issued it	—	116
Progress of Protestant Opinions—Authors of the two Prayer Books the same	—	117
Question of Cranmer's Sincerity—Rapid Progress of Opinions during Revolutionary Times—Gardiner an Instance	—	118
Change of Opinions not necessarily Knavery	—	119
Rebellions in Yorkshire, Devonshire, and Norfolk—Misgovernment of the Council	—	120
Fall of Somerset—The Protestant Faction still remains in power	—	121

	DATE	PAGE
Publication of the Ordinal—Bishop Heath sent to the Fleet—Bishopric of Westminster dissolved—Ridley made Bishop of London	1550	122
Hooper's Contention about the Vestments—Reasonableness of Bucer and Peter Martyr—Establishment of John a Lasco's Congregation in London—Publication of Ridley's Injunctions—Deprivation of Gardiner, Heath, and Day.	1551	123
Robbery of the Bishop's Lands and continued Misgovernment of the Council—General Distress and Discontent—Change of Religion not the Principal Cause . . .	—	124
Execution of the Duke of Somerset—Preparation of the Forty-two Articles—Revision of the Prayer Book . .	—	125
Dispute as to the Authority of the latter—Change of Doctrine in it	—	126
The Homilies and the *Reformatio legum ecclesiasticarum*—Northumberland's Conspiracy to change the Succession .	—	127
Edward himself enters into it—Cranmer's Conduct in the matter	—	128
Changes in the Position of the Church in Edward's Reign—In its relation to the State far less than in Henry's—Greater Independence of Parliament	—	130
Great Changes in Ritual—Doctrinal Changes greater in Fact, but not in Principle, than under Henry	—	131
Popular Effect of Changes in Ritual greater than of any other	—	132

CHAPTER VII

REIGN OF MARY

Collapse of Northumberland's Conspiracy—Mary's previous Life	—	134
Her short-lived Popularity—Finds herself Supreme Head—Restoration of the Deprived Bishops	—	136
Meeting of Parliament—Repeal of the whole of Edward's Ecclesiastical Legislation—Henry VIII.'s Ritual restored—Possible Popularity of these Changes	—	137
Cranmer, Ridley, and Latimer sent to the Tower—Spanish Marriage determined on—Its Unpopularity . . .	—	138
Its Advantages and Disadvantages	—	139
Mary's Aim the Restoration of the Roman Church—Her Statesmen and Advisers all differ, both from herself and from each other	—	140
The Commons remonstrate against the Spanish Match—Sir Thomas Wyatt's Rebellion	—	143

CONTENTS

	DATE	PAGE
Execution of the Dudleys—Elizabeth sent to the Tower	—	144
Mary's Letter to Bonner—Commissions to eject seven Bishops	—	145
This done by the Supremacy only—Marriage Bill passed—Gardiner's Bills rejected	—	146
Parliament dissolved (May 5)—Marriage of Philip and Mary (July)—Their Characters	1554	147
Bonner's Visitation—Discontent	—	148
Parliament meets (November)—Reverses the Attainder of Cardinal Pole—Repeals the Anti-papal Legislation of Henry VIII.—Refuses to restore the Church Lands	—	149
Reconciliation with the Church (Nov. 30)—Parliament refuses to exclude Elizabeth from the Succession, to Repeal the Præmunire, or the Mortmain Acts—Rejects a Regency Bill in Philip's favour, and is dissolved (January)—Mary's Success	1555	150
Its Limits—Unsatisfactory to herself	—	151
She commences a Persecution	—	152
Gardiner's, Bonner's, and Pole's Shares in it respectively	—	153
Character of Pole	—	154
Convocation in Mary's Reign—Its Doings	—	155
Is overshadowed by Pole's Synod—Pole obtains a Warrant under the Great Seal to permit to assemble it	—	156
Arbitrary Character of Mary's Proceedings—Remonstrances against them from unlikely quarters	—	158
Mary's single-minded Fanaticism—Her Conduct to Cranmer and Gardiner respectively	—	159
Not accounted for by their Conduct in regard to her Mother's Divorce—Gardiner's Reaction probably due to Cromwell's Policy	—	160
Character of Gardiner	—	161
Character and Later History of Cranmer	—	162
Character of Mary	—	171
Effects of her Persecution	—	172
Death of Mary	—	174

CHAPTER VIII

REIGN OF ELIZABETH

General Rejoicing at Elizabeth's Succession	—	175
Another Ecclesiastical Revolution—Cecil, Elizabeth's Chief Adviser	—	176
Changes before the Meeting of Parliament slight	—	177

xvi   CHURCH AND STATE UNDER THE TUDORS

	DATE	PAGE
Revision of Edward's second Prayer Book—Meeting of Parliament and Convocation (January)	1558 1559	178 178
Changes in the Views of Convocation between 1549 and 1559	—	179
This Convocation more independent than any of the Century —Unanimously Roman—The Vicar of Bray and the Bishop of Llandaff Types of the Clergy of the time . .	—	180
Proceedings of Parliament	—	181
Acts of Supremacy and Uniformity—Their Effect . . .	—	182
Convocation ignored—Disputation at Westminster—Elizabeth's first Ecclesiastical Commission—Her Interview with the Marian Bishops	—	184
They refuse the Oath, excepting Kitchin of Llandaff, and are deprived—Bonner committed to the Marshalsea—Oath of Supremacy exacted from the Clergy . . .	—	185
Very few refuse—Probable Reasons why the Bishops refused	—	186
Matthew Parker made Archbishop of Canterbury . . .	—	188
His Consecration	—	189
The Queen's Visitation and Injunctions.	—	190
The Beginning of Difficulties with Scotland—Scotland as much a Foreign Country as France	—	192
Elizabeth's Foreign Relations	—	193
Mary Stuart as a Rival—Philip of Spain, Elizabeth's only Ally	—	194
Elizabeth's temporising Policy	—	195
Removal of Roods and Images	—	197

CHAPTER IX

REIGN OF ELIZABETH (*continued*)

Parliament meets, and also Convocation—Defenders of the Pope's Authority subjected to Præmunire	1562	199
Revision of Edward's Articles	—	200
Attempt of Convocation to do away with the Habits, &c.—Nearly succeeds—Humble Protestation appended to its Acts	—	201
More Commissions issued by the Queen under 1 Eliz. Ch. I. —Re-establishment of the Dutch Church . . .	—	202
Grindall, Bishop of London, becomes its Superintendent—Calvin's Negotiation with Parker	—	203
Bonner's Lawsuit with Bishop Horne	—	204
Consequent Act of Parliament for the Validity of the Bishops' Consecrations	—	205

CONTENTS xvii

	DATE	PAGE
Personal Supremacy of Elizabeth	—	206
Rise of the Puritans	—	207
Elizabeth's Dislike of them	—	208
Her Bishops mostly sympathise with them	—	209
The Advertisements—State Regulation of Foreign Protestant Churches	1564 1567	210 210
Elizabeth and the Jesuits	—	212
Different Views of her Conduct towards them	—	213
Elizabeth excommunicated	1570	214

CHAPTER X

REIGN OF ELIZABETH (continued)

Change of Policy produced by the Excommunication	—	217
Legislation of the thirteenth year of Elizabeth (13 Eliz. c. 12)	1571	218
Elizabeth's Personal Government of the Church	—	219
Enforcement of Conformity—Deprivation of Cartwright	—	220
Elizabeth's Religious Views	—	221
English Protestantism of the Swiss Type	—	222
Elizabeth and Archbishop Grindall	—	223
Grindall Sequestrated—Religious Differences increasing	—	224
Legislation of XXIII. of Elizabeth and of XXIX of Elizabeth	1581 1587	225
And of XXXV. of Elizabeth	1593	226
Whitgift becomes Archbishop—The Bishops mere Tools of Elizabeth	1583	227
Whitgift an Enemy of the Puritans—Whitgift an extreme Calvinist—Case of Dean Whittingham	1578	228
And of Travers	1584	230
The Martin Marprelate Controversy	1590	233
Bitterness of the Puritans and Harshness of the Bishops	—	234
The Oath *ex officio*—Inquisitorial Character—Trifling Character of the Points in Dispute	—	235
A Moderate Party exists notwithstanding	—	236
Bancroft's Sermon of 'Trying the Spirits' first suggests a Divine Right of Bishops	1588	237
His extreme Doctrine of the Royal Supremacy—Bilson's Perpetual Government of Christ's Church	1591	238
It was the State which persecuted, not the Church	—	240
The Predestinarian Controversy and the Lambeth Articles	—	241

xviii CHURCH AND STATE UNDER THE TUDORS

	DATE	PAGE
Cecil's Letter to Whitgift—The Sabbatarian Controversy arises	1595	242
Elizabeth's high-pressure System	—	243

CHAPTER XI

REIGN OF ELIZABETH—SUMMARY

Elizabeth's exceptional Position	—	244
Her System absolutely Erastian	—	245
The first two Acts of her Reign are passed independently of the Clergy	—	246
Church afterwards governed by the Queen and Council—Instances which show this	—	247
Elizabeth, Pope of England—How qualified for such an Office by Nature and Education	—	250
Peculiar Characteristics of the Church of England mainly due to her—State of Parties during her Reign—Difficulty of her Work	—	254
Her System hard and narrow, but successful nevertheless	—	256

CHAPTER XII

GENERAL SUMMARY AND CONCLUSIONS

Preliminary Sketch—Church not National before the Reformation	—	259
Made National by Henry VIII.	—	262
Henry no Protestant—His Motives in breaking with the Pope	—	263
Difficulty of the Situation—Completeness of the Schism	1534	264
Under Edward the Council rules—The Protestant Faction supreme in the Council	—	266
Rapid Changes in Opinion—Mary's tyrannical Reaction	—	267
Could never have succeeded—Commencement of Elizabeth's Reformation	1559	268
The Clergy have no Share in it	—	269
Elizabeth's Personal Supremacy	—	270
Leads to the Development of Nonconformity	—	
Tudor System completely Erastian	—	271
The Church of England the Creature of the State	—	272
Elizabeth's Divines were Swiss Protestants	—	274
Conclusions to which the History of Church and State under the Tudors leads	—	276

APPENDIX I.

Note I. P. 62.

Evidence as to the Divorce—Chapuys' Despatch to Charles V. . 283

Note II. P. 68.

Despatches from Chapuys, &c. 283

Note III. P. 72.

Probable Date of Anne Boleyn's Marriage—Mr. Pocock's Evidence 288

Note IV. P. 116.

Mr. Pocock on Edward the Sixth's Prayer Books . . 288

Note V. P. 145.

Queen Mary's Letter to Bonner 290
Her Commissions for turning out Edward's Bishops . . . 291

Note VI. P. 233.

Orders in the Church of England 293

Note VII. P. 253.

The Protestantism of Elizabeth and her Advisers 305

Note VIII.

Alleged Corruption of the Clergy in the Sixteenth Century . . 312

APPENDIX II.—STATUTES. . . 320

CHURCH AND STATE UNDER THE TUDORS

CHAPTER I

INTRODUCTION

It is proposed in the present essay to investigate the relations of Church and State in England during the reign of the Tudor sovereigns, with the object of throwing some light upon the respective shares of each in what is commonly known as the 'Reformation settlement.' In order to do this intelligibly it is, however, necessary to give a short account of the state of these relations in far earlier times, and also a slightly fuller one of the position which they occupied during the reign of the Plantagenet and subsequent kings, since in historical as in other investigations into the actual course of facts, however violent may be the contrast which any given state of things may present to that which preceded it, there are constant relations of cause and effect to be discovered between the two. The best, perhaps the only practicable, mode of treating history may be to divide it into periods; but we must ever remember that no given period could have presented the actual phenomena which we see in it had that which preceded it been other than it was.

It is also necessary to give some slight account of the machinery, so to speak, by which in early times the two powers were brought into relation, although this subject is far from being as clear as might be wished.

For this last subject, as well as for the earlier part of my sketch, I shall adopt as my chief guide the report of the late commission on the constitution &c. of the ecclesiastical courts, and therein and mainly the learned appendices to the same by the present Bishop of Oxford.

I. From these, then, we learn that in the early Saxon times a great deal of power, in ecclesiastical as in other matters, lay in the hands of the king. This we should expect from the fact that the Saxons had in those times been but recently converted, and that it must therefore have been largely by the permission or the co-operation of the king that the missionaries were permitted to exercise their functions at all, and so any relations of Church and State were established. We learn, further, that the king's power was by no means accurately defined, and depended in a great measure for its practical effect upon the strength or weakness of character of the individual king for the time being. But the example chosen by the commissioners to illustrate this fact is not an Anglo-Saxon king at all, but Charles the Great, whom they refer to as the type of a strong monarch, and whose influence on ecclesiastical affairs was certainly undeniable. No doubt, however, influence such as his was exercised in its degree by the Anglo-Saxon kings. During the whole of the præ-Norman period the ecclesiastical court appears to have been the court of the bishop, who sat together with the ealdorman, and took, as we might say, the ecclesiastical causes while the latter functionary disposed of the secular, much as in our own day the criminal and civil cases are disposed of by two judges of assize.

The whole account as given in the report has an air of vagueness and uncertainty about it, depending mainly, no doubt, on the scarcity and remoteness of the evidence, but which seems to suggest also, what was doubtless the fact, that the powers of the judges named, no less of the king himself than of the bishop and the ealdorman, though large, were vague and undefined, and partook more of the character of visitorial authority than of strict legal power. Indeed it is abundantly clear that in those early days the 'authority' of any man who from rank, birth, or office had become an important individuality carried with it an amount of actual power, efficient both for good and for evil, which we living in the latter end of the nineteenth century find it difficult adequately to realise.

Beyond the point which we have already indicated, the report does not go in defining the constitution of the courts which administered the law in ecclesiastical cases in those early times, or their mode of procedure.

It does, however, describe the law administered in the ancient English Church as comprising,[1] first, 'a body of canonical law containing the Holy Scriptures, the Creeds, and the canons of general councils, *which were authoritative in the whole of the Western Church*; and, secondly, the decrees of national councils, supplemented in application by the less authoritative manuals of discipline known as Penitentials, by the collections of foreign canons, and by the coincident legislation of Christian kings,' and this is a matter important to be remembered.

The commissioners note further, here as elsewhere in

[1] Report of the above Commission, p. xvii.

this portion of their report, adopting almost verbally the statements made by Bishop Stubbs in his careful and able historical survey constituting Appendix I.,[1] that 'in the historical growth of ecclesiastical judicature in national Churches three principles are involved: (1) the existence of an ecclesiastical law independent of and, in modern states, anterior to the national secular law; (2) the acceptance by the nation of that law, so far as it is of general obligation, as the law of religion of the National Church; and (3) the annexation, by the nation, to the sentence of the law so accepted, under varying limitations, of the coercive power by which alone the sentences can be enforced upon the unwilling.

Now it seems clearly to follow from these three principles (1) that 'the Church' is something anterior to and independent of the nation which accepts it, and (2) that its acceptation by the nation is the act of the nation itself, and, as Lord Penzance rightly says in his own report (p. lxiv.) 'what the sovereign of his own supreme authority with the advice of his Council or Parliament set up and created, the sovereign, with the advice of Parliament, may well alter and amend.'

Hence we must be very careful in this matter to distinguish between 'the Church' and 'the National [2]

[1] Reports xvi.

[2] The term National Church, though susceptible of a distinct meaning, is often so used as to be ambiguous and misleading. If England had adopted the Roman law, or still better for purposes of illustration the Code Napoléon, would it be right to speak of it as a national system of law? Is it not rather the fact that English law differs from the law of other nations which makes it national? And, similarly, if the English nation accepted the Church with its then existing canon law, does it not tend to obscure rather than to illustrate the history of the Church in England to speak of it as the National Church?

Bishop Stubbs states repeatedly and expressly that the Church of England was not even in Anglo-Saxon times merely the religious organisation of the nation, but a portion of a much greater organisation; the exact limits of its relations to foreign Churches were possibly disputable,

Church.' To take the earliest instance, the Church was the Church before the time of Constantine, but it did not, and could not, become the national or (in this case) the imperial Church until his time. Further, the law of the Church is binding on Churchmen as such; it is binding on citizens only so far as it is accepted by the State—so far, that is, as it has been made a part of the law of the State.

II. Proceeding downward, still under the guidance of the commissioners and Bishop Stubbs, we find that in ecclesiastical as in other matters very considerable and very important changes followed upon the Norman conquest. 'That event,' in the words of the commissioners, 'placed the English Church in closer connection than before with the Churches of the Continent, introduced a new school of ecclesiastical administrators, and coincided in time with a revival of the study of civil and canon law.'[1] From this time dates the establishment of the ecclesiastical courts as separate tribunals, of which[2] those now in existence are the legitimate descendants; the creation of a large class of professional ecclesiastical lawyers; and of a system of appeals ultimately to the courts of Rome.

Of the law administered by these courts we are told that while no new code was imposed, the 'episcopales leges' were to be followed so far as they were 'secundum canones.'

Bishop Stubbs believes that 'they were already drawn out and codified *in conformity with the usages of foreign Churches.*'[3] It is to be borne in mind, further, that the Roman canon law was not formally imposed, nor

but the fact of the incorporation was admitted on all sides. Appendix I. p. 23. *See* also previous page *sub fin.*

[1] Report, p. xviii.   [2] Appendix I. p. 27 *sub fin.*
[3] Appendix I. pp. 24-5.

were its provisions permitted to stand where they came into conflict with the statute law of England; yet it served as the groundwork upon which the English Canonists John of Ayton and Lyndwood worked, and a knowledge of it was part of the equipment of an ecclesiastical lawyer. Further, we are told that 'very much of the ecclesiastical law,' after as well as before the conquest, 'was customary;' that the declaration of the law still remained in the mouth of the judge, who 'declared it out of his own knowledge and experience, *without reference to any authoritative text*;' that the judge was either the bishop or his nominee, and before the end of the Conqueror's reign nearly all the sees were filled by 'foreign bishops to whom all that was national and insular in the Church law of England was entirely strange;'[1] that if the judge erred 'his error could be corrected at Rome if the suitor was able to reach the supreme court of Church judicature there;' that the archdeacons, the early substitutes for bishops as judges, were mostly educated at foreign universities. All these taken together make it a difficult matter to resist the conclusion that Roman canon law became practically the Church law of England, except in the few cases in which local custom held its own because it was worth no one's while to upset it, or in those in which it came into actual conflict with the statute law of the State. This conclusion is confirmed by the fact that the procedure in the new ecclesiastical courts, which at first appears to have had a tendency to retain its own præ-Norman form, was after a brief period 'adapted to the customary procedure of the Roman law,'[2] and that a regular system of appeals to Rome was established, which Henry II. and other sovereigns were able to restrain

[1] Appendix I. pp. 24-5.   [2] Appendix I. p. 27.

and modify only to a very limited extent, and that only by pleading a privilege specially granted by the Apostolic See, which excused English subjects from the liability of personal attendance at Rome.[1] Another point which must not be passed over is the fact that for some four centuries, from 1127 to 1534, with slight exceptions and interruptions, the Archbishops of Canterbury held the office and bore the title of legate of the Apostolic See.[2] When the popes had for some time used the institution of legates to exercise active interference in the internal affairs of England, and when not only the kings but on some occasions the primates also had found their so doing inconvenient, and at the same time had failed to prevent it, the latter got over the difficulty by accepting the office for themselves, thus at once adding to their own authority and, without detracting, in appearance at least, from the papal power, lessening the jealousy with which it was regarded when exercised by foreigners. The Archbishop became *legatus natus* instead of *legatus a latere*; but this probably only increased the flexibility of the whole arrangement. The ultimate advantage to the archbishops was, however, a questionable one, since it led in the end to a doubt as to how much of the authority they claimed belonged to them as primate of England and how much as legate of the Pope.[3]

It is hardly necessary to refer in detail to the better-known historical facts which illustrate the more direct and ostensible relations of the Church and the State during this long period. Whenever there was a king weak either in character or in title, then the Church became the predominant power; when the monarch was strong

---

[1] Appendix I. p. 30, *sub fin.*
[2] E.g. Anselm; *see* Appendix I. p. 27.   [3] Appendix I. p. 27.

and his right unquestioned, this predominance became less marked.[1] William, the very type of a strong monarch, had maintained his own supremacy in Church as well as in State; so to almost an equal degree had his able and politic son Henry I.; but the balance had inclined in the other direction by the time that Henry II. was compelled to give up the constitutions of Clarendon, and the power of the State was hopelessly outweighed when John had consented to hold his crown as a fief from the successor of St. Peter. From his time downward not even Edward I. and Edward III. were able to shake off the control of the Church, though they and their successors attempted from time to time, and with more or less success, by measures such as the Acts of Provisors and Præmunire, to restrain it within endurable limits.[2] These and similar measures seem, however, to have had an incurable tendency to fall into abeyance, and during the wars of the Roses, the kings, especially those of the House of Lancaster, were often ready to prop up their own doubtful authority by the powerful help of the clergy, without always considering the price which they had to pay for it.

There was generally, during these ages at least, a constant tendency to a rivalry between Church and State, which not unfrequently deepened into a sharp contention. When the ordinary division of parties became temporarily altered in times in which the State was divided against itself, the Church would side now with one party and now with another, and there was at

---

[1] Appendix I. p. 25.
[2] Appendix I. p. 30, *sub fin.*, wherein Bishop Stubbs defines the object of the statute of *Præmunire* as being to 'prevent the recourse to Rome *upon points which the civil tribunals at home were competent to settle*,' not, as some people seem to fancy, to prevent such recourse altogether.

least one famous instance in which the process was reversed, and the factions of the State succeeded for the moment in arming the different powers of the Church against one another, when Archbishop Langton incurred the censure of the Pope by joining the barons against that most dutiful and exemplary son of the Church King John. But it is just this very fact that a rivalry did exist, during the period now under review, between Church and State, which makes it difficult to attach any meaning which is other than misleading to the phrase 'National Church.' Contending parties *in* the State all ages have seen, and all ages have in a greater or less degree understood; but it is not so easy to understand the existence of a party *against* the State, unless it be one which aims at nothing less than the entire subversion of the State.

The Western Church was and remained until the Reformation one and indivisible, and the very fact that it had, as we have seen, its own laws and its own organisation, and that prior to and independent of the very existence of any nation of modern Europe, was in itself enough to prevent its becoming in any intelligible sense of the word 'national.' It extended into all the nations of Europe, and was national in none of them. Its own laws, its own customs, ceremonies, usages, prevailed throughout its whole extent, and the powers and prerogatives of its officers, and its own claims on the allegiance of mankind, were quite unaffected by the locality in which they chanced at any moment to be exercised. Its ritual, nay, its very language, was the same throughout the world, so that not only a priest in Germany was a priest in Italy, but if a priest travelled from one country to another he could join and officiate in the services of the Church, as Luther did when he made his journey to Italy, in Rome itself and elsewhere. Such differences as did exist in the usages of the Church in different countries were due, no doubt, partly to the different character of the people—emphasised perhaps by the difficulty of communication and consequent rarity of intercourse between Churchmen of distant countries—and partly also to the nature and circumstances of the bargain which the Church had been able to make in each case with the State, and to the character and aim of the ruling powers of the State for the time being.

It will be said, perhaps, that some of the statements which I have now made, carry with them the implication of a considerable degree at least of freedom on the part of the Church from State control, and this is no doubt true; but then it is just because it was not national, and just so far as it was not national, that this independence existed. It would be a thing not only beyond the experience of historians but beyond the conception of political philosophers that two co-ordinate powers, such as the Church and State appeared to be in Plantagenet times, should ever have co-existed in one nation if they had both belonged to that one nation; but it was just because the Church in England was not in truth the Church of England, but was an organic portion of the one great Western Church, and able to carry on its own diplomacy and enter into its own alliances, that it was enabled to occupy the position of independence, and sometimes almost of supremacy, in which we find it. It is this double position of the Church which alone makes intelligible the history of England, and indeed of most other European nations, during the centuries preceding the Reformation. The Church was at once in the nation and not of it; it formed a part of a vast organisation extending throughout—nay even beyond—the civilised world; its officers, while in every nation numbered amongst the great ones of the earth, belonged at the same time to an independent theocratic State, whose sovereign, as such, was the earthly equal of earthly kings at the same time that, as the declared vicegerent of God, he claimed superiority over the highest of them. It was thus, and thus only, that the rivalry between Church and State in so many countries, and in England especially, arose and was maintained. Had the Church been in truth the Church of England it would have been a mere *imperium in imperio*, and would never have been able to hold its own generation after generation and century after century against the State, often represented by powerful and able monarchs such as Henry II. or Edward III. It was just because it was not the Church of England but a mere extension into England of the powerful Western Church, having its rights and its interests and its officers in every nation, and its independent seat of empire at Rome, and thus enabled to enlist one nation against another, or a nation against its own rulers, that it became in a greater or less degree, and for periods varying in different countries, independent of the State, and a rival of the State. Had the Church in England been in truth the Church of England, a Becket or even a Dunstan would have been impossible; it was just because they could fall back upon a foreign power independent of and formidable to the Government of their own country, that those prelates were enabled to treat with their own sovereigns as on equal terms.

No author of repute, however insular his point of view, would venture to write of one of the great religious orders—the Cistercians, say, or the Franciscans, or the

Templars—as a great 'national' order; such a title would be at once recognised as a misnomer. It would be answered that they were in no sense national. They were powerful orders of men, bound by their own rules, subject to their own officers, settled, indeed, in every nation of Europe, and so far—and so far only—bound by the instinct of self-preservation to keep on good terms with the law of the several countries within whose dominions they lived, and by whose protection they enjoyed their possessions, but acknowledging no nationality but that of Christendom as a whole, and deriving their power, their grandeur, and their influence mainly from the very fact that they did acknowledge none. And yet this is but comparing small things with great. If this be true—as surely it is true—of the great religious orders of the Church, much more is it true of the Church herself—the one great nationality, if I may so call it, which those great religious orders owned, the one great mistress and mother whom alone they acknowledged and obeyed.

CHAPTER II

INTRODUCTION (*continued*)

WE may take the cessation of the anarchy which subsisted under Stephen as the point at which to commence our preliminary sketch of the relations of Church and State in England previously to the Tudor times. We cannot but observe that the power of the Church had in the interval since Henry I.'s time largely increased, for we find that, as Mr. Green points out,[1] what Henry II. endeavoured to do in the Constitutions of Clarendon, was little else than to restore the system of William the Conqueror; but that, though he was a strong man, he was unable to accomplish it successfully.

From his time on we find three contending parties in the State—the king, the baronage, and the Church, and somewhat later a fourth, viz. the people, gradually emerging into importance. The last of these, indeed, did not play any great part until the reign of Edward I., from which time, first as represented in Parliament, and afterwards on more than one occasion by insurrection, the people rose gradually into the position of a power which had to be reckoned with, and in the reign of Edward III. and Richard II. they became for a time very formidable. During the interval, the barons and the Church had between them acted as checks upon the power of the Crown, but each of the three had varied in their relations to one another; each two making

---

[1] Green, *History of the English People*, vol. i. p. 165.

common cause against the third as their own interests from time to time persuaded them. Then followed the long agony of the wars of the Roses, and when they were ended a vastly different state of affairs had developed itself. The baronage had almost burnt itself out; not only had it lost its greatest men, but constant battles, defeats, attainders, exiles, and executions had utterly extinguished some of its most powerful families; above all, it had lost its character, and with it its power of revival.[1] The great barons, demoralised by the French wars, had become marauders and mercenaries on a grand scale, more greedy of wealth than of honour, more anxious to increase their own possessions than to do justice or defend right, whether their own or other people's.

The fortunes of the Church, as the subject with which I am more immediately concerned, require more minute examination. Its condition underwent great variation during the long period before us. Its power was somewhat diminished by the end of it, and was soon to undergo a vastly greater diminution; but its decline was not steady or regular, and it is far from being an easy matter to trace the vicissitudes which it underwent, since not only did it ally itself, as we have said, now with one and now with another of the contending parties in the State and outside of it, but it was all the time more or less divided against itself, although its divisions could often suddenly heal up for the purpose of presenting a solid front to a common enemy. It had also always a foreign element in its composition, arising from its intimate relations with the Papacy, the number of foreign ecclesiastics in official positions in England, and from the constitution of the

[1] *Green*, vol. ii. pp. 15-16.

monastic orders, which belonged, as already noticed, to all countries alike.

Almost at the beginning of the period with which we are concerned this division became visible. At the very time when Becket was contending with his sovereign almost on equal terms, Walter de Map, himself a churchman, was working up his portrait, or rather his caricature, of the churchmen of his day in his character of Bishop Golias. Nevertheless, we must remember that it was Becket and not Walter de Map who was the representative churchman of the time. Walter was but the clever literary semi-professional man of the world—a sort of twelfth-century 'Saturday Reviewer,' whose churchmanship just supplied him with enough knowledge *ab intra* to make him a pungent critic, but whose point of view was not that of the man who made history, but of the clever, somewhat cynical bystander; and his pictures those, not of the great portrait-painter, but of the great caricaturist of his day. In those days Church and Crown fought each 'for his own hand,' and, as I have said, almost on equal terms. They sought the alliance; one of the Pope, the other of the baronage; but while the one sought the aid of the Pope as a vassal that of his lord, the other, not always with success, claimed the assistance of the barons as a lord commanding his vassals, and both alike made but little account of the people.

What we are to trace in this chapter is not alone a struggle between the Pope and the Crown, though this is constantly recurring, but there are, besides these two, the barons, the clergy, and the people, all more or less parties to the struggle, and shifting in their alliances between the one side and the other as their particular interests at the time persuade them, and the perplexity of the situation is still further increased by the division of the Church against itself to which I have just referred—the bishops, the monks, and the secular clergy, and from Henry III.'s reign also the friars—all in a greater or lesser degree jealous of one another, and all ready to enter into a temporary alliance with any of the contending parties, whenever by so doing they could obtain an advantage against one or another of their rivals.

The history of the Church, whether as a whole or in England, is one of much complication and difficulty, and is rendered all the more so by the fact that most of those who have written it, have written party pamphlets in the guise of history. The inordinate power which lay in the hands of the clergy during the middle ages, and which had reached its highest point in this country in the very period with which we are now dealing, arose, no doubt, directly or indirectly from three sources, viz.: (1) the supernatural powers with which they were believed to be invested, and which all the recent developments of the Roman faith had tended to increase; (2) the monopoly which they possessed not only of all the learning (in the modern sense of the word) which then existed in the world, but even of those mere rudiments of knowledge, the tools for the acquirement of learning, which we now understand by the term elementary education; and (3) the vows of the monks and the enforced celibacy of the seculars, which at once marked them out as separate from the rest of mankind and welded them together into a caste by themselves. The first of these was an abundant source of wealth; the second was a direct source of power; and the third, while it did not secure them from internal divisions, gave class interests and *esprit de corps*, and so made their wealth and their power dangerous to the State. To these sources of power and influence another has yet to be added. The power of the Papacy was the band which bound together the bundle of sticks, that is to say, which sufficed for a long time to outweigh all the jealousies between regulars and seculars, between monks and friars, between dignified and lower clergy, and to bind the whole sacerdotal order into one vast army, with the Pope for its emperor and generalissimo. That army, extending into and quartered in every civilised country in the world, was at all times ready to obey orders from headquarters, and though bound by ties of natural feeling and considerations of self-preservation, to keep some sort of terms with the civil government of each of them, yet was ready, always in idea, and very commonly also in practice, to sacrifice those feelings and considerations to the supposed higher law imposed upon them by the Church.

The ideal of the Papacy was perhaps the noblest which has ever entered into the heart of man to conceive. According to it, the Pope was to be the High Priest of God and Vicar of Christ, higher than the kings of the earth. He was to sit above the kings of the earth, surrounded by an atmosphere of tranquillity and holiness, and thence was to act as their visitor, moderator, and peacemaker, swayed by no meaner consideration than the desire to carry out the very law of Christ and the spirit of His Gospel, and thus to make in very deed of the kingdoms of the earth the kingdom of God and His Christ. The contrast presented to this lofty ideal by the spectacle displayed to the world in the courts of the Borgias and the Medici—the swinish sensuality of Alexander VI., the all but undisguised paganism of Leo X., the cowardly and pettifogging politics and unabashed lying of

Clement VII.—may suffice to make us wonder that the reaction of the Reformation was not far more sweeping than was actually the case, unless, indeed, we are prepared to re-echo the sentiments of Boccaccio's Abraham. Nevertheless the idea was not without its value. It held its ground, no doubt, more easily in various countries in proportion to their remoteness from the monstrous reality, but it served for many generations to nourish the loyalty of innocent and guileless souls. Just as in our own time we have heard of Irish peasants sending hard-earned Peter's-pence to Rome, in the honest hope of mitigating the rigour of the imprisonment which they were taught that Pio Nono was suffering at the hands of the godless Italian Government, so in the middle age, and even up to the very end of it, to all those quiet, honest, homespun souls who have through all our history made up the staple of the English nation, and constituted the very salt and savour of English religion, the Pope remained as at first, the symbol of all that was at once holy and venerable and orthodox, and the rumours of the actuality of the Curia and court of Rome, which could not but reach their ears from time to time, were put aside as the suggestions of mere wicked malice, or at best as the wild exaggerations of disappointed suitors or angry and unscrupulous partisans.

The development of the papal power as a whole from the stage of that of the great spiritual adviser of kings—confessorial power as I may call it—through that of an authoritative visitor, up to the fully developed supremacy which we find claimed and exercised by Gregory VII. or Innocent III., it is beyond my province to trace. It is sufficient for me to show that there is no ground for the assertion, that when so established it was less in England than elsewhere in Europe. Dean Milman [1] says on this point, 'With all the Teutonic part of Latin Christendom the belief in the supremacy of the Pope was coeval with their Christianity. It was an article of their original creed as much as the Redemption; their apostles were commissioned by the Pope. To him they humbly looked for instruction and encouragement, even almost for permission to advance upon their sacred adventure. Augustine, Boniface, Ebbo, Anschar, had been papal missionaries.' Almost 100 years before Augustine,[2] Pope Innocent I. had put forward a claim to the filial obedience of the Churches planted by Peter and his successors, and in 347 A.D. the Council of Sardica had countenanced the metropolitan claims of Rome. Thus the Church in England was in every sense a daughter of the Church of Rome, or rather was an extension into England of the one great Catholic Church of the West whose metropolitan seat was Rome. And the papal power remained in England, in varying degrees no doubt, but continuously, until it was abruptly ended by the antipapal legislation of Henry VIII.

In the century following Augustine, we find Wilfrid obtaining his episcopal authority from Rome, and Theodorus sent direct from Rome to Canterbury. In the seventh century, Bishop Stubbs tells us, Augustine's succession had almost, if not entirely, died out; and towards the end of the eighth, King Offa set up Lichfield as an archbishopric by papal authorisation, obtained, as he suggests, by a 'liberal tribute;' and from that time, or even earlier, until the 25th of Henry VIII. Peter's-pence continued to be paid to Rome.[3] And so we

[1] *Lat. Christianity*, vol iv. p. 4.   [2] *Milman, op. cit.* vol. i. p. 115.
[3] Stubbs's *Const. Hist.* vol. i. pp. 238, 250, 251.

might go on tracing a constant connection between the Church in England and Rome, and a constant dependence of the former upon the latter through the intervening times, through the era of Dunstan and that of Edward the Confessor down to the Conquest, and from the Conquest to the times with which we are more immediately concerned, and with one only result, that, though not without checks depending upon the personal characters of individual popes or kings, or the political circumstances of the time, the connection becomes closer and the dependence more plainly visible, until we arrive at that remarkable period when John became a vassal of the Holy See and held his kingdom of Innocent III.

From Innocent III. downwards until we come to the age of the Reformation itself, there is not the slightest ground for maintaining that the Church in England was less papal than elsewhere in Europe. It might even be contended with some show of reason that it was more so. Milman quotes as a common saying in the reign of Henry III. that 'England was the Pope's farm.'[1]

The papal character of the Church in England in the century immediately preceding the Reformation is admitted even by Dean Hook,[2] who asserts, however, that up to the pontificate of Martin V. (1417) it had maintained its independence, and had subsisted under a sort of royal supremacy differing little from that established, or, as he would rather say, re-established under Henry VIII. There is no doubt, indeed, that when the papal power revived under Martin V. its renewed vigour was felt in England as well as elsewhere;

---

[1] *Latin Christianity*, vol. vi. p. 235.
[2] *Lives of the Archbishops of Canterbury*, vol. v. p. 100.

but the theory of its previous independence may well be called in question.[1] It seems to rest partly upon the long series of antipapal enactments which extended from the 35th of Edward I. to the 9th of Henry IV., and partly upon the weak and degenerate condition of the papacy during the Avignon 'captivity' and the subsequent schism. Of the latter it may at once be said that it is exactly an instance of what I have stated above, viz. of the variation which took place in the stress of papal power in all ages in direct ratio with the capacity and vigour of the individual Pope for the time being, and in inverse ratio to that of the King, and that it affected other countries equally with England. It is further to be remarked that, as Professor Creighton[2] well observes, the Popes at Avignon were partisans, if not dependants, of France; hence during Edward III.'s wars the feeling against them in England.

With regard to the antipapal statutes, there is somewhat more to be said.

1. The period during which they were placed upon the statute book coincides almost exactly with the period of general papal depression to which I have just referred.

2. They were in a great measure the mere counters which the King of England used in playing his game for power with the barons, the clergy, or the people, or any of these who happened for the moment to be in alliance.

3. They were constantly broken, and as constantly

---

[1] Creighton's *Papacy*, vol. ii. p. 28, who remarks that 'Martin V. exercised a more direct authority over the machinery of the English Church than had been permitted to any pope *since the days of Innocent III.*,' and again that 'his successors had no reason to complain of the independent spirit of the English bishops.'

[2] *Papacy*, vol. i. p. 47.

re-enacted, and mostly accompanied with a pardon for the offenders against them in times past, or with provisoes for rendering them dispensable by the King at his pleasure; and, as a fact, they were used or disused in a perfectly arbitrary fashion.[1]

There were thus causes, both general throughout Christendom and others specially appertaining to England, why the papal power should have reached its lowest point during this period.

It would, nevertheless, be a great mistake to suppose that it was small even then. To give but a few instances of what the popes could do in England, and of what English kings could admit that they could do.[2] Henry III., on one occasion, when in want of money, told his Parliament, October 13, 1252, that *the Pope had given him* an entire tenth of the revenues of the Church of England. Again, years later, the nuncio Raymond raised a tenth for the purpose of a crusade. In Edward I.'s time, Peckham, Archbishop of Canterbury, and William de Wickwar, Archbishop of York, were both appointed by the Pope on his own authority, and the former openly declared that, whatever oaths he had taken, he should feel himself absolved from them if they interfered with his duty to the Pope.[3] Yet, of all the self-relying and independent monarchs who ever reigned in England, Edward I. stands foremost, and Professor Creighton[4] even says that it was under his wise government and patriotic care that 'the spirit of national resistance to the claims of the Papacy to exercise supremacy *in temporal matters* was *first developed.*' 'If they do these things in a green tree, what shall be done in the dry?'

---

[1] *Burnet*, vol. i. pp. 185–6. [2] Hook's *Archbishops*, vol. iii. p. 270.
[3] *Hook*, vol. iii. p. 346. [4] *Papacy*, vol. i. p. 17.

Dean Hook, whose thorough English honesty and candour is constantly making wild work with his preconceived theory of the Church of England, remarks in regard to another prelate of the same reign, Archbishop Winchelsey, that 'he had only the one object, of introducing a novel assumption of papal power which would have reduced the country to a mere province of Rome.'[1] He makes a very similar remark concerning each of the three immediate predecessors of Winchelsey, viz. Archbishops Peckham, Kilwardly, and Boniface, and accounts for the alleged fact by two of them being friars and the third a Savoyard. Winchelsey was none of these, but an Englishman and a secular; and yet Hook constantly speaks of the English bishops as being opposed to the claims of Rome.

Coming now to the reign of Edward II., we find that king actually applying to the Pope, Clement V., to annul the election by the Chapter of Canterbury of Cobham as archbishop, and to provide for the see by nominating Walter Reynolds, the King's own candidate—a proceeding which affords a good example of the mode in which the kings occasionally allied themselves with the Pope, in order to suppress any attempt at independence on the part of the body with whom the election of a bishop nominally lay. In the same reign also, in 1319, two nominations were made to the vacant see of Winchester —one by the King, and another by the Chapter. The dispute was referred to the Pope, John XXII., who rejected both candidates and nominated his own nuncio. The Archbishop sided with the King, and refused to consecrate the Pope's nominee. In the end, however, he had to yield, and permitted his consecration to be performed by the Bishop of London.

[1] Hook's *Archbishops*, vol. iii. p. 408.

The reign of Edward III. is remarkable in many ways in connection with the history of the Church. It was, from the causes already specified, a time of the deepest depression of the papal power; and there were especial causes, as we have seen, why greater hostility should be felt towards it in England than elsewhere. We might therefore expect to find it of very slight account in England. Yet even now, the facts with which we meet are hardly of a kind to justify such an expectation. Throughout the reign the bishops were almost all appointed by papal provision, and though in the latter half of the reign several laws were enacted intended to act in restraint of the Pope's power, yet, as we shall shortly see, the King himself was the first to infringe them.

The period at which we are now arrived is one of very great importance in the history of the Church in England. From the middle of Edward III.'s reign to the close of his successor's, a space of about sixty years, was the time when the papal power in England was subject to more depression and opposition than at any other period between the Conquest and the Reformation. It saw by far the greater part of that long series of antipapal legislation which looked so formidable but effected so little, until, long after it had fallen practically out of use, and was almost forgotten, Henry VIII. suddenly revived it to suit his own purposes, and Chapuys[1] wrote of it to his master that it was a 'law no person in England can understand, and its interpretation lies solely in the King's head, who amplifies it and declares it at his pleasure, making it apply to any case he pleases.' It witnessed also the rise of Wycliffe and the Lollards, that premature birth of

[1] *State Papers*, Feb. 14. 1531.

Protestantism which smouldered on for more than a century, but never obtained the upper hand, and seems to have been almost extinct before the Reformation came. It witnessed also a vast rise in importance of the common people, and last, not least, the first preaching in England of those very socialistic doctrines, which, after a lapse of five centuries, are again making themselves heard among us in forms as crude and impracticable as when John Ball preached them.

The Statutes of Provisors were passed in the 25th and 27th years of Edward III., yet we find this very king on the death of Archbishop Stratford applying to Pope Clement VI. to supersede the election of Bradwardine to the archbishopric and appoint John de Ufford by provision.[1] On Bradwardine's death, almost immediately afterwards, the Pope inserted in the bull appointing Simon Islip his successor the words, 'Per provisionem apostolicam spretâ electione factâ de eo.'[2] This was but a few months before the passing of the first Act of Provisors. On two other occasions at least did Edward III. disregard his own antipapal legislation, viz. first in the case of Stretton, Bishop of Coventry and Lichfield, who was elected at the instance of the Prince of Wales, and rejected by Archbishop Islip as incompetent, when the King and Prince concurred in an appeal to Rome;[3] and again at a later time, when Archbishop Langham was made a cardinal and resided at Avignon, Edward, though compelling him to resign the archbishopric, yet permitted him to retain a prebend at York, the deanery of Lincoln, and some other preferments in England.[4]

[1] Hook's *Archbishops*, vol. iv. p. 103. [2] *Ib.* p. 114.
[3] *Ib.* p. 148. [4] *Ib.* p. 214.

A year of Jubilee was ordered by Pope Clement VI in 1349, shortly after the visitation of the 'black death, on which occasion Edward III. prohibited his subjects from making pilgrimages to Rome. The Pope remonstrated, but to no purpose. The King's conduct was probably prudent, and his wisdom was vindicated by a renewed outbreak of the plague on the Continent, from which England was exempt. In connection with this story Hook remarks that it gave rise to a feeling of doubt in the minds of the English people as to the complete infallibility of the Church, and that from this time forth hostility towards Rome became a predominant feeling among them. This led, he thinks, to two important results, viz. to a determination on the part of the laity to compel the clergy to retire from politics and restrict themselves to their proper calling; and, on the other hand, it converted a large part of the superior clergy into partisans of Rome. For these statements Dr. Hook cites no authority whatever. I conclude, therefore, that they are inferences of his own from the facts adduced.[1]

The former of the two is doubtless true. Such a conclusion would be but the reaction natural under the circumstances. The people, brought up in a belief of the infallibility and almost unlimited power of the Church, would certainly be looking forward—would probably be taught by their priests to look forward—to some judgment of God as likely to fall upon the nation for its neglect of the commands of the Vicar of Christ. None such came; so far from it that as they watched they beheld the plague fall on the nations who had obeyed, and saw themselves, though disobedient, escape. Naturally, like the people of Melita, they changed

[1] *Hook*, vol. x. pp. 126-7.

their minds, though in this case in the opposite direction. They had looked on the Pope as something very like a god. In this belief they had submitted to his ceremonies and his pilgrimages, sometimes even to his exactions. Now they found that he was not a god, and they were ready naturally to conclude that he was an impostor. Whether there was at this time any great change in the feeling of the superior clergy towards Rome seems to me a more doubtful matter. That after this period the bishops were far from being hostile to or even independent of Rome, is admitted by Hook in the passage here referred to, and also stated by Creighton;[1] but the facts as here cited do not seem to bear out Dean Hook's assertion that they had been so previously. In a note on this subject in his 'Life' of Archbishop Stratford he treats it as a mere delusion of modern times to suppose that the English bishops took sides with the Pope. The Pope, he says,[2] was perpetually encroaching on the bishops' rights, and it is therefore unlikely that they should side with him. The argument is a plausible one, and may be taken for what it is worth, but it can hardly avail against the constant individual instances in which the same author mentions primate after primate as a partisan of the Pope. We may fairly argue that however much a bishop, when made, became the Pope's slave, it was mostly or very often to the Pope that he was indebted for being made a bishop at all, and the Pope was at all times almost as much the fountain of honour in the Church as the King was in the State, and with the difference in his favour that promotion in the Church was possible to a man of any nationality, and might be found in any country by the man who

[1] *Papacy*, vol. ii. p. 28. [2] *Hook*, vol. x. pp. 71-2, *note*.

proved himself thoroughly useful to the Head of the Church. We have seen in our own day, in the history of Pius IX. and the Vatican Council, how obedient bishops can be to the Pope, even when that obedience appears to be rendered against their own interests and in derogation of their own offices.

The closing years of Edward's reign, and the whole of that of his successor, were a time of intrigue, faction, insurrection, and confusion generally, in which we find the Church involved as well as the State; and they were especially fruitful in those singular changes of alliance between one and another of the contending parties in the State to which I have already referred.

Simon Langham,[1] on his appointment as archbishop, 1366, solemnly renounced all expressions in the Pope's bull which militated against the royal prerogative, or infringed upon the laws lately enacted, viz., of course, the Acts of Provisors. This is a remarkable fact, for on the one hand it affords something very like a precedent for the famous reservation made by Archbishop Cranmer in his oath of obedience to the Pope, which created so much scandal in 1533, though on the present occasion it seems to have passed without remark; and, on the other, it is almost the direct converse of the declaration of John Peckham in Edward I.'s reign, that whatever oaths he might have taken, he should feel himself absolved from them if they interfered with his duty to the Pope.

At a congress held in Bruges in 1374, Pope Gregory XI. undertook to abstain from reservation on condition that the King should so far relax the provisions of the Acts of Provisors as to permit the aliens at that time in possession of benefices in England to retain them.[2] How

---

[1] Hook's *Archbishops*, vol. iv. pp. 198-9.   [2] *Ib.* vol. iv. p. 253.

far these acts had really effected their professed purpose may be judged from a petition of the Good Parliament (so called) in 1376, in which they affirm ' that the taxes paid to the Church of Rome amounted to five times as much as those levied for the King; that the Pope disposed of the same bishoprics by reservation four or five times, and received each time the firstfruits; that the brokers of the sinful city of Rome promoted for money unlearned and unworthy caitiffs to benefices of the value of a thousand marks, while the poor and learned hardly obtain one of twenty . . . that the Pope's revenue from England alone is larger than that of any prince in Christendom . . . that his collector remits yearly to the Pope 20,000 marks, sometimes more.'[1]

The clergy at the same period complain that ' the tax paid to the Pope of Rome for ecclesiastical dignities doth amount to fourfold as much as the tax of all the profits as appertain to the King by the year of the whole realm.'[2]

The above may serve to represent the condition of the papal power in England in the end of the reign of Edward III. In the intrigues with which its closing years and the whole reign of his successor were filled we find a constant recurrence of change of parties and of alliances between parties. Archbishop Sudbury is attached on the one hand to John of Gaunt, but is also loyal to the Pope, and John of Gaunt himself belongs mostly to the antipapal, but sometimes to the papal party, yet generally has a leaning towards Wycliffe, against whom the Pope is furious.

As in other matters so also in ecclesiastical affairs,

---

[1] Milman's *Lat. Christianity*, vol. viii. pp. 173-4.
[2] Hook's *Archbishops*, vol. iv. p. 256.

the reign of Richard II. is something of a puzzle. No period was more fruitful in antipapal legislation. The Statute of Provisors was renewed and strengthened, the mortmain laws were tightened up, and the great statute of Præmunire in 1393 imposed a penalty of forfeiture of goods on the offence of obtaining bulls or other instruments from Rome.[1]

Yet, all this notwithstanding, Bishop Stubbs[2] tells us 'the statutes against Roman aggressions were multiplied but disregarded, and notwithstanding the schisms in the Papacy the Bishop of Rome drew his revenue and promoted his servants in England as he had done so long.' Lollardism so called spread and increased, but underwent curious vicissitudes. Wycliffe himself, who appeared at the beginning of the reign under the patronage of John of Gaunt and the Princess of Wales, died before the end of it—unmolested, indeed, but having lost his royal patrons, though he had increased his influence among the Commons, and especially the Londoners.[3]

After the disturbances which led to the summoning of the Merciless Parliament in 1388, when many of Richard's lay advisers were condemned and executed, the Archbishop of York (Neville) and the Bishop of Chichester were handed over to the Pope (Urban VI.), and by him translated to Scotch or Irish sees—an indirect equivalent for banishment, and which I notice only to show how at this time it was by the Pope alone that a bishop, even though a traitor, could be punished, for treason was the charge under which their lay confederates fell. Archbishop Courtenay, who was primate during the greater part of the reign, was in no way

[1] Stubbs's *Const. Hist.* vol. ii. p. 507.
[2] *Ib.* p. 492.   [3] *Ib.* p. 464.

remarkable for independence of the Pope. He applied to him for leave to levy a rate on ecclesiastical property to pay the expense of his visitation, and also obtained a bull permitting him to nominate to all such benefices as had by remaining vacant lapsed to the Pope.[1] His own translation from London to Canterbury had also been effected by permission of the Pope.

On this subject Dean Hook[2] remarks that 'notwithstanding the Statute of Provisors the opinion very generally prevailed, and was hardly denied by the Government, that the Pope had the supreme power in what related to translations. The Chapter might elect, but he only could sanction the divorce of a bishop from the see to which in consecration he had been wedded.'

According to the same authority Archbishop Courtenay seems to have inclined much to the papal faction during his later life, though he found it necessary to acquiesce in the passing of the act of Præmunire.

The reign of Henry IV. occupies an almost unique position in relation to ecclesiastical affairs. At home, the Archbishop of Canterbury during the whole reign was Thomas Arundel, brother of the Earl of Arundel, who was one of the foremost of Richard II.'s ministers during his tutelage, but was executed by him in 1347, at which time also the Archbishop was, at the King's request, translated to St. Andrews by Pope Boniface IX. and sent into exile.[3] Arundel had begun his public life by being made Bishop of Ely by papal provision at the age of twenty-two, and he was, while a stern churchman and a bitter persecutor of the Lollards, at least as

---

[1] Hook's *Archbishops*, vol. iv. p. 374.　　[2] *Op. cit.* p. 339.
[3] *Ib.* vol. iv. pp. 50-1.

much devoted to the King as to the Pope—when that king was Henry of Lancaster, the author of the statute De Hæretico Comburendo, which first legalised the slaughter of heretics as such. Antipapal statutes continued to be passed in this reign also, and in one instance at least the penalties of a Præmunire were incurred and exacted, viz. that of William de Lynn, Bishop of Chichester, who, having quarrelled with the Earl of Arundel, procured a citation from the Pope ordering the Earl to appear personally at Rome. Arundel was the chief instigator of the bloody suppression of the Lollards, which marked the closing years of Henry IV.'s reign and the commencement of his successor's.

Another domestic transaction of this reign, important from an ecclesiastical point of view, was the punishment of the rising in the North in the year 1405, under Lords Northumberland and Nottingham, Scrope, Archbishop of York, and others. In this case, for the first time in our history, one measure was dealt out alike to layman and priest, and the Archbishop was treated with the same severity as the rebellious lay lords, and was summarily hanged, as was also, on the renewal of the outbreak three years later, another dignified ecclesiastic, viz. the Abbot of Hales.[1]

It is remarkable that we find no trace of any papal

---

[1] *Green*, vol. i. p. 533. Stubbs's *Const. Hist.* vol. iii. p. 52. Bishop Stubbs speaks of the execution of Archbishop Scrope as a 'judicial murder,' far more inexcusable, as far as the King was concerned, than the assassination of Becket; because Henry IV. was certainly and directly chargeable with the one, while Henry II. was only secondarily and perhaps doubtfully guilty of the other. That it may have been an unwise, as it seems to have been an unpopular act, no one would probably deny; but it is difficult to see why, from the point of view of strict justice, when three or four men appear as the leaders in an insurrection, and are all as such condemned and executed, the execution of one of them is to be stigmatised as a murder for the sole reason that he is a clerk and the others are laymen.

censure or remonstrance as having followed upon this flagrant and unprecedented invasion of the immemorial privileges of the Church; but the Papacy was, as we have seen, at its lowest point of depression; Henry IV., like the succeeding Lancastrian princes, was the dutiful and obedient son of the Church, with whom it did not suit the Pope to quarrel; and he had, besides, purchased a right to some indulgence by granting in the Statute of Heresy some four years before, also for the first time in English history, a licence to the bishops and clergy to put men to death for holding erroneous opinions.

Abroad, the Papacy itself had reached its lowest point in the years immediately preceding the assembling of the Council of Constance. The closing years of the reign of Henry IV. saw the Council of Pisa solemnly depose two rival popes, describing them both as notorious schismatics and heretics, guilty of enormous iniquities and excesses, and annulling their official acts; and following upon this the still further scandal of three popes at once, all arrogating to themselves the super-human dignity of supreme pontiff and vicar of Christ, all denouncing one another as heretics and Antichrists, and all equally debasing and discrediting the character of the Christian Church.

There is in one respect a curious resemblance between the state of things at this time in England, and that which existed in the later years of Henry VIII. after the enactment of the Six Articles, for in both cases there was a hot persecution of heresy instituted by the King, and existing coincidently with a depreciation of the papal and an exaltation of the royal authority. But the difference is far greater than the similarity, for the depression of papal authority was in the one case slight and temporary, in the other deep and permanent; in the one case it arose mainly from the weakness and disgrace of the Papacy itself, in the other from the self-will and determination of the King. Henry IV. persecuted the Lollards chiefly as a matter of policy, because he sought to fortify his precarious tenure of the throne by conciliating the Church, as one of the strongest powers of the State. Henry VIII. persecuted Catholics and Gospellers alike only in carrying out the general scheme of making himself absolute ruler both in Church and State, pope and king at once.

The reign of Henry V., though only nine years in duration, formed a turning-point in ecclesiastical affairs. The King himself, a great soldier, a vigorous governor, a man of strong character, whether for good or for evil, had in him a large element of the fanatic, and the policy which he inherited from his father warned him to stand well with the Church and the priesthood. Within about three years of his accession followed the final acts of the Council of Constance, the deposition of the three scandalous popes, the election of Martin V., and the commencement of the great revival of the Papacy; and following upon it, as might have been expected, the close of the era of antipapal legislation in England, and the gradually more and more complete desuetude of the antipapal laws which remained upon the statute-book.

Throughout what may be called the age of papal depression the English nation had retained its devotion to Christianity and to the Church, mixed up, no doubt, with no small amount of superstition, and would, had it been possible, have retained its loyalty to the Pope also. But the position and conduct of the popes themselves forbade it. When the popes were maintaining an openly dissolute court; when they were throwing aside their impartiality and becoming mere dependants on the Kings of France, the open and hereditary foes of England; when there were two or even three popes, bidding against one another with as little scruple or decency as so many rival brokers; and when all these things took place at Avignon, close to the borders of what was for years together English territory, it was little wonder if, while the English nation retained its old attachment to the Christian religion, it had lost in a great degree its loyalty to the popes. The wonder is not that it retained so little but that it retained so much—that when, at so apparently auspicious a time, the great Wycliffian anti-sacerdotal movement began, the old beliefs should have shown the vitality which they did show; and this will appear even a greater wonder when we come to examine some of the relations which subsisted between clergy and laity and among the clergy themselves. No sooner, however, did the Council of Constance remove the worst scandals, and Martin V. once more figure as a pope whom it was possible for decent people to respect, than the natural conservative feeling of the nation reasserted itself, and for another hundred years it remained the acknowledged duty of a Christian man, king or not, to 'obey the Pope.'

The history of Archbishop Chicheley, famous as the founder of All Souls College in Oxford, may serve to illustrate some of the above remarks. Chicheley, like so many of the great churchmen of the period, was a lawyer by profession. In this character he was retained by the Pope in 1402, and in reward for his services was nominated by papal provision to a prebend in Salisbury, and to a canonry in the collegiate church of Wilton, whenever they should become vacant, and, as Dean Hook says, 'in direct contravention of the law.'[1] He

[1] Hook's *Archbishops*, vol. v. p. 11.

was afterwards promised the bishopric of St. Davids by the King, but, being in Rome at the time when the vacancy occurred, and being desirous to be consecrated by the Pope, the Pope took the opportunity to appoint him by provision and ignore altogether the royal nomination, so that his appointment may be represented as due either to the King or to the Pope. On a subsequent occasion Chicheley was desirous of resigning some of his preferments. It happened, however, that they were held under a dispensation from the Pope, and therefore could only be resigned with his consent. A bull could easily be had, but to introduce it into England would subject him to the penalties of a Præmunire. Hence a royal mandate had to be obtained containing a *non obstante* clause with reference to the statute of Præmunire.

Chicheley also, according to the same authority, set the precedent of confiscating the property of the monasteries for the service of the State.[1] This was, however, in the case of alien priories, which had a natural tendency to raise international difficulties, and which obviously stood on a different footing from others.

It is unnecessary for my purpose to follow this subject to a later date. Even so stout a champion of Anglican independence as Dean Hook gives it up at this point. In commenting on the rebukes administered by Martin V. to Archbishop Chicheley he says: 'Henceforth the Church of England, to the time of the Reformation, was to be accounted only as a branch of the Church of Rome; and at the head of what had hitherto been the national Church was to be, not the Archbishop of Canterbury, but the Bishop of Rome.'[2] Coming from such a

[1] Hook's *Archbishops*, vol. v. p. 43.   [2] *Ib.* p. 103.

quarter, this is a very full admission, and it is no more than is demanded by the actual state of things. From this time on, the presence of a cardinal or a legate or a cardinal-legate in England is almost continuous, and the antipapal statutes, though still in force, and although their repeal was resolutely refused by the Parliament, fall more and more out of use. There is therefore no dispute as to the correctness of the view which Dean Hook gives of the condition of the Church of England between the time with which we are now dealing and the separation under Henry VIII. The question is, whether the facts known to history, some few of which only I have just passed in review, are such as to justify his assertion as to its previous condition of independence; and the only possible answer is that they are not. It is clearly shown that there was throughout the period which I have reviewed a constant and close relation between the ecclesiastical authorities of England and Rome, and that that relation was one of dependence and deference on the part of England, and of authority on that of Rome.

The general tax of the Peter's-pence, trifling as it was in amount, was not trifling as a principle, and still less so as an evidence of the kind of relation subsisting; and this, be it remembered, continued from the remotest period down to the separation. So also did the much more formidable taxation of the clergy, of which I have given several instances above. Again, we find that the appointment of bishops, although it was formally disputed from time to time between the Pope, the King, and the Chapters, lay for the most part in the hands of the King; yet this was not without exception, and even throughout the period of the lowest depression of the papal power, the Pope's consent was still necessary for translation from one see to another, and he was still able to claim the appointment of the successor to any dignitary, bishop or other, who died *in Curia*, as it was called, i.e. while in attendance on the papal court.[1] The one great fact to be alleged on the other side is to be found in the series of antipapal statutes from the reign of Edward III. to Henry V. inclusive; but while the existence of these statutes is strong evidence of the existence of the state of things which they affected to remedy, yet their constant repetition is equally good proof that they failed to remedy it. Had they been efficient they would not have needed repetition, and when at last they ceased to be repeated, it was, as we have seen, not because the papal power had languished, but because it had revived; not because they had effected their purpose, but because their failure to do so had become manifest. The true account of these statutes I take to be something of this kind. In the mutual jealousies which subsisted between the various parties in the State, the power and influence of the Papacy became from time to time an important makeweight, and to the King especially it was oftentimes of great moment to be able to employ it for his own purposes. At the same time papal exactions, oppressions, and interferences were not popular in the nation at large, and were often not relished by one or other party among the Churchmen themselves, who had to pay dearly for the support and influence which the Papacy afforded them. Thus these statutes came to be passed partly to gratify the popular demand for protection against papal oppression, partly to enhance the power of the Crown, which was always exalted in proportion as that of the Pope was depressed.

[1] Hook's *Archbishops*, vol. v. p. 279.

And when they were passed they were, as we have abundantly seen, either employed, or neglected, or the infringements of them condoned, exactly as might suit the convenience of the King or his minister for the time being. The clergy were a very powerful, sometimes the most powerful, body in the State, and it became the interests of the other three parties—the Crown, the Baronage, and the Commons—to enlist them on their own side; while they themselves, on their part, held a divided allegiance. They owed a duty to the Crown and another to the Papacy; and when the two were incompatible, their choice between them was likely to be governed by a more or less enlightened regard to their own corporate interests; and though, as we have seen, these were divided, yet they were probably less so than those of any other party, because their separating interests were those of a few great corporate bodies rather than those of families or individuals. The instances given above of the oaths taken by the primates to the King and the Pope respectively, and of the diverse interpretations given by different primates to the conflicting terms of these oaths, may serve as a good instance of all the three points which I wish to insist upon in regard to the papal power in England, for they show, (1) that the allegiance of the clergy throughout this period was in England, as elsewhere, a divided allegiance; (2) that this division remained a very real and important one even through the period of papal depression; and (3) that its inclination to one side or the other differed from time to time in accordance with the varying circumstances of the times, and with the differing interests, characters, dispositions, and abilities of the kings, the popes, and the prelates concerned.

It is scarcely necessary to go into a comparison between the condition of the papal power in England and in other countries during the period with which we are now dealing. In its main features it was much the same in most countries; i.e. the Papacy was, in spiritual matters, always in theory, and mostly in fact, the supreme authority. In matters temporal the reverse—again as a rule only—was the case; while in those numerous affairs which could not be classed exclusively as temporal or spiritual, there was a constant liability to dispute, and their actual position varied from time to time with the circumstances and the capacities of the contending parties. In France, certainly, taken as a whole, the papal power was less, and that of the kings was greater, than was the case in England from Louis IX., the contemporary of Henry III., down to Francis I., the contemporary of Henry VIII., when the two countries took new departures in this particular, almost in diametrically opposite directions, and Francis I. sacrificed all that remained of the so-called Gallican liberties to the Pope in order to obtain the surrender of the rest to himself, while Henry VIII. absorbed into his own person the authority of pope and king at once.

The further subject of the social and moral influence of the clergy during this period also need not detain us long in this place. It will be necessary to discuss it at greater length in the body of the work; and there is no reason, so far as I can learn, for supposing that it underwent any sudden or marked alteration at any particular epoch. The condition in which it was found when the great dispute with Rome commenced was but the gradually developed result of the slow growth of centuries. It will be sufficient if I adduce the following few statements, all of them from the works of authors themselves clergymen, and none of them disposed to be over-severe judges of the order to which they belong.

Dean Hook says[1] 'the celibacy imposed upon the monks, whether in holy orders or not, had a more demoralising influence upon them than it had upon the secular clergy. The secular clergy took to themselves wives, though in so doing they felt themselves to be lowered in the estimation of their neighbours; but the monks, being in community, could not evade the law in this manner, and the licentiousness of their conduct became proverbial.' Again, he says 'the condemnation of the clergy, regular and secular, is most emphatically proclaimed by the institution of the mendicant orders. The mendicant orders came into existence because in the task of evangelising the people the clergy were unwilling or incompetent to do what the circumstances required. The superior clergy were, as we have seen, absorbed in the world of politics. The inferior clergy were employed in prosecuting rather than instructing their flocks; while those among them who endeavoured conscientiously to discharge the duties of a pastor were involved in a routine of ceremonial observances. The monks were living as country gentlemen, not always of high repute.' Further on in his Life of Archbishop Islip is a noticeable passage.[2] Complaint being made of the abuse of 'benefit of clergy,' and of the inadequacy of the punishment inflicted upon the delinquencies of clerks, the Archbishop says that he and his suffragans are fearful that the abuses (which they, in fact, admit)

---

[1] Hook's *Archbishops*, vol. iii. pp. 44-7.   [2] *Ib.* vol. iv. p. 131.

should turn to the prejudice of—'clerical privilege'! Again, at a later time, in the primacy of Kemp, he tells us[1] that 'every act of legislation in the Church tends to show the low condition of morals among the clergy, and their neglect of duty.' They are charged, besides, with constant quarrelling and litigation with one another, with frequenting taverns, shows, cells of suspected women, and unlawful games. And in general terms he says, speaking of the middle of the fifteenth century, 'It is admitted by all persons and by all parties that the Church from this time and a century before till the age of the Reformation was in point of morals and legislation in a very degraded state.'[2]

Professor Creighton[3] also quotes from Von der Hardt a frightful account of the licentiousness of the clergy, and adds: 'Denunciations to the same effect might be quoted from writers of almost every land. . . . Lamentations over the corruptions of the clergy were not confined to a few enthusiasts: men of high ecclesiastical position and undoubted orthodoxy spoke openly of the abuses which everywhere prevailed.'

Finally, Bishop Stubbs,[4] in a passage to which I will only refer my readers in this place, gives similar evidence.

The same authority has also an interesting passage concerning the effect of the clergy in keeping alive through the darkest period some sparks of learning and education. He says: 'Some forms of intellectual culture were spread everywhere, and although perhaps it would still be as easy to find a clerk who could not read as a layman who could, it is a mistake to regard even so dark a period as the fifteenth century as an age of dense

[1] Hook's *Archbishops*, vol. v. p. 238. [2] *Ib.* p. 289, note.
[3] *Papacy*, vol. i. pp. 262-5. [4] *Const. Hist.* vol. iii. pp. 380-5.

ignorance. In all classes above the lowest, and especially in the clerical class, men travelled both in England and abroad more than they did after the Reformation had suspended religious intercommunion and destroyed the usefulness of ecclesiastical Latin as a means of communication.'

CHAPTER III

REIGN OF HENRY VIII

NOTHING is more difficult, glibly as it is often talked and written of, than successfully to place ourselves in the circumstances of men living in another period of history, or even in another climate or under another government. So vastly do the circumstances of our daily and hourly lives, the atmosphere of the society which we meet, the tone of the books and newspapers which we read, mould every thought which we think and modify every view which we take of the occurrences which surround us, that it is all but an impossibility to judge how those best known to us, or how even we ourselves, would think or speak or act in a set of circumstances widely different from those in which our actual experience has been cast.

The Tudor times are often and justly thought of as being those in which modern history took its rise, in which the great inventions and the great discoveries—the revival of learning, the printing-press, the discovery of America—tended of themselves to evolve great ideas and to develop great men; but when we are discussing the characters and achievements of those great men, we are apt sometimes to underrate the difference between their surroundings and our own—to forget, for instance, that they lived under a 'reign of terror,' as complete as that which has obtained that name in the history of modern France, and far more permanent. It is doubtless this fact, the difficulty which we experience in realising the men of comparatively modern ideas acting under circumstances so very much the reverse of modern, which makes the characters of some of the more distinguished men of that period such a puzzle to us, and which causes them to be painted in such widely different colours, by writers who are far removed from mere prejudice or conscious partisanship.

This is a reflection, the truth of which will strike us more and more as we proceed. The statesmen of Henry VIII.'s reign were men of like passions with ourselves. Had they lived in other times they might have been like the statesmen that have followed them—like Walpole or Pulteney, Chatham or Bute, Pitt, Peel, or Palmerston; but it is surely not too much to say that these modern statesmen would have been very different from what they were, had they lived all their time with a halter round their necks, and worked under a master who, upon almost any displeasure conceived against them, instead of merely accepting their resignation would have ordered them at once to the block. When we perceive the difficulty which a modern statesman finds in preserving a strict integrity, when the price he may have to pay for it is the loss of office and popularity, and the defeat at worst of some cherished plan for the benefit, as he conceives it, of his country, and that loss in most cases a merely temporary one; and when he is left in possession, at the worst, of wealth and friends and high social position, and the prospect of restoration to more than his former greatness by the next turn of the political wheel, can we wonder if Wolsey and Cranmer and Cromwell and Gardiner, when, in addition to all this, the stake for which they played included their own heads and the complete finality which decapitation involves as well, should have failed to maintain on all occasions the high level of an ideal morality?

In studying the history of the Reformation in England, nothing is more necessary than to keep its different stages distinct from one another. We are too apt to think of the Reformation as if it had been all one process, or at least as if some person or persons had deliberately set it going, with a distinct perception of the results to which it was to lead, and had consciously adapted the means employed to the production of those results. Such a notion is not only not true, but is almost the direct reverse of the truth. The many recent additions to our materials for the history of the Reformation in England, all seem to me to point to the conclusion that, of several persons who may be named as the chief agents in bringing it about, the only one who set a distinct object before his eyes and worked constantly for it was Thomas Cromwell; and with him the Reformation of religion was not the object at which he aimed, but was only incidentally connected with it. Cromwell intended to make Henry VIII. absolute master of England, and himself absolute master of Henry VIII.[1] He succeeded in the first object, and the absolutism which he constructed maintained its ground in a greater or less degree as long as there remained a Tudor sovereign to wield it, and even subsisted through more than a generation of Stuart feebleness and triviality. In his second object he very nearly succeeded also, but at last he fell into the error, so often fatal to strong and successful statesmen, of overrating his own power, thinking that what had already done so much could

---

[1] He is said to have boasted that in brief time he would bring things to such a pass that the King, with all his power, should not be able to hinder him. (See Green, *Short Hist.* p. 848.)

surely do a little more—that fortune, who had so often stood his friend, would not desert him just at the last moment; and thus he fell a victim to the tyrant whose will he himself had made irresistible.

The first and greatest distinction, then, of which we are never to lose sight in considering the history of the English Reformation, is that between the separation from Rome and the reformation of doctrine. That these two facts were closely related is true; that many of the same causes which brought about the one also conduced to the occurrence of the other, is also true; but I think that a fair consideration of all the circumstances will tend to show that the connection between them was one which depended upon special circumstances of the times, and not one arising out of the necessity of the case. That this is the true connection between these two important facts, seems to me to be suggested by the different relations in which they stood to one another on the Continent and in England. Thus in Germany and in Switzerland the reformation of doctrine preceded and brought about the separation from Rome. In England the separation from Rome preceded the reformation of doctrine, and contributed to bring it about. Luther professed the utmost deference for the Pope's person and authority long after he had protested against indulgences and had begun to preach justification by faith only.[1] Henry VIII. and his satellites had begun to call the Pope bad names long before they attempted to meddle with the generally accepted doctrines of the Church. Separation from Rome was necessary to the completion of Cromwell's designs; change of doctrine followed as a consequence, partly of the separation itself, partly of the machinery by which

[1] See D'Aubigné, *Ref.* vol. i. p. 287, 3rd edition.

it was accomplished. The time at which Henry and Cromwell chose to separate from Rome on grounds which had nothing to do with doctrine, chanced to coincide with that at which other persons elsewhere were doing the same thing for reasons distinctly doctrinal, and at which doctrinal differences with Rome were rising up all over the civilised world. Hence it became impossible but that the fact of the separation itself should tend to foster the doctrinal differences already growing up in England, though these were in themselves not only not shared by Henry but positively distasteful to him.

Whatever we may think either of the moral characteristics of the man, of the ends for which he worked, or of the means which he employed in pursuing them, it will hardly be denied that the world has seen no bolder statesman than Thomas Cromwell, and few more original; yet, like all so-called original ideas, his were not the spontaneous offspring of his own brain, but were suggested to him in a great degree by the phenomena which he saw around him. Cromwell had been for years Wolsey's confidential man of business; had watched his modes of working from a ground of vantage, and had been employed by him in the business of the suppression of the small monasteries, out of which Wolsey founded his colleges at Oxford and at Ipswich. From all this Cromwell had not failed to learn much. He had seen Wolsey concentrating all the power of the State in the hands of the King, and so indirectly in his own, and he had, further, seen him use his position as cardinal and legate to intercept, as it were, the stream of ecclesiastical administration in its natural course between England and Rome by deciding most of the appeals himself, though always professedly as the

Pope's delegate, and thus concentrating still more completely in his own hands the power of the Church. The state of things which Wolsey had thus brought about as a temporary phenomenon, the result of special circumstances (not absolutely without precedent in earlier times), Cromwell proposed to himself to render permanent and normal. What he proposed he also carried out, and in so doing he effected a revolution both in the civil and ecclesiastical government of the country; but the civil revolution was as nothing by comparison of the ecclesiastical, because the Parliament which acted as a check in the one case became an active ally in the other. The civil revolution was but the establishment of the King as an absolute monarch, and he remained, after all, absolute only by the consent, or we might almost say the connivance, of Parliament. Parliament retained its constitutional position and powers, and Henry VIII. showed on more than one occasion his consciousness that his own power, absolute as it practically was, was so only so long as he could reckon upon that connivance. The ecclesiastical revolution was vastly more thorough and complete, for not only did it increase to a great extent the previously existing power of the State over the Church, but it concentrated this power in the hands of the Crown; it destroyed for ever the double government in ecclesiastical matters which had existed in varying degrees in every state of Europe, and in England itself from the time of Augustine downwards; and above all, by placing a preponderating power in the hands of a lay sovereign and his lay vicar-general, and this not as a matter of mere personal submission but as a matter of law, it invaded the region of hitherto exclusively clerical rights in a manner never before seen in the history of the Christian Church.

The history of the celebrated Præmunire will serve well to illustrate both these propositions. The outline of the well-known story is as follows. After using the statute of Præmunire as an instrument in the overthrow of Wolsey, it seems to have occurred to Henry, or more probably to Cromwell, that it might be further usefully employed for the purpose of improving the position of the Crown. The whole nation, therefore, the clergy first and the laity afterwards, were held to have become involved in the penalties of this law, as having been abettors of Wolsey in his illegal exercise of papal authority; but the course followed with the two classes of offenders was widely different. The clergy were compelled to purchase forgiveness by a heavy payment in money, and, what was of infinitely more importance, by passing in their convocation the famous 'Submission of the Clergy,' whereby they accepted the King as supreme head of the Church, and gave up all claim to legislate for the Church except by his permission and consent. Parliament, on the other hand, showed such a temper that Henry recoiled before it, and, in the words of Chapuys, 'granted the exemption which was published in Parliament without any reservation.'[1]

These few facts speak volumes. They serve to account at once for the widely different measure which Cromwell dealt out to the clergy and to the laity, and, by demonstrating how much more easy it had become to trample on the former than on the latter, may serve as a measure of the little hold which the clergy had retained over the hearts and affections of the people.

[1] *State papers*, Feb. 14, 1531.

Of this fact there is ample evidence at hand, though it would be beside the mark were I to discuss it at the present moment. Unimpeachable contemporary evidence on this subject is afforded by the despatches of Chapuys to the Emperor Charles V., recently published in the volume of State papers for this period (1530–1).

Cromwell did a great work, and narrowly missed doing a far greater. Yet the outcome of his work, as of every man's work, was greatly modified by the nature of the material with which he performed it; and one of the great modifying agents was the personal character of Henry VIII. I will not enter here into the interminable dispute as to how far a great man modifies his age, and how far he is himself modified by it; but I think it must be admitted that, in the whole history of our own country at least, there has been no single man who has fixed so strongly or for so long a time upon its institutions, its laws, its history, its whole subsequent national life, the impress of his own vices, virtues, and even caprices as King Henry VIII. There is no man, also, of whose character more divergent estimates have been formed. It is, indeed, a character most difficult to estimate. He was not in any worthy sense a great man, for there was a vein of pettiness as well as a vein of selfishness running through his character from first to last; but he was a man endowed with great talents and versatility, considerable learning, and withal with a vast amount of courage and force of character of an irregular kind, which made him always a powerful force, but one the direction of which could not be calculated beforehand. We should never forget, in trying to unravel the character of Henry VIII., that the son of Henry VII. was also the grandson of Edward IV. He seems to have inherited some of the virtues and almost all the vices of both. From the Lancastrian Henry he inherited in a great degree the shrewdness, the intellectual ability, the love of learning, and the tenacity of purpose, which had made the latter one of the ablest monarchs that ever sat upon the English throne, and also the hard selfishness and grasping acquisitiveness which had made him one of the most unpopular. From the Yorkist Edward he derived his fine person, his frank soldierlike bearing, his popular manners, but also his sensuality, his want of self-restraint, his profusion, and his caprice. Personal courage on the one hand, and a tendency to cruelty on the other, seem to have come to him almost equally from both. The contrary tendencies of some of the above characteristics and the prominent development of them all seem to account in a great degree for that element of versatility and uncertainty to which we have already drawn attention. If we allow due weight to all of these, and consider, further, the peculiar circumstances in which they found their sphere of action—the early age at which he came to the throne, the sudden change from a somewhat strict subjection to his father to the enjoyment of almost unlimited power in his own hands, the constantly increasing development of the autocratic element in government during his reign, and the difficulties in which his own tyranny and caprice were constantly involving him—we may perhaps be able to reach a fairly accurate conception of Henry's character, and one almost as far removed from the mere brutal, sensual, and capricious tyrant which some historians would have us believe him, as it must be from the politic, patriotic, self-restrained hero which Mr. Froude has persuaded himself to present to us. It is also entirely consistent with such a character, and with his early attainment of autocratic power, that Henry VIII. should have become more arbitrary, more capricious, more unscrupulous, and altogether more unmanageable as age and irresponsible power increased—and both did increase together; and accordingly we find that each of his chief ministers in succession at last fell under his displeasure, and each in successively shorter periods. Wolsey maintained himself for nearly twenty years, Cromwell for ten only. After his fall no minister established the same ascendency over Henry which these had held. Norfolk held the highest position, and he too, after some six years of power, was overthrown, and was saved from the headsman only by the King's own death. It is a significant fact that the only one of Henry's really intimate advisers who continued to be such through the latter half of his reign, and maintained his position to the end of it, was Cranmer—a man who combined beyond a doubt great talents and much learning with many virtues, but also with one capital defect, that he had positively no character at all.

The sixteenth century, not in England alone but throughout Europe, was the golden age of personal government, and it would seem that it was beyond the capacity of human nature to endure the semi-deification which was accorded to all the great sovereigns of that period, without undergoing a process of moral degeneration. In those days kings governed as well as reigned; their will to a very great extent was law, and it was impossible that youths of nineteen or twenty, as were all the three great European monarchs of the period when they ascended their respective thrones, should endure such a trial without damage to their moral nature; and accordingly we find that each one of them succumbed to it. The moral standard of all of them was certainly what we should now consider low; and, low as it was, they failed to live up to it. But it is no more than just to remember, that the standard of the sixteenth century was not that of the nineteenth,[1] and that Henry VIII., though very far from irreproachable, shows favourably in this respect when compared with Francis I., or even with Charles V.

Wolsey's dying speech in regard to Henry has been quoted and eulogised as a striking testimony to the great defect in his character, till even its combined force and accuracy and the pathos of the circumstances which surrounded its utterance, fail to save its iteration from becoming wearisome; but it seems scarcely to have been observed that it is almost equally remarkable as a testimony to the character of the age as to that of the King. 'Rather than want any part of his pleasure he will endanger the half of his kingdom.' What king but a sixteenth-century king would have thus acted? But, again, what minister but a sixteenth-century minister would have submitted to a master so acting, and continued to be his responsible agent and adviser? But no scruple or difficulty on this point ever seems to have

[1] There seems to be an inclination even in some of the best writers of the present age to question this. (See Brewer, *Henry VIII.*) I may have occasion to discuss the subject more fully when I come to the story of the general condition of the clergy. At present I will only refer to a single case, which is, however, so remarkable that the mere possibility of its occurrence marks a condition of public opinion almost inconceivable to ourselves. It is that of Nicholas Udall. This person—of whose excellence as a scholar there is, I believe, no question—was head master of Eton from 1534-43. At the latter date there occurred an inquiry into a robbery at Eton, to which he was accused of being privy. In the course of the investigation a charge was brought against him of nameless immorality in relation to his own scholars. He was not only convicted of this but he *confessed* it; yet a few years afterwards, about 1554, this same man was made head master of Westminster, having in the interval made much interest to be re-appointed to Eton! See Maxwell Lyte's *History of Eton College*, p. 113, and references there given.

occurred to a minister of that age, with perhaps the single exception of Sir Thomas More. 'The King's will' was the *ultima ratio* with ministers, bishops, and judges alike, and the only excuse, however inadequate, for many of the judicial decisions of the period is to be found in the fact that prosecution, when the Crown was prosecutor, was itself equivalent to condemnation.

Henry VIII. came to the throne in the year 1509, at the age of eighteen years. For our present purpose, the early years of his reign, illustrated though they were by the brilliant career of Wolsey, need not detain us long. He found himself in a far better position than any king of England since Edward III. His title was for the time undisputed, and though possible rivals existed the country was in no mood to listen to them. His exchequer was full; his own manners, appearance, and character were all calculated to ensure his popularity, and personally popular he was and continued to be till the end of his reign. The position of the Church at the beginning of his reign was peculiar—in some respects not unlike that of the French Monarchy at the accession of Louis XVI. It apparently retained to the full all its old wealth, grandeur, and power. The Archbishop of Canterbury was Chancellor, the Bishop of Winchester was Secretary, the spiritual peers formed a majority of the House of Lords.[1] The King's own marriage had depended upon a dispensation of the Pope, and within a very few years of Henry's accession, Wolsey—abbot, archbishop, cardinal, and legate *a latere*—became the foremost man, not only in England but in all Europe. The King himself was a professed theo-

---

[1] See this worked out with great skill in Book V. chapter i. of Green's *History*.

logian, and rejoiced in none of his possessions more than in his title of Defender of the Faith.

The antipapal statutes still remained upon the statute book, but they had lain dormant so long as to have been almost forgotten, and Rome obtained its Peter's-pence and its annates just as before. But underneath all this external magnificence there were not wanting signs that all was not sound. The monasteries were hopelessly corrupt, the friars being probably rather worse than the monks; their estates were mismanaged, wasted, and alienated. The men of the new learning were beginning to spread abroad a contempt for shrines and relics, pilgrimages and modern miracles; and above all, the people hated the priests. Morton and Warham had each made an attempt to reform the monasteries and the ecclesiastical courts, but neither was strong enough to succeed; and Wolsey, who possibly might have been, was too fully occupied with the larger and weightier objects of foreign policy to find leisure, or perhaps inclination, to cleanse such an Augean stable. The general corruption of the clergy, and more especially of the monks and friars, is, in point of fact, undeniable. Most of the more recent and better informed historians of this period have been themselves clergymen, and have, either consciously or unconsciously, held a brief for their predecessors; but the ablest and most learned of them have practically had to give up the case. Dean Hook, who makes no secret of his advocacy, and never disguises his prejudices, is nevertheless transparently honest and diligent, and constantly supplies material for the refutation of his own views; but even Dean Hook has to make so many admissions that, for all intents and purposes, he gives up his own case.[1] Bishop Stubbs also, in an elaborate chapter upon 'The Clergy, the King, and the People,' says, in regard to the moral influence of the clergy, that 'the records of the spiritual courts of the middle ages remain in such quantity, and in such concord of testimony, as to leave no doubt of the facts; among the laity as well as among the clergy of the towns and clerical centres there existed an amount of coarse vice which had no secrecy to screen it or prevent it from spreading.'[2] This is no exaggerated statement, and to say, as Canon Dixon does say, 'that no proof of deep corruption has been made good against the English clergy,'[3] is simply to fly in the face of the evidence, not only of satirists and lampooners but of annalists and historians, of records and of law reports.

Such was the state of things when Henry VIII. came to the throne. Of the changes which took place before he left it, the following chapters will contain the record.

[1] Hook's *Archbishops*, vol. vi. p. 229.
[2] Stubbs's *Const. Hist.*, vol. iii. pp. 384-5.
[3] Dixon, *op. cit.* vol. i. p. 86.

CHAPTER IV

REIGN OF HENRY VIII (*continued*)

HENRY VII.'s reign had been one of great quiet and apparent prosperity to the Church. The King had been on good terms with the Papacy, and had, especially in the later years of his reign, been a munificent builder and decorator of churches. His greatest ministers had been great ecclesiastics. Morton and Fox had risen to fame and eminence in his reign, and Wolsey had begun to display those great powers which were soon to make him the most important man in Europe, in the last few years of it.

At the same time we must not suppose that the reverence felt for the Pope by Henry VII. and other contemporary sovereigns was very genuine or deep, or was of a kind which promised any great permanence to his influence in Europe. Thus there is a despatch from Ferdinand and Isabella (the Catholics *par excellence*) to Henry's ambassador, in which they recommend the King to send his contributions to the crusade, either at once in a fleet to be built in England, or else to send the money direct to Rhodes by some person of great trust, 'for if they should send it to the Pope it is certain that he would expend it for some other purpose, and not on account of the said expedition.'[1]

This state of things continued unchanged in its main features through the first half of his son's reign also. Though, as we have seen, there were signs for

[1] Bernard André, *Memorials of Henry VII.*, by Gairdner, p. 414.

those who were wise enough to read them, which might suggest that all was not as sound in the Church as it appeared to be, yet it was not until the divorce question came into agitation that they became visible to ordinary men. Not only was the divorce question the main cause of the fall of Wolsey, but it also led directly to that quarrel with the Pope which brought on the whole antipapal legislation of Henry VIII. and the destruction of the monasteries, and had no little connection with the especial and peculiar form taken by the English Reformation.

One previous occurrence, arising out of the trial of Dr. Horsey, the Bishop of London's chancellor, for the murder of a citizen named Hun, which took place in the years 1513 and 1514, seems to show something both of the strained tone of feeling which subsisted between the clergy and laity, at any rate in London, and also of the extreme sensitiveness of the King in regard to anything which appeared to touch his own prerogative.[1] The case involved the whole question of the liability of clerical felons to the jurisdiction of the ordinary criminal law; it seems to have been taken up warmly by the clergy on one side and the lawyers on the other, and argued with no little acerbity on both sides before the King in person. A certain minority of the clergy, represented on the present occasion by Dr. Standish, afterwards Bishop of St. Asaph, and Dr. Veysey, dean of the Chapel Royal, and afterwards Bishop of Exeter, maintained the view that the clergy might be, and in England had been, amenable to the ordinary criminal courts; but it seems to have been a very small one. The King's remark at the conclusion of the arguments is given by Burnet as follows: 'By the permission and ordinance

---

[1] The story is told at length by Burnet, vol. i. pp. 38-49.

of God, we are king of England, and the kings of England in times past had never any superior but God only. Therefore know you well that we will maintain the right of our crown and of our temporal jurisdiction, as well in this as in all other points, in as ample manner as any of our progenitors have done before our time. And, as for your decrees, we are well assured that you of the spirituality go expressly against the words of divers of them, as hath been showed you by some of our council; and you interpret your decrees at your pleasure; but we will not agree to them more than our progenitors have done in former times.' In this particular instance Henry seems to have thought that he had sufficiently vindicated his authority by having the clerical delinquent brought to the bar, and the case was in the end withdrawn from the jury; but it required the utmost efforts of the Cardinal and the Archbishop of Canterbury to bring about this result, and the state of feeling which existed is plainly shown in a letter of the Bishop of London to Wolsey, in which he says: 'Assured I am that if my chancellor be tried by any twelve men in London, they be so maliciously set *in favorem hæreticæ pravitatis*, that they will cast and condemn any clerk though he were as innocent as Abel.'

It is quite conceivable that had the question of Henry's divorce not arisen, the Reformation in England might have been postponed for some years, for Henry VIII. was essentially an absolutist, and his first bias was, as is well known, in favour not only of Roman doctrine but also of Papal power, and he hated Luther and all his works. But it is not conceivable that if there had been no question of the divorce there would have been no Reformation in England at all. It was impossible but that the great movement which began in Germany and Switzerland and spread with greater or less force, completeness, and permanence over every country in Europe, succeeding best in those which were most akin to England, should have spread to England sooner or later; and, as we have seen, it would find, as it did find, all the elements there which it needed for its success. It required a motive applied to the King himself which should call up all his strongest personal feelings and range them actively against the Pope and the clergy, instead of more or less languidly in their favour as they had previously been, in order to make him the champion and leader of the anti-Church movement instead of its moderator or even suppressor, as in other circumstances he might have been; and just this required motive was supplied by the question of the divorce and the particular treatment which it received at the hands of Clement VII.

Into the history of the divorce it is unnecessary to go here at length. It has afforded, and will afford, matter for dispute so long as the history of their forefathers continues to be a subject of interest to mankind, and each man's ultimate decision upon it will be governed, as it ever has been, very much by his sympathies and antipathies. But so much has the subject been obscured by heated discussion that it seems advisable in this place to state the main points of the case as plainly as possible. It will, I think, appear that the old belief so much in fashion a generation ago that many persons even now can hardly hear it questioned without a shock, that the divorce was taken in hand merely to gratify Henry's caprice, and the scruples only put forward as a decent veil wherewith to cover it, must be abandoned by every one who makes the slightest pretence to impartial judgment or to any capacity for weighing evidence.

It is, then, obvious that, *primâ facie*, the King had

right on his side. In every Christian land it was and is the law that a man may not marry his brother's wife, and the dictum of the Lutheran doctors, 'fieri non debet, factum valet,' is but a very lame and unsatisfactory way of getting over the difficulty. To take a case in some respects parallel, and which, if I mistake not, has actually happened in one of the English noble families within the last century. A and B live together unmarried, and after the birth of a son, C, they see the error of their ways and marry, and another son, D, is afterwards born. D, and not C, is the heir to his father's title and estates, and no subsequent act of the parents can alter their respective positions. So, too, the marriage of Henry and Katherine being unlawful from the beginning, mere lapse of time or other subsequent occurrence could never make it valid. Then comes the question of the papal dispensation on which alone its claim to validity could rest, and on this there were three possible views, some of which admit of subdivision, and all of which were actually adopted by different parties to the dispute. The extreme antipapal view would be that the dispensation made no difference—that that which was unlawful before was unlawful after it. The moderate view would raise the further question whether such a marriage was void by the law of God, or only by human enactment, and declare the dispensation valid or not according to the answer. The extreme papal view, on the other hand, maintained that whether the invalidity depended on the law of man or of God, the Pope's dispensation was an adequate remedy. Finally, the subject was still further complicated by the question raised as to whether Katherine had ever really been the wife of Prince Arthur or not, and which made the validity or invalidity of the dispensation turn on the answer to it. On this point it is hardly possible to avoid two remarks. First, that there was ample evidence of the fact to have convinced an ordinary court in an ordinary case; and, secondly, that, in an age when a mere contract of marriage with one person was held to invalidate any subsequent marriage with another, to raise such a question at all seems rather like a proposition to swallow a camel after straining vehemently over a previous gnat.[1] The whole subject is manifestly one upon which an irreconcilable difference of opinion might, and may, legitimately exist; though I confess that to my own mind it appears perfectly clear that great as may be the sympathy which is naturally called up in our own minds by the hard measure dealt out to Queen Katherine, yet that in fact and in law she never was the lawful wife of Henry, and the Princess Mary was *ab initio* illegitimate. Again, the notion—if any one still entertains it—that Clement VII. ever felt any real scruple on the subject, or that he would have hesitated for a single moment to grant the divorce had not Charles V. stood in the way, is absolutely destitute of foundation. Of the many odious characters which meet us in the history of the sixteenth century, that of Clement VII. is the most despicable by far. As one reads in the State papers the letters and despatches from men representing every side of the question, it is impossible not to see plainly that Clement is troubled by no scruple whatever, I will not say regarding the prostitution of his high office as the vicar of Christ, but even regarding the most elementary considerations of right and wrong. His primary object is to save his own skin; his next, to improve his position as a petty

[1] See Appendix, Note I.

Italian prince. Beyond these ideas he never once soars, and for either of these he is prepared to commit any iniquity and to inflict any wrong, and this under the highest and holiest sanctions.

But though the divorce cannot be rationally looked upon as itself the cause of so mighty a change as that involved in the success of the Reformation in England, it is difficult to over-estimate the effect which it exercised indirectly over the especial measures by which it was brought about, and which gave it a character so different from that which it assumed in other countries.

It is a familiar commonplace to say that the peculiarly conservative character of the English Reformation arose from the fact that the impulsive force which originated it came from above, not from below; that instead of being a popular movement acquiesced in by the rulers of the State, as in Germany, for instance, it was initiated by the rulers of the State, and, for many years at least, only partially accepted by the people; but when we remember that the rulers of the State in this case meant Henry VIII. and his ministers, and that of all personal rulers Henry VIII. was the most individual, then we see that it was from his individual character that this conservative bias proceeded, and there is no difficulty in convincing ourselves that no motive less immediately personal than that supplied by the divorce question would ever have placed the defender of the Seven Sacraments, and the antagonist of Luther, in the anomalous position of an opponent of the Catholic Church.

Thus, though the divorce question was certainly opened as early as 1527, the first attack upon the privileges of the Church appears to have been the introduction of the Mortmain Bill in the parliamentary session of

1529; and although this may be represented as only a measure of necessary reform of what was felt to be a gross and irritating abuse of the power of the clergy—and there are ample indications in contemporary literature of the actual irritation felt by the lay people in consequence of such abuses—yet, coming as it does after the minds of Henry and his ministers were fully possessed by the divorce question, it admits also of being represented as the commencement of a system of reprisals on their part to meet the delays and hesitation of the Pope in granting the relief which Henry required.

The Parliament of 1529 met on November 5, almost immediately after the disgrace of Wolsey (October 18), and it opened with a speech from Sir Thomas More, announcing that the King intended to carry out an ecclesiastical reform. This was followed immediately by the petition of the Commons against the abuses of ecclesiastical administration, which led to prompt legislation—the session lasting only six weeks. The three most important acts passed, viz. 21 Henry VIII. 5, 6, and 13, dealing with probate, mortuaries, and the trading, the pluralities, and the residence of the clergy, embodied the chief points of the petition, and were passed in the teeth of the bishops in the Lords, and not submitted to Convocation at all.

With the exception of the proclamation issued by the King in September of the following year forbidding the introduction of bulls from Rome, and which was founded upon the old Plantagenet legislation, no important step was taken till 1531. This proclamation is, however, worthy of notice, as depriving of any little rag of value which might be supposed to cling to it, an assertion which has become fashionable of late with certain writers, viz. that the *first suggestion* of an assumption of independence of the Pope was made by the clergy in their petition against annates in the year 1532.

The year 1531 is one of considerable moment in our history. The only important Acts of Parliament are the 22 Henry VIII. c. 15 and 16, which relieved the clergy and laity from the penalties of Præmunire; but the preliminary step which constituted the condition on which alone this relief was granted, was one of the most momentous in the whole history of the Reformation, being nothing less than the famous submission of the clergy, wherein they acknowledged the King as *Ecclesiæ Anglicanæ . . . supremum caput*, albeit with the qualification appended *quantum per legem Christi licet*—of which we shall hear more by-and-by.

The legislation of the next year, 1532, was in itself very important. Acts were passed—23 Hen. VIII. c. 1, 9, 11, and 20—all of which altered materially the relations of the Church to the lay people and the State, by (1) limiting the range of 'benefit of clergy' by means of which hitherto clerical or quasi-clerical criminals had been able to evade punishment; (2) limiting the power by which persons could be cited to ecclesiastical courts to the diocese in which the cited person dwelt; (3) bringing within the law convict clergy who escaped from prison; and (4) restraining the payments of annates to the See of Rome.[1]

Over and above these legislative Acts there were in this year also three petitions more or less closely connected with them, and of a highly important character. There was the petition of the Convocation against the payment of annates, which some writers[2] will have, as

---

[1] This refers to the *first* Annates Act.
[2] Blunt's *Hist. of the Ref. in Eng. Ch.* vol. ii. p. 584.

already noted, to have been at once the first suggestion for separation from Rome, and a spontaneous act of the clergy themselves; though others,[1] and amongst them the late Mr. J. R. Green, not certainly a strong partisan of the Protestants, treat it, as it plainly was, as merely an attempt on their part to leave a position with some show of dignity, from which it was evident that they would otherwise have been ignominiously driven. There was also the famous complaint of the Commons[2] against the clergy, consisting of twelve articles, which formed the groundwork for most of the legislation of the session, and of which the first article was that 'canons were made in Convocation without royal assent, or lay assent, and in derogation of the royal authority.' And there was a petition of the clergy of the province of Canterbury to the King, containing four articles, of which the third ran thus: 'That as the clergy are much impoverished by recent Acts annulling the liberty of the Church, *et sanctiones canonicas*, to the peril of the souls of those who made the Acts, in the framing of which *they were not consulted*, and as these Acts are so capricious that it is difficult not to violate them, that the same fathers whose business it is to declare the truth of the canons may provide a remedy.'[3] The words of this petition might in themselves surely furnish a sufficient answer to the pretence that the clergy were in any sense free agents in the ecclesiastical legislation of Henry VIII. That legislation became, notwithstanding, the law of the land, and remains in a very great measure the law of

---

[1] *Short History*, p. 329; Convocation *was made* to propose the withdrawal of payment, &c.

[2] *Stubbs*, Appendix iv. pp. 88–90.

[3] *Ib.* p. 92.

the land still; and by it, as we shall see more and more clearly as we advance, the Church surrendered or was driven from every rag of independence of the State.

The final achievement of this important session was the formal resignation by Convocation itself of whatever independent power of legislation it ever had, by agreeing to the articles which enact that it should neither pass nor execute any ordinance whatever without the King's approval and assent.[1] These articles were brought down to the House on May 10 by Edward Fox, the King's almoner, with a message 'that the King willed that all should subscribe.' Subscribed they were, accordingly, on May 13; the Convocation was prorogued forty-eight hours later, and the members were at liberty to depart to their several homes, having fairly, to use a modern phrase, 'contracted themselves out' of any quasi-independence which they ever fancied they possessed.[2] The despatches of Chapuys and other documents to be found among the State papers supply an ample refutation of the theory of Dr. Hook that the royal supremacy existed in England almost as completely before the time of Henry VIII. as it has done since. Thus, in his despatch of February 14, 1531, he says, speaking of the submission, 'The thing that has been treated to the Pope's disadvantage is that the clergy have *been compelled* under pain of the said law of Præmunire to accept the King as head of the Church, *which implies in effect as much as if they had declared him Pope of England.*'

Again, a week afterwards he writes, while blaming the Pope's proceedings, 'If the Pope had ordered the

---

[1] *Stubbs*, Appendix iv. p. 92.
[2] See Appendix, Note II.

lady to be separated from the King, the King would
never have pretended to claim sovereignty over the
Church. . . . 'There is none who do not blame this usurpation except those who have promoted it.' . . . Again :
'The Nuncio has been with the King to-day.' . . . 'The
Nuncio then entered upon the subject of *this new papacy
made here*,' &c. And again on March 8 he writes : 'The
clergy are more conscious every day of the great error
they committed in acknowledging the King as sovereign
over the Church.' Once more, on June 6 of the same
year, he gives his master an account of a visit of some
of Henry's counsellors to Queen Katherine, and he
quotes her as saying that ' the King is sovereign in his
realm as far as regards temporal jurisdiction, but as to
the spiritual it was not pleasing to God either that the
King should so intend, or that she should consent, for
the Pope was the only true sovereign and vicar of God,
who had power to judge of spiritual matters, of which
marriage was one.'

Such extracts, if they do not prove that Henry's
ecclesiastical legislation was in truth a new departure,
are at least conclusive of the fact that those nearest
his throne and most immediately affected by it believed
it to be so.

Bishop Stubbs[1] gives quite a different account of the
relations of Church and State in England during the
middle ages, and it is one which, while far more consonant than that of Dr. Hook with the actual facts, is
also totally irreconcilable with it. He says that the
clergy 'recognise the King as supreme in matters
temporal, and the Pope in matters spiritual. But then,'
he adds, 'there are questions as to the exact limits
between the spiritual and the temporal, and more im-

[1] *Const. Hist.* vol. iii. ch. xix. p. 290, and the chapter generally.

portant questions touching the precise relations between the Crown and the Papacy. On mediæval theory the King is a spiritual son of the Pope, and the Pope may be the King's superior in things spiritual only, or in things temporal and spiritual alike.'

The mediæval popes had grasped after, and to a great extent obtained, power over matters which, if they belonged to the borderland of spiritual and temporal at all, belonged almost more to the latter than to the former; and the constant effort of the kings had been to limit this borderland as narrowly as possible; and this, and nothing more than this, is, and was always at the time, supposed to be the scope of the antipapal legislation of the Plantagenet and Lancastrian Kings. Henry VIII. took a bolder and a different course, and, ignoring to a great extent the distinction between spiritual and temporal, made himself, with the connivance of Parliament and the forced acquiescence of Convocation, the supreme arbiter of both, and thus, as Chapuys called him, 'Pope of England.'

To this year belong also one or two other matters which, though not directly affecting the relations of Church and State, serve to throw some light upon them. On February 24, just six months before his death, Archbishop Warham drew up his famous protest against all enactments made against the Pope's authority or the ecclesiastical privileges of the Church of Canterbury. The same archbishop, who but a few months before had, in his capacity of president of the Upper House of Convocation, put to the vote the submission of the clergy, and as a peer of Parliament had been involved in the whole of the antipapal legislation, now, in his own palace at Lambeth, with the full consciousness that death is at hand, and feeling that the hopes and fears of the present world are gradually fading and growing dim, looking back upon the stormy times which the last years of his primacy have proved to be, at last summons courage to do what can no longer avail him or his Church, and records his solemn disavowal of the legislation of the last two years.

Another matter deserving of notice is that the Commons in this session decisively rejected a bill on what was called primer scisin, sent down to them by the King, and which affected at once his revenue and their own disposal of their property; thus showing that there was a limit to the 'servility' of which we hear so much, when the subject of legislation was one which touched private property and nearly concerned its owners.

The following year was full of important events, affecting both directly and indirectly the relations of Church and State. The great legislative measure of the year was 24 Henry VIII. c. 12, the Statute of Appeals, by which *all appeals* to Rome, of whatsoever kind, were from henceforth prohibited, and the court of the Archbishop made the final court of ecclesiastical appeal, except in cases 'touching the King,' in which an appeal lay to the Upper House of Convocation. This, so far as appears, was purely and simply an act of the Parliament; and though the records of the contemporary Convocation are full, there is no indication that the subject of the statute was brought before it. That assembly was, however, far from idle during the year. It was now completely subservient to the King, and under his influence it now put forward the first great practical defiance of Rome (April 5)[1] by pronouncing

---

[1] *Stubbs*, Appendix iv. p. 96.

that his marriage with Queen Katherine was null and void, and that he was therefore at liberty to marry another wife. This was promptly followed by Cranmer's formal sentence (May 23) as to the nullity of the former marriage, and the coronation of Anne Boleyn (June 1).

Much discussion has arisen about the date at which Anne Boleyn's marriage took place. From the expression ' about St. Paul's Day ' (January 25), used in a letter of Cranmer's to Hawkins, his successor as ambassador to Charles V., together with the date of Elizabeth's birth, viz. September 7, it has been too hastily assumed that Anne Boleyn had become Henry's mistress before she was married to him.[1] Mr. Pococke, however—certainly no partisan of Anne Boleyn or of the Protestant party —has shown good reason to believe that this inference is not warranted, and certainly the general probabilities of the case appear to support his view. Henry's character and conduct generally would not lead us to suppose that he would be likely to make his mistress his queen; nor is it probable, on the other hand, that Anne, who had kept him at a safe distance for several years, should have endangered the great object of her ambition, viz. the chance of becoming queen, when almost within her grasp, by yielding to him at last prematurely.

The subsequent history of Anne Boleyn, and especially the vexed question of her guilt or innocence of the charges on which she was divorced and beheaded, infinitely as it affects the characters of the various persons concerned in her condemnation, does not properly belong to my subject. It is well that it does not, for no more insoluble problem is to be found in history.

[1] See Appendix, Note III.

The materials do not appear to exist—certainly have not been brought to light—which might alone enable us to solve it.

The next year, 1534, was even more momentous than its predecessor. More and heavier blows were dealt against the papal authority in this year than in any previous one, and two or three important Acts, which had been already passed, but which by an unusual provision had been left in suspension during the King's pleasure—that is to say, had for all intents and purposes been weapons placed in his hands, to be used by him if milder measures failed and the Pope proved recalcitrant, —were now definitely put in force; so that from this year we may date the complete cessation of the papal power in England.

The most important of the Acts passed were:—

25 Henry VIII. c. 14, an Act imposing some limitation on the power of printing heresy;

25 Henry VIII. c. 19, the Act for the submission of the clergy;

25 Henry VIII. c. 20, restraining payment of annates;

25 Henry VIII. c. 21, restraining payment of Peter's-pence, and other exactions of the Pope; and

26 Henry VIII. c. 1, the Supremacy Act, the latter being passed in a second session which commenced in November.

The Act for the submission of the clergy sums up and turns into law at once a great deal of what had formed the subject of the petitions and proceedings of previous sessions of both Parliament and Convocation. Thus, while it stereotyped into law the surrender by the Convocation two years before of its legislative powers, in the act of so doing it also adopted the language of the petition of the Commons against the clergy. It further re-enacted the Statute of Appeals of the previous year, with the important addition of a right of further appeal from the Archbishop to the King in Chancery, which was to work by means of a commission under the Great Seal.[1] The Annates Act,[2] again, was a repetition in a much more thoroughgoing form of the Act of two years before, and is further remarkable as containing also the provision for the appointment of bishops on the royal nomination, and with a merely colourable election by the Chapter, which was again restored under Elizabeth, and which has given rise to so much discussion and animadversion in our own days.

The previous Annates Act had been a measure evidently intended partly as a reform of an acknowledged abuse, and partly as a warning to the Pope of what might be in store for him in the future.[3] This is plainly seen in the fact that bulls were, under it, still to be obtained from Rome for the appointment of bishops, though the sums to be paid for them were diminished, and that the King was empowered to suspend the Act, and in the meantime to negotiate with the Pope for a settlement on moderate terms. This Act, on the other hand, forbids not only all payments but all bulls also, and, together with the following Act forbidding payments to Rome of other kinds and on other occasions, constituted an entire practical repudiation of the Pope's authority.

While it was yet the springtime of 1534, the sessions of both Parliament and Convocation came to an end, but the Acts of this important year were far from being

[1] See the Act *in extenso* in the *Eccl. Courts Com. Report*, p. 216.
[2] P. 218
[3] *Eccl. Courts Com. Report*, vol. i. p. 211.

completed. Both bodies assembled again in November, for a short session of some six weeks.¹ Convocation was employed in a more or less unsuccessful crusade against heretical books, and in requesting the Archbishop to urge the King to put them down, and forbid religious controversy, and at the same time to have a correct translation of Holy Scripture made and 'delivered to the people for their instruction.'

The Archbishop, too, ordered that in formal documents the word ' metropolitanus ' should be substituted in his title for the ancient style ' apostolicæ sedis legatus.'

All these are important matters; important less perhaps in themselves, or even in their consequences, great as some of these have been, than as indications of the ferment of opinion which was characteristic of the times, and as showing how, at one and the same time, while the ecclesiastical authorities were prepared to treat liberty of conscience at once as a chimera and a crime, they were themselves carried away by the irresistible current of antipapal reformation into taking the very measures—such as spreading a knowledge of Scripture amongst the people—which could not but lead directly to it. Meanwhile Parliament was wielding weapons more immediately trenchant and formidable. There were some nine Acts dealing roughly enough with ecclesiastical matters, and among them 26 Henry VIII. c. 2, the Act which compelled all the King's subjects to take an oath to submit to the arrangements made in the previous session for the succession to the Crown—an Act which is made famous, or infamous, by its having given the immediate occasion for two other Acts about the infamy of which posterity has had little doubt, viz. the Acts of attainder of Bishop Fisher and Sir Thomas More.

¹ *Stubbs*, Appendix iv. p. 110.

But even these are dwarfed by the great Act which stands at the head of the labours of the session, 26 Henry VIII. c. 1, the Supremacy Act.

This Act is of such momentous import to the whole subsequent history of the Church of England, that I think it well to print it at length—it is very short—as it stands upon the statute-book, that my readers may see in its own words how tremendous a revolution it involved, and in what uncompromising and comprehensive terms it announced it :—

'Albeit the King's Majesty justly and rightly is, and ought to be, the supreme head of the Church of England, and so is recognised by the clergy of this realm in their Convocations, yet nevertheless, for corroboration and confirmation thereof, and for increase of virtue in Christ's religion within this realm of England, and to repress and extirp all errors, heresies, and other enormities and abuses heretofore used in the same; be it enacted by authority of this present Parliament that the King our Sovereign Lord, his heirs and successors, kings of this realm, shall be taken, accepted, and reputed the only supreme head in earth of the Church of England called Anglicana Ecclesia, and shall have and enjoy annexed and united to the imperial crown of this realm as well the title and stile thereof as all honours, dignities, pre-eminences, jurisdictions, priviledges, authorities, immunities, profits, and commodities, to the said dignity of supreme head of the same Church belonging and appertaining; and that our said Sovereign Lord, his heirs and successors, kings of this realm, shall have full power and authority from time to time to visit, repress, redress, reform, order, correct, restrain, and amend all such errors, heresies, abuses, offences, contempts, and enormities, whatsoever they be, which by any manner, spiritual authority, or jurisdiction ought or may lawfully be reformed, repressed, ordered, redressed, corrected, restrained, or amended, most to the pleasure of Almighty God, the increase of virtue in Christ's religion, and for the conservation of the peace, unity, and tranquillity of this realm, any usage, custom, foreign laws, foreign authority, prescription, or any other thing or things to the contrary hereof notwithstanding.'

Not only, as has been so often observed, was the quasi-saving clause 'quantum per Christi legem licet,' with which the members of Convocation had attempted to gild the bitter pill which they were enforced to swallow, omitted in the Act which became the law of the land equally to layman and to clerk, but so comprehensive are the terms used, so entire is the absorption of the powers of all 'manner of spiritual authority' into the prerogative of the Crown, that we feel that it justified to the full, and if possible even more than justified, the language already quoted from the Spanish ambassador when the subject was in debate in Convocation three and a half years before, that it was 'in effect as much as if they had declared him (the King) Pope of England.' This is in fact, though not in name, what both the Convocation and the Parliament had done; it is what Henry VIII. fully intended that they should do. Pope of England he was, and Pope of England he remained, and so did his successors after him; and though Edward, from the necessity of his age, and Elizabeth from a certain sense of personal dignity and the fitness of things, placed their papal authority, if I may say so, 'in commission,' neither of them dreamed of abdicating it. It continued on, less vigorously exercised, but not always less offensively asserted, through the reigns of the feebler Stuarts, and it appears prominently in the curious clause of the Act of Uniformity,[1] which gives to that 'most religious and gracious sovereign' Charles II. a power of dispensing in the case of certain foreigners with episcopal orders, as a qualification for the cure of souls, and has only disappeared in practice with the recent gradual absorption of the royal prerogative in the powers of the Houses of Parliament.

The great Acts of the following year, 1535, were less legislative than external and executive Acts. They did not so much alter the legal relations between Church and State as show how much those relations had been already altered; they were like the heavy and dangerous swell that agitates the sea after the gale which produced it has for the time abated. Cromwell received his commission as vicegerent; the King issued a proclamation by which the Pope's name was ordered to be erased from the service-books. Fisher and More were beheaded. Pope Paul III. replied to the abrogation of his power in England by excommunicating Henry and his abettors, and a new departure was made by the King in his ecclesiastical policy by the first visitation of the monasteries; but neither Parliament nor Convocation sat.

With the year 1536 we commence another period of legislative activity. The famous Parliament of 1529 held its last session at the beginning of the year, and was dissolved on March 31, having sat through seven such years as England never saw before or since. Convocation, as usual, followed the same course. The latter assembly does not seem to have signalised its last session by any very important discussions. In Parliament no less than nine Acts more or less affecting the

---

[1] 13 and 14 Car. II. c. 4, s. xv.

Church were passed, of which 27 Henry VIII. c. 15, which re-enacted the permission to the King to nominate a commission for making ecclesiastical laws (which, however, never took effect), and 27 Henry VIII. c. 28, which dissolved the smaller religious houses, and gave their possessions to the King, were the most important.

A new Parliament and a new Convocation assembled in June. The primary business of both was to deal with the miserable affair of the dissolution of Henry's marriage with Anne Boleyn, and the subsequent execution of that unhappy person. Into the right or wrong of this matter it is quite beyond my province to inquire; it is enough to know that priests and lawyers, Parliament and Convocation, all and equally concurred in condemning her; and though it has been made, with most of us in modern times, almost an article of faith to believe her innocent, it is somewhat difficult to believe that all these dignified and highly reputed and responsible authorities concurred in the perpetration of a deliberate and atrocious crime.

The ecclesiastical legislation of this short Parliament, for it lasted but a single session, being dissolved on July 18, is a matter which more immediately concerns us, and it was not altogether of an unimportant character. Amongst its Acts were two which tended to extinguish completely any lingering rights or quasi-rights of the See of Rome in England, and others which dealt with the discipline of the clergy. The proceedings of Convocation in this session are of greater interest. Now, for the first time, the lay vicar-general appeared and took his seat next the Archbishop, and signed documents, so far as appears, even before him. Now also the Supreme Head began to exercise his functions in a very practical way, by sending down to the Convocation the first set of articles of faith and ceremonies, drawn up in his own handwriting.[1] These were not introduced till July 11, and seem to have been agreed to the same day;[2] at any rate they can have been but little debated, since the Convocation was dissolved nine days afterwards, and a good deal of other business of importance was got through in the interval, viz. some ordinances on the observation of festivals, and a bill showing the causes why the King should not appear in the General Council recently summoned by the Pope.[3] The two facts of the articles being in Henry's handwriting, and of the speed with which they were enacted, afford sufficient answer to the hypothesis that they were the spontaneous and willing work of the English clergy.

These Acts finished the work of the Parliament and Convocation elected and dissolved in 1536, and no Parliament or Convocation met again till the end of April 1539. But though legislation was thus suspended, this period of almost three years was far from wanting in occurrences affecting the relations of Church and State. On the contrary, soon after the rising of Parliament appeared a set of injunctions about religion and the conduct of the clergy, issued by the vicegerent on the King's authority. These, according to Burnet, gave much offence to the clergy as being the first act of supremacy on the part of the King, and done withal without the consent of Convocation.

The year 1539 is again a year of primary importance in the history of the relations of Church and State.

---

[1] *Froude*, vol. iii. p. 67.
[2] *Stubbs*, Appendix iv. p. 114
[3] *Ib.* p. 116.

The same policy is continued, and for the present under the same influences. The Acts gravely affecting the above relations are:—

- 31 Hen. VIII. c. 8, *i.e.* the Act of Proclamations, which had the effect of giving to the King's proclamations the force of law.
- 31 Hen. VIII. c. 9; enabling the King to make bishops by letters patent.
- 31 Hen. VIII. c. 13; decreeing the dissolution of abbeys and giving them to the King.
- 31 Hen. VIII. c. 14; an Act for abolishing diversity of opinions. This was the famous Act of Six Articles, or Whip with Six Strings.

It is of importance that we should know not only the fact of the passing of this last Act, but as much as can be learned as to the mode in which it passed, the source from which it sprang, the influences by which it was affected, and the feeling with which it was regarded by contemporary persons. Its origin may surely be attributed to the mind of Henry himself, acted upon by Cromwell. It was but one step, though an advanced step, and, as it turned out, almost the last which Cromwell was to take in his general policy of rendering the Crown of England supreme both in Church and State, and using Parliament as the means of establishing its supremacy. Yet it was a step taken, not because it formed a natural part of that policy, but because it was necessary in order to accommodate it to the circumstances of the moment, and the predilections of the King. Like other able artificers, Cromwell found it necessary to modify his work in accordance with the tools wherewith he had to perform it, and the material which he had to use.

Henry loved power, and he hated restraint, and hence he had been well pleased with the earlier steps of Cromwell's policy, which had made him, as we have just seen, *il re papa*, as it were—at once Pope and Emperor as far as his dominions extended: but he never forgot that he had been himself the champion of the Faith against Luther, he never loved Protestants or Protestantism, he could not endure the name of heretic; and he seems at this time to have been seized with some misgiving, as to whether his previous articles had not gone a little too far, and to have been anxious to show that his repudiation of Roman authority did not mean that the supreme head of the English Church would himself appear as a patron or condoner of heretical opinions. This reaction in Henry's mind was itself due no doubt mainly to the recent rebellion in the north, the famous Pilgrimage of Grace. The movement had been an alarming one, and the fact that it was occasioned in a great degree by discontent with the King's recent religious measures, may have given him reason to reflect on his course. His council always contained a reactionary element, to which such an event was certain to give strength and prominence; and Cromwell's influence was even then beginning to wane. Thus it came to pass that the Six Articles, which were in all probability Henry's own composition, represented exactly his own opinions, and were regarded, and rightly regarded, by the Protestants as reactionary—as, with their penal enactment attached to them, they soon were proved to be. Such being the character of this famous document, the history of its enactment is strictly accordant with it. Its introduction is preluded by a statement to Parliament by the Chancellor [1]

---

[1] *Stubbs*, Appendix iv. p. 116.

that 'it is *the King's especial desire* that all differences of religious opinion should be eradicated,' and that 'it is *his will* that some persons should be chosen to examine such opinions and report on them in the present Parliament.' On this a Commission was appointed consisting of Cromwell, as representing the supreme head, the two archbishops, and six bishops, of very different opinions.[1] These were appointed on May 5, and upon their having made no progress in their somewhat hopeless task by the 16th of the same month, the Duke of Norfolk introduced the Bill of Six Articles, with a penal clause attached, at once, into the House of Lords on that day. Nothing more appears to have been done until after a short prorogation from May 23 to 30, on which latter day[2] the Chancellor announced it to be the '*King's will* that a penal statute should be made on the Six Articles.' It was agreed that two forms of statute should be framed—one by the Archbishop of Canterbury and the Bishops of Ely and St. Davids, with the assistance of Dr. Petre; and the other by the Archbishop of York and the Bishops of Durham and Winchester, with that of Dr. Tregonwell. Meanwhile Cromwell lays the Six Articles before Convocation, *in the form of questions*, on June 2, and gets their affirmative answers apparently on the 5th. On the 7th the bill is read a first time in the Lords; and notwithstanding the subsequent introduction of a proviso in the Commons, which necessitated its reappearance in the Lords, it is through both Houses[3] on the 16th, and Parliament is prorogued before the end of the month.

[1] These were, Canterbury (Cranmer), York (Lee), Bath (Clerk), Ely (Goodrich), Bangor (Bird), Worcester (Latimer), Durham (Tonstall), Carlisle (Aldrich).

[2] *Stubbs*, Appendix iv. p. 118.

[3] *Ib*. p. 120.

Nothing surely can prove much more distinctly than does the history of this Act, how completely Henry VIII. and Cromwell had, to adopt a favourite modern phrase, made the supreme headship a 'reality.' Here is a direct and emphatic and authoritative statement of doctrine which is introduced into Parliament as 'the King's will,' is hurried by Parliament into a bill, to which is appended—also because it is 'the King's will'—a penal clause, and the whole is passed by Parliament into an Act, and, as such, becomes the law of England, binding upon clergy no less than laity. And what is the share of Convocation in this important Act? It is simply asked whether it approves of the doctrines—*i.e.*, it is consulted in the same way as, at the present day, the College of Physicians sometimes has been consulted—simply as a professional body of experts—on the advisability of some intended legislation about leprosy or cholera. Even the ordinary forms of legislation in use in Convocation are omitted. The vicegerent comes and asks what the members think of the doctrine, and that is all; and even that is done with as little respect as may be, and with no regard even to the appearance of permitting liberty of discussion. The questions are asked and the answers given between Monday and Thursday of the same week;[1] and the deliberation, if there was any deliberation, took place under the immediate superintendence of the lay Vicar-General.

To this year also (Nov. 12) appertains another very remarkable document, printed by Burnet, vol. iv. p. 410 (185), which shows how truly Chapuys spoke of the supremacy as 'a new papacy,' viz., the commission taken out by Bonner from the King for the exercise of his episcopal functions. It is probable that other

[1] *Stubbs*, Appendix iv. p. 118.

bishops also, and it is rumoured that Cranmer himself, received similar commissions from King Henry VIII., as it is certain that he did at the beginning of the next reign.

The following year also is full of ecclesiastical legislation and ecclesiastical government; but the clergy, individually and collectively, are bound hand and foot, and by this time they have become aware of the fact, and their part in what goes on is either none at all, or that of mere catspaws. In this, perhaps, they have little to regret, for it was a year with the doings of which they, or the honester part of them, would have been glad, no doubt, to avoid even an enforced complicity. At the end of seven Acts more or less concerning the discipline and the pecuniary position of the clergy, and of which one only—viz., the subsidy—seems to have been submitted to Convocation, are three of more permanent importance—viz., 32 Hen. VIII. c. 24, giving the possessions of the great order of the Hospitallers of St. John to the Crown; 32 Hen. VIII. c. 25, the Act for the dissolution of the *pretended* marriage of the Lady Anne of Cleves; and 32 Hen. VIII. c. 26, an Act concerning Christ's religion.[1] Of these last two Acts, while the latter was the consequence of the appointment *by the King* of two Commissions which were respectively to settle the moot points in the doctrine and ceremonies of the Church— and was meant to give their decisions, when made, the force of law, and, so far as appears, neither sought nor received authority from the clergy in any form—to the former, the most scandalously unrighteous of all Henry's divorces, was duly appended the instrument by which Convocation had declared, in accordance with his wishes, that the marriage was invalid. July 28 of this year saw the dissolution of Parliament and Convocation, and,

[1] *Stubbs*, Appendix iv. p. 124.

at the same time, the execution of Cromwell and the marriage of his hardened master to Katherine Howard.

In the year which followed there was held neither Parliament nor Convocation.[1] Cromwell, indeed, was gone, but his policy was not altogether gone with him. The Duke of Norfolk was once more in power, who would willingly have reversed it, who, with longer life, and under the influence of the constant irritation of Cromwell's action, had now become thoroughly reactionary, and had been known to say, 'It was merry in England afore the new learning came up; yea, I would all things were as hath been in times past.' That speech represented a frame of mind almost as much out of harmony with the middle of the sixteenth century as it would be with the end of the nineteenth; and so unable was the Duke to resist the current of the times that we find in this year a proclamation issued—having, be it remembered, the force of law—requiring that a Bible should be placed in every church: certainly of all measures the least likely to bring all things back to the state in which 'times past' had left them, albeit the Duke himself declared, 'I never read the Scripture, nor never will.'[2]

In this year, too, some of the service books were printed[3] omitting the name of the Pope as impugning by its presence there 'the statute of our most Christian King.'

In January of 1542 both assemblies resumed their activity. Parliament, besides the dismal work of passing bills of attainder against the Queen and Lady Rocheford, was employed with a number of enactments on ecclesiastical matters such as the rearrangement of bishops' sees and the civil status of the unfrocked monks,

---

[1] *Stubbs*, Appendix iv. p. 126. [2] Green, *Hist.* vol. ii. p. 204.
[3] *Stubbs*, Appendix iv. p. 127.

&c.—matters which would scarcely have come before Parliament at all in previous reigns, and could not assuredly have been settled by it without the intervention of Convocation, and probably also of the Court of Rome; but which seem small and insignificant when compared with the doings of the previous Parliaments of Henry VIII. Meanwhile Convocation, which does not seem to have been consulted on these Acts, was busy upon other and not unimportant matters. The Houses were informed,[1] at the commencement of the session, that it was the '*King's intention* that they should deliberate on the bad state of religion, and on the remedies; and should correct and reform where it was necessary.' They accordingly discussed the revision of the translation of the Bible, the abolition of the lights burned before images, the erasure of the names of the Pope and Thomas à Becket from the service books, decreed the uniform employment of 'the use of Sarum' throughout the province of Canterbury, and introduced propositions concerning the reform of various practical disorders among clergy and laity, upon which it was determined to 'consult the King.'

One remarkable occurrence took place which, when taken in connection with other events before and after, illustrates in a curious manner the relations subsisting at the time between Parliament and Convocation.

A bill was introduced into Parliament to enable bishops-chancellors to marry, and yet to retain their offices, with the powers thereto belonging for pronouncing suspensions, excommunications, and other ecclesiastical censures,[2] 'as priests do'; also that they who held these offices should have sufficient fees of the ordinaries to find them *and their families.* To this bill the bishops

[1] *Stubbs,* Appendix iv. p. 126.   [2] *Ib.* p. 128.

objected, 'for the great slander which might thereupon ensue,' and it was withdrawn in consequence.

Much stress has been laid by certain writers upon this transaction as showing the greatness of the power which Convocation still retained, when it thought fit to use it. When it is considered how small a matter this was in comparison with the innumerable larger ones mentioned in the course of this chapter, and which were passed, either without the concurrence of the clergy, or in the teeth of their opposition, it will be seen at once how weak a case those writers must have when they make so great a matter out of it. Such as it is it avails them nothing, since another bill with the same object was passed only three years later—to all appearance unimpeded by Convocation. The probable explanation is simply that the King, who had just insisted in the Six Articles on the continued celibacy of the clergy, had not quite made up his mind as to whether these chancellors, amphibious beings as they were, half clergy and half lawyers, were or were not to be included in the ranks of the former, as hitherto they always had been; and thus it was not yet determinedly 'the King's will,' which was at this time the measure of the action of Convocation even more certainly than of that of Parliament.

The year 1543 was distinguished by the publication of the famous 'King's book, a necessary doctrine and erudition for any Christian man.'[1]

There was a long and busy session of both Parliament and Convocation. The Acts passed by the former, however, having reference to our subject are but few. The most important of them was the 34 and 35 Hen. VIII. c. 1, called 'an Act for the advancement of true

[1] *Stubbs*, Appendix iv. p. 135.

religion, and for the abolishment of the contrary,' or, as it is named in the Lords' Journals, ' the bill for abolishing erroneous books.' Convocation, in response to an announcement from the Archbishop that it was the *King's will* that 'the service books should be reformed, by omitting all mention of the Pope and legendary and superstitious matter, and the abolition of the commemoration of saints not mentioned in Scripture or by authentical doctors,' appointed a committee for that purpose, consisting of the Bishops of Sarum and Ely, together with six members of the Lower House.[1]

It also ordered that every Sunday and holiday a chapter of the Bible should be read in English by the curate in every church, without exposition ; and it sent up several petitions to the King, among them one for the ecclesiastical laws of the realm to be made according to the statute.

It likewise compiled expositions of the Sacraments, the Decalogue, the Lord's Prayer, and Twelve Articles of the Faith, and treatises on justification, works, and prayer for the dead (which, in point of fact, constituted the work entitled, as above, the King's book).

The principal Acts of the following year (1544) were :

35 Hen. VIII. c. 1, a succession Act.

35 Hen. VIII. c. 3, a bill for the King's style.

35 Hen. VIII. c. 5, a bill concerning (modifying) the Six Articles.

35 Hen. VIII. c. 16, a bill for the examination of the Canon laws by a commission of thirty-two persons.

The last being another renewal of the former legislation on this subject.

Convocation appears to have been busy mainly with questions of money, tithes, and subsidies.

[1] *Stubbs*, Appendix iv. pp. 131-2.

At the end of the session, which terminated at the end of March, both assemblies were dissolved.

Towards the end of November 1545 [1] opened the first session of what was to be the last Parliament of Henry's reign. The King had in the previous May published his Primer in Latin and English. Several Acts were passed more or less affecting the Church and clergy, of which the two most important were:—

37 Hen. VIII. c. 4, which delivered up all colleges, chantries, and hospitals to the tender mercy of the King; and

37 Hen. VIII. c. 17, an Act enabling the married doctors of civil law to exercise ecclesiastical jurisdiction.

The record of the proceedings of Convocation in this year is not preserved.

The above are, in fact, the last Acts of the reign.

In the following year neither Parliament nor Convocation met, and the session of 1547 was brought to an abrupt termination, by the sudden death of the King about a fortnight after its opening, and when its only act had been to pass the bill of attainder against the Duke of Norfolk and Lord Surrey, with his assent to which, on the day before his death, Henry characteristically concluded his reign.

---

[1] It is a fact, noted by Mr. Green (*Hist.* vol. ii. p. 219) as not unimportant, that in this session a bill for the abolition of heresies and of certain books infected with false opinions, which was introduced in the Lords, disappeared when it reached the Commons. In fact, the history of the bill is remarkable, for it seems to have been read no less than five times in the Lords, and at last agreed to '*nemine repugnante*' in a House which must have been a full one for that time, no less than thirty-six members voting; but, after all, it never became law. *Stubbs*, Appendix iv. p. 188.

CHAPTER V

REIGN OF HENRY VIII. (*continued*)

AFTER the enumeration of the actual legislative measures affecting the Church contained in the last chapter, let us now endeavour to take stock of the entire amount of those changes, and to see how far the position of the Church at the end of Henry's reign differed from what it was at the time when Wolsey fell. This will be a question of the more interest, in that we know there are writers, on the one hand, who will tell us that the true Reformation in England was complete at his death, and that the subsequent changes have been for the most part for the worse; and, on the other hand, some who consider that the real Reformation was in his time hardly begun, and that what he had established was merely popery without the pope. Here it is before all things necessary to bear in mind the distinction already pointed out between the separation from Rome and the reformation of doctrine. The separation from Rome was as complete years before the end of Henry's reign as it ever has been since. The Act of Appeals (24 Hen. VIII. c. 12); the Act for the submission of the clergy (25 Hen. VIII. c. 19); the Act restraining the payment of annates (25 Hen. VIII. c. 20); and that restraining the payment of Peter's-pence and other exactions of the Pope (25 Hen. VIII. c. 21)—had put a stop to all the existing relations between the Church in England and the Papal See, and finally the great Act of Supremacy (26 Hen. VIII. c. 1) had transferred, as completely as language could do it, the papal authority to the King—had made Henry, as we have seen, Pope of England. On the other side, Paul III. had retaliated by a bull of excommunication and deposition against Henry and all his abettors, thus making the separation as complete as possible on both sides.

To estimate fairly the changes in doctrine and ritual is a less easy matter. There was nothing very revolutionary in the Articles of 1536, and still less in those of 1539; and neither Henry nor probably Cromwell had any great sympathy with the Protestants: but the air was full of new doctrines and new views, and such measures as the destruction of shrines and images, and the translation of the Scriptures, tended to encourage the Protestant sectaries; while the separation from Rome, and the establishment of the King as the highest ecclesiastical authority, did the same in a still greater degree, by the shock which it gave to the old and time-honoured belief in the absolute unchangeableness and stability of the Church. The system of the Roman Church before the Reformation was, as it has since remained, a solid and consistent whole, each portion of it resting upon the same foundations, and guaranteed by the same warrants; and it was in the sixteenth century, as it remains still, impossible to throw over one part of it without exposing other parts to the same danger.

But these changes in doctrine, slight as they appear in comparison with those made in the following reign, and far, as we see by Hooper's letter,[1] as they fell short of satisfying the Protestants, were none the less fatal to the catholicity of the English Church. They

[1] *Infra*, p. 94.

broke the unity of the Church, they rent the seamless coat, they altered, in however slight a degree, the doctrines of the Catholic Church, and all this they did, not by the authority of a General Council or a Papal Consistory, but by the mere motion of a despotic king and an unscrupulous minister, or, at best, of a national synod, which moved but as its strings were pulled by a lay supreme head, or a lay vicegerent, or even a lay vicegerent's lay deputy. The changes in ritual were probably slighter still, and with ignorant people these are apt to be felt and resented when changes in doctrine may pass almost unperceived. The mass of the English people would scarcely have discovered the difference had Henry confined his action to the changes actually made in the doctrines and services of the Church. That which really caused what popular discontent existed—and there can be little doubt that some did exist—was the abolition of pilgrimages and holy days, the destruction of images and shrines, and still more the demolition of the monasteries, and the consequent cessation of their doles and alms.

The last few years of Henry's reign show us the first experiment that was made in maintaining what was afterwards known as the Anglican *via media*—the only one, in fact, which was tried with the combined advantages of unlimited power and unscrupulous use of it; and how it appeared in the eyes of as disinterested and well-informed a spectator as the times could afford, we may learn from the despatch of Marillac, the French Ambassador, to his master Francis I., quoted by Mr. Froude. He is speaking of the simultaneous execution, on July 30, 1540, of three Protestants for heresy and three Roman priests for treason, and, after mentioning the indignation excited among people of the most opposite opinions, he adds:[1] 'It is no easy thing to keep a people in revolt against the Holy See and the authority of the Church, and yet free from the infection of the new doctrines, or, on the other hand, if they remain orthodox, to prevent them from looking with attachment to the Papacy. But the Council here will have neither the one nor the other.' And again he says: 'It was a strange spectacle to see the adherents of two opposite parties die there on the same day and at the same hour; and it was equally disgraceful to the two divisions of the Government who pretended to have received offence. The scene was as painful as it was monstrous.' This was the opinion of a statesman, impartial as between the two, but impartially condemnatory of Henry's policy regarded from either one side or the other. What the Papal party thought of it we know abundantly from Paul III., from Cardinal Pole, and innumerable other writers; while the Protestant view is best explained in the well-known letter of Hooper,[2] afterwards one of Edward VI.'s bishops, to Bullinger, written apparently in 1546, in which he says: 'Our King has destroyed the Pope, but not Popery. . . . The impious mass, the most shameful celibacy of the clergy, the invocation of saints, auricular confession, superstitious abstinence from meats, and purgatory, were never before held by the people in greater esteem than at the present moment.' This last letter is important. It shows, from strictly contemporary evidence, three things—viz., first, how entirely the schism between the two Churches of Rome and England was completed in Henry's time; secondly, how entirely both parties were conscious of the fact; and, thirdly, it shows what Protestant doctrines really were, and how far the Anglican

---

[1] *Froude*, vol. iii. p. 534, *note*.   [2] *Zurich Letters*, vol. i. p. 33.

Church of Henry VIII. was from adopting them—and all this it shows on the authority of a man who was himself a pronounced Protestant, and who, certainly without becoming less a Protestant, was made a bishop in the same Church in the following reign. It is not easy to imagine Henry VIII. making Hooper a bishop!

If, then, we can find, as we have now done, a view of any particular transaction which is shared at the time by both friends and foes alike, and also by one standing, as nearly as a contemporary can stand, in the position of an indifferent spectator, we may feel pretty sure that it represents the actual state of the facts. And in this case we may be certain that what had actually happened to the Church in England, in the ten momentous years which intervened between the fall of Wolsey and the enactment of the Six Articles, was that while a complete division was effected between the Churches of Rome and England, with whatsoever effect upon the ecclesiastical position of the latter that division may be held to involve, no essential or even very important change had been effected in the doctrinal position of the latter Church. And that this was held for a century afterwards so to be, we shall have ample opportunity of seeing as this work proceeds; but I will here cite one passage in proof of it, because it comes from a learned and authoritative writer of the seventeenth century, and coincides remarkably with those already quoted. Archbishop Bramhall says:[1] 'The many Acts which were passed in the reign of Henry VIII. declaring the independence of the Church of England, were passed by Roman Catholics when there were no thoughts of any Reformation. If it was this separation from Rome which constituted a schism, then

---

[1] See the passage quoted at length in Hunt, *Op. Cit.* vol. i. p. 331.

the authors of it, Heath and Bonner, Tunstall and Gardiner, Stokesly and Thirlby, were the schismatics. The separation was made to our hands. It was not till Edward's days that the Church of England embraced the doctrines of the Reformation.'

It is worth while, before concluding this short summary of the results of Henry VIII.'s ecclesiastical legislation, to call attention emphatically to the authority by which all these changes were made.

It would seem, then, that, of the various measures which we have noted in the last chapter, the work of the session of 1529, though it may not impossibly have been discussed in Convocation, was actually performed in Parliament alone. It consisted mainly in the passing of the 21 Hen. VIII. 5, 6, and 13, regulating the fees to be received by the clergy for probate and mortuaries, and also their residence, pluralities, farming, trading, &c. The next step was the King's proclamation forbidding the introduction of bulls from Rome, with which, of course, neither Parliament nor Convocation had any concern. The year 1531 is mainly famous for the celebrated Præmunire, the consequent submission of the clergy in Convocation, and the passing of the two bills in Parliament 22 Hen. VIII. c. 15 and 16, concerning the pardon of the clergy and laity respectively.

The proceedings of the year 1532 are of a more complicated character. On the one hand, we have several Acts of Parliament, as above noted, dealing somewhat roughly with the privileges of the clergy; and we have also the complaint of the Commons against them, and the Three Articles founded upon the latter, brought to the Convocation by Edward Fox, the King's almoner, and, after some discussion, agreed to. We have, on the other hand, the petition of the Convocation to the King to take away the annates from the Pope, and also their petition to him (1) 'that the Church may enjoy her privileges,' (2) 'that the limits of Præmunire may be defined in Parliament,' (3) 'that as the clergy are much impoverished by recent Acts annulling the liberty of the Church and *sanctiones canonicas*, to the peril of the souls of those who made the Acts, *in the framing of which they were not consulted*, &c., that the same fathers whose business it is to declare the truth of the canons may provide a remedy.' This last is, and can be nothing else than, a formal and explicit disclaimer, on the part of the clergy, of all share in, and all responsibility for, the ecclesiastical legislation of Henry VIII.; so that we know not only that they did not originate it, but that they were not even asked to concur in it up to this time. The Act of Appeals and that for the apparel of the clergy (24 Hen. VIII. c. 12 and 13) in the following year do not appear to have been submitted to Convocation at all.

The legislation of the year 1534[1] was, as we have seen, that which completed the great schism which entirely divided the Anglican from the Roman Church, and which actually provoked the papal excommunication in the following year. The share which the clergy took in it appears to have been the passing of an abstract resolution to the effect that 'the Pope had no greater jurisdiction in the realm of England conferred on him by God in Holy Scripture than any other foreign Bishop,' and a concurrence in the Act for the Submission of the Clergy —the reduction into law of their own submission of two years before, made by them simply and almost avowedly with the knife at their throats in the trenchant shape of an indictment of Præmunire. Before Convoca-

[1] *Stubbs*, Appendix iv. p. 106.

tion sat again for despatch of business, Cromwell had received his commission as vicegerent, and from that time till his own attainder he himself or his deputy became its virtual, if not actual, president and master. After this we have the Act extinguishing the power of the Bishop of Rome, Cromwell's injunctions, the King's proclamation about rites and ceremonies, the Act for the King to make bishops, the Act for the Six Articles and for the demolition of abbeys, and many other Acts affecting the discipline, ceremonies, and even doctrines, of the Church in a greater or less degree. It is scarcely too much to say that all these were the acts of the State and not of the Church. They were the acts of the King and Parliament, and Convocation was either not consulted at all or was allowed no free agency in the matter. It is clear, of course, that the warning with which Bishop Stubbs commences his work, in the Appendix IV. so constantly referred to, must be duly regarded, and that no argument can be drawn from the absence of records of Convocation that that assembly was not engaged on a particular measure at the time; but we may, on the other hand, fairly conclude that when a certain important bill was discussed and finally passed in Parliament, and when there is evidence of some other work done in Convocation, but no sign that it discussed this one, that it was not, in fact, consulted about it, and did not concur in it. Thus it appears that the Act of Appeals in 1533 did not come before Convocation at all; and though, in the following year, some clauses on this subject were appended to the bill in Parliament for the submission of the clergy, they were omitted from it as it appeared in Convocation. Take, again, the case of the famous Six Articles in 1539. Convocation was consulted in this case, as in a great many others, in no way as a body possessing concurrent legislative powers with Parliament, but simply as a body of professional experts whose opinion it was advisable to have for the avoidance of technical blunders. Cromwell went to Convocation on June 2, and demanded the opinion of the Houses on certain definite points of doctrine which had previously been formulated in the House of Peers by the Duke of Norfolk. On the 5th he received definite answers to these questions, and they were afterwards drafted into a bill, which was read a first time on June 7, and passed through both Houses of Parliament by the 16th.

In the following year, also, it is at least doubtful how far they were consulted—deferred to they clearly were not—about any of the important ecclesiastical Acts of the session. On the other hand, it is not doubtful at all that they were very busy about the dirty work of finding excuses for the repudiation of the King's marriage with Anne of Cleves, just as they had previously been in finding pretexts for the divorces of Catherine of Aragon and Anne Boleyn.

The whole history of the years in question, as it is read in the State papers and drawn out in Appendix IV. to the Report of the Ecclesiastical Courts Commission, shows plainly that the great changes brought about in the position of the English Church were entirely the work of Henry and of Cromwell, with the willing co-operation of Parliament, but that the clergy were helpless tools in their hands throughout—they were either not consulted or else dragooned.

During one year only, viz. 1534—a very important year, no doubt—have they even the appearance of having been free agents, for, as we have seen, they themselves repudiated the legislation before that year, and after it their whole constitution was despotically changed by the introduction of the lay vicegerent; and if we remember what the acts of that one year were, and what was their own previous and subsequent conduct with regard to those acts, we shall not easily believe that they were really any more spontaneous on their part than were those which preceded and followed them. The two important acts of Convocation in 1534 were the resolution that the Pope has no more power given him by God in England than any other foreign bishop; and the concurrence in the Act for the Submission of the Clergy. The latter was a mere repetition of the action which had been forced upon them by the Præmunire two and a half years before, and which they therefore well knew that they could not escape; and how much the former was a really voluntary act on their part may be seen from the fact that a quarter of a century later, on the accession of Elizabeth, after the thirteen years' trial of Henry's *via media* had been followed by twelve more years of bitter struggles between the opposing faiths, and of alternate government by the bigots of each side, Convocation declared, by a unanimous vote, not only for transubstantiation and the mass, but for the supremacy of the Pope and the authority of the priesthood in matters of faith and discipline. It appears clearly that throughout Henry's reign, while Parliament was his active, though humble and somewhat servile, coadjutor, Convocation, on the other hand, was but his convenient and utterly helpless tool. The reason of this state of things is not far to seek. Henry entered upon his reign with high notions of his own prerogative. The circumstances of the times, both at home and abroad, tended to foster them, as we have already seen, and also to induce the Parliament to become his abettor in carrying them out. The abuses existing in the Church were great and oppressive; the clergy, both regular and secular, were unpopular. The nobility were too weak to offer effectual opposition to the King. From this state of things it followed that the clergy, who alone stood in a position to do so, had many enemies, and no ally except the Pope. But the Pope (Clement VII.) was worse than no ally at all. He was a man totally destitute of any high ideal—he was, if I may so say, a Medici first and only Pope afterwards; that is to say, he was essentially a petty upstart Italian princeling, who cared far more for his own family ascendency in Florence than for all the interests of Christianity over the civilised world, and was ready at any moment to employ, and even to endanger, the authority which the Papacy gave him amongst the clergy of all Europe, for the sake of some beggarly family intrigue or dynastic interest. Nevertheless, low as the Papacy had sunk at the beginning of the sixteenth century, it still retained an immense prestige. The Pope was still supreme over the clergy in every State, though his right may have suffered in some degree in each, and still drew a large revenue from them, both in England and elsewhere. Hence, as soon as Henry quarrelled with the Pope on the matter of the divorce, his plain policy was to attack the clergy at home, since by this means he carried out at once his secondary object of punishing the Pope, and his primary object of making himself absolute. By the help of his Parliament he coerced the clergy into joining him in repudiating the Pope, and he punished the Pope not only by annulling his authority, but by depriving him of his revenue; and then he proceeded to transfer both authority and revenue to his own person, while all the time he maintained the Church in appearance very much as it was before, and made it, in fact, far more subservient to himself than it ever had been to the Pope. This was shown very remarkably in the share which Convocation had to take in his various divorces. The people had been used to regard divorce as an especial prerogative of the ecclesiastical power. Accordingly, when Henry wanted a divorce, Convocation and the Archbishop had to provide him with the excuse for it, and to pronounce the judgment, so as to make it appear to receive the sanction of the Church, in a manner at least superficially regular; but for the anti-papal legislation there was neither the possibility nor the need of a regular precedent, and accordingly it was mostly enacted without troubling Convocation for their consent.

The bearing of all this upon the progress of the Reformation, strictly so called, will be best discussed in relation to the commencement of the next reign.

CHAPTER VI

REIGN OF EDWARD VI

THE reign of Edward VI., from January 1547 to June 1553, is a period of great importance, but one also with which it is difficult to deal. Cromwell's system was kept up till the end of his master's life to the full extent of that degree of completeness to which he himself had brought it; but it ceased to move forward from the moment of his own death, or perhaps, more strictly speaking, from the moment when his influence began to decline, and Cromwell's system may be shortly defined as an absolutism in Church and State, established and maintained by the connivance of Parliament. It is almost inconceivable that such a system could have lasted long in any case; though we may see, from its partial resuscitation under Elizabeth, that it was more possible in the sixteenth century than it could have been before or after. Still to us, looking at the matter by the help of that somewhat profitless wisdom which comes to us so readily after the event, it seems obvious enough that a system which admitted the full rights of Parliament, and calculated upon Parliament always lending its support to the King, could hold good only so long as Parliament chose actually to grant that support; and as soon as circumstances should arise to cause some wide divergence between the interests or wishes of Parliament and the King's will, the alliance between them would break down, and not improbably be changed into a sharp opposition. Not only do we know as a fact that this actually happened less than a century after Henry's death, but we see that it appeared as a serious danger more than once in the reign of Elizabeth, and, what is more to the purpose still, there were various indications of it even in Henry's own lifetime. On two occasions at least—viz., the Præmunire, as it affected the laity, and the Bill of Uses in 1532—the Commons resisted the King successfully, and on several others they showed that they were quite capable of doing so when they had sufficient inducement. Henry himself also on several occasions used the probable opposition of Parliament as a diplomatic weapon, saying that he could not agree to such-and-such a condition, as, if he did, his Parliament would not accept it; a proceeding which, though it might be held to show taht he had, on the occasion in question, no great reason to fear their opposition, also proves that he was aware that they had it in their power to oppose effectually. These remarks, however, apply only with considerable limitation to the case of ecclesiastical government, inasmuch as there can be little doubt that Henry and Cromwell alike considered that by means of the Act for the Submission of the Clergy and the Act of Supremacy they had stereotyped the power of the Royal prerogative to govern the Church absolutely; and this view continued to be held and acted upon, though with constantly-diminishing success and constantly-increasing difficulty, down to the time of Charles I.

But the circumstances which followed upon Henry's death were such as at once put the strength of Cromwell's system to a severe trial, and that it stood the test even as well as it did, is sufficient evidence how wonderfully great that strength was.

The King's health had been manifestly declining for a considerable time before his death; his son was a little boy; there was no statesman left of the calibre of Wolsey or of Cromwell. It was therefore impossible but that speculation and intrigue should have been rife as to the hands into which power was likely to fall during the approaching minority. Two parties had existed for years in Henry's Council, between whom his hand had held the balance. It remained to be seen how it would adjust itself when that hand was withdrawn. The Act of Six Articles, and the persecution which followed it, had marked the extreme point of the reaction which had been induced in Henry's mind, partly at least by the Pilgrimage of Grace. As time went on and Henry's health became weaker, the influence of Katherine Parr and of the Seymours seems to have gradually increased; and though he still maintained his enforced religious truce, the King became gradually less severe in his treatment of heretics, and rumours went about of an intended further religious reform. Still, up to within a very few months of Henry's death, it might well have seemed that the reactionary party in the Council had the better chance of success. In the main it consisted of the nobles of 'the old blood,' headed by the Duke of Norfolk and his son Lord Surrey, together with Gardiner, Bishop of Winchester, and Lord Wriothesley, the Chancellor, who, though himself one of the new nobles, seems to have adhered to the Catholic party. Their opponents consisted mostly of the nobles of 'the new blood'—*i.e.* the Seymours, Lord Parr, Lord Lisle, Lord Russell, and others: men who had risen from positions of comparative obscurity, had been ennobled by Henry himself, and grown rich upon the spoils of the monasteries. They had as their great ally Archbishop Cranmer; but though some of them, and Lord Hertford in particular, had shown considerable capacity, their weight in the country was small compared with that of their opponents. Their position as men who had thriven upon the spoils of the Church inclined them naturally to the new order of things; and they were driven still further in the same direction by the fact that the Protestants were the only section of the nation upon whom they could certainly count as supporters. Henry had contrived for some years to keep the peace between these two factions by his own vigorous methods of ruling; but Henry felt that he could not live long, and, in the absence of a man whom he could thoroughly trust, had arranged a council of executors in which the two parties seem to have been carefully balanced, in the hope—it is to be supposed—that they would keep one another in check. All at once however, only about three months before Henry's death, an event occurred which entirely falsified his calculations, and in the end overthrew all his arrangements. Lord Surrey, in many ways the most brilliant and remarkable member of the reactionary party—but, at the same time, the most bitter in his hatred of the new men, and the most unrestrained in his contemptuous expression of it—was accused of having altered his coat of arms, and quartered the royal arms upon it, in a position which could not but suggest a claim on his part to a very near place in the succession to the throne. He was known to have spoken boastfully of his father as being the person most fit to be entrusted with the guardianship of the prince, and to have used vague threats of what the new men should suffer when the King was dead. All these matters, trifling in themselves, derived importance from the circumstances of the times—the King's now dangerous illness, and the prince's tender age—and suggested that the Howards were looking forward to a protectorate over the young King which might not impossibly develop into a succession to his throne. Henry's jealousy was aroused, and an investigation followed, ending in the implication of the Duke also, at least to the extent of a guilty knowledge of his son's acts. Mr. Froude[1] tells us that the execution of Lord Surrey has been unanimously treated by historians as a gratuitous murder, but he has himself shown very good reason to doubt the correctness of their verdict; and one is inclined to think that the generally brilliant reputation of Lord Surrey, and his high literary and poetical fame, have conspired with the general belief in the despotic and sanguinary character of Henry's government to induce the historians to undervalue some very damaging evidence against him, notably that of his sister, the Dowager Duchess of Richmond. However this may be, the result of the charge was that Surrey was tried, condemned, and executed, and a bill of attainder passed against the Duke of Norfolk, who was saved only by the King's death. Thus, whether the alleged misdeeds of these two noblemen were real, or whether they owed their fall only to a successful intrigue of the opposite party, the result was the same, for when Henry died the reactionary party was left without its leaders, and the new men were able to reap the advantage thereof.

Between these two extreme parties, however, it is hardly necessary to say there were many persons who held different shades of opinion. Many, of whom Gardiner was the type, had entertained no great affection

[1] *Froude*, vol. iv. pp. 510-23.

for the Pope, and had been willing to embrace Henry's ideal scheme of a Church which should throw off the authority of the Pope, but retain the accepted doctrines of Catholicism with little or no alteration; and many more would have submitted to it for a time, while they turned their eyes to that coming General Council which was the centre of so much hope on the part of good and single-minded men, anxious for the purification of the Church and not for its destruction. But in revolutionary times moderate parties rarely produce much effect. A moderate man may be, and often is, the best-informed, the most rational, the most highly-gifted man of his time, but his very virtues, moral and intellectual alike, tend to disqualify him for the position of a great party leader. For this the requisite is enthusiasm, real or pretended; and for enthusiasm the first condition, in most cases, is either an intellectual incapacity for seeing more than one side of a question, or a moral obliquity which prevents a man from acknowledging another when he does see it. In such times men, even of the coolest tempers and the fairest and clearest judgments, find themselves compelled either to take a side and keep to it, often in defiance of their convictions and their conscience, or else to stand on one side and leave society, including themselves and all that are nearest and dearest to them, to be victimised by leaders less clear-sighted or more unscrupulous than themselves. If they choose the latter, they sink out of sight, and history knows them no more; if the former, we see them gradually losing the clearness of their intellectual vision, and rubbing the bloom off their moral natures, till they sink gradually into something not much better, but only very often less efficient, than the coarser natures who have plunged blindly or unscrupulously into party warfare from the beginning of their career. So it was throughout the reigns of Edward VI. and Mary. On both sides moderation was cast away, and a revolution and reaction, each of the most violent kind, took place, creating a religious and political tempest which it took the utmost efforts of Elizabeth and her statesmen to still, and the effects of which continued for a century beyond her time.

During the whole of the sixteenth century and almost over the whole of Europe it may be said that religion—*i.e.*, in fact, the relation of religion to the State—formed one of the most important questions of the day, and was intimately intermixed with both the internal and foreign policy of every State; but just at the period with which we are now dealing it became in England the absolutely paramount question, so that in this and the following reign the history of the Church is almost the history of the State as well. There was no problem, whether of domestic or foreign policy, into which the religious question did not enter, and in most cases as its most important element.

It needs not here to repeat the full account, which may be better read elsewhere,[1] of how adroitly Lord Hertford, assisted by the most subtle statesman of the time, Sir William Paget, made use of Henry's will to defeat its own objects, overset the balance between the two parties, which Henry had been at so much pains to adjust, and finally emerged from the turmoil, which he had himself created, in the character of Duke of Somerset, governor of the young King's person and Lord Protector of the kingdom. Somerset was, it seems likely, sincerely attached to the reformed opinions; but even had he not been so, he had no choice but to

---

[1] Green, *Hist.* vol. ii. pp. 220-4 and Froude, *Hist.* vol. v. ch. i.

fall back upon the reforming party. This was pretty clearly shown after his fall by the fact that his successor, Lord Warwick, did the same, though at his death he showed that such belief as he really had, attached itself to the old religion.

The later years of Henry's reign, after the fall of Cromwell, may well have appeared to his contemporaries,[1] to whichever party they belonged, to be years of steady reaction in the direction of the old faith; but there are many indications that the reaction was but skin deep. Apparently the system had been a hard-and-fast maintenance of Henry's ideal Church—Catholicism, with a substitution of himself for the Pope, and accompanied by a tightening-up of the bonds of orthodoxy by the substitution of the Six Articles for the more liberal Ten, and a sharpening of the persecution of Protestants. But all this time, as we have seen, Papists so called (that is, the genuine adherents of the old religion) had been persecuted too—not, it is true, as heretics, but as traitors; and other changes were made, such as the omission of the Pope's name in the service books,[2] the order for the revision of these books and the omission therefrom of all superstitious and legendary matter, and for the public reading of the Bible in churches, the publication of the King's book, &c.

Thus the reaction, though it existed, was of a kind calculated rather to exacerbate both parties than to satisfy either. Both parties were held in check, but, while neither was permitted to reap a substantial victory, neither was effectually discouraged.

The greater part of the year 1547 was occupied, first by the settlement of the Protector's government

---

[1] *Green*, vol. ii. p. 217 *et seq*.
[2] Feb. 21, 1543. *Stubbs*, Appendix iv. pp. 131-2.

and the showering of honours and emoluments upon himself and his partisans, and then by the war with Scotland, culminating in the very complete but very unprofitable victory of Pinkie Cleugh. This victory, however, though it rendered the realisation of Henry's great object of uniting the two countries by means of a marriage between Edward and Mary more unlikely than before, yet served the purpose of increasing for the moment the popularity and reputation of Somerset. But, in the midst of these occupations, the Protector found time to proceed with certain other measures, which must have given the Catholics some foresight of what was in store for them. Thus, the bishops were compelled to take out commissions for the execution of their episcopal office, which proceeded upon the distinct assumption that all ecclesiastical, as well as all civil, authority was derived from the Crown. This, it is true, was no new thing, having been carried out nine years before by the late King—at least, in individual instances —and was a strictly logical result of the terms of the Act of Supremacy: now, however, it was to be made the regular condition of the episcopal jurisdiction, and the first to accept the new condition was Cranmer himself, the successor of Augustine and of Becket. Injunctions were issued for the purification of churches, though the curate and churchwardens of St. Martin's in London were compelled to restore the crucifix which they had removed from their church without legal warrant. A book of Homilies was issued, and a royal visitation announced, and the bishops temporarily suspended from their functions. Bonner and Gardiner alone attempted resistance; but Bonner and Gardiner, in consequence, went to the Fleet, where, in the course of a week, the former gave up his opposition, while

'Gardiner, persisting in his, presently exchanged the Fleet for the Tower.

On Somerset's return from Scotland, Parliament met, and the measures of this Parliament were not a little remarkable. In them we see the first sign of the failure of Cromwell's scheme of absolutism. The very first Act was one against such as should irreverently speak against the Sacrament of the Altar; but while it was thus directed against the profane and indecent proceedings of the extreme Protestant sectaries, its final clause enacted for the first time that the cup should be administered to the laity,[1] a resolution in favour of which was passed through Convocation during the progress of the bill through the House of Lords. The second was an Act for the election of bishops, which did away with the remaining phantom of capitular election, and directed that they should be nominated immediately by the King. But another Act (1 Ed. VI. c. 12) made even these somewhat strong measures appear moderate. It proceeded to sweep away at once not only the old Plantagenet and Lancastrian anti-Lollard Acts, 5 Ric. II. c. 6, and 2 Hen. V. c. 7, but also several very important Acts of the last reign, viz. 25 Hen. VIII. c. 14, for the punishment of heretics; 31 Hen. VIII. c. 14, the Act of Six Articles; 34 and 35 Hen. VIII. c. 1, the Act for the Advancement of True Religion, otherwise called the Act for Abolishing Erroneous Books; and, above all, 31 Hen. VIII. c. 8, the Act of Proclamations.[2] It would be difficult indeed to believe that a mere desire of conciliating the Protestant party would have induced the Protector to repeal this statute if we are to accept Burnet's state-

[1] *Eccl. Courts Com. Rep. Hist.* App. v. pp. 142-8 (Dr. Stubbs).
[2] *Burnet*, vol. i. p. 423 (263).

ment that upon it were grounded the great changes in religion made during the minority of Edward VI. It appears a more rational supposition that these changes, so far as they were made without the concurrence of Parliament, rested rather upon the Act of Supremacy which was interpreted to place the government of the Church in the hands of the sovereign personally rather than in those of Parliament. However, the changes made by this extensive repealing Act were in any case very considerable, and were all, especially the last-mentioned, in the direction of mitigating the system of absolute personal government which Cromwell had established, but were all at the same time calculated to re-awaken the religious strife which Henry's iron hand had so long forcibly restrained. But while so much was done in the direction of relaxation of the laws existing against the new opinions, there was one point in which this Act tightened the grasp of the law to the detriment of the old: section 6 made it high treason to impugn the supremacy of the King. The one remaining ecclesiastical Act of the year was a renewal of 37 Hen. VIII. c. 4, the Act giving colleges and chantries to the King. Another Act, though only affecting ecclesiastical in common with all other legislation, was 1 Ed. VI. c. 11, which altered a provision made in the last reign to the effect that the young King, on attaining the age of twenty-four years, should be at liberty, by his letters patent, to annul any laws enacted during his minority as if they had never been. The new Act limited this power to annulling such enactments for the future only, but not so as to render void the acts done under them in the interval between the time of their passing and the King's majority.[1]

[1] *Burnet*, vol. ii. p. 94 (41).

The Convocation contemporary with this Parliament, besides agreeing to the resolution above mentioned, presented several petitions of more or less importance,[1] viz. (1) for the reformation of the canon law according to the Acts framed under the late King; (2) that the inferior clergy might sit in the House of Commons, which they affirmed to have been the ancient custom of the nation, or else that no Acts concerning religion might pass without the sight and assent of the clergy; (3) that the work of the bishops and others appointed in the late King's time to alter the services of the Church 'might be brought to its full perfection' (Burnet), or (a somewhat different thing) 'might be produced and laid before the Lower House' (Lathbury); and another (4) regarding the maintenance of the clergy during the first year of their incumbency, in which they were charged with first-fruits. To this they added a desire to know whether they might safely speak their minds about religion without the danger of any law; a request which shows how vivid was their remembrance of the Præmunire. They also carried a vote in favour of removing all restrictions on the marriage of the clergy by a majority of fifty-three to twenty-two.[2]

The year 1549 is famous, amongst other things, as the year which saw the authoritative issue of the first English Book of Common Prayer. Of the significance of this act Mr. Green gives the following striking and accurate account: 'The old tongue of the Church was now to be disused in public worship. The universal use of Latin had marked the catholic and European

---

[1] *Burnet*, vol. ii. p. 103 (47); also Lathbury, *Hist. of Convocation*, pp. 134-5.
[2] Lathbury, *op. cit.* p. 135.

character of the old religion; the use of English marked the strictly national and local character of the new system. In the spring of 1548 a new Communion service, in English, took the place of the Mass: an English Book of Common Prayer—the Liturgy which, with slight alterations, is still used in the Church of England—soon replaced the Missal and Breviary, from which its contents are mainly drawn. The name Common Prayer which was given to the new liturgy marked its real import. The theory of worship which prevailed through mediæval Christendom—the belief that the worshipper assisted only at rites wrought for him by priestly hands, at a sacrifice wrought through priestly intervention, at the offering of prayer and praise by priestly lips—was now set at naught. The laity, it has been picturesquely said, were called up into the chancel. The act of devotion became a common prayer of the whole body of worshippers. The Mass became a Communion of the whole Christian fellowship. The priest was no longer the offerer of a mysterious sacrifice, the mediator between God and the worshipper: he was set on a level with the rest of the Church, and brought down to be the simple mouthpiece of the congregation.'

The authority of this First Book of Edward VI. is in all points complete. It had the sanction of Convocation as well as that of Parliament and King, although, as we have seen before and shall have to see again, the first of these was, in a vast number of instances, both before and after, held quite unnecessary, and the second not much less so.

It would be out of place to enter here into a discussion as to the theological peculiarities of this book, and its difference from those which followed it in 1552, and again in the reigns of Elizabeth and Charles II.; but it is worthy of notice that, as to the intention of those who compiled and issued it, two quite different theories are held by two differing sections of the modern High Church party. Until recently, the prevailing view has been that the Prayer Book of 1549 was perfection—that its compilers fully meant it to be final—but that before its successor was published, the Reformation had, so to speak, fallen into bad hands, and that the second Book, consequently, was in direct contradiction to the first, and was all that was uncatholic and bad; that the changes introduced under Elizabeth and Charles II., though not all that could be wished, were still mostly in the right direction, and served to restore the Prayer Book of the Anglican Church to something like a respectable standard of Catholicity.[1] Of late years, however, a more extreme, but, at the same time, a more logical and accurately historical, section of the party, represented by Mr. Pocock, have maintained that there was in Edward's Council 'an avowed intention, from the very first, to proceed further and further, though the alterations were gradually introduced, for fear of shocking the prejudices of those who adhered to the older forms of religion'; and, again, that Edward's first Book 'was never meant to be final, and that the Council, with the Protector at their head, went as far as they dared at the time, leaving future changes to take their chance as occasions for making them might arise.' Now, when we consider that the principal movers and the principal agents were the same throughout, we can hardly doubt that the latter is the real account of the

---

[1] *The Principles of the Reformation Shown to be in Contradiction to the Book of Common Prayer*, by Nicholas Pocock, M.A. (B. M. Pickering, 1875), pp. 12 and 19. See also Appendix, Note IV.

matter. It is probably true that the Duke of Somerset was, to some extent at least, sincere in his reforms, and that his successor was not so; but Northumberland had little choice, if he meant to prosecute his ambitious schemes, but to throw himself upon the support of the Protestant party,[1] and the Protestant party was running constantly into greater extremes: added to which a man who is not really himself by conviction a member of the party with which he acts, or which he aspires to lead, is certain to ally himself with its extreme wing. Thus the substitution of Northumberland for Somerset rather urged on than retarded the changes made. The moving powers among those actually engaged in the work were in both cases Cranmer and Ridley. Cranmer was a man always, in a greater or less degree, under the influence of those about him; and we know that under that of Ridley, and of the foreign Protestants, his opinions progressed rapidly, during the later years of his life, in the direction of more and more extreme Protestantism. When, upon the occasion of his second trial at Oxford, Dr. Martin [2] said to him, 'Then from a Lutheran you became a Zwinglian, and for the same heresy you did help to burn Lambert the Sacramentary,' &c., he did not deny it, but merely answered, 'I grant that I did then believe otherwise than I do now, and so I did until my lord of London (Ridley) did confer with me,' &c.

[1] Edward himself had inherited no small portion of his father's determination and self-assertion, and although it seems absurd to attribute any considerable influence to a mere boy, as he was, yet it is to be remembered that he was an absolute monarch in the making, that his intelligence was very precocious, that he was fanatically Protestant as far as he was able to be anything, and that he was surrounded by influences which made him even more so. His nearest relative, Somerset, was the head of the Protestant party, and his domestic tutors and governors, Aylmer and Cheke, belonged to the same faction.

[2] *Foxe* (Edit. 1641), vol. iii. p. 656.

So that there can be little room for doubt that to the extent just indicated Mr. Pocock is probably right. At the same time, it must be observed that in the charges of insincerity which he is constantly hurling at Cranmer and his abettors, he appears to make no account of the rapid growth and development of views and opinions which always takes place during periods of great and sudden change. At such times, when a man has once chosen his side or his party, his opinions, which have vacillated before, will often progress even to extremes in a very short time, and harden and stiffen in them. No better instance of this kind of development in the time with which we are now dealing can be found than that of Gardiner himself. When Gardiner exchanged the service of Wolsey for that of his master, and for some years after, he appeared to be as facile a tool in the hands of Henry VIII. as any other of his ministers or courtiers. When he was ambassador to the Pope, it is probable that what he saw in Rome had the same effect on his mind as it had on those of others, and he was ready to go all lengths with the King. After his return, his early impressions became gradually less intense, the evil side of the Reformation presented itself with more and more insistance to his mind, and he became gradually more and more conservative in his tone. Nevertheless, so long as Henry lived, Gardiner supported and defended all or most of his ecclesiastical measures, and remained in the main subservient to his will. On Edward's accession, he first openly attempted to stem the tide of change, assuming—probably for the purpose of gaining time—the indefensible position, that he had been willing to yield to the supremacy of the late King, and would be equally willing to do so to the new one, but protesting against the exercise of that supremacy by the council of regency during the minority; and finally we shall see him, in the following reign, throwing himself heartily into the reaction, flinging reform to the winds, and taking the lead in the submission to that very papal supremacy, which he had aided and abetted Henry in subverting and trampling on.

It is, however, by no means necessary to believe, with the modern partisan historians, that the leaders, either on the one side or on the other, were the thorough-paced knaves and scoundrels which these writers represent them. When a great cause is in dispute among men, it is seldom or never true that all the right is on one side and all the wrong on the other, and still less that all the good men are on one side and all the bad men on the other. In the tangled web of human affairs, no man but a complete fanatic, or an entirely selfish and unscrupulous person, can ever act from a single motive, and the man who professes to do so is mostly one so ignorant of his own nature, and so blind to his own faults, that he entirely overlooks the real springs of his actions. If we could suppose a person quite free from selfishness, prejudice, and all other human errors and weaknesses, even such a man could hardly act in a complicated case from a single motive, and, if he did, would probably produce an effect totally different from that at which he aimed, because the very faults from which he was himself free, were still present both in those with whom and those against whom he was acting. In practice, however, every man enters on his career biassed in one direction or another by the influences of birth, family, friendship, education, interest, association, sentiment, or inclined to take one side rather than another by the mere intellectual constitution of his mind; and even these several motives act mostly not alone but in combinations of the most various description—one or more in one direction being modified or overcome by the combined influence of others acting against them. Moreover, when a man has once chosen his party and taken his side, his convictions, as we see constantly in the example of a modern party politician, are very apt to deepen and harden with the effect of time and exercise. He becomes surrounded by a partisan atmosphere. He reads the publications of his own party, and listens to their conversation and their speeches; and when he hears a speech on the other side, he looks upon it as the mere one-sided harangue of a professional advocate, and fixes his own attention mainly on what there is to be said against it. Thus, after a time, he begins to act as if he believed, and sometimes even really to believe also, that his own party has an absolute monopoly of truth and right, and at last, if, as in the case before us, the contention concerns religion, that his own party are the servants of God, and their adversaries, therefore, the ministers of Satan. That party organisation tends to foster knavery may be admitted without qualification; but it does not necessarily follow that every party leader is therefore a conscious and deliberate knave.

The remaining principal transactions of the year 1549 are almost all of them connected directly not only with the change of religion, but also with the relations of Church and State. Thus the rebellions in Yorkshire and Devonshire were in some measure due to the unpopularity of the religious changes, though that in Norfolk appears to have been more of what we should call a socialistic character. But in all three cases alike they were considered as so many offences against the State, and were met and put down as such; and although, no doubt, the religious changes had something to do with these revolts, it is probable that the general misgovernment of the time, the shameless greediness of the courtiers, the financial distress, and the depreciation of the coinage had at least as much, probably a good deal more. But the contentions about the Princess Mary's mass, the execution of Joan Bocher, and the deprivation of Bonner, were all of them directly ecclesiastical transactions.

The close of this year, however, was distinguished by an event of a peculiar and very significant character. In the King's council, no less than in the nation at large, it had become recognised that Somerset's administration was a failure. Abroad and at home it had been equally unsuccessful, and the knot of unscrupulous new nobles who had at first accepted him as their leader, finding that he was unequal to the post, at last compelled him to resign it. Somerset, in fact, had ruled as chief of a faction of rapacious upstarts, who had cared throughout more for their own gain than for the good of the country. They had absorbed the Church lands, and enclosed the commons, and raised the rents, and ruined the tenants. When the revolts took place, they were thoroughly alarmed; but, being many of them men of great energy and courage, they took what means lay ready to their hands, used their own resources freely, and risked their own lives, and thus at last put down the revolts. Thus it was that the same faction remained at the head of affairs; but Somerset fell, and Warwick (better known as the Duke of Northumberland), the most successful of the leaders against the rebels, became his successor, and thus it was also that Warwick, though any religion which he had appears to have been of the older sort, came into power on the implied condition that he still maintained the ascendency of the Protestant faction. How completely the general condition of affairs was, in these respects, unchanged, is shown by the two ecclesiastical Acts of the session which commenced in November—one (3 and 4 Edw. VI. c. 10) for the abolition of images, and ancient service books, and the other (3 and 4 Edw. VI. c. 11) a renewal of the old Act of Henry VIII., for the appointment by the King of two-and-thirty persons to revise the ecclesiastical laws—and also by the fact that Bonner's and Gardiner's petitions for a rehearing of their cause were either unnoticed or rejected.

Almost with the beginning of the year 1550 appeared the first form for the ordination of bishops, priests, and deacons. This had been arranged for by an Act passed in the session just referred to.[1]

It was drawn up by the same committee of twelve—six bishops and six other divines—as had composed the first liturgy, and it is remarkable, as a sign of the times, that Heath, Bishop of Worcester (afterwards Chancellor and Archbishop of York under Mary), who was one of them, was sent to the Fleet for declining to agree with his colleagues in accepting it.[2] The committee was appointed by council, and the use of the form which they should draw up was provided for, as we have seen, in advance by Act of Parliament; but whether the form itself was ever accepted by, or even submitted to, Convocation does not appear to be equally clear.[3] In the early part of this year, also, the bishopric of Westminster, first instituted by Henry VIII., was dissolved, and Ridley was translated from Rochester to London, to fill the place of the deprived Bonner. The year was,

[1] Strype, *Mem.* II. i. 290.   [2] *Burnet*, ii. 251.
[3] At least, it is not mentioned either by Strype, Burnet, or Lathbury.

in fact, full of religious disputes and controversies. In the course of it[1] occurred the famous quarrel about vestments, consequent on the promotion of Hooper to a bishopric, in which Cranmer's foreign *protégés*, Bucer and Peter Martyr, appear to have shown a degree of moderation and good sense which contrast favourably with the hair-splitting fanaticism of Hooper himself and many other divines.

In this year also occurred the authoritative establishment by the King[2] of John a Lasco's congregation of Germans (Netherlanders?) and others in London, the first legalisation of any body of Nonconformists in England. Of these curious and utterly anomalous bodies we shall have occasion to hear more in the reign of Elizabeth. Following upon this, in the autumn, appeared Bishop Ridley's[3] injunctions for the removal of altars in his diocese, prohibiting also certain motions and ceremonies used in the time of the Holy Communion as 'counterfeiting the popish mass,' which appear to have been further enforced by the Privy Council.

The transactions of the year 1551 showed plainly how little improvement was to result from the substitution of Warwick for Somerset as the leader of the gang of adventurers who misgoverned in the name of the King. Gardiner, Heath, and Day were deprived of their sees, on the ground of their unwillingness to carry out the reforms of the council, and to fill the place of the first,

---

[1] *Strype*, II. i. 350.

[2] See the King's letters patent in *Burnet*, vol. v. p. 305, where an especial command is addressed to all sorts of authorities, archbishops and bishops, among others, that this congregation is to be permitted to use and enjoy its own rites and ceremonies and ecclesiastical discipline, 'non obstante quod non conveniant cum ritibus et ceremoniis in regno nostro usitatis.'

[3] *Burnet*, vol. v. p. 309, and Strype, *Mem.* II. i. 355.

Ponet was translated from Rochester and Scory put in his place, while the other two sees were left vacant for the time. Every change was attended by the robbery or fraudulent exchange of some of the possessions of the see, most of which were lavished upon the courtiers, and friends of the successful faction; and all this deliberate malversation of what was treated as the property of the State, took place at a time when the King's debts were large and increasing, when the coinage was deliberately debased, and when the nation at large, and the poor in particular, were suffering from scarcity, from the sweating sickness, and from the general rise in rents which followed upon the transference of the Church lands to lay landlords, mostly belonging to the class of '*nouveaux riches*.' Before we acquiesce altogether in the currently-received view that the risings in this reign were due to the attachment of the people to their old religion, and the unpopularity of the reform, we ought in fairness to remember that the rapacity of the upper classes, the financial errors of the government, and the general distress and misery of the people, were such as have rarely been equalled in England; and there can be little doubt that much of the unpopularity of the religious measures of the time was due to the fact that they appeared to proceed from the same hands as did all its other evils. It is certain that papal supremacy was never popular in England, and it is also certain that in Henry VIII.'s time the priesthood was in no better odour with the people than the Pope, and that Henry carried popular opinion with him in his measures against both; and it seems unlikely that any very great feeling would have been aroused in favour of either, had Edward's counsellors moved on with any degree of mildness or moderation, or had they not shown, in their general government, an entire absence of regard for either religion, justice, or even common humanity. It seems to have been assumed by historians that because the religious question appeared on the face of the Articles presented by the rebels in Devonshire, therefore the rebellion arose mainly, if not solely, from dissatisfaction with the King's reforms; but it should not be forgotten that the priests were in general the persons who would draw up such documents, being, in fact, almost the only persons of any education to be found in the country districts, and that the priests were of all men, in the nature of things, those most disaffected to religious reforms. It is therefore probable that, although these had a considerable share in the production of the revolts, they had a far less one than they have been generally credited with.

Of the domestic occurrences of the year 1551, besides the squabbles over the Princess Mary's mass, and the execution of the Duke of Somerset, the principal were the preparation of the Forty-two Articles, and the revision of the Book of Common Prayer, neither of which was, however, published till the following year. The two former, if they affected the Church at all, did so only indirectly, and need not occupy us here; but the others were two of the most important events in the history of the English Church.

There has been a vast amount of controversy as to the exact authorship of the Forty-two Articles, which appears hardly necessary, since Cranmer distinctly took it upon himself, when answering Dr. Martin at his second trial at Oxford.[1] They were the earlier form of the existing Thirty-nine Articles, from which they differ but little. It is of more immediate consequence to us to determine, if possible, the exact authority by

[1] *Foxe*, vol. iii. p. 657.

which they were imposed, but this it is far from easy to do. Strype states distinctly, quoting the Warrant Book as his authority, that they were 'agreed upon by the bishops and other learned men *in the synod* at London, in the year of our Lord 1552, and many other authorities [1] follow on the same side; and, on the whole, it seems probable that it was the case. With respect to the Prayer Book of 1552 there is greater doubt. The Act of Parliament by which it was authorised was passed early in the year 1552, and is called 5 and 6 Ed. VI. c. 1. It does not seem by any means clear that it ever was formally submitted to Convocation. It was drawn up by a committee of bishops and other divines appointed by the King—*i.e.* by the Council—but Cranmer himself was its principal author.

The comparison of the second Book of Edward VI. with the first, as well as the consideration of the Articles and of all the facts that have come to light concerning their history, seems to point to the theory of Mr. Pocock —at least, with a slight modification—as that which best accords with them. For while the doctrine has visibly progressed in a direction towards a Swiss rather than a German form of Protestantism, the persons responsible for the authorship of the two books are mainly the same; and as the distance of time is very short, it affords an excuse for suspecting that they may have intended to proceed to still greater extremes. At the same time, as already noticed, the opinions of Cranmer, and probably also of many of his coadjutors,

---

[1] E.g: Lathbury, quoting Wilkins and Heylin, Bishop Harold Browne, who cites the authority of Cardwell, &c. On the other hand Canon Dixon, *Hist. of the Church of England*, vol. iii. pp. 513-14, perhaps turns the balance once more in the opposite direction. The practice, however, of the times tended so greatly to the exaltation of the royal supremacy, that the authority of Convocation was gradually becoming of little account.

were changing rapidly, and the two books may therefore represent their sincere convictions at the time of publication. In any case, the differences are well worthy of notice, especially in their relation to the course taken on the resumption of the work of reformation in Elizabeth's reign.

Two other compilations of some importance call for notice in this place, viz. the book of Homilies and the *Reformatio Legum Ecclesiasticarum*, though the latter never acquired a legal sanction.

The Homilies appear to have been begun before the death of Henry VIII. Cranmer was what we should now call the responsible editor, but the authors were various, and were men of the most diverse position and character. Thus those on salvation and faith and good works are attributed to Cranmer himself; that against brawling to Latimer; that against adultery to Becon; while that on charity has been assigned, of all men in the world, to Bishop Bonner. The *Reformatio Legum Ecclesiasticarum* was intended to be the final outcome of the often repeated Acts of Henry and Edward, whereby the canon law was to be revised, codified, and re-enacted. This also was due to Cranmer, assisted by a committee of divines and lawyers; but its confirmation was prevented by the death of Edward, and it has never obtained any legal authority.

Edward's reign was now at an end. It needs not here to repeat the often-told tale of how the poor young king faded away, as his uncle and his half-brother had done before him; of how Northumberland gradually increased his power and influence, drew most of the Council, willingly or otherwise, into his conspiracy, and, working on Edward's fanaticism, at last persuaded him to attempt to set aside his father's will, to deprive his half-sisters of their inheritance, and to endeavour to set up Lady Jane Dudley as his successor on the throne. All this may be read elsewhere in greater or less detail. The one point in it which interests us here is the conduct of Cranmer. Cranmer had floated on the full tide of prosperity during Edward's reign. On the whole, his conduct had been good. He may have been somewhat inclined to harshness in his treatment of Gardiner and Bonner, but his chastisements had been but with whips as compared with the scorpions which they themselves dealt out to their opponents both before and after. But at the last moment a real trial came upon him, and then he showed, as he did all his life, a want of that element of hardness, that backbone as it is sometimes called, which is an indispensable constituent in a really great man in troublous times. Northumberland, as we have seen, had all but completed his scheme by gaining over the young King himself, as well as the most important members of his Council. The King himself, in his zeal for what he called 'the religion,' became impatient for the completion of the arrangement which he had made for its maintenance. He was manifestly dying, and after having by his own personal urgency almost compelled the judges, in spite of their remonstrances, to draw up the letters patent, he turned to the Archbishop, whose name was still wanting, and expressed his hope that he alone would not 'be more repugnant to his will than all the rest of the Council.'

Cranmer's case was a hard one, that is undeniable. Edward was his sovereign, and that in an age when to be a king was to be a demigod: he was also as dear to him as his own son. He had answered for him at the font in his infancy, and had been his father's favoured counsellor in his childhood, and his own guardian and adviser in his youth; and now Edward lay a-dying, and this was his last request to him, and was made in the interest of that very form of religion which Cranmer himself had done more than any living man to establish. It was a case in which even a strong man might have yielded, and Cranmer was not a strong man: in which a hard man might have been softened, and Cranmer was not a hard man. He did wrong, no doubt, but surely not without excuse or from base motives.

It is argued by some that Cranmer's reluctance was a mere pretence—that as he, of all men, had most to lose by the accession of Mary, so he went heartily with the Duke of Northumberland, and with the extreme section of the Protestants, who were his only real adherents. But it must be remembered that he was on the worst of terms with Northumberland himself, who, as he said in his letter to Mary afterwards, had sought his destruction; that if he meant to join him from the beginning, he had no reason to spoil the act by hesitation and pretended unwillingness; that he had been a lawyer and a statesman before he became a reformer, and therefore, like many other statesmen of the time, had probably no great confidence in the hasty and ill-contrived scheme of Northumberland; and must at least have known that, unless it succeeded, to join it was to throw away his last chance of safety, whereas to take active measures against it would have been the most obvious means of averting Mary's anger from himself. It was simply another, and this time a fatal instance of that inherent weakness of character, which had made Cranmer so often unable to withstand his sovereign, even when the choice lay between his sovereign and his own conscience, his better judgment, and his peace of mind.

K

If now, in conclusion, we come to sum up the difference in the position of the Church at the end of this reign from what it was at the beginning, we shall find it greater in some respects, less in others, than seems to be generally believed. The reign of Edward VI. seems to be generally looked upon as the time when the great revolution took place in the Church of England— as pre-eminently *the era* of the Reformation ; but if we examine the statute book we find no Acts in this reign which affect the fundamental relations of Church and State in any way at all comparable to the Act of Supremacy and the Act for the Submission of the Clergy in the previous reign. There are several Acts already noticed above, such as the two Acts of Uniformity and others, of great importance to the Church; but they are all of a quite different class from the great Acts just mentioned, and, in fact, grew out of them. They are Acts dealing with the constitution and management of the Church, and are the legitimate and natural results of that transfer of the government of the Church from the Pope and the clergy to the sovereign, which those two great Acts had effected. In fact, the Parliament of Edward VI. was far more remarkable for what it refused to do than for what it did. In 1552 it (and in this case 'it' means the House of Commons) rejected a Heresy Bill, it rejected the attainder of Bishop Tunstall, and it completely remodelled a Treason Bill. These were all Northumberland's measures, and he consequently dissolved the Parliament (April 15). But early in the following year he was compelled to summon another, and this, though carefully and unscrupulously packed, refused to pass a bill against ecclesiastical impropriation, and another which would have renewed the system of monopolies abolished in the twelfth year of Henry VII.

These proceedings show plainly the breakdown of Cromwell's system of absolutism. We have here come a very long way from the Parliament of Henry VIII., ready in almost every case to register the 'King's will,' and give the sanction of law to his every caprice. It is in the executive rather than in the legislative acts of the reign that we find the true justification of its character as a revolutionary era. Henry VIII., as we have seen, while he had completely revolutionised the relation of Church and State, had made but little change in the condition of the churches or in the character of the ritual. He had abolished some images, which had already become scandalous, and had done away with the shrines of a few saints, whose wealth had almost become a by-word, and the pilgrimages to which had already given rise to notorious abuses; but in the main he had left the churches and their services very much as they were. The altars stood as of old, the priests wore their gorgeous vestments and offered their masses as before, the choirs chanted, the organs rolled, the incense arose in clouds above the bowed heads of the worshippers, exactly as old men remembered it in their youth, and as they supposed their fathers had seen it before them. The transition from all this to the second Prayer Book of Edward VI., with the altar pulled down and replaced by a plain table in the middle of the church—an oyster-board, as the men of the old faith called it in derision—with all the images and shrines removed, the priest changed into a minister in a simple white surplice—sometimes without even that, and mostly murmuring at being compelled to wear it—was as great as that which we should see if we walked out of St. Paul's into the nearest Primitive Methodist meeting-house—nay, it was even greater. The doctrinal changes, though far greater in fact, were not greater in principle; for, although the changes from the doctrines hitherto held by the whole Western Church were more thorough and more intimate under Edward than under his father; though the standard of the Forty-two Articles was very different from that of the Six or even of the Ten; yet the severance from Rome had been as complete under Henry as it ever became afterwards, and the severance from Rome was in itself a revolution in doctrine. But where doctrine appeals to one man, ritual affects a thousand; and though the masses may now and then take up a cry for or against a particular doctrine, they have mostly been awakened to its existence by a change in the outward ritual which expresses it. Thus, though Henry's changes had been, as regards doctrine, not inconsiderable, and, as regards polity and the general relation of the Church to the State, incomparably greater than those inaugurated under Edward, they had given far less offence, and stirred up infinitely less enmity, because they had in the main let alone those external observances by which only the mass of mankind are sensibly affected. Even had Henry's life been prolonged, it is difficult to conceive that his system could have been maintained for many years in the then existing condition of Europe. The civilised world was still in all the ferment into which the revival of learning and the invention of printing had plunged it. Protestantism had sprung up into a formidable power, and the air was full of it: it followed the new learning and the newly awakened spirit of inquiry into every country of Europe, and under such circumstances it was impossible to separate a single country from the old unity of the Western Church without giving Protestantism a vast advantage in it. If any existing consideration could justify the breach of the unity, and the consequent revolt against the unique authority of the one universal Church, much more could similar considerations justify an assault upon some of those practical abuses which the best and noblest of her sons could not deny to exist within her, and which they had endured only because her own authority alone stood high enough to initiate a reform. The breach once made was as the letting-out of water, and Henry it was who made it; and though his authority and determination proved sufficient to limit it for the moment, yet even his powers of repression would, in all likelihood, have failed had they been tried much longer.

CHAPTER VII

REIGN OF MARY

WE have witnessed the worst excesses of the reforming party. We have seen how the Lords of the Council cared little enough for either religion or morality, or the prosperity of the State or the good of the people, or any other thing except power and honour and wealth for themselves and their friends. We are now to see how, the moment the pressure was taken off, the Catholic party ran into excesses even more extreme than those of their opponents; how the reaction even exceeded the action which provoked it, and that to such an extent that its effects have continued, though in a gradually diminishing degree, up to times within the memory of still living men.

It is unnecessary here to enter into the mere facts of the political history; how Northumberland's ill-arranged and almost childish scheme fell to pieces and collapsed, and how, within a few days of Edward's death, Mary found herself undisputed Queen of England, and those who opposed her had not only gained nothing, but had put themselves entirely at her mercy. Mary was herself, perhaps, as unfit to rule as any sovereign who ever arrived at a throne in mature age. Of the Roman Emperors it has often been remarked that those who had attained mature years before they ascended the throne mostly became good rulers. But with Mary it was not so. Again, we are told that 'sweet are the uses of adversity,' and Mary's life of thirty-seven years before her accession had been one long course of adversity, but to her its uses had not been sweet. Her life had been throughout a most unhappy one. The estrangement between her father and mother began when she was still a mere child, and from that time till her mother's death her life was made miserable, not only by witnessing the constant persecution, injustice, and indignity, with which her mother was treated, but by enduring a full share of similar ill-treatment in her own person. On Katherine's death she became formally reconciled to her father, but in order to do so was compelled to write to him acknowledging his supremacy, the unlawfulness of her mother's marriage, and her own illegitimacy, and thus retained no right to the succession except what it pleased Henry afterwards to assign to her in his will. During her brother Edward's reign, her constant adhesion to the old faith—or, at any rate, her opposition to the further development of the Reformation—was a source of continual complaint to the Council and continual annoyance to herself. Her life, moreover, had been, for a person in her situation, a very secluded one; and thus her knowledge of the world and of mankind had not only been very limited in amount, but had been warped and coloured by the constant feeling that the world, so far as she knew of it and heard of it, was all going wrong, and that her first duty, if ever she came to take an active share in its government, would be to head it back, and lead, or rather drive, it once more into the ancient paths. Mary possessed by inheritance her full share of the pride and sternness of her Spanish mother, as well as the self-will and vehement temper, and also the courage and energy, of the Tudors, and the reaction produced by a sudden change from a life such as I have described to a position of almost unchecked power, upon such a temperament, was not unlikely to drive her to some excesses.

In the first weeks after her accession, when, for almost the only time in her life, Mary found herself welcomed and apparently beloved by her people, she displayed for a brief moment some small measure of that geniality and frankness which made her father, and afterwards her sister, despite their rough dealings and choleric tempers, the most popular of sovereigns: but she seems to have expected every obstacle to give way at once before her; and when opposition and disappointment came upon her, and ill-health speedily followed, she sank at once into a soured, disappointed, angry zealot, rendered only the more self-willed, the more unscrupulous, and the more cruel, by the constant ill-success of all her efforts and the miscarriage of all her schemes.

The actual relations of Church and State during her reign changed more strangely than even during her father's. Mary found herself by law on her accession *Ecclesiæ Anglicanæ supremum caput*, albeit the assumption of such a title must have seemed to her the extreme of blasphemous presumption. Yet even Mary did not venture, in the first weeks of her reign, to show openly her intention of bringing England once more into bondage to the Pope, although the general disgust and disaffection, caused by the misgovernment of Edward's Council, might seem to have afforded an unusually good opportunity for so doing. Gardiner was released from the Tower and restored to the Council board. Edward's bishops were removed, and those expelled by him were restored to their sees, and Acts were passed—1 Mary, Sess. 1, c. i., repealing some of the recent extensions of the Treason-felony and Præmunire Acts; 1 Mary, Sess. 2, c. i., declaring the Queen's legitimacy and repealing any Acts in a contrary sense; and, lastly, 1 Mary, Sess. 2, c. ii., the famous Act which repealed almost the whole of Edward VI.'s ecclesiastical legislation and re-established Divine service and the administration of the Sacraments as they existed in the last years of Henry VIII.

To this point it seems likely that the Queen carried the general feeling of the country with her. Though the reformed religion had progressed since Henry's death, it is probable that the majority of the nation still retained their preference, if not for the old faith, at least for the old ritual and ceremonies. It is certain, in fact, that they did so in most parts of the country, though apparently not in London nor in the eastern counties. Moreover, the outrageous proceedings of Edward's Council had for the moment alienated very many who, left to themselves, would have taken the side of the Reformation, and made them look back upon the later years of Henry's reign as a time of moderation and comparative tranquillity. But indications were early given, though not so early generally understood, that Mary did not intend to rest in this illogical though generally acceptable position; for in the inhibition[1] from preaching, published on August 18, she speaks of herself as 'of that religion which she had professed from her infancy,' and limits her previously-promised toleration of other opinions 'till public order should be taken of it by common assent.' The expulsion of the Edwardine bishops from the sees whose previous occupants had been removed to make room for them,

[1] *Burnet*, vol. ii. p. 894.

and the restoration of the latter, were also acquiesced in as a necessary consequence of the righteous reversal of the high-handed measures taken during the Protectorate. There can be no reasonable doubt that, as a rule, the Londoners preferred Ridley to Bonner; but they probably felt that Bonner had received hard measure from the party which had just fallen from power, and that, as there could not be two kings of Brentford, his restoration was the natural consequence of their fall, and Ridley's expulsion a necessary preliminary to it.

In September, Archbishop Cranmer, who had hitherto simply been ordered to confine himself to his own palace, was sent, together with Ridley and Latimer, to the Tower. How far the immediate cause of this was the manifesto against the Mass, which he seems to have written but not published, but which became known, and was acknowledged by him before the Council, is not easy to determine; nor is it of much importance, since it seems clear that, when he had once resolved to remain in England, his final doom was no longer doubtful, or was only rendered so by his own subsequent vacillation.

With the beginning of the third session of her first Parliament,[1] Mary's brief popularity may be said to have come to an end. She now decided, contrary to the advice of her wisest councillors, on the marriage with Philip of Spain, a match which was abhorred by all her subjects, except the small section who were, to adopt a modern phrase, 'Catholics first and Englishmen only afterwards.' To the nation in general no proposition could have been more hateful. It had, it is true, one and one only recommendation, viz. that it secured Spain as a permanent ally against France,

[1] Strictly speaking this was a new Parliament, though the Acts are reckoned as if it were the same.

and thus did away with the virtual subjugation of
England to the latter power, which was threatened by the
marriage of Mary of Scotland, the heir nearest in blood
to the English crown, with the Dauphin of France. But
even this advantage was more apparent than real, as
was proved by the subsequent policy of Elizabeth, which
proceeded on the assumption that the mere instinct of
self-preservation would compel Spain to continue in alliance with England in order to check the growth of the
power of France. In the meanwhile the disadvantages
were evident enough. The power of England in Europe
at the accession of Mary was a mere shadow of what it
once had been; while Spain was, at the moment, the
most powerful nation in the world. Hence it was clear
that if the two were to become one, Spain, and not England, would be that one. Treaties and paper arrangements would be useless, and should the issue of Mary's
marriage with Philip be an only son, there would plainly
be nothing but the uncertain life of Don Carlos between
him and the combined crowns of Spain and the Indies,
England and the Low Countries, and England would
become a mere permanent appendage to Spain. But,
besides these prospective evils, hateful to all Englishmen, Catholic and Protestant alike, there was also the
more immediate certainty that all Philip's influence
would be thrown into the scale in favour of the Queen's
known desire for an immediate and unreserved reconciliation with the see of Rome. To the thorough-going
Protestants this meant not loss or inconvenience, but
actual persecution; and the religious persecution of the
sixteenth century wore no kid gloves. To the forty thousand families who had profited by the spoliation of the
monasteries it meant loss, impoverishment, in many
cases ruin; to the mass of the nation, even to those

whose faith was what it had ever been, it implied the renewal of all those annoyances, scandals, and practical inconveniences and oppressions, from which Henry VIII.'s drastic measures had, as they hoped, delivered them for ever. Only to the really enthusiastic and bigoted Papists, a minority probably smaller even than that of the Protestant fanatics, could the Spanish marriage be a truly welcome measure.

Mary's great aim was undoubtedly the restoration of England to the unity of the Catholic Church. In this aim she was, as Mr. Green [1] very truly tells us, almost alone, and that she should have succeeded in it as far as she did, was due to the curious complication of political and religious aims and circumstances by which she was surrounded. Lord Paget looked upon the matter from a purely political point of view, and regarding, as he did, the peril to England from the impending union of Scotland with France, he was disposed to support the marriage with Philip as the best course for the safety of the country, though he loved neither the Pope nor religious persecution. Renard and his master, though objecting to neither of them when the times were suitable to them, advised a degree of caution and moderation in religious matters which were little in accord with Mary's fanatical enthusiasm; but their views of the religious question were quite overshadowed by their paramount anxiety to create a power in their own hands which should outweigh that of France. Gardiner, the ablest and most influential of Mary's ministers, Paget perhaps excepted, appears at this time to have held a view different from either of them, and far more in accord with that of the bulk of Englishmen of the time. Gardiner had been brought up by Cardinal Wolsey, and

[1] *Green*, vol. ii. p. 247.

was a kind of survival of the old ecclesiastical politician; but the politician in him always preponderated slightly over the ecclesiastic. He had seen much of the evils of the Roman supremacy, and had gone with Henry VIII. in his subversion of it; and though later on he became one of the Roman party, it is not credible that he was really sincere in his wish for its restoration. His efforts, up to this time, had always been directed towards the revival of the system which had prevailed in the later years of Henry, viz.: the maintenance of the old faith and the old ritual almost unaltered, together with a rigid intolerance of difference of opinion, and with little or no diminution of the authority of the clergy, but with the substitution of the Royal for the Papal headship. He wished Mary to marry a subject, and to send Elizabeth to the Tower, and he hated the Spanish match as certain to lead to the re-establishment of the Papal power in England, and probably by violent means. Mary herself possessed all the self-will of the Tudors, reinforced by the obstinacy of her Spanish forefathers; and partly by playing off the different parties against one another, and partly by insisting obstinately on her own personal right to marry as she pleased, she gained her point at last. The only real ally whom she had throughout was Reginald Pole, a man as fanatical, as narrow, and, though from different causes, as politically ignorant, as herself, but without a tithe of her courage or her patience, who had been in exile for years, and was not even yet permitted to return to England, and whose knowledge of England was therefore obtained at second-hand and coloured by all the fancies of an enthusiast and a dreamer.

Mary's determination to marry Philip was—at least in the first instance—simply a means to an end, and the end in question was the restoration of England to the unity of the Catholic faith. She was probably quite sincere in her reiterated statement that she was content as she was, and had no wish to marry at all; but this she conceived to be the appointed task of her life, and as soon as she had come to the conclusion that the true means to accomplish it was by a marriage with Philip, to marry Philip became part of her duty as Queen. That she afterwards nursed herself into an enthusiastic desire for the marriage itself, and was disappointed just in proportion to her enthusiasm, is a mere incident in the history, and serves only to show how really great her ignorance was, and how completely she had fallen into the hands of a single party in the State. That she should have looked upon Philip as the person who would enable her to carry out her reactionary views, may seem strange when we consider the repeated exhortations[1] to caution and moderation in her dealings with religion which she received from both Philip's father and his ambassador Renard at the beginning of her reign: but she may well have considered that their advice was due to an exaggerated view of the number and influence of the Protestant party in England, such as an ambassador, drawing his conclusions mainly from what he saw in London, would be not unlikely to form; and she knew that both Philip and his father were pretty deeply committed on the orthodox side. That she was right in the main, the later history of her reign shows plainly enough. The action and reaction of the different parties concerned, and the curious modes in which their various aims crossed and partially defeated one another, all seemed, at this period, to

---

[1] See despatches in the *Granvelle Papers*, vol. iv.; quoted also by *Froude*, vol. vi. p. 43.

work together to enable the Queen to carry out her own, which, as already said, concurred with no one's else.

Besides the restoration of the Papal power the other great object was the exclusion of Elizabeth from the succession to the throne.

Gardiner, it would seem,[1] would even have backed her in this latter design, but Gardiner did not approve of the marriage with Philip and was at this time less than lukewarm in his zeal for the Pope. Paget, the sole advocate of the marriage, was earnest in maintaining the claims of Elizabeth, and even the necessity of recognising them to the full. He was a latitudinarian in religion, and certainly not anxious to restore the Pope. All the more moderate Catholics went with Gardiner.

The Protestants, on the other hand, could not go with Paget: they had a dread, only too well founded, of Philip and his Spaniards.

Hence, while nobody supported the Queen heartily, none were, except the Protestants, heartily opposed to her. Parliament, it is true, was opposed to the Spanish match, and the House of Commons even ventured to remonstrate with Mary on the subject. They gained nothing by their motion but a rebuke for their presumption from the Queen, together with the reply that 'on this matter she would take counsel with God, and with none other.' This famous interview occurred on Nov. 16. Two months afterwards broke out the rebellion of Sir Thomas Wyatt. But the rebellion was badly led. Courtenay was a coward and a weakling, if not even a conscious traitor. He betrayed Carew to Gardiner, and precipitated the whole movement.

Carew hastened off into Devonshire, but was unable to effect a rising, and had to make his escape. Suffolk

---

[1] Renard, as noted by *Froude*, vol. vi. p. 120.

was equally unsuccessful in the Midlands. But even so there was a time when the danger was extreme: Wyatt had London and the Queen's person almost at his mercy, and it appeared to be almost certain that he would succeed. At this point of extreme peril the Queen's own courage and determination saved her. She rode to the Guildhall and appealed in person to the Corporation to defend her, pledging herself at the moment to give up the Spanish marriage if it should not appear to Parliament that it would be for the benefit of the whole realm.[1] This was the turning-point of the movement. Wyatt reached the south side of London Bridge, and found it closed against him; and before he could make his way round by Kingston, the Queen and the City were better prepared, his own troops were exhausted, and the enterprise was hopeless. The results of its failure were soon apparent: not only were the leaders executed, but Lady Jane Dudley, as well as her father, her husband, and her brothers, were put to death, and the preparations for the marriage went on as before, the proxy marriage taking place on March 6.

Every effort was made by Gardiner and Renard to incense the Queen against Elizabeth, and she was sent to the Tower, and escaped but narrowly, and only by means of the active intervention of several of the Lords of the Council. It was not, however, only in the revenge taken upon the rebels, and their friends as such, that the failure of Wyatt's rebellion showed its fruits. It was looked upon specially, and probably with justice, as pre-eminently the rising of the Protestants; and its failure furnished a pretext, as well as a motive, for further action against them. Accordingly, we find

[1] *Green*, vol. ii. pp. 250-1.

three remarkable documents,[1] which have been printed by Burnet, all bearing dates in March 1554—in the interval, that is to say, between the suppression of Wyatt's rebellion and the meeting of Parliament at the beginning of April. The first of these is a letter to Bishop Bonner, containing a number of injunctions (articles they are called) to be put in execution without delay throughout his diocese. They command, among other things, the use of all the ecclesiastical laws and canons which were in use in Henry VIII.'s time, not being directly contrary to the laws of the realm; the disuse by the bishop of the phrase '*regia auctoritate fulcitus*,' and of the oath of supremacy; the deprivation or divorce of all married clergy; and rigid care on the part of the bishops for the exclusion of all Sacramentaries and other heretics from holy orders. This is in several respects a remarkable document; it describes itself as given under *our signet* at our palace, &c., and, although addressed to the Bishop of London to be put in execution *in the whole diocese*, most of its items begin with the words 'That every bishop,' &c., as though intended, as it doubtless was, to be observed through the whole realm. The second and third are commissions given to the Bishops of Winchester, Durham, London, St. Asaph, Chichester, and Llandaff; the first, in Latin, to eject the Archbishop of York and the Bishops of St. Davids, Chester, and Bristol, from their sees on account of their having contracted marriage; and the second, in English, to eject those of Lincoln, Gloucester, and Hereford, on the ground that they held their sees by the late King's letters patent with the express clause '*quamdiu se bene gesserint*,' and had since, both by teaching erroneous doctrine, and also by

[1] *Burnet*, vol. v. pp. 381-8, also Appendix, Note V.

inordinate life and conversation, declared themselves very unworthy of that vocation and dignity in the Church.

All these three important documents would appear to rest upon the royal authority only; that is, upon that very 'supremacy' which Mary was so anxious to resign and repudiate. The time chosen to issue the two latter was dictated, in all probability, not only by the feeling of irritation caused by Wyatt's rebellion, but also by considerations of policy,[1] to diminish the hostile votes in the House of Lords, when, in order to redeem her pledge to the City of London, the Queen would be compelled to submit the Spanish marriage to the final decision of Parliament. During all this time the disputes in the Council had been so hot, the general disgust of the people at the severity with which Wyatt's rising had been punished so great, and party spirit had run so high, that Renard had more than once threatened that the arrival of the Prince of Spain must be deferred until the country became more tranquil.[2]

Early in April Parliament met, but though the Marriage Bill was permitted to pass, the House showed no great complacency in other matters. Thus, of three bills introduced by Gardiner, viz. (1) for restoring the Six Articles, (2) to revive the Lollard statutes of Henry IV., and (3) to restore the episcopal jurisdiction, the first never reached a second reading at all, and the other two, though they passed the Commons, could not be got through the Lords, and Parliament was dissolved while they were still unpassed. It is to be noted that in these cases, as in several others about this time, the reactionary measures of Gardiner and his mistress were carried through the Commons with more ease than

[1] According to *Burnet*, the new bishops were sixteen in number: vol. ii. p. 444. [2] *Froude*, vol. vi. p. 221.

through the Lords. It may, however, be doubted whether the compliance of the Commons in such matters can be taken as a fair proof of the general consent of the nation. That pressure of all kinds was unscrupulously used, not only during elections, but upon members themselves when elected, in these times [1] is notorious, and there is no reason to suppose it was less on this occasion than on others. Parliament was dissolved on May 5, but it was not till June 19 that the news arrived that Philip was on his way to England; and at last, towards the close of July, the marriage took place.

And what a marriage it was! The bride more than ten years older than her husband, haggard and wizened and older even than her age, and utterly destitute of all those personal charms which might have attracted, and for a time at least retained, the affection of such a man as Philip, but withal worked up by the combined effect of vanity, enthusiasm, and the constant flattery of interested attendants, to a pitch of persistent and demonstrative fondness more repulsive in such a person than the most chilling indifference. Her mind, doubtless, was more attractive than her person, or might have been so, for Mary was an educated and accomplished woman: but she was a religious enthusiast, and her religion was of the narrowest, the most fanatical, and the most superstitious type; and she had so completely assimilated the dogma that the end justifies the means, that there was scarcely any method, however cruel or treacherous, which she would hesitate to adopt for the good of the faith. The bridegroom was young enough —indeed, far too young for his wife—but he was undersized, pale, feeble, and, if the truth must be told, cowardly, repellent in manners and repulsive in feature,

---

[1] *Burnet*, vol. ii. p. 447; also *Green*, vol. ii. p. 252.

and already a thorough sensualist; a man of a dark, gloomy, and mercilessly cruel temper, selfish to the extreme to which selfishness can go, destitute of natural affection, and absolutely unfeeling, as well as unscrupulous in regard to those who stood in his way. He was as bitter and narrow a bigot as Mary herself; and this was, indeed, their only point of sympathy. But there was a difference between the two. Mary was thoroughly single-minded: if she sacrificed others, she was ready to sacrifice herself as well. Philip always kept an eye on his own interests, and when they were at stake could be as hard on the Pope as on a heretic. The one was a bigoted fanatic, the other a fanatical hypocrite. In all the long array of historical portraits, of whatever age, we can scarcely find any one single character more entirely detestable, or more absolutely destitute of redeeming features, than that of Philip II. From such a marriage what good could follow to Mary or to England?

In the autumn a visitation of the dioceses by their bishops took place, largely in the spirit of the Queen's letter to Bonner already referred to. Bonner's own visitation articles still remain in his register, and are quoted by Burnet and Wilkins, though with some variations, and probably from different copies. These articles, as we learn from Renard,[1] created a ferment in London, and Bonner found it necessary to defer his proceedings.

It is worthy of note that Renard anticipated the probability of similar trouble in other dioceses; a prognostication which seems to suggest two things, viz. that other bishops were about to follow a similar course to Bonner's, and that practical returns of this kind to the old ecclesiastical order of things were not altogether popular even elsewhere than in London. The ambas-

[1] *Granvelle Papers*, iv. 329.

sador's letters at this time have a certain tone of uneasiness throughout, and he seems to rest his hopes of continued tranquillity chiefly on the fact that the malcontents had no head, and were unable to trust one another.[1] Parliament was to meet in November, and every sort of pressure appears to have been used to influence the elections in the Lower House and to gain over the members of the Upper; and, judging by the results, with much success. When assembled, its subservience was as conspicuous, though not quite so complete, as it had ever been even under Henry VIII. Its first work was to reverse the attainder of Cardinal Pole, and thus pave the way for his return to England; and then it proceeded to pass some of the very measures which the preceding Parliament, some six months before, had rejected. The Act of 1 and 2 Philip and Mary, c. vi., revived the bloody legislation of Richard II., Henry IV., and Henry V., for the punishment of heretics; and 1 and 2 Philip and Mary, c. viii., repealed at once the anti-papal legislation of Henry VIII. from his twentieth year onwards; that of Edward VI. having, as we have seen, been already abolished in the second session of Mary's first Parliament—though, as a condition precedent to this, the Houses insisted on, and received, a distinct assurance, in the Pope's name, that the holders of Church lands were not to be molested. But not even so was the humiliation of the British Parliament, or of the British nation in its Parliament, complete; for in the interval between the passing of the repeal of Pole's attainder and the other legislation just mentioned, the two Houses had humbly petitioned the King and Queen to sue for their absolution to the legate, and had received it on their knees, and been re-admitted into the unity of

[1] *Granvelle Papers*, vol. iv. p. 317.

the Catholic Church. But, great as were the successes of the Catholic party under the exceptionally favourable circumstances of the early part of Mary's reign, they were far from coming up to the level of the wishes and hopes of Pole or Gardiner and the Catholic clergy. Parliament had stoutly refused to exclude Elizabeth from the succession, or to permit Philip to ignore the conditions imposed upon him on his marriage, or to remove or define the Præmunire, or to meddle with the Mortmain Act beyond a temporary suspension, or to restore the Church lands, or even to take away the impropriated tithes from their lay owners.[1] Thus, though much was given, much also was withheld; and Pole and the Court party were but imperfectly satisfied.

An unsuccessful attempt to give additional power to Philip by a Regency Bill brought about a dissolution of Parliament in the middle of January 1555. Thus, in eighteen months after Edward's death, the whole, not only of his religious system, but of his father's also, was swept away, and the power of the Pope, and of the Catholic clergy, was re-established in England as it had been in the early days of Henry's reign—so far, at least, as it was in the power of law to re-establish it. But the England of 1555 was not the England of 1525: the thirty years which had elapsed since Henry first openly agitated the question of divorcing Mary's mother, had been years which had brought more change in the social, moral, and intellectual condition of the country than the whole previous century; and though Mary had succeeded in sweeping away, for the time, almost the whole legislation of the period, the other factors in the condition of the nation were beyond the powers even of a Tudor monarch. Mary's success had, indeed, been

[1] *Froude*, vol. vi. pp. 292-306.

marvellous, and in the main it was all her own work.
Her one idea, when she arrived at the throne, was to
restore religion; that is to say, the sway of the Pope and
the Roman Church. With that view she had brought
about the Spanish marriage, against the opposition of
Gardiner himself, the leader of the Catholic clergy, and
with no support beyond that of Paget and a small knot
of latitudinarian statesmen; and, with the additional
influence derived from that marriage, had succeeded in
bringing about the complete legislative revolution which
we have just seen. For the revolution was now, indeed,
complete, and even the most important of the subsequent Acts of the reign (2 and 3 Philip and Mary, c. 4),
by which the Crown renounced the first-fruits and
tenths, were but matters of detail, however important
they might be in their effects. But, wonderful as it was,
Mary's success was not complete. Nor was it satisfactory to herself. She had failed in excluding Elizabeth[1]
from the succession; she had failed in securing any
power to Philip beyond the term of her own life; and
not only had she failed in effecting a restoration to the
Church of the lands and goods torn from it by her
father, but the spirit which had been displayed when
she had raised the question, was such as may well have
aroused a doubt in her own mind, as it clearly did in
those of others, as to the sincerity and permanence of the
change which she had effected. Some such thought as
this, no doubt, urged on Mary in the course of severity
which she now adopted. Of her sincerity there can be no
doubt, and she may well have felt that her work was but

[1] In the despatches of the period there is a constant repetition of the statement that if Elizabeth succeed there will surely be a recurrence to heresy. See for example Renard's despatch of June 27, 1555, quoted by *Froude*, vol. vi. p. 355, where he says that the succession 'must fall to Elizabeth, and with Elizabeth there will be a religious revolution.'

half done; that, by the recent legislation, she had cleared the way and acquired the means for effecting her object, but the object itself was as yet far from being attained.

Half her own ministers were either latitudinarians, like Paget, or concealed heretics, like Cecil. Elizabeth was her inevitable successor, and Elizabeth belonged to the latter category; and Mary most probably felt that her own life was uncertain, and that, unless she could root out the tendency to heresy, which she saw all around her, in her own lifetime, all would relapse at her death, and her labour would be in vain. Whatever the constraining motive, or, as is more likely, the combination of motives, there is no doubt of the fact that with the close of the first Parliament of Philip and Mary began the cruellest, the most relentless, and the longest persecution which has ever been seen in England ; and that, in the main, it is to Mary herself personally that this persecution is due.[1] Gardiner's share in it is not so clear, for though it is evident that at first he was in its favour, it seems also clear that he did not long remain so. Incapable of religious zeal himself, he seems to have doubted, until repeated trials had cleared up the doubt, whether the Protestants believed any more sincerely than he did—whether, when it came to the point, they would think their particular views were worth defending at the cost of their lives.

From the position which Gardiner held in Mary's esteem and counsels, there can be no hesitation about fixing the charge of the commencement of the persecution upon him—at least, it could not have commenced without his concurrence or against his will; but

---

[1] See Renard in State papers quoted by *Froude*, vol. vi. p. 197. See also the commission to Bonner, Thirlby, and others, for a severe way of proceeding against heretics (*Burnet*, vol. v. p. 469).

he probably thought that a very few executions would be sufficient to check the zeal of the Protestants, and when he found that he was mistaken he did not care to go on. It is true that two important factors may have contributed to diminish Gardiner's zeal, viz. the fact that Pole arrived in England only a few weeks before the outbreak of the persecution, and that Gardiner's own health began to fail very shortly after this; for he died on November 13, 1555, exactly a year after Pole left Brussels on his journey to England, and had been ill probably for some months before.[1] The other principal agent in the persecutions, Bishop Bonner, seems to have received rather hard measure both from his contemporaries and from posterity. That he was a man of coarse mind and brutal manners there is no room for doubt; and, having chosen his party from whatever reasons, he went all lengths with it, with little pity and no scruples, and often with a malignant satisfaction in paying off old scores upon his personal enemies with somewhat large usury. Such a man is likely to be, and often is, popularly accepted as the embodiment of the system of which he is the expression, when, in fact, his part is that rather of the executioner than of the judge. But we all recognise the fact that Jack Ketch is not a popular character, albeit he may deserve his unpopularity far less than the Judge Jeffreys who calls his services into requisition; and Bonner, who was the hand rather than the head or heart of the persecution, probably obtained a larger share of its unpopularity than fairly belonged to him. His return to his see, at the commencement of Mary's reign, seems to have been popular; and we know at

---

[1] De Noailles to the Queen of Scots, Sept. 9, 1555.—*Ambassades de M. M. de Noailles*, vol. v. p. 127.

least of one occasion on which he appears to have tried to save a victim, even against his own will. Another person who shares to some extent the responsibility of the persecution is Cardinal Pole. But to him, on the other hand, historians appear to have been most unaccountably lenient. He may possibly have deserved his early reputation as a learned and studious man, and he seems to have been sincere, and fairly free from selfish and personally ambitious schemes; but he was a pedant, and what would in modern days be called a prig. As a negotiator he was incompetent, and as a statesman beneath contempt. He held the seals for a few months after Gardiner's death, until he received an intimation from the Pope that his legate must not serve two masters, when he retired to make room for Archbishop Heath; and at this time De Noailles describes Mary as so regarding the legate that 'she neither will nor can do anything without him.'[1] This is the very winter, also, when the horrors of the Lollards' Tower and Bonner's coal-house were perpetrated. Added to this, his own injunctions to the bishops, of February 1555, for the reconciling of their dioceses to the Church, introduced a register of all persons in each parish who had been reconciled, with a promise of a future visitation of a very significant character. Moreover, towards the latter part of the persecution, in no place did it rage more hotly than in Pole's own diocese of Canterbury: and although it is alleged that Thornton, the Suffragan of Dover, and Archdeacon Harpsfield, were the principal agents in the matter, yet it ought not to be forgotten that Thornton and Harpsfield were but Pole's subordinates, and there is no reason why the rule '*qui facit per alium facit*

---

[1] *De Noailles*, vol. v. p. 256.

per se' should not be applied to the full in such a case as this. It is therefore quite futile to endeavour to relieve Pole from the charge of complicity in the abominations of the Marian persecution. But neither, to do him justice, is there any good reason to believe that he would have disowned his share in it.

The ecclesiastical counter-revolution of Mary's reign was in many respects very remarkable. It seems that the English Church, in any intelligible sense of the words, had very little to do with it, and that little was of a kind which reminds one of the Japanese institution of happy despatch. Mary's methods were precisely those of her father and Cromwell, but the process to which they were applied was the reverse of that for which they had employed them. Parliament, as we have seen, she was unable to control with the completeness with which Cromwell had done it, though even with Parliament her success was surprising; but Convocation [1] was far more compliant, and how it became so is sufficiently indicated by the fact that, whereas the assembly of the previous year had authorised the Forty-two Articles, and, as seems almost certain, Ponet's Catechism also, the new Lower House contained but six members who declined to sign Weston's bill declaring the latter 'pestiferous and full of heresies.'

The first of Mary's Convocations conducted the well-known disputation on the Sacrament of the Lord's Supper, at St. Paul's, and decided, as of course, in favour of the Roman doctrine. The second managed the still more famous disputations with Cranmer, Ridley, and Latimer, at Oxford. The third Convocation synchronised with the first Parliament of Philip and Mary,

[1] *Lathbury*, pp. 148–9.

and its proceedings show the greater boldness which had been infused into the Roman party by the Queen's marriage with Philip. Not only did they receive the Pope's absolution, at the mouth of Cardinal Pole, with becoming humility, but they petitioned, and petitioned successfully, for the repeal *en masse* of the whole anti-papal legislation of Henry VIII. from the twentieth year of his reign onwards. The one point in which they failed was that of the restoration of the Church lands, and in this their failure was as conspicuous as was their success in other matters. Yet, had Mary's reign been prolonged, or had the birth of an heir perpetuated the sway of the Spanish dynasty, it seems that the English clergy would have been indeed in evil case as a result of their own success. They had sold themselves to the Pope more completely than their predecessors had ever done; and yet, if we look at the share which the Crown had had in the bargain, it might be fairly doubted how far they had efficiently emancipated themselves from State control, as the next reign, indeed, sufficed to show; and in the meanwhile they had failed to regain that position of wealth, and of the independence which wealth gives, which had for ages gone so far in enabling them to oppress the people, and to make their own terms often with the Crown itself.

The subsequent Convocations of this reign were of little importance, inasmuch as they were practically over-shadowed by the Legatine Synod which Pole assembled in November 1555. It is worthy of notice that Pole thought it necessary, or at any rate wise, to obtain a warrant under the Great Seal as a condition preliminary to assembling this Synod,[1] since it showed,

[1] *Lathbury*, p. 152.

in the first place, a sense of the necessity of obtaining the licence of the civil powers for his proceedings, and, in the second, a truly remarkable forgetfulness of the fact that Wolsey, less than half a century earlier, had obtained the same licence to perform the same act, yet it had failed to shield him from the Præmunire, the very same law which the utmost efforts of Pole's friends in Parliament had failed to get repealed. But, whatever may be thought of the security, or the reverse, of Pole's position, it is clear that the English Church, so far as that mysterious entity was represented by Convocation, had got itself placed effectually between the upper and the nether millstone.

And now there remains but little more to be said of the relations of Church and State in Mary's reign. The Church in England now meant nothing but the Popish clergy, and of the Church in that sense of the word Mary was the abject slave: but Mary was a Tudor monarch, and a Tudor monarch could say, with as much truth as Louis XIV. a century later, '*L'état c'est moi*'; so that the whole country was delivered up to the tender mercies of the Popish clergy, and truly is it said that the tender mercies of the wicked are cruel. True, these saintly men would not embrue their hands in human blood; but they would, and they did, arrange with the State that from their judgment there should be no appeal, and that their convicts should die by the cruellest death which human wickedness has ever yet invented.

There are one or two matters connected with Mary's persecution which, although they do not come directly within the category of matters affecting the relations of Church and State, yet concerned those relations so intimately, that it appears necessary to notice them in this place. One of these is the arbitrary character of the proceedings instituted against heretics.

Burnet[1] prints the original letter of Philip and Mary to the justices of Norfolk, ordering them in the plainest terms to make investigation into the behaviour of private persons, to employ informers, to call before them such as may 'probably be suspected,' and compel them to give an account of themselves. That this letter is but a sample is further proved by another, addressed to Bishop Bonner, and expatiating upon his slackness and want of zeal, in which their Majesties speak of having sent letters similar to the above to 'the justices of the peace within every of the counties in this our realm.' This seems to have been the completest instance on record of the introduction into England of the practical methods of the Inquisition, which Gardiner,[2] as we are told, had been anxious, still earlier in the reign, to set up in England; and it is worthy of notice that it was now introduced apparently on direct royal authority alone. Instances are to be found of remonstrance against Mary's policy of persecution from even the most unlikely quarters—from Charles V.,[3] from Renard, from Philip II.[4] (at least, indirectly), and even from Gardiner[5] himself—but they all seem to have

---

[1] *Burnet*, vol. v. pp. 427 and 429.

[2] Renard as quoted by *Froude*, vol. vi. p. 197.

[3] At the beginning of her reign, as we have seen, and again after the burning of Hooper. See also *Granvelle Papers*, vol. iv. pp. 393, 402.

[4] Philip had made Alphonsus à Castro (!) preach a sermon before him, in February 1555, against taking away men's lives for religion. *Burnet*, vol. ii. p. 490.

[5] Gardiner, followed by her other bishops, sitting to try Rogers, shifted the responsibility for the persecution from their own shoulders to the Queen's (*Burnet*, vol. ii. p. 484). Also Pole's instructions to the bishops

been in vain: some, doubtless, were insincere, and those which were not so, coming from whence they came, can be attributed to policy only, and not to honest conviction; but, by whatever motive dictated, they all met the same fate. Mary went on her way without pity, without remorse, and not less without reason. And yet Mary's conduct must, in fairness, be attributed to pure religious fanaticism. It breaks from her at every opportunity, from the beginning of her reign to the end of it. Her reply to the Commons, when they remonstrated about the Spanish marriage, that in this matter she would take counsel of God, and of none other; her statement, also to Parliament, on the subject of the firstfruits and tenths, that she could not take them with a clear conscience; her profound belief that she had been preserved, almost miraculously, for the special purpose of restoring England to the unity of the Catholic Church; all these and other indications, while they are no way inconsistent with the self-willed, narrow, sour, and ignorant woman which Mary certainly was, all point also to one completely under the power of a dominant religious belief, as sincere and brave as it was narrow and mischievous. Nay, it would almost seem, if the whole circumstances be fairly considered, that the very act of her reign which has been especially pointed out as dictated by private and personal revenge, viz. her ferocious persecution of Cranmer, was really due to the same conviction.[1] On what principle, or for what reason, was Mary's conduct to Gardiner and to Cranmer so widely different? During the greater part,

and their officials especially concerning the keeping of a register of those reconciled to the Church, and summoning before them those unreconciled, and proceeding against them (*Burnet*, vol. vi. pp. 866-9).

[1] *Burnet*, vol. ii. p. 535; where it is to be observed that he quotes no authority for his statement.

if not the whole, of Henry's reign, Gardiner had been fully as much her enemy, and fully as much her father's tool, as Cranmer had been, and with her mother's divorce he had to the full as much to do. He had been sent to Rome, as one of Henry's ambassadors on the subject, long before Cranmer had any concern with it. He was Henry's principal counsel at the famous trial before the two legates; and he sat with Cranmer, and concurred in his judgment, at the final conclusion before the Court at Dunstable.[1] Cranmer, therefore, could not easily, on this ground, be more obnoxious to her than Gardiner was; and, on the other hand, Burnet tells us, though again without giving his authority, that at a time when her father was much incensed against her, Cranmer ventured upon the not altogether safe office of interceding for her, when Gardiner himself and the Duke of Norfolk stood aside and left her to her fate.[2] From the very beginning of the divorce negotiations Gardiner had been one of the prime agents of the King, and had continued to be so to the very end of them; and up to and beyond the passing of the Supremacy Act—indeed, till after the death of Katherine of Arragon—Cranmer and Gardiner had acted together; nor is there any evidence that the former had acted more rigorously against the Queen than the latter —indeed, the supposition is negatived by the character of the two men. The first indication of any divergence between their views appears in the discussions preceding the Act of Six Articles. It was, in fact, doubtless Cromwell's reduction of the bishops to mere State officers, after the Supremacy Act, which first inclined Gardiner to a reactionary course; and it was the fact

---

[1] *Burnet*, vol. i. pp. 135, 219.
[2] *Burnet*, vol. ii. p. 387.

of his becoming reactionary, and more and more reactionary as time went on, which made him change gradually from Mary's bitterest enemy to almost her closest and most trusted friend; and his so doing shows how completely Mary could overcome her most natural and most sacred private feelings at the bidding of her religious fanaticism, and in the interests of her cherished Church. And just as Gardiner had moved in a retrograde, so had Cranmer moved in an advancing, direction from the time when he sentenced Frith for denying the Corporal Presence in the Eucharist, to that at which he adopted Frith's words on the very same subject, and incorporated them in a note into his own Communion Office.

Is it not possible, too, that in Cromwell's later legislation we may find the key to Gardiner's later and reactionary course? His early career showed that he had little real regard for the Papal claims or the unity of the Church; but nothing in his whole life ever gave rise to a suspicion that he undervalued the privileges of the clergy or the power and dignity of a bishop.

He cared little whether Pope or King was called Head of the Church, but he cared a great deal for the bishop's revenues and the bishop's courts and rights and jurisdictions; and when he found out that the royal supremacy was to be a reality, and not a mere title, and that it meant a lay vicar-general presiding in Convocation, and a Church made really subject to one master, instead of maintaining a position in which it might alternately despise each of two, then the scales fell from his eyes, and he began to perceive that the clergy were in danger of exchanging 'King Log for King Stork,' and that the Pope in Italy, with all his exactions and extortions, was a better bargain than the

King in England, intent upon obedience no less than taxation, and always at hand to enforce his authority. Hence, perhaps, his enmity to Cromwell first and to Cranmer afterwards, his obstructive tactics under Edward VI., and his active retrogression under Mary.

There is probably no single character in history of which it is more difficult to arrive at a tolerably accurate and fair estimate than that of Archbishop Cranmer. Not only was his a 'strangely mingled' and highly complex nature, but it was cast upon the most perplexed and stormy period of all modern history; therein to occupy a post of the very greatest difficulty and danger. But, over and above all this, Cranmer was the most prominent leader of a party, at a time when party spirit ran its very highest, when every leader and every follower fell, and could not but fall, into errors, and when every error was seized upon by a hundred malignant enemies, and painted for all posterity in the blackest colours. He has suffered, too, almost as much from the exaggerated encomiums of excited partisans, as from the slanders of unscrupulous opponents. In a word, his reputation has been the chosen battle-ground of the most embittered party warfare that the world has ever seen, and a task eminently difficult in itself has been rendered almost impossible by the struggles of the combatants.

If we lay aside the merely rhetorical slanders of malignant opponents, we shall, I think, arrive at the conclusion that the main charges brought against Cranmer's character resolve themselves into three, viz. (1) that he was insincere in his oath to the Pope when first made Archbishop of Canterbury—that he never meant to observe it, and was guilty of deliberate perjury; (2) that he perpetually yielded to the wishes of Henry VIII. in regard to his divorces and other matters, and must have done so in divers cases against his own conscience, and with full knowledge that he did wrong; and (3) that in his last struggle under Mary he recanted several times in the hope of saving his life.

(I.) The first of these charges need not detain us long. It belongs almost to that very class which we have just excluded from notice. Cranmer had, like every archbishop for many centuries, two oaths to take, one to the Pope and another to the King. Like almost every similar pledge, when a functionary owes allegiance to two different authorities, these oaths, if strictly interpreted by a man of scrupulous conscience, would be found to be more or less incompatible. That they were felt to be so in older and less difficult times, is proved by the fact that Archbishop Langham,[1] in Edward III.'s time, 'solemnly renounced all expressions in the Papal bulls which militated against the Royal prerogative, or infringed upon the laws lately enacted' (the laws in question being no other than the Statute of Provisors); while, on the other hand, in the reign of Edward I., Archbishop Peckham[2] 'openly stated that whatever oaths he might have taken (*e.g.* to the King), he should feel himself absolved from them if they interfered with his duty to the Pope.' To quote a more modern instance, the case is exactly similar to the charge brought against the Heads and Fellows of Colleges in Oxford and Cambridge, in regard to their oaths to obey statutes, &c., for several years previously to the appointment of the Royal Commission of 1850.[3] But though

---

[1] Hook, *Archbishop of Canterbury*, vol. iv. pp. 198-9.
[2] *Ib.* vol. iii. p. 346.
[3] Chaps. iv., v., vi., and vii., of the late Sir William Hamilton, *Discussion on Philosophy, Education, &c.* (Longmans, 1852).

these truly shocking accusations were thus freely dealt around, and all the Heads of Colleges were held up to contempt as so many perjurers, yet no man ever really thought the worse of them, nor did one of them suffer either in person or reputation; in other words, no one really believed the charge. It is singular also, and worthy of remark, that these charges against Cranmer are mostly heard now from the mouths of clergymen of a particular party in the English Church, every one of whom has committed the same offence as Cranmer, only in a more flagrant form than he, and without his excuses, when he has declared his belief in the Thirty-nine Articles of the Church of England.

We must never forget that, to a mind like Cranmer's, versatile and subtle by natural constitution, and trained, and we may also say sophisticated, by a life-long familiarity with every phase and shade of controversial learning, it is almost, perhaps quite, impossible to put a question in a way which will admit of a perfectly unqualified answer, or which will present itself to it for simple denial or affirmation; and when such a mind is accompanied by a temperament naturally nervous and timid, and placed in a body depressed and weakened by age, imprisonment, and ill-treatment, it must be a *very* immaculate or a very Pharisaical accuser who will dare to cast the first stone at him. Every man is to some extent the victim of circumstances, and every man is to a still greater extent limited by the constitution of mind and body with which he came into the world. These are the facts which make the command that we judge not others as perfect a precept in philosophy as it is a rule in morals, since a really just judgment of another is impossible to man. We may, in many cases, be compelled to pass a judgment, and justified in passing one without qualification; but it must always be an objective judgment—*i.e.*, a judgment on the conduct of a man in its relation to others, not an absolute judgment on the moral value of the man himself.

II. The second charge is a far graver one, and there is, alas! less to be said in Cranmer's defence. Still, it is less than it appears to us of the present day, when we look at it in the light—or the darkness, I should perhaps better say—of the times in which he lived. Of Henry's three divorces, the circumstances were all different. In regard to the first, and most important—that from Katherine of Arragon—there is no doubt whatever that it was defensible, and that Cranmer believed it was right. The question of Anne Boleyn's guilt or innocence is one which most historians, of late years, have given up as insoluble; but if any man really knew the rights of the question at the time, Cranmer was that man.

The divorce of Anne of Cleves seems to have been, on the King's side, the most groundless and inexcusable of all; but it must be conceded, as far as the judge is concerned, that she herself appears to have concurred in it.[1] Thus, if we take the charges against Cranmer of having violated justice in deference to the royal wishes, we shall find ourselves compelled, so to speak, to grant him an acquittal in two out of the three, and a verdict of not proven in that of Anne Boleyn. Now, when we take into consideration the fact so often referred to, that in Tudor times to be prosecuted by the Crown was practically equivalent to being condemned, and that the only two men who openly stood out against Henry's will were More and Fisher, both of whom lost their heads in consequence, we can hardly be surprised that any man should object to doing the same *in a doubtful case.*

[1] Oughton, *Ordo judiciorum*, p. 320.

More and Fisher may have died for what seems to be a small point, but it was, at any rate, a point about which they had no doubt. They clearly thought that they would violate their consciences by taking the oath required of them; Cranmer, on the other hand, in the cases the particulars of which we know, did not think that he was doing wrong in pronouncing the divorce, and we may, therefore, fairly give him credit for similar conduct in that of Anne Boleyn, which we do not know.

In the matter of the divorces, then, we may say that, in regard to those of Katherine of Arragon and Anne of Cleves, Cranmer clearly did that which was his duty as a judge, holding the beliefs that he actually held, and that which every just judge would have found himself compelled to do. In the remaining case, we have to admit that we have too little information to justify us in either condemning or acquitting him. The charge of having assisted in the condemnation of Frith and Lambert, which comes also under this heading, resolves itself really into a statement that Cranmer had not completely assimilated a doctrine which, if it existed at all in his time, did so only as a theory, and which, even now, is but very imperfectly followed—viz., the doctrine of toleration. A Puritan divine at the epoch of the Rebellion, almost a century later, speaks of a toleration as 'the grand design of the devil!'

On this head, also, there is much to be put down to Cranmer's credit. He, and he alone, ventured on three several occasions to intercede, though mostly in vain, for some of the victims of Henry's ferocious tyranny—viz., for Anne Boleyn, for Cromwell, and, as we have just seen, according to Burnet, for the Princess Mary herself; and again, in the matter of the Act of Six Articles, he steadily, and from beginning to end, opposed Henry's will.

He not only declined to advocate it, but he also declined to abstain from opposing it, and did oppose it throughout its course in the Lords.[1]

Thus, it will be seen in regard to the charge of habitual and unworthy yielding to Henry's will, that in respect to the divorces he could do no other than he did, if we admit that we are not fully enough informed to condemn him in the case of Anne Boleyn; while, on the other hand, he, a constitutionally timid man, ventured to oppose Henry's will on several occasions, and to an extent, in the case of the Bill of Six Articles, —as Bishop Phillpotts, no great admirer of him, has pointed out—which More and Fisher never equalled. Of his error in regard to Northumberland's conspiracy I have already spoken.

III. We come, therefore, in the last place, to speak of the recantations between his trial and his execution, of which so much capital has been made by his detractors. That these require much excuse it is impossible to deny, but that they are absolutely inexcusable let him only assert who has stood firm in equally trying circumstances.

Cranmer had great reason—apart from the unwillingness to die which most men feel—to desire to live: He had done much to build up a Protestant Church in England, and seemed almost within reach of the end of his labours, and the crowning of the work, when Edward's death brought it to a sudden end. He may well have longed to finish it; he may well have indulged a hope that something would occur to frustrate Mary's plans, or even to alter her designs (for before his death her hopes of offspring had disappeared, and her health was manifestly failing), and have longed to

---

[1] *Bishop Phillpott's Correspondence with Lord Macaulay,* p. 4. Murray, 1861.

be still alive when the good time came, and to have his share in the completion of that on which he had spent so much labour, and for which he had gone through so many perils. Added to all this, he was an old man, and he went through misery enough in the last months of his life to have worn down the resolution of a stronger man than he; and had been worried by the perpetual arguments of Dr. Soto and his fellows—arguments always reinforced by the deluding hope of life and pardon—till his half-starved and weakened frame had, in all probability, reacted, for the time at least, both upon his intellect and his moral power. And so he fell—and no more pitiable fall than his is recorded in the long roll of history. But even that fall, grievous as it was, was not altogether unatoned for. At the last moment he found that his weakness and humiliation had been all in vain. His enemies had strained and twisted even their own pitiless laws in order to prevent his escape, to put him through the lowests depths of humiliation, and finally to bring him to the cruellest of deaths. They were just anticipating the final scene of triumph. They were to wreak their vengeance to the utmost on the man who had done more than any other man to perpetuate the schism from Rome, and to organise the English Protestant Church. They brought him out to die, and expected to hear him, in the face of a whole congregation, openly confess that Rome was the true Church of God, that the Pope was the legitimate Vicar of Christ, that Protestantism was utter heresy, that the system which he had established was utterly rotten, and himself a hypocrite, an apostate, and a too-late repentant heretic. But the scales had at last fallen from Cranmer's eyes—all his illusion had at last departed. He saw all at once the cruel craft of his enemies, and his own folly and baseness and cowardice. It was as if the evil spirit had departed from him, and he was once more in his right mind. All at once he recovered his manliness and his courage.

Cole, the preacher, at the end of his sermon had said: 'Lest any man should doubt the sincerity of this man's repentance, you shall hear him speak before you. I pray you, Master Cranmer, that you will now perform that you promised not long ago—that you would openly express the true and undoubted profession of your faith.' Then Cranmer spoke, and, after a prayer for forgiveness, he entered upon a kind of sermon, in which he solemnly warned his hearers, with all the earnestness of a dying man, against what he considered the prevailing vices of the time; and finally, when the interest of his hearers was wound up to the very highest pitch, he began with the words: 'And now I come to the great thing that troubleth my conscience more than any other thing that ever I said or did in my life'—words which might, quite naturally, lead up to a recantation of his heresy. Then followed—' and that is the setting abroad of writings contrary to the truth, which here I now renounce and refuse as things written with my hand contrary to the truth which I thought in my heart, and written for fear of death, to save my life, if it might be; and that is all such bills and papers as I have written and signed with my hand since my degradation, wherein I have written many things untrue; and forasmuch as my hand offended in writing contrary to my heart, my hand, therefore, shall first be punished; for, if I may come to the fire, it shall be first burnt.' The consternation produced by this bold speech seems to have been so great that, for the moment, those in authority forgot to stop the speaker, and he was able to add the final and important sentence: 'As for the Pope, I utterly refuse him, as Christ's enemy and Antichrist, with all his false doctrine; and as for the Sacrament, I believe as I have taught in my book against the Bishop of Winchester.' Then, indeed, there arose shouts of 'Pull him down!' 'Away with him!' 'Stop his mouth!' and so on. Further speech was not permitted. He was haled off to the stake, pursued to the last moment with the arguments and reproaches of the disappointed friars, and there took his death, without shrinking and without bravado, stood and held his right hand in the flame, and 'never stirred nor cried' till life was gone. Surely a death like this was some sort of atonement for the weakness and the fall which went before it. Whether it were so or not, at least it was a heavy blow to the Catholic party. They had striven hard to win a double triumph, and had violated justice, and been crueller than their own cruel laws to make their triumph and their vengeance complete. They had spared no effort to secure his recantation, had lured him to it by hopes of life, and, when they had succeeded, they would take his life as well. Then, at the last moment, he had turned upon them, flung back his recantation in their teeth, and, like Samson, to whom Mr. Froude has well compared him, 'the dead that he slew at his death were more than they that he slew in his life.' It is with no less truth than eloquence that Mr. Green has told us that 'it was with the unerring instinct of a popular movement that, among a crowd of far more heroic sufferers, the Protestants fixed, in spite of his recantations, upon the martyrdom of Cranmer as the death-blow to Catholicism in England. For one man who felt within him the joy of Rowland Taylor at the prospect of the stake, there were thousands who felt the shuddering dread of Cranmer. The triumphant cry of Latimer could reach only hearts as bold as his own; while the sad pathos of the Primate's humiliation and repentance struck chords of sympathy and pity in the hearts of all. It is from that moment that we may trace the bitter remembrance of the blood shed in the cause of Rome, which, however partial and unjust it may seem to an historic observer, still lies graven deep in the temper of the English people.'

Of Mary herself, by far the most charitable, and not improbably the truest account, is, that from a period shortly after her marriage with Philip, she ceased to be fully responsible for her actions. Early in 1556 De Noailles, the French Ambassador, describes her as ' in a continual state of excitement because she could not enjoy either the presence of her husband or the affection of her subjects'; and again he says : ' She sleeps but three or four hours, and spends the rest of her time in weeping, and regretting, and writing to bring her husband back, and anger against her subjects.' She is described as constantly breaking out into the most violent and abusive language when speaking of her heretical and disaffected subjects; and Henry II. (of France), in writing to De Noailles, speaks of her as '*possédée et maniée.*' And when at last there came upon her the evident disgust and desertion of Philip, the constantly-recurring libels and lampoons which manifested the growing hatred of her subjects, and, finally, the disgrace and danger involved in the loss of Calais, she sank into a condition of dull, miserable despondency and gloom, from which one might suppose that even death itself must have been a welcome deliverance. There is, in fact, a good deal of contemporary evidence which suggests the above conclusion. The fits of despondency into which she fell alternated with passion which vented itself in the most violent language. Her habits of wandering about her palace at night, and of sitting for hours on the floor, with her knees drawn up to her face, and her further habit of perpetually looking out for miracles, and regarding the most ordinary occurrences as miraculous, all point in the same direction, and we may fairly, as well as charitably, believe, that at any rate from the time that she recognised the fact that she could bear no child, and that Elizabeth must be her inevitable successor, Mary Tudor was no longer responsible for her actions. So considering, we may regard her as the most pitiable of human beings; otherwise she can hardly be relieved from the opprobrium which for three centuries has been attached to her name.

Little enough of the acts and deeds of Mary's Government took any permanent place in the constitution or laws of England. Most of her work was to undo that of her two immediate predecessors—her father and brother. Hers, in its turn, was mainly undone by her sister and successor; yet is there no sovereign who ever sat on the English throne, unless it be Henry VIII. himself, who has produced a greater or more permanent effect upon the subsequent history of the country. The loathing which Mary's persecution produced in the minds of Englishmen did more to establish the Reformation in England than any other single cause. 'You have lost the hearts of twenty thousand that were rank Papists within this twelvemonth,' wrote a lady to Bonner. The courage and the faith which ennobled and made heroes of 'prentices and herdsmen produced its natural effect, and the combined horror of the cruelty of the one party, and admiration of the courageous endurance of the other, produced a fixed hatred of the Roman Church and of Roman churchmen in the bulk of the English nation which was at least as immovable as it may have been unreasoning, which was kept alive for many years afterwards by the conspiracies against Elizabeth and the famous Gunpowder Plot, which lasted for three centuries, and of which traces still remain.

Another result of the persecution was that many of the Protestant divines who had flourished under Edward were driven into exile, and sought refuge, not among the Lutherans of North Germany, but among the Zwinglian and Calvinist communities of Switzerland and the Upper Rhine. This is a fact which has a double significance, and is of much importance. It shows, in the first place, the strong tendency towards the Zwinglian form of Protestantism which had developed itself in the English Church during Edward's reign, for the exiles would naturally direct their steps towards those amongst their co-religionists with whom they most strongly sympathised; and it accounts, as has been often pointed out, for the further development of the same or similar tendencies which took place in Elizabeth's reign.[1] The strength of this tendency in the Swiss towns to which the exiles went, naturally affected their minds, and, reinforced as it was by the cordiality and kindness with which they were mostly received, and the sentiments of gratitude and affection thus awakened in them, soon made a conquest of them altogether, and this form of Christianity became in their eyes the only

[1] See this point argued out by Mr. Pocock in the *English Review* and in his lecture. Grindal, in the early days of Elizabeth's reign, writes of 'Lutherans and semi-Papists' as if synonymous. See above, p. 116.

one really worthy of the name. But while most of these men, filled with love and admiration of Bullinger, Martyr, and some other of the Swiss leaders of reform, were content to enjoy their friendship and imbibe their doctrines, a few others—of whom Whittingham (afterwards Dean of Durham) was the most notable—became enamoured of their discipline as well, and, bringing their passion for it also back to England with them, laid the foundation of the Puritan movement, and of all its momentous results.

Mary died on November 16, 1558, and the total result of her reign had been misery to herself and disgrace and wretchedness to her country. She had ascended the throne, little more than five years before, amidst all but universal joy and gratulation. Her subjects, apparently, moved by that curious sympathy so constantly shown to monarchs, rejoiced to see her emerge from the clouds of undeserved misfortune which had surrounded her early life, and, themselves smarting under the selfish government of Edward's Council, indulged freely in all those vague and groundless hopes which so often usher in the beginning of a new *régime*. In those few years all was changed, and the rejoicings which proclaimed the accession of Elizabeth were more than half due to the relief felt at having escaped from Mary's tyranny.

CHAPTER VIII

REIGN OF ELIZABETH

ONCE again, on the accession of Elizabeth, was there a general outburst of relief and joy throughout England. Similar demonstrations, no doubt, had occurred when Mary began to reign; but the present rejoicings were more general and heartfelt, and far more long-continued. The relief felt at the relaxation of the Protestant tyranny of Edward's Council was slight compared to that experienced at the cessation of Mary's massacres; and the outcries of the Protestants, in the one case, formed a more audible note of discord than did the murmurings of the Popish clergy on the other, so true was the statement of Bishop Bonner's famous lady correspondent, that 'the very Papists themselves begin now to abhor your bloodthirstiness, and speak shame of your tyranny.'

In this reign, also, we shall find religious matters occupying an important—and, as it would appear to modern eyes, a disproportionately important—place; but they do not form the one completely dominant consideration which they did in the last two reigns, and especially in the last. Indeed, it was impossible that they should do so. The perils by which England was surrounded, both at home and abroad, were too pressing, too varied, and too immediate, to permit a new sovereign to rule, as Mary had done, on purely fanatical principles, even if the new sovereign had been—as Elizabeth pre-eminently was not—in anywise disposed to do so. Nevertheless, the reign commenced with an ecclesiastical revolution almost as complete, though not so rapid and violent, as that which we have seen in Mary's reign. Indeed, it could hardly have been otherwise; for while Mary's legislation had replaced the Church, theoretically, in the most authoritative position which it had ever held in England, her administration had tended to reduce the theory to practice in its cruellest and most unmitigated form. This was to bring about a state of things which had never been popular in England; and if, as we see no reason to doubt, all the earlier part of Henry VIII.'s anti-Papal policy had been carried out with the full assent of the bulk of the nation, it is scarcely possible to suppose that Mary's reversal of it could have been permanently acceptable. When, to these general considerations, we add the almost universal disgust occasioned by Mary's continual burnings, and the enthusiasm stirred up by the courage and boldness, for the greater part, of the victims, we need be at no loss to account for the general ill-feeling which existed at the close of her reign. But it must not be supposed that other causes of discontent were wanting. There existed also scarcity, high prices, heavy taxation, and a debased coinage, and, to complete all, a deep feeling of national humiliation at the loss of Calais. These last potent causes were amply sufficient of themselves, as they have often proved, to account for general disaffection; but they were all, as it were, brought to a focus, by the circumstances of the times, upon the one point of religion.

Elizabeth's chief adviser, from the very moment of

her accession—and, indeed, even before it—was the celebrated Sir Robert Cecil, afterwards Lord Burleigh, the direct ancestor of the present Marquesses of Exeter and Salisbury. Cecil was a man of the most consummate ability and prudence. He was a man much under the influence of religion, yet totally free from fanaticism—a combination very rarely found in the sixteenth century, and not very common at any time. Like Elizabeth herself, he had outwardly conformed in Mary's days; but in his case, as in hers, nobody doubted that his real attachment was to the Reformed religion. Under his influence, which coincided to a great extent with the natural bent of her own disposition, the religious revolution under Elizabeth was neither so rapid nor so violent as that under Mary. In the first month of her reign very little outward change was effected, and several of Mary's old Ministers kept their seats at the Council Board. Yet it is clear that everybody felt that mighty changes were impending; else why, though the Ritual was apparently unaltered, did the bishops, with only a single exception, steadily refuse to assist at the coronation of Elizabeth? There is, in fact, observable a very curious similarity between the beginning of the two reigns of Mary and of Elizabeth. The earliest steps of the two queens were taken in almost parallel lines, though in opposite directions. Thus, just as Mary waited for the meeting of Parliament before she resorted to revolutionary measures, so also did Elizabeth; but both in the interval put a stop to unlicensed practices, and prohibited unauthorised innovations in Church services. Elizabeth's action was, however, as might be expected, in all this more moderate than Mary's; for while the latter had at once, and without legal authorisation, caused Edward's Prayer-book to be disused, and put some of his bishops in prison, Elizabeth, on the other hand, contented herself with discountenancing the Elevation of the Host, and setting free the prisoners confined for religion at Mary's death, putting an immediate stop to the burnings, and permitting the return of the Protestant exiles. In each case, too, these moderate and apparently necessary acts were generally, and in the main rightly, interpreted as unmistakable indications of what was to follow. The only other overt acts by which Elizabeth displayed the inclination of her own feelings, previously to the meeting of Parliament, appear to have been that she ordered the Litany, the Lord's Prayer, and the Creed to be used in English, and that, when the Marian bishops came to meet her, and offer their congratulations on her accession, she is said to have refused the ordinary royal courtesy to Bonner.

One of the most important transactions of the beginning of Elizabeth's reign was a secret consultation of a number of Protestant divines at the house of Sir Thomas Smith, in Cannon Row, in which the alterations in Edward's second Prayer-book, which were shortly to be submitted to Parliament, were discussed and determined on. An anonymous paper in which this appears to have been suggested to Cecil is given by Burnet, Strype, and others, with several, mostly slight, variations; and the consultation itself was resolved on, and probably took place, before the Parliament met. But the meeting of Elizabeth's first Parliament was not long delayed. Mary had died on November 17, and Parliament met for the despatch of business on January 25.

Parliament and Convocation, as usual, met about the same time, though in this case, in consequence of a slight indisposition of the Queen, Convocation appears to have had the advantage by a day. The gyrations of this latter assembly during the years from 1549 to 1559 are something quite marvellous, and the different policy pursued towards it by Mary and Elizabeth, in the early part of their respective reigns, gave more ample scope for their performance than would have been the case had the latter sovereign acted with the vigorous decision which, in matters ecclesiastical, characterised the former. As we have already seen, in Edward's reign Convocation was becoming steadily more and more Protestant, and almost its last acts were the approval of the Forty-two Articles and Ponet's catechism. Mary showed her true colours, from the very beginning of her reign, by dismissing Edward's bishops, and reinstating Gardiner and Bonner; and Convocation, with a minority of only six, pronounced the latter of the above documents to be 'pestiferous and full of heresies,' and continued to endorse the whole of Mary's reactionary proceedings, until it was itself superseded in a great measure by Pole's Legatine Synod. Again there was a change: Mary died, and Elizabeth succeeded. But Elizabeth proceeded with a caution unknown to Mary, and though, no doubt, every one believed that the Reformed faith would be restored, little or nothing was actually done in the first weeks of her reign which indicated to what extent she would go. Again Convocation met, but this time its conduct was exactly the reverse of what it had been before. It did very little, but that little consisted in a presentation of Articles by the Lower House to the bishops, which comprehended all the chief points in dispute between the Roman and the Protestant Churches, decided in favour of the former, with a request that they should be presented to Parliament. Presented accordingly they seem to have been, at least by Bonner, the President of Convocation, to the Lord Keeper, the Speaker of the House of Lords; but no further direct effect was produced by them.

It is a fact, to which modern historians of the English Church do not frequently draw attention, that the only Convocation during the earlier Reformation period which was evidently elected without any pressure from the Government, and was the freely-chosen representative of the clergy of England, should thus have declared its opinion, to all appearance unanimously, in favour of the Roman faith and the Roman obedience.[1] It is idle to pretend that this was not, as fully as any other Convocation, a fair representative body. On the other hand, its out-and-out opposition to the Queen and the Government of the day prove plainly that it was so, and, further, very strongly suggest that it was so in a much greater degree than any other Convocation of the period; while the completeness with which its decisions were ignored shows clearly how very little the opinions of the clergy as a body really affected the course of the reformation of the Church. If we compare this Convocation with its predecessors in the reigns of Edward and Mary, we cannot but be struck with the remarkable opposition which exists between the decisions at which they arrived: nor can we avoid noting the fact, that at no time during the period does there appear to have been any general eviction of the clergy from their livings, such as that which took place a century later, in the reign of Charles II.; and the only possible conclusion seems to be, that the celebrated Vicar of Bray must have been the type of a very large class among the clergy. It is,

---

[1] Cox, writing to Weidner in May 1559, says that 'none of the clergy' joined the Reforming party. See the *Zurich Letters* (Parker Society), vol. i. p. 27.

indeed, a somewhat curious fact that, while every one has heard of, and is ready to laugh at, or to rebuke, that unfortunate person, few people, comparatively, seem to be aware of the existence of the far more conspicuous example of tergiversation presented by Anthony Kitchin, Bishop of Llandaff, who contrived to continue in possession of that dignity from 1545 to 1567, accommodating himself to all the various changes introduced, and taking, we may add, all the incongruous oaths required by Henry, Edward, Mary, and Elizabeth. Bishop Kitchin, indeed, may probably be taken as a fair type of the clergy who elected the Lower House of this Convocation, for he has left us in no doubt of his real sentiments, since his name appears, with the other bishops, in the list of the minority which voted against the Acts of Supremacy and of Uniformity, and other ecclesiastical measures of Elizabeth's first Parliament; yet, unlike the other bishops, when the Oath of Supremacy was tendered to him, he chose to accept it rather than to lose his see.

But while Convocation thus answered all the burning questions of the time by one general '*Non possumus*,' and effectually effaced itself by so doing, the real work of reformation was being performed by Parliament. The work, as we shall presently see, was fairly thorough—more so, indeed, than some of our modern historians are disposed to admit—and when we read the literature of the period, and fully realise the exasperation and bitterness[1] which existed on both sides, we can only wonder that any moderation at all was observed. It seems, in the main, to Elizabeth herself and Cecil that the avoidance of far greater extremes was due. The Acts actually passed and which brought

---

[1] See the letters even of Jewell of about this time—*e.g.*, two quoted by *Burnet*, vol. iii. pp. 475, 476.

about the entire ecclesiastical counter-revolution, were but five in number, viz :—

- 1 Eliz. c. 1. An Act to restore to the Crown the ancient jurisdiction over the estates ecclesiastical and spiritual, and abolishing all foreign powers repugnant to the same.
- 1 Eliz. c. 2. An Act for the uniformity of Common Prayer and service in the Church, and administration of the Sacraments.
- 1 Eliz. c. 4. An Act for the restitution of the firstfruits to the Crown.
- 1 Eliz. c. 19. An Act giving authority to the Queen's Majesty, upon the avoidance of any archbishopric or bishopric, to take into her hands certain of the temporal possessions thereof, recompensing the same with parsonages impropriate and tenths.
- 1 Eliz. c. 22. An Act giving authority to the Queen during her life to make ordinances in collegiate churches and schools.

It is necessary to examine a little what was the actual effect of the first two of these Acts, in order that we may see how far the state of things established by them differed from that which existed at the death of Edward VI. Mary had, as we have seen, by two sweeping Acts abolished, first, all Edward's Protestant laws; and secondly, all Henry's anti-Papal ones; taking advantage, in the first case, of the reactionary feeling which followed on the death of Edward and the Northumberland *fiasco*; and in the second, of the temporary improvement in her position and strength which followed upon her marriage with Philip. Elizabeth and her Parliament had neither the will nor the power to carry out a similarly high-handed policy. What they really did by this first year's legislation was this :—

(1.) They restored in full the ecclesiastical supremacy established by Henry VIII., merely avoiding the revival of the style and title of Supreme Head. Thus, while this change was made by the enactment of 1 Eliz. 1, s. 16 to 19 inclusive, the 26 Hen. VIII. c. 1 and 1 Ed. VI. c. 12, s. 7 were not revived in terms; on the other hand, 25 Hen. VIII. c. 19—the Act of the Submission of the Clergy—was restored in full, so that nothing but the mere title was renounced, and the whole power was reserved to the Crown.

(2.) The Act of Uniformity was varied to the extent of two specified alterations in the Book of Common Prayer, but otherwise restored.

(3.) For some reason, not very obvious, the appointment of bishops directly was dropped, and the old method of indirect appointment by means of a merely colourable election was resumed.

(4.) The marriage of the clergy was not yet re-legalised, in deference, apparently, to a private caprice of Elizabeth.

In all other respects the Reformation Statutes of Henry and Edward were restored, with the exception of those which were merely temporary or trivial. One partial and temporary exception, however, may be alleged—viz., that the Act of 3 and 4 Ed. VI. c. 10, for abolishing and putting away divers books and images, which had been included in Mary's repeal, was not revived in terms. It was, however, no doubt partially obsolete, as many of its provisions were, doubtless, pretty completely carried out in the iconoclastic times of Edward, and others were provided for by Elizabeth's Act of Uniformity, and afterwards by later Acts. At this time, however, as is well known, Elizabeth herself retained some taste for crosses and other ecclesiastical ornaments.

It will be well to give a somewhat full and detailed account of the ecclesiastical proceedings of the earliest years of Elizabeth's reign, because, as no further Parliament or Convocation was held until the fifth year, it is clear that, whatever transactions took place before that time, depended solely for their legality upon the Acts of the Parliament just narrated, since Convocation, as we have seen, had no part nor lot in them.

Some time in March, and while Parliament was still in session, one of those formal disputations, of which so many took place in the previous reigns, was held in Westminster Abbey between some bishops and other divines of the Roman Church on the one hand, and an equal number of the champions of the Reformation on the other, with the usual result that, while no one was really convinced on either side, the henchmen of the ruling party were credited with the victory, though in fact it was but a barren display.

One of the earliest of Elizabeth's measures after the dissolution of Parliament was the issue of a Commission to value the bishops' lands, with a view to carrying out the provisions of 1 Eliz. c. 19, which seems to have pleased the Protestants who were likely to become bishops as little as it did their predecessors.[1]

In the course of the summer Commissioners were appointed under the recent Act to administer the Oath of Supremacy to the bishops and other clergy. Strype tells us, on the authority of a MS. of Sir Henry Sidney, that Elizabeth had an interview with the bishops previously to the Oath being offered to them, and on their

[1] Strype, *Annals*, vol. i. pt. i. 142-9.

spokesman, Archbishop Heath, assuming a high tone, and exhorting her to follow her sister's example, replied in a bold, if somewhat theatrical speech, beginning with a quotation from Joshua, that she and her house would serve the Lord, and continuing with a very plain announcement that she would make no terms with the 'Bishop of Rome.'[1] It is said, further, that papers left behind by Mary showed that several of the bishops had been, even in Edward's time, carrying on an intrigue with Rome. However this may be—and it certainly closely resembles one of those mere stories which are told of every party or every important person when the spirit of partisanship runs high—it is certain that within a few months the Oath was tendered to all the bishops, and that all, except Kitchin of Llandaff, refused it, and were in consequence deprived by the Commmissioners. Some of these were imprisoned, though without any rigour, for various terms, and afterwards sent to live under the surveillance of various Protestant bishops; others were left at liberty to dwell where they pleased; some went abroad to Rome and elsewhere. Bonner alone was committed to the Marshalsea, there to remain till his death in 1569, though one or two others were imprisoned again at a later time in consequence of new offences.[2] Towards the end of this year took place a curious interchange of letters between five of the Marian bishops and Queen Elizabeth, in which they urged her to follow the example of her sister, and submit herself and her realm to the Pope; and she, in her reply, attributed the conversion of England, not to the Papal Mission, but to Joseph of Arimathæa—a touch, no doubt, of Archbishop Parker's antiquarianism. The Oath was now exacted gradually from all the beneficed

[1] Strype, *Annals*, vol. i. pt. i. pp. 206-8.   [2] *Ibid.*

clergy of the kingdom. According to Camden, these numbered 9,400, and out of that number less than 180 refused it altogether! and of these, more than half were dignitaries. It may fairly be asked, why so many dignitaries should have declined to swear, or, if they did so decline, how it was that more than 98 per cent. of all the parochial clergy should have accepted the Oath. Of the former, certainly many, as remarked in the Queen's reply[1] to a letter of the Emperor in their behalf, had made no difficulty about doing the same thing in Henry's and in Edward's days. In some cases, even their writings remained to prove the fact; and it is not, perhaps, at first sight easy to see why those who had (upon no slight pressure, no doubt) been induced to swallow the revolutionary changes of Henry, and the pronounced Protestantism of Edward, should suddenly resolve to give up place and power and wealth rather than accept the same treatment at the hands of Elizabeth in slightly more moderate doses. They were, assuredly, under no compulsion, and the one instance of Kitchin of Llandaff is enough to show that, had they conformed, they might have retained their sees, as he did, to the end of their lives. Their opponents have shown no want of ingenuity in inventing discreditable motives, both for those who did and for those who did not take the Oaths. Both, probably, had better excuses than have been generally allowed to them. The circumstances of the times were not only cruel and difficult—they were also quite unprecedented. The changes made must have appeared to many minds to involve the very foundations of religion and morality, yet they were made—in England at least—by an authority which, in that king-worshipping age, must have seemed little less

[1] Strype, *Annals*, vol. i. pt. i. p. 221.

than divine; and they were made, and unmade, and remade with a rapidity and violence which must have involved an ordinary mind in the most hopeless perplexity and terror. We must add to this, the general consideration that, in any age of the world, the proportion of men in whom there exists the true stuff of which martyrs are made is but very small, and is found, generally, in larger proportions on the side of new opinions, with new hopes and new aspirations, than on that of old ones, which have become to some extent matters of inheritance, or education, or habit, rather than of intense personal conviction; and also the particular consideration, to which I have already had to refer, and which will be amply proved ere long, that the moral standard of the age was a low one, and was lower, rather than higher, among the clergy of both sides than among other people. Under all these circumstances, it is far from surprising that the recusants were few in number.[1] Nearly all the clergy, in fact, remained the Papists which they always were.

The action of those few dignitaries who, having conformed under Henry and Edward, refused to do the same under Elizabeth, is easily intelligible, and is certainly creditable to them, as far as it goes. The suddenness and violence of Henry's onslaught took them by surprise, and they yielded to it, doubtless, further than their consciences justified them in doing; but, in fact, a man with a knife held to his throat is not in a favourable position for either cool judgment or dignified action. Once surprised into yielding, they may well have waited to see what further changes were to come, and the somewhat reactionary character of Henry's later government may have fed their hopes for

---

[1] Jewell says "*none* of the clergy."

a time. In Edward's reign, the King's youth, and the mere fact of a regency, and the consequent certainty that the existing system would be but temporary, with the discontent of the people and the misgovernment of the Council, all pointing to a coming change, may well have inclined them to the belief that their strength was to sit still. The accession of Mary seemed to bring the reward of their patience, and they at once rebounded to their old position of Popish priests and prelates inflamed with all the additional zeal born of years of repression and adversity. Then they became agents, or at least accessories, in the persecution which was at once the disgrace of Mary's reign, and the chief cause of the final establishment of Protestantism in England. When, in the midst of this, and of the rising tide of popular indignation against it, Mary died and Elizabeth succeeded, they could no longer buoy themselves up with any reasonable hope that the new changes were temporary : Elizabeth, they knew, could never acknowledge the Pope, since to do so was to proclaim herself a bastard, and her mother a harlot ; they themselves were no longer young, and their faith, conscience, consistency, self-respect—every consideration which affects the minds of religious or honourable men—concurred to keep them loyal to the cause for which they had struggled, intrigued, and persecuted through some thirty stormy years.

The bishops being thus all deprived, or in process of deprivation, it became necessary to fill their sees with others.[1] Matthew Parker was chosen to be Archbishop of Canterbury—a man of learning and moderation, and who, besides his peculiar fitness as a consistent, but not a fanatical, reformer, for the difficult position which he

[1] *Burnet*, vol. ii. p. 637.

was to fill, may have been supposed to have a sort of personal claim upon the consideration of the Queen, as having once been one of her mother's chaplains. A certain difficulty appears to have arisen in his obtaining regular consecration. His election took place, upon the usual *congé d'elire*, at the beginning of August, by the Dean (Dr. Wotton) and a portion of the Chapter— the absent members being, probably, recusants. Early in September a warrant was issued to the Bishops of Durham, Bath and Wells, Peterborough, and Llandaff, and also to Bishops Barlow and Scory, requiring them to consecrate him. At this point the proceedings came for a time to a standstill, probably because the first three of these refused, and the fourth either may also have been indisposed to act, or others may have been unwilling to let him, except in the last resort. On December 6 another warrant was issued, in which the first three names were omitted, and to the other three were added those of Coverdale, late Bishop of Exeter; and Hodgkins, Bishop-Suffragan of Bedford; John, Suffragan of Thetford; Bale, Bishop of Ossory, or any four of them. At last, on the 17th of that month, Barlow, Scory, Coverdale, and Hodgkins met, and carried out the consecration at Lambeth Chapel, according to the form contained in King Edward's book. It must have been a curious and suggestive ceremony, with most of the ancient pomp omitted, and with grim old Bishop Coverdale, even on such an occasion, stiffly rejecting the ordinary episcopal vestments, and habited only in a long, woollen gown, reaching down to his ankles; and the Suffragan of Bedford apparently endeavouring to face both ways, by apparelling himself like Scory in the earlier part of the ceremony, and like Coverdale in the later.

The Archbishop once constituted, it became a comparatively simple matter to consecrate bishops to the remaining sees, and, accordingly, sixteen more were made in the course of the next two years, besides Barlow and Scory, who, being bishops already, were settled into their new sees of Chichester and Hereford respectively.

In the meanwhile, the Queen had commenced and proceeded with a General Visitation, for which certain Articles of Enquiry[1] were drawn up, and in which the famous Injunctions of Queen Elizabeth were delivered to both clergy and laity, 'to receive and truly to observe and keep,' as it is expressed in the preface[2] printed with them. This Visitation was worked by means of a number of Commissions[3] appointed for various districts of the country, and each consisting of several noblemen and gentlemen, a divine, a doctor of civil law, and one or more other lawyers, with, in many cases at least, the lord-lieutenant of the county or the president of the district at their heads.

There are various points of considerable interest in these documents. Thus, while, as we have seen, Elizabeth herself had a feeling in favour of the retention of, at any rate, some images and various other adjuncts of the more ancient form of worship, we find in Injunctions 2 and 18 the most ample and uncompromising directions for the doing away with all the old paraphernalia connected with them, and for the abolition of all processions as well. Again, although, as we lately saw, the law of Edward VI. for the marriage of priests had not been revived, yet in the Injunction 29 we find a special clause introduced to permit it, and to fence it round with special safeguards,

---

[1] Bishop Sparrow's *Collection*, edit. 1675, p. 65. [2] *Ibid.* p. 66.
[3] Strype gives lists of several: *Annals*, vol. i. pt. i. p. 245 *et seq.*

intended, apparently, not to hinder it, but to ensure it against any possible scandal.

These are evidently the result of the remonstrances of the Protestant divines, some of which are preserved to us by Strype[1] and Burnet,[2] and are instances of that remarkable tact which so often enabled Elizabeth to yield her own opinions exactly at the right moment. Two other provisions may be noticed, the source of which is, perhaps, not quite so evident. Thus, in 20 the clergy are bidden to teach their parishioners 'that they may with a safe and quiet conscience, after their common prayer in the time of harvest, labour upon the holy and festival days, and save that thing which God hath sent,' &c. Surely a wholesome and truly Christian doctrine, which must, however, have been as unwelcome to the Puritans of that age as some other provisions in these Injunctions were to the Papists, or as it would now be to the less-excusable Sabbatarians of our own days. In 45, again, there is a direction to the Ordinary to 'exhibit unto our Visitors their books, or a true copy of the same, containing the cause why any person was imprisoned, famished, or put to death for religion'— a provision apparently intended to put on record what had actually taken place in Mary's reign, to be published, probably, should there appear any danger of a serious reaction in favour of the old religion.

Elizabeth's Injunctions are not only anti-Papal—they are thoroughly Protestant, and that is a fact which we shall have to consider when we come to sum up the ecclesiastical results of her reign. To these same early years—the interval between the first and second Parlia-

---

[1] Strype, *Annals*, vol. i. pt. i. p. 331.
[2] *Burnet*, vol. ii. p. 629.

ments of Elizabeth—belongs also the commencement of that Scottish imbroglio which was to last for so many years, and to occasion so many complications, and to darken Elizabeth's reign with the most piteous tragedy that belongs to it, whatever may be the amount of her own responsibility for the results. Into the full particulars of this it is, happily, not my business to enter—it forms a portion of the foreign policy of the reign; but it is, nevertheless, absolutely necessary to give some consideration to it, in order to form anything like an adequate conception of the situation in which Elizabeth was placed, and which accounted for, and to some extent excused, many of her most questionable actions. Modern Englishmen, accustomed for more than two centuries to regard the whole island as one kingdom, the home of a single nation, though they know, as a fact, that in Elizabeth's reign the affairs of Scotland were as truly foreign affairs as those of France, find a difficulty in fully realising it. True it is, that for more than one generation kings and statesmen on both sides of the Border had begun to recognise the fact that it would be best for both nations could they be amalgamated into one; but even kings and statesmen had hardly come to look at it as more than a remote contingency to be hoped for, rather than as the end and aim of a practicable policy: and, for everyone alike, the hopes which may have begun to dawn with the marriage of James IV. and Margaret Tudor had been drowned in the blood of Pinkie Cleugh, and buried, apparently for ever, in the grave of Edward VI. When Elizabeth came to the throne, it was certainly true that the relations of Scotland with France were both far more intimate and far more friendly than they were with England. The King of France, as was truly said, 'bestrode the realm, having one foot in Calais and the other in Scotland.' Its relation to foreign States, and to Scotland among them, formed, as it were, the physical conditions of the life of the England of Elizabeth's reign, and very complex relations they were; and, unless we have a fairly clear comprehension of at least their principal complications, we can no more hope to understand the life of England, than we could understand the life of an animal without knowing something of the atmospheric and other conditions which surround it, and of the part these play in its life. I must repeat too, even at the risk of some tediousness, that in the sixteenth century the religious question was the pivot upon which turned the policy, not of England alone, but of every State in Europe. It is in the light of these facts that we must look at Elizabeth's position, and upon the bearing which her foreign relations had upon it. It is impossible to exaggerate the perils with which she was surrounded: without money, without generals, without trained soldiers, and with her own people divided into two bitter religious factions, to one of which she was herself bound by the conditions of her birth and history, but to offend either of which was to add the danger of rebellion to that of foreign hostility. The most pressing danger at the moment was that of a conquest by France, and this was enormously enhanced by the intimate alliance existing between France and Scotland. Elizabeth's relations with Mary were, from the nature of the case, extremely delicate. Not only was Mary the daughter of a French princess, and the wife of a king of France, but she was also the next heir to the throne of England itself. Moreover, this relation, difficult enough in itself, was complicated by the fact that

o

Mary was a Catholic, and her present title to the Crown appeared to most English Catholics to be better than that of Elizabeth herself; and thus she was likely to become, even without her own consent, if need were, the natural head of the Catholic party in England, and the centre of all their hopes. But that her own consent was not wanting was amply shown by the fact that she and her husband had already assumed the arms and titles of King and Queen of England. Individually, moreover, Mary of Scotland, if once acknowledged as a rival, was the most formidable rival that can be imagined. She is one of those few characters in history the charm of whose personality has been such as to enlist an enthusiastic party in her favour in despite of the most odious crimes, and to retain it to remote generations. She was acknowledged in her lifetime—whatever modern criticism of old portraits may say to the contrary—as the most beautiful woman of her time. She was highly educated and variously accomplished. Intellectually clever, shrewd, and capable, she was on a level with the ablest politicians and statesmen of her time, and she possessed in perfection that fascination and charm of manner which is more effective than beauty itself. To all these womanly graces she added brilliant health, wonderful physical strength and activity, and that light-hearted courage and natural contempt of danger which, in a man, makes a leader the idol of his soldiers, and which, when found in a woman, never fails to arouse the wildest enthusiasm and devotion. Such, then, with the whole power of France at her back, was Elizabeth's most formidable foe.

Her only ally was Philip of Spain. Yet the very circumstances which determined her policy at home, without leaving her any real liberty of action, were of a kind calculated, above all others, to estrange him from her. Philip was the acknowledged champion of orthodoxy, and, as it were, the official leader of the Catholic world. Elizabeth had overthrown the whole polity which he had been at so much pains to establish in England, had slighted his Ambassador's advice, and had refused his own offer of marriage, and was now trifling with that of his cousin and nominee, the Archduke of Austria. The religious policy which, as we have seen, she was compelled to follow, was, therefore, just what was best calculated at once to embitter her enemies and to estrange her single ally. Need we wonder, then, if her policy became a by-word all over Europe for crookedness and duplicity, the perennial resource of the weak and the over-matched? She has been called the evil genius of Scotland, and she may have been so; but self-preservation, we are told, is the first law of Nature, and it is hard to blame a monarch if he saves his own people at the expense only of their enemies. Elizabeth was not a person who overvalued, and many would say that she undervalued, the accessories of religious worship, though it is fairly clear that, as a mere matter of taste and private inclination she liked pomp and ceremony in church, as she did elsewhere. Hence, on the one hand, when she found that her bishops and divines strongly objected to images and such things, she yielded her own wish, and ordered their abolition; but, on the other, it is hardly surprising that she should have retained something of ritual in her own chapel, and the more so when she hoped thereby to disarm the enmity of her Catholic subjects, or to mollify the rising anger of her only ally by holding forth to them a delusive hope that she might possibly be veering towards their opinions. Yet I confess it seems hardly fair to say of her, with Mr. Froude,[1] that 'she constructed her Church for a present purpose, with a conscious understanding of its hollowness. The next generation might solve its own difficulties—Elizabeth was contented if she could make her way, undethroned, through her own.' Her conduct admits of a more charitable, as well as a more probable, explanation, and one, at the same time, far more consistent with the complete despotism over the Church which she assumed in the years then approaching. Thus, if we take the main alteration made in her Prayer-book—that, namely, in the words used in the administration of the Communion —the words themselves might be understood, as, in fact, they now are, and have been in a greater or less degree ever since her time, in a quasi-Roman, or in a purely Protestant, or in any possible intermediate sense; and they were no doubt intended, as Mr. Froude would have us suppose, to be as comprehensive as possible, the object of the framers being to add one more inducement to conformity, which should smooth the way of the half-hearted Catholics, whose children, it was no doubt expected, would thus, in the course of a few years, become habituated to the Service, with all its Protestant characteristics, and would gradually forget the original gloss which had enabled their fathers to conform. Such conduct may savour more of policy than of godliness, but it is a very different thing from the deliberate construction of a delusive Church for the mere purpose of retaining the Crown, and is far more likely to have been acquiesced in by the divines who actually made the revision of the Prayer-book, and whom, because they were not martyrs, we need not stigmatise as

[1] *Short Studies*, vol. iii. p. 168.

mere knaves. It is common in all such cases, that what appears to a man of moderate views to be but a prudent avoidance of unnecessary offence, will seem to a zealot an unworthy sacrifice of truth to mere worldly expediency; and Elizabeth's revisors had certainly one precedent at least for their moderation, in the case of the Preface to Edward VI.'s Ordinal, which, though suggesting and almost implying the necessity of episcopal ordination, carefully abstains from actually asserting it. This document was composed at a time when there was certainly no thought of conciliating Catholics, but there was, on the other hand, a very strong desire to avoid anything like a direct condemnation of the foreign Protestant Churches. The above words may also have been introduced with a view to conciliate the Lutherans rather than the Catholics. One of Elizabeth's bishops, namely, Cheney of Gloucester, is said to have held Lutheran opinions.

Whatever may have been Elizabeth's private tastes and sentiments, there is no room for doubting the fact that her Visitors did, in the latter half of the year 1559, cause the removal of altars, roods, and other similar ornaments from the churches in London generally, and particularly from St. Paul's; and when this fact is taken in connection with the Acts passed in the previous Parliament, and the Injunctions issued by the Queen on her own authority, there can remain no reasonable doubt of the thoroughness of the Reformation in these her first years.

We may criticise Elizabeth's consistency as much as we please in that, while retaining the crucifix in her own chapel, she yet permitted the destruction of roods and altars in Westminster and St. Paul's; but there are small incidents which seem to point clearly to a genuinely

Protestant conviction in her own mind, as, for instance, the story minutely told by Strype of her rebuking the Dean of St. Paul's for having placed in her seat in the cathedral a profusely-illustrated Prayer-book. She would hardly have gone out of her way to notice such an apparent trifle, had she not really felt what she said.

CHAPTER IX

REIGN OF ELIZABETH (*continued*)

THE year 1562—in legal language, the fifth of Elizabeth, though when it began she had been little more than three years upon the throne—was remarkable for the assemblage of the second Parliament and the second Convocation of the reign. Again, the first measure passed by the Parliament was one relating to religion— viz., 5 Eliz. c. 1—'An Act for the assurance of the Queen's royal power over all estates and subjects within her dominions.' This Act made it penal in any person to maintain or defend the authority of the bishop or see of Rome within the Queen's dominions, subjecting offenders against it to the pains and penalties of the Statute of Præmunire. One of its clauses (14) incidentally explains that the Oath of Supremacy enacted by 1 Eliz. c. 1, acknowledges in her Majesty 'none other authority than that was challenged and lately used by the noble King Henry VIII. and King Edward VI., as is set forth in an Admonition annexed to the Queen's Majesty's Injunctions published in the first year of Her Majesty's reign.' What that authority was we have already seen in considering Henry VIII.'s Act of Supremacy. This was the only ecclesiastical Act of this Parliament of primary importance, those for the due execution of the '*writ de Excommunicato capiendo*' (5 Eliz. c. 23), and some others, being of little permanent interest.

The concurrent Convocation was one which has been considered to have done very important work. Its work was to revise the Forty-two Articles of Edward VI., and re-enact them in their revised form. The changes made in them would appear to most persons in the present day to have been but slight, and to have consisted mainly in the omission of some few dogmatic statements upon obscure theological questions, such as the mode of our Lord's descent into hell, or the condition of the soul in its intermediate state—*i.e.*, between death and resurrection. It is, however, often difficult for men of one generation to sympathise with the difficulties and doubts of those of another, and the whole of Christian theology in the sixteenth century had been thrown, as it were, into the caldron whence the most eccentric and dangerous opinions had come forth, which, so long as it was considered that opinions as well as actions came within the province of government, no Government could, in some cases, avoid taking notice of; and if it took notice of opinion in one case, it was not always easy to avoid doing so in another, where the practical results were not equally important. Hence we must not be surprised to meet with enactments, and, still more frequently, propositions for enactments, which to modern eyes appear at once trifling and inquisitorial. But though the revision and republication of the Articles was the principal work actually accomplished by this Convocation, it had a vast deal more brought before it which it did not accomplish, partly from the wide differences of opinion existing among its members, and partly, apparently, also because a somewhat abrupt prorogation, simultaneous or thereabout with that of the Parliament, brought its labours to a premature termination; and for several years afterwards it met only to be prorogued again.[1] A vigorous attempt was made in this Convocation to do away with the habits—except the surplice—with organs, and with the sign of the cross in baptism, and to make kneeling at the communion optional—an attempt, moreover, which was extremely near succeeding, since on a division the proposers of these alterations had an actual majority of those present, but lost their motion, when the proxies also were reckoned, by a single vote, 27 members abstaining altogether.[2] Even more strongly Puritan suggestions had been previously made by Nowel, the Dean of St. Paul's, Sampson, Dean of Christ Church, and some others. It would have been interesting to see how such proposals would have been received by Elizabeth had this trifling majority been reversed. It is more to my immediate purpose, however, to observe two things in regard to this Convocation—viz. (1) That it[3] first obtained the Queen's permission to revise the Articles, and (2)[4] That the following protest was appended to the signatures attached to them when revised:—'*Ista subscriptio facta est ab omnibus sub hac protestatione, quod nihil statuunt in præjudicium cujusquam senatus consultum: sed tantum supplicem libellum petitiones suas continentem humiliter offerunt*'—thus apparently declaring themselves subject, not only to the Crown, but also to Parliament.

Several incidents occurred during these first years of Elizabeth's reign which, though they had no direct bearing upon either the establishment or the modification of the relations of Church and State, yet may be referred

---

[1] See Lathbury, *op. cit.* p. 173.   [2] Strype, *Annals*, vol. i. pp. 502-6.
[3] Lathbury, *op. cit.* p. 164, note.   [4] Strype, *Annals*, vol. i. p. 491.

to in this place, since they seem in various modes and degrees to illustrate those relations. First of these, we should note the commencement of that issue of Commissions by the Queen to various persons chosen by her, for the purpose of inquiring into and regulating the ecclesiastical affairs of the whole kingdom, or a whole province, or a single diocese. These Commissions, whether permanent, such as that which developed into the Court of High Commission, or temporary, and intended only for some particular occasion, were issued under the Queen's letters patent, were directly authorised by the 1 Eliz. c. 1, sec. 18, and formed the regular mode in which the sovereign's supremacy was brought to bear upon the government of the Church, until the commencement of the discontents which preceded the great Rebellion in the sixteenth year of Charles I. It, in fact, enabled the sovereign to govern the Church with the aid of the Privy Council alone, independently alike of Parliament and of Convocation. We shall have ample occasion to see,[1] in the course of this reign, how far this personal government of the Church was actually carried into practice.

The congregation of Dutch Protestants[2] which had been established, under the permission of Edward VI., by his letters patent, and had been driven away and dispersed under Mary, petitioned Elizabeth for the restoration to them of the church given them by Edward, and the renewal of their charter, which they appear shortly after to have obtained.[3] Of this Presbyterian church, as

---

[1] Strype, *Life of Grindal*, bk. ii. chaps. 8 and 9.
[2] *State Papers*, Edward VI., July 24, 1550.
[3] *State Papers*, Eliz. vol. xi. 24, Feb. 1560: The Queen to the Marquess of Winchester, empowering him to deliver over the Church of the Augustine Friars to the Bishop of London for the celebration of divine service by the strangers in London.

also of another French one, Grindal, being Bishop of London, became the official superintendent, and in that capacity undertook and exercised careful supervision of their discipline. There is in the State Papers [1] a recantation of certain false opinions prepared for Hadrian Hamsted, one of the ministers of this church, by Bishop Grindal, in which he is made to speak of himself as '*decreto domini episcopi Londinensis ministerio depositus atque excommunicatus*;' of the Bishop as '*utriusque peregrinorum ecclesiæ superintendentem*'; and again of himself as '*optimo jure hoc promeruisse et ordine a dicto episcopo meum fuisse actum.*' The fact that Hamsted refused to sign this document is of little importance, since it was drawn up by the Bishop, and may be taken to prove his own view of his legalised position in regard to the Dutch Church in London. This is not by any means the only instance of the official interference of the Bishop with the affairs of these churches, as their regular and legitimate superintendent.

Very soon after Parker's consecration [2] as Archbishop of Canterbury, he received a letter from Calvin containing suggestions for the union of the Protestant Churches. On Calvin's part this appears to have been a reopening of an earlier negotiation with Cranmer in Edward VI.'s reign, which had been brought to an abrupt conclusion then by the accession of Mary, as it was again, now, by his own death, which took place in 1564. From the characteristics of Calvin's own mind, it is likely that he would appreciate to the full the disadvantages under which Protestantism laboured even then — as it has done ever since—from its want of organisation and its tendency to split into sects; and the task of attempting to

---

[1] *State Papers*, Eliz. vol. xxiii. 67, July, 1562.
[2] Strype, *Life of Parker*, vol. i. p. 138.

unite them into one powerful body, was one congenial at once to his courageous temper and his genius for organisation. In this place, however, the matter comes under our notice, not so much from the point of view of Calvin's motives in suggesting it, as of the mode in which it was received by Parker. So far as appears from Strype's account,[1] drawn, as he tells us, from his own manuscripts, Parker seems to have consulted no bishops or divines about the matter, but to have gone straight to the Queen and her Council, and taken from them his instructions as to how Calvin's proposals were to be received. These were, in effect, that the Council 'liked his proposals, which were fair and desirable; yet, as to the government of the Church, to signify to him that the Church of England would still retain her episcopacy, but not as from Pope Gregory, who sent over Augustine, the monk, hither, but from Joseph of Arimathæa, as appeared by Gildas, printed first, anno 1525, in the reign of King Henry VIII.'

An attempt, made by Horne, Bishop of Winchester, to enforce the Oath of Supremacy upon Bonner, at that time a prisoner in the Marshalsea, and therefore within his jurisdiction as diocesan, led to a lawsuit in the Queen's Bench, in which Bonner's main ground of objection was that Horne was not lawfully Bishop of Winchester at all, and therefore had no authority to require him to take the Oath. This case was before the Court in Michaelmas Term 6 and 7 Eliz.; and whatever might be the real force of Bonner's plea, it appears to have been considered necessary, in consequence of it, to bring a Bill into Parliament, which finally took the form of a very notable Act, viz., 8 Eliz. c. 1, entitled an 'Act declaring the making and consecrating of the archbishops and

[1] Strype, *Annals*, vol. i. pt. ii. pp. 2-8.

bishops of this realm to be good, lawful, and perfect.' This Act, which asserts the validity of the consecrations already made by reason of the Act of Supremacy and of the Act of 5 and 6 Edward VI. c. 1, and the revival thereof by 1 Eliz. c. 1, also alleges that (2) the Queen, 'by her supreme power and authority, *hath* DISPENSED with all causes or doubts of any imperfection or disability that can or may in any way be objected against the same'; and has a further clause, apparently intended expressly to meet Bonner's case, (6) 'that no person shall at any time hereafter be impeached or molested by occasion or mean of any certificate by any archbishop or bishop heretofore made, or before the last day of the present session of Parliament to be made, by virtue of any Act made in the first session of this present Parliament, touching or concerning the refusal of the Oath declared and set forth by Act of Parliament in the first year of the reign of our said Sovereign Lady, Queen Elizabeth, anything in this Act or any other Act or Statute heretofore made to the contrary notwithstanding,' and (7) that all tenders of the said Oath made by any archbishop or bishop aforesaid, or before the last day of this present session to be made by authority of any Act established in the first session of this present Parliament, and all refusals of the same Oath so tendered, or before the last day of this present session to be tendered by any archbishop or bishop by authority of any Act established in the first session of this present Parliament, shall be void and of none effect or validity in the law.'

We may now see plainly what was the theory of the relation between the Church and State in England in the early part of Elizabeth's reign, and we shall see further as we proceed how entirely that theory was carried into practice. The revival of Henry's Act of Submission, and of his Act of Supremacy, in everything except the particular title of Supreme Head, by 1 Eliz. c. 1, was now clearly held, as the words of the Act just quoted are sufficient to show, to mean that the government of the Church was a part of the prerogative of the Crown, and machinery was appointed by which this authority should be exercised—viz., one or more Commissioners, to be appointed by the Sovereign by letters patent under the Great Seal. How far into what may be called spiritual matters this authority of the sovereign was intended to go, is also well shown by the words of the Act now under discussion, wherein she does, by her own *dispensing* power, take upon herself to make good any defects whatever, which may be supposed to have existed in the order of the bishops or other ministers already made.

The Church of England is thus seen to be in very deed the creature of the State, and to be in all things subject, in Tudor times at least, to the personal government of the sovereign, and this as completely under Elizabeth as under Henry or Edward. As we follow the history during Elizabeth's reign, we shall have occasion to see how very much the mere personal predilections of the sovereign herself have affected the course of affairs in that Church, both in her own time and in every subsequent age to the present. Hitherto we have seen but one contest proceeding—that between the Reformed Church in England and the Church of Rome. The former, from the separation downwards, we have seen following the fluctuations, first of Henry VIII. and of Edward's Council, and then, after its temporary extinction under Mary, revived on the accession of Elizabeth; but through all this period Rome has been theologically and ecclesiastically its only acknowledged adversary. Now we are to see a new foe arise, in the shape of Puritanism, which increased in bitterness as well as in strength in proportion as the danger from Rome became less immediate, until in less than a century it overwhelmed State and Church together. We are concerned with Puritanism in this place simply as its rise affected the relations of the Church with the State, which it did to a greater extent than might have been the case, had the Church been less under the personal control of the sovereign, and had Elizabeth herself been less arbitrary, and less personally disliked it.

Camden gives the year 1568 as the date of the rise of Puritanism, and it was certainly about this time that it became a power with which the Government had to reckon. The thing itself, however, had existed already for many years. Hooper's controversy about the vestments under Edward VI., and, even earlier than this, his letters to Bullinger and others in Henry's reign, show plainly that, almost from the time of the separation, two different tendencies existed among English Protestants. The one was represented by men like Parker and the majority of the Elizabethan bishops, who, while they were in the main thorough Protestants of the Zurich type, yet seem to have been anxious to comprehend as widely as possible, to give as little shock as might be to the prejudices and habits of men, and therefore to change only those forms and ceremonies which they deemed absolutely necessary, and whose feelings of reverence and subordination and order made them anxious to maintain whatever they could of the ancient and venerable rites of the Church's worship. The other party had much less reverence for antiquity, and vastly more confidence in themselves, and when they had once taken up the false principle that they ought to make their worship as unlike that of the old Church as they could, and that they could draw the exact type of their Church government and discipline from the Bible itself, it soon became obvious that, good men as many of them were, they could not be brought under any uniform and orderly government at all, and would perpetually differ, even amongst themselves. The trials which many of the men of this party had undergone under the Act of Six Articles, and afterwards in Mary's reign, together with the circumstances of their exile at Frankfort, Strasburg, Geneva, Zurich, and elsewhere, had both intensified their hatred of Popery, and attached many of them greatly to one or another of the Continental forms of Protestantism, and had thus accentuated the differences between them and the moderate party.

We must remember, nevertheless, that these differences, in the times with which we are now dealing, were only as those between the different wings of a modern political party, and were scarcely yet ready to be displayed in the face of the enemy. It was Elizabeth's own decided adherence to the former party which at once gave it a decisive preponderance, and aggravated the discontent of its rival. It would be entirely inconsistent with Elizabeth's character and intellect to suppose that she really cared one jot for the points in controversy between the two; but she did care for order and pomp and appearances in other things, and in religion too; and, above all, being a Tudor, she did care to have her own way, and she looked upon the Church of England as her own Church, over which her own personal authority was supreme, and to find fault with which was to call in question her own judgment and her own arrangements.

Many, if not even most, of Elizabeth's bishops and divines, at least in the earlier part of her reign, sympathised in a great degree with the Puritans, even while they were unwilling, for the sake of a square cap or the use of the sign of the Cross in baptism, to risk the whole cause of establishing a national Church which should at once, as they hoped, be pure from the corruptions of Rome, and maintain a position of dignity and influence in the nation and avoid anarchical and fanatical extravagances. Jewell may safely be taken as an example of the very best of the Elizabethan divines, and Jewell's sentiments are thus expressed [1] in his own words : 'The contest, about which I doubt not you have heard either from our friends Abel or Parkhurst, respecting the linen surplice, is not yet at rest. The matter still somewhat disturbs weak minds; and I wish that all, even the slightest, vestiges of Popery might be removed from our churches, and above all from our minds. But the Queen, at this time, is unable to endure the least alteration in matters of religion.' It seems, then, that it was to Elizabeth's personal caprice, rather than to any scruples on the part of the divines of the Church of England, that the first beginnings of organised Puritan discontent are due ; but, as usually happens, the longer the dispute continued, the more bitter it became, and those who at first differed about mere questions of habits or ceremonies, by dwelling constantly upon their points of difference, and forgetting their far more numerous and important subjects of union, drew gradually farther apart until the Puritan

[1] *Zurich Letters*, pp. 148-9, Jewell to Bullinger and Lavater, Feb. 3, 1566.

P

became almost as great an enemy to the English Churchman as the Papist had always been. Elizabeth, it is true, displayed the same vacillation in her management of the Church as she did in every other department of policy, and, as in other matters, so in these, she too often left her servants to bear the consequences of her own indecision. Thus, early in 1564, she addressed a sharp letter [1] to the two archbishops complaining of the diversities in the services and ceremonies of the Church, and ordering them to 'provide such other further remedy, by some other sharp proceedings as should percase not be easy to be borne by such as should be disordered.' Upon receipt of this, the archbishops, with such bishops as were on the Ecclesiastical Commission, and one or two others, drew up the book of 'Advertisements,' so called, containing certain orders for the regulation of the clergy in the matters complained of: but when they were drawn up Elizabeth declined to sign them, alleging that the authority of the archbishops and the Commissioners was sufficient; and it was two years or more before they obtained the royal authority, after undergoing some revision.

An incident occurred, at the close of the year 1567, which shows how the government of the Church by the State extended to some degree beyond the bounds of the establishment. It is curious that both Edward VI. and Elizabeth, while as regards their own subjects they tolerated no nonconformity, yet took under their patronage certain Netherlanders and others driven from their own country on religious grounds. These persons, while they were permitted to settle in London, Norwich, Colchester, Canterbury, and elsewhere, and to exercise their own (Presbyterian) form of religion, were at the

[1] Strype, *Annals*, vol. i. pt. ii. pp. 128-9.

same time placed under the special care of the bishops of the dioceses in which they settled, who, in some cases at least, as we have seen in the instance of Grindal, became their official superintendents. By this means they became amenable to the authority of the Ecclesiastical Commission; and at this time this authority took occasion to redress certain disorders among the Dutch Protestants in London, to compel certain members who had revolted from it to return, and to decree 'that the said Dutch Church should continue in its first constitution, under its own discipline hitherto accustomed, and in its conformity with other the Reformed Churches, confirming the ministers, elders, and deacons of the same Church in their ministries and administrations.' It then exhorted all strangers abiding in the City of London who professed Christ and His Gospel, to join themselves to that Church and submit to its holy appointments; and further declared all such as had made a defection from this Church, and had caused the late disturbance in it, to be unquiet and stubborn persons, until by repentance they had returned and gave satisfaction to God and His Church —reserving to themselves the further restraint and correction of them.[1]

---

[1] Strype, *Annals*, vol i. pt. ii. p. 250. Strype quotes this decree as given under the seal of the Commissioners on December 19, 1567.

He refers also to an instrument of Bishop King, of London, nearly fifty years later, in which, after much laudation of the same body, and of a similar Church at Colchester, he enjoins that no member of the same churches that had offended, and thereby deserved their censures, should depart from these congregations and join themselves to any parish church, before he had either been censured for his offence, or had otherwise reconciled himself with his respective congregation.

A similar instance may be quoted from the *State Papers* for 1621, under dates January 21, September 25, and October 10, from which we learn that a certain Denis l'Ermite, a freeman of the city of Norwich, had left the Walloon congregation and attended an English church, and declined

Another matter which touches the skirts of my subject rather than properly belongs to it, but which it is impossible entirely to omit, may be noticed here—viz., the question whether the deaths of the Jesuits and others executed under Elizabeth can rightly be used, as by Roman Catholic writers they always have been, as a set-off to the burning of the Protestants under Mary.

In considering such a question as this, in order to arrive at a reasonably fair conclusion, it is absolutely necessary to take into account the different views which prevail at different periods; and by this I mean, not only what we may be pleased to consider the moral advance which would enable us in these days to condemn all political assassination in the lump, and which has given occasion to a good deal of very ill-founded self-complacency in some modern historians, but also that more subtle result of political and religious action and reaction, which gives rise to a tendency in each successive generation to take a different, and a more or less antagonistic, view of any subject from that held by its predecessor, and this the more strongly in proportion as the previous opinion has been firm and general.

to pay the rate for the support of the ministers of the church he had left. Complaint was made to the Council, who directed a Commission of inquiry, on which were the Bishop, the Mayor, and others. The Commissioners report, and in their report request that such persons as the aforesaid L'Ermite, though born in England, shall be ordered to continue, and be of that Church, and submit to its discipline, and that ' such of them as shall not conform themselves thereunto, and shall not, in case of their Church discipline, submit themselves to be ordered therein by the Bishop of Norwich for the time being, and in case of civil government by the Mayor and justices of the peace of the said city,' may have to appear before the Council to answer for their contempt and disobedience. The report is signed by the Bishop (Harsnet), the Mayor, and others. The Council, in their reply, order that Denis l'Ermite and all others of the Walloon congregation in Norwich, although born in England, shall continue to belong to that Church, and to submit to its discipline, on bond to appear before the Council in case of disobedience.

Thus the ascendency of Protestantism in England, from the reign of Elizabeth to a time within the memory of living men, was so complete and so universal, that all the questions concerning it had come to be looked upon by the mass of Englishmen as finally settled, and had ceased to be a subject of study or interest even with the majority of educated persons, who were mostly bred up with the notion that all the right was, and had always been, on the Protestant, and all the wrong on the Roman, side of all questions between the two parties.

It is no exaggeration to say that this was the general opinion of Englishmen of all classes throughout the reign of George III. and for some years after its close. Two causes mainly have led to a reaction since—the great spread, in later years, of a taste for historical and antiquarian research, consequent upon the institution of the Camden and other Societies, and of the enormously increased facilities recently given for the consultation of ancient records in every direction and of every kind; and, secondly, the extension to England of the great Catholic reaction, which began on the Continent towards the close of the last century and dates with us from the rise of what is known as the Tractarian movement in 1833. The first of these, by letting men see the letters and writings of members of the defeated party, put matters in a new light, and displayed, for the first time, the other side of the Reformation questions—the many good points of the sufferers, and too often the meanness, tyranny, and unfairness, on the side of the victors—and so at last there were found English Churchmen who began to write as if the Reformation had been the triumph of wrong, and the real martyrs of the sixteenth century were to be found among the disciples of Allen and Parsons rather than in the victims of Mary's persecution. Now, when a few more years are past, when researches have been still further extended, and there has been time and opportunity to see that the new side of the question is no more the only side than the old one was, we may hope that a more judicial and rational view may be taken, and that we may learn that the ideas of the value of the Reformation which prevailed for almost three centuries in England were, on the whole, nearer the truth than those which have for the moment almost superseded them ; that they never would have retained their hold upon the English nation so long and so firmly otherwise ; and that they lost it for the time, mainly because this ascendency had been so complete, that men forgot the possibility of holding any other views, and had lost sight even of the grounds upon which they held these. And certainly there is no point in which all the research which has taken place can only serve to re-establish the old opinion in the view of any person who comes to the question with an open mind than the one now before us.

Elizabeth's justification for the execution of Jesuits and Seminarists is in all points complete. It was on May 15, 1570, that Pius V.'s bull of excommunication was found nailed up against the Bishop of London's palace at Fulham. Up to that time no execution had taken place in Elizabeth's reign which could in any way be said to be due to intolerance of Popery ; so far from it that, albeit for other reasons, priests, known to be such, had been permitted to retain their livings, and recusants generally, though sometimes worried, were not punished. It was in July 1571 that the first conspiracy was hatched at King Philip's council-table for the assassination of Elizabeth ; and from that time till the final scene at Fotheringay had closed the tragedy of Mary Stuart's existence, Elizabeth's life was the mark of unceasing plots and conspiracies, of which Jesuits and Seminarists were both the brain and the hands, even though they had received the unqualified approval of kings, popes, cardinals, and nobles, who, while they would not stain their own hands or risk their own skins by assassination, were willing enough to encourage others to do it, and to profit by the deed when done. The evidence of all this is unimpeachable, and comes from their own side.[1] There is no room for reasonable question or doubt about it. An English convert in his sermon at Rheims had said, 'Pity it was there could not be found any of that courage to bereave her (Elizabeth) of her life'; and Pope Gregory XIII. had said to Ballard and Tyrrel that he 'not only approved the act, but thought the doer, if he suffer death simply for that, to be worthy of canonisation.' In the face of these precepts given by the highest Catholic authority, and followed by the actual attempts which were made at assassination, the declamation about 'our religion only is our crime' is felt to be mere bluster. If a

[1] *Records and Memorials of Cardinal Allen*, London, 1882, p. 412; also the remarkable reasoning in the historical introduction to the same, pp. 48–51. See also *Green*, vol. ii. p. 416; and *Froude*, vol. xi. ch. xxviii. *passim*, and especially pp. 303–5. Also Simpson's *Life of Campian*, pp. 342–3, where he says, 'To be a conspirator generally implies a readiness to swear that you are not one. That is but a lame plot when the plotters are not ready to deny it at the bar. But Allen and Parsons put all the English Catholics in this position, that they were obliged to risk life, liberty, and lands, rather than take the oath of allegiance, which denied the Pope's right to depose princes; and, at the same time, they were obliged by their position to deny, with any amount of imprecation, their complicity in any plot, or in any general design or intention, under any circumstances, to enforce this Papal claim. Hence grew up a suspicion which has always remained in England of the inherent falsehood of Catholic morality,' &c. The whole passage is well worth perusal.

man, be he a Jesuit or a Thug, will make murder a part of his religion, he may place his religion *pro tanto* outside the pale of toleration by civilised society; but he does not palliate his crime, nor make it the duty of society to tolerate that which is incompatible with its own existence.

CHAPTER X.

REIGN OF ELIZABETH (*continued*)

THE consideration of the incidental matters referred to in the latter part of the last chapter, while it has interrupted the proper course of the history, may nevertheless be excused, inasmuch as the history itself could scarcely be intelligible without it. The whole course of legislation, and not of legislation only, but of State policy also, so far as it affected religion, was profoundly modified by the bull of Pope Pius V., and by the Catholic conspiracies which followed it. Up to the time of the publication of that bull, Elizabeth and the Church of England were in the position of a province in rebellion, indeed, against the empire of which it had formed a part, but not yet separated from it. The bull was the final and fatal act—not its own, indeed, but that of the Catholic Mother Church—by which the Church of England was recognised as separate, and by the very recognition condemned as hostile to the Church Catholic, and the enemy of God and man.

Up to this time, however much Catholic Englishmen may have disapproved Elizabeth's ecclesiastical proceedings, they were not called upon peremptorily by authority to oppose them actively; now they were placed once for all under the uncomfortable necessity of taking a decided line one way or the other.

The general result of this bolder line of policy

adopted by the Roman Church was, in the first place, to embitter the quarrel between the Roman and Protestant parties in England, and to endanger the person of the Queen; and, in the second, to compel Elizabeth to a more decided Protestant policy, and, by imperilling the very existence of the nation, to force men to decide whether they would be Catholics or Englishmen, and ultimately, by the constant formation and detection of Jesuit plots and intrigues, to possess the mass of the population with a thorough distrust and detestation of Romanism which three centuries have not entirely washed away.

The thirteenth year of Elizabeth was the next important epoch of ecclesiastical legislation. There was again a Parliament and also a Convocation which was permitted to perform its functions. The Acts of the former were :—

13 Eliz. c. 2, a reprisal for Pius V.'s excommunication, in the shape of an enactment against the introduction of bulls or instruments, and 'other superstitious things,' from the see of Rome, subjecting offenders to the penalties of a Præmunire, and containing also a clause forbidding the importation or use of an Agnus Dei, pictures, or cross, &c.;

13 Eliz. c. 10, providing against frauds by spiritual persons upon their successors in the matter of dilapidations, &c.; and

13 Eliz. c. 12, entitled an Act for the Ministers of the Church to be of Sound Religion.[1]

---

[1] This Act is sometimes referred to as in no way admitting non-Episcopal orders, and it is said to be a disabling Act, aimed at the surviving Catholic clergy, and requiring them, so to speak, to give security for their loyal behaviour towards the Queen and the Established Church. This, no doubt, is true, but not the whole truth. An Act of Parliament is judged by what it says, and the same words admitted non-Episcopal as well as

This last Act is one of very considerable importance. It provides: 1. That every person under the degree of a bishop which doth or shall pretend to be a priest or minister of God's holy word and Sacraments by reason of any other form of institution, consecration, or ordering, than the form set forth by Parliament in the time of the late King of most worthy memory, King Edward VI., or now used in the reign of our most gracious sovereign lady &c., shall declare his assent and subscribe all the Articles of Religion . . . . and shall bring a testimonial of such assent, and shall openly read in church the said testimonial and Articles;

2. That he shall be deprived if he affirm or maintain any doctrine directly contrary to the said Articles;

3. That he shall be twenty-three years old, at least, and a deacon, and must read himself in within two months; and

4. That he must have due testimonials, &c.

Also another Act, 13 Eliz. c. 20, touching leases for benefices and other ecclesiastical livings with cure, &c.[1]

In this Parliament two notable instances were given of Elizabeth's jealousy in the matter of her prerogative as supreme governor of the Church. A bill was passed in the Commons for the conservation of order and unity in the Church, and was duly sent up to the Lords; but an answer came from the latter to the effect that 'the Queen's Majesty having been made privy to the said articles liketh very well of them, and mindeth to publish them, and have them executed by the bishops, by direction of her Highness's royal authority and supremacy of the Church of England, and not to have the same dealt

---

Roman orders. That it was considered so to do is proved by two passages from the works of *Bishop Cosin*, vol. iv. pp. 403–7 and 449–50.

[1] Lewis, *Reformation Settlement*, p. 267, *note*.

in by Parliament'; and when a member (Mr. Strickland) brought in a bill to amend the liturgy, the House resolved not to proceed with it until the Queen's pleasure were known. Even so, however, at the dissolution, the Lord Keeper, by the Queen's command, administered a sharp rebuke to those members who had meddled with matters not pertaining to them, and above their understanding, as well as contrary to her express admonition.

In Convocation, the Articles were once more reviewed, and subscriptions of all clergy who had not already subscribed was insisted on, and some canons were passed, which, however, were not ratified by royal authority.

The rule of conformity was now more and more rigidly enforced against those, on the one hand, who held too much to the old customs of the unreformed Church, especially in the northern and midland counties, and against the Puritans also, who seemed more than ever bent upon assimilating the English worship and discipline to that of Geneva. Cartwright, who was Margaret Professor of Divinity at Cambridge, and Fellow of Trinity, and at this time the most conspicuous Puritan leader, was deprived and expelled the University.

A careful consideration of the extravagances of both sides during the years intervening between the thirteenth of Elizabeth and the next epoch of serious ecclesiastical legislation—viz., the twenty-third of her reign—would surely go far to relieve Elizabeth and her counsellors from that charge of deliberate hypocrisy which Mr. Froude so constantly brings against them.[1]

---

[1] Grindal's answer to Bullinger's letter on the 'habit' question. He says that when the bishops who had been exiles in Germany could not persuade the Queen and Parliament to remove these habits out of the Church, though they had long endeavoured it, by common consent they thought it best not to leave the Church for some rites, which were not

During all these years the air was full of Jesuit conspiracies. Mary Stuart was a prisoner in England, and, with her will or without it, was the focus of them all. Elizabeth's life was the one hope for the independence of England, and Elizabeth's life was the point at which they all were aimed; and the Massacre of St. Bartholomew, and Pope Gregory's Te Deum, showed the spirit of Popery and the lengths to which it was prepared to go.

With all these forcible 'dissuasives from Popery' added to the associations connected with her mother's marriage, and her own subsequent life during her sister's reign, it might have been expected that Elizabeth would have thrown herself into the arms of the Protestants without reserve; and if she had gone all lengths with the most extreme of them, there would have been no cause for surprise. Yet she was far from doing so, and, as we have seen, it was her personal predilections alone which preserved to the Church of England its singular and unexampled form and character. There are some minds—and Elizabeth's was one of them—whose actions are directed more by their taste than by either reason or conscience; and the canting phraseology and external precision of the Puritans seem to have been as revolting to Elizabeth's taste as their extravagant doctrines were to her reason. Having them on the one hand, and the Romanists on the other, before her eyes, she, and many others with her, might well be led to ask whether it was not possible to avoid Scylla without falling at once into Charybdis. Anyone

many nor in themselves wicked, especially since the purity of the Gospel remained safe and free to them. Nor had they to this present time repented themselves of this counsel; for their churches, God giving the increase, were augmented much, which otherwise had been prey to Lutherans and Semi-papists. Strype, *Grindal*, p. 156.

who will contrast, for instance, the language of the Admonition to Parliament with that of the correspondence of Bullinger or Peter Martyr, and with that of Elizabeth's bishops, will scarcely fail to be struck with the difference of tone between them, and will be ready to admit the difficulty of working with the Puritan leaders. Other motives, no doubt, combined with taste in directing Elizabeth's action against the Puritans. She had scarcely the materials for arriving at James I.'s subsequent formula, 'no bishop, no king'; but a Tudor had ever a keen scent for disobedience, and the general revolt against authority which was implied in Puritanism, would of itself have been sufficient to secure it her disfavour, while its direct tendency to split up the Protestant body was a manifest disadvantage in the struggle against the old Church. Elizabeth liked no authority but her own, and as she found herself often compelled to yield in matters of State, she became all the more arbitrary in her government of the Church. It should further be considered that during nearly the whole of Elizabeth's reign, as also in the latter part of Edward's, there had been and was no doubt as to the essentially Protestant character of the Church of England. The whole of the lives and writings of the Elizabethan divines, with the single and perhaps doubtful exception of Bishop Cheney, of Gloucester, agreed in doctrine with the Churches of Zurich and Geneva, and would almost certainly have followed them in practice also, but for the personal predilections of the Queen.[1] The passage already quoted from Jewell is sufficient to show

[1] See, for example, Norton's letter to Whitgift in Strype, *Whitgift*, vol. i. pp. 58-9. See also Archbishop Hutton's letter to Lord Cranborn at the beginning of the next reign; Strype, *Whitgift*, vol. iii. p. 420. Also extract from Archbishop Sandy's will in Strype, *Whitgift*, vol. i. p. 548. Also *Annals*, vol. iii. pt. ii. pp. 67-8.

this, and innumerable others might be cited. They constantly refer to themselves as of the same religion with their Swiss correspondents, and as constantly speak of the Pope as antichrist, and even sometimes use the phrase 'Christian religion of Protestantism,' in a way which, by implication, excludes Romanism from the name. Indeed, it must be evident to any candid reader of the English divines of the sixteenth century,[1] that it was a doubtful point with them whether the Roman Church were within the pale of salvation. With regard to ritual also, and whatever is implied by it, it should be observed that Hooker,[2] in his answer to Travers, refers incidentally to the fact that in the Temple Church in his time the practice was to receive the Communion sitting, and that Travers had introduced the use of the standing position. Hooker refers to it as in itself a matter of indifference.

Perhaps the most perfect instance of Elizabeth's personal government of the Church is to be found in her treatment of Archbishop Grindal,[3] who had succeeded Parker at Canterbury in 1576. The clergy, in several places, had adopted a habit of meeting together from time to time to explain and discuss the Scriptures, one being elected as Moderator, and each member of the assembly taking his own part in the discussion. These meetings, it appears, were more or less of a public character, taking place in the principal church of the town in which they were held, and not excluding the laity as spectators and hearers. Grindal, who was shocked at the ignorance of many of the clergy, encouraged these meetings as likely

---

[1] The controversy between Hooker and Travers, and Archbishop Whitgift's remarks upon it, in Walton's life of Hooker, Keble's *Hooker*, vol. i. pp. 54-65.

[2] Keble's *Hooker*, vol. iii. pp. 578-4.

[3] Strype, *Grindal*, pp. 325-86.

to improve their learning, though, at the same time, he imposed rules upon them in order to avoid scandals. The Queen, however, who hated liberty of speech, and did not care for overmuch preaching, was dissatisfied with Grindal's rules,[1] and required him to suppress these meetings (exercises or prophesyings, as they were called) altogether. Grindal, like an honest man, refused, and intimated, in his letter to the Queen, in very plain terms, that he was a better judge in the matter than herself, and had a higher duty than that towards her. The result was that the Queen suppressed the prophesyings herself by a letter addressed to the bishops, and sequestrated the archbishop and confined him to his house, and would, if she had been able, have deprived him. This last proceeding, however, she found to be difficult, and was compelled to content herself with the former; and Grindal accordingly remained in disgrace, and practically suspended, until his death in July 1583.[2]

Thus Elizabeth's reign went on. The Catholics, most of whom probably had conformed up to the time of Pope Pius V.'s bull, became less conformable every day, and the Puritans set the example, so fatally followed by their opponents since, of obstinately retaining their preferments in the Church while deliberately violating the conditions on which they held them. Many of both parties were deprived, but it is obvious from such passages as that just quoted from Hooker, from the report of Archbishop Sandys on the condition of things in the North, and many similar writings

---

[1] See her letter to Whitgift, Bishop of Worcester, in Strype, *Whitgift*, vol. i. pp. 163–4.

[2] Convocation had petitioned for the removal of Grindal's sequestration in 1581, and in 1582 he made a submission, and was restored. The Queen even then wished him to resign, but the arrangements for his doing so were not completed at the time of his death, in July 1583.

of the time, that conformity was not so strictly enforced as the law required, or as Elizabeth wished, and that irregularities in both directions were winked at.

In 1581 the 'English Mission' organised by Cardinal Allen and his abettors had borne its sufficient fruit in treason and plots of assassination and gave occasion to the passing of another Act (23 Eliz. c. 1) 'to retain the Queen's Majesty's subjects in their due obedience.' This Act makes it treason to convert or to be converted from the established religion to that of Rome, and involves all abettors of such conversions in the guilt of misprision of treason. It also enacts penalties for the saying or hearing of Mass, and reiterates and strengthens the penalties against persons absenting themselves from church, and against Nonconformists in general. It was followed some few years later by a still more stringent Act (27 Eliz. c. 2) called, 'An Act against Jesuits, Seminary Priests, and other such like disobedient persons,' in which the persons named were forbidden the realm, or, if remaining in or returning to it, treated as traitors, and persons harbouring or relieving such subjected to the penalties of præmunire; and other penalties are denounced against those who send their children to be educated in foreign seminaries, or who, knowing of the presence of Jesuits or the like in the country, conceal the facts. There is a saving clause for such, if they should submit and take the oath prescribed in 1 Eliz. c. 1, provided that they do not come within ten miles of the place in which the Queen happens to be.

A still further enactment of a somewhat similar character followed in this year, 1587 (viz. 29 Eliz. c. 6), called 'An Act for the more speedy and due execution of certain branches of the statutes made in the twenty-third year of the Queen's Majesty's reign, and entitled "An Act to retain the Queen's Majesty's subjects in their due obedience,"' and two others in the year 1593 (35 Eliz. c. 1 and 2) called respectively 'An Act to retain the Queen's Majesty's subjects in their due obedience,' which inflicted penalties on those who did not come to church, on those who persuaded others to impugn the Queen's authority in ecclesiastical causes, or who were present at unlawful conventicles for religious purposes, and required any such person, if he did not conform within three months, to abjure the realm or to forfeit to the Queen all his lands, tenements, and goods during his life; and 'An Act for restraining Popish recusants to some certain places of abode'—a measure whose scope is pretty fairly indicated by its title. These also, it should be observed, were to abjure the realm if they refused to submit themselves.

Such measures as these are certainly vigorous, and to modern ears they sound arbitrary and even tyrannical to an extreme degree, but they have at least the merit of dealing pretty equal measure to offenders on both sides, and showing little or no more favour to the Protestant Nonconformist than to the Popish. They bear evident witness also to the truth of what has already been stated as to the increasing bitterness of the Puritan leaders and how they progressed from one thing to another; and whereas they had begun with few or no objections to the doctrines of the Church, but merely to the habits and a few of the ceremonies, the two parties had by this time talked and written themselves gradually wider apart, until in some of Cartwright's diatribes against it we find the Church of England spoken of in language little different from that which was commonly applied to Rome.

Whitgift succeeded Grindal as Archbishop of Canterbury in the year 1583, the twenty-fifth of Elizabeth, and his primacy lasted during the remainder of her reign. It was a period of very great importance to the Church of England. The series of Acts just enumerated made Nonconformity almost as penal as Popery, and without the same provocation which could be alleged in excuse for severity in the latter case. Nonconformists, in Tudor times at least, always professed to be and probably were loyal subjects; their quarrel, according to their own account, was not with the Queen but with the bishops. Yet it is sufficiently evident that the bishops were but the tools of the State, and that to quarrel with them was to quarrel with the State, and, further, that in this particular department even more than in any other, Elizabeth herself was the State. To arrive at any sound conclusion on this matter it is necessary to look at the reign as a whole and then to see wherein the latter half of it differed from the earlier. We shall find on so doing that Elizabeth herself retained the same disposition, the same tastes and inclinations throughout, but that as times changed and opinions progressed, so the action of this constant force became modified, and the results which it produced modified still more. The opinions and wishes of most of Elizabeth's earlier bishops, Grindal, Jewell, and others, differed, as we have seen, little or nothing from those of the earlier Puritans, and there can be no reasonable doubt that but for the personal distaste of Elizabeth herself, very great modifications in the ceremonies and ecclesiastical habits in use in the English Church would have been introduced.[1] Certain it is that in the Convocation of 1562 the pro-

---

[1] *Burnet*, vol. iii. p. 518, and *Strype* as there referred to.

posal to accept the principal Puritan modifications was defeated in the Lower House by one vote only, and this in the face of the fact that its acceptance would have involved all the difficulties of procuring a change in the law but recently passed in Parliament, as well as overcoming the opposition of the Queen herself. But as time went on further changes took place. Both parties gradually hardened in their opinions. Whitgift may be taken as the typical bishop of the latter part of Elizabeth's reign almost as completely as Jewell was in the early part, and Whitgift is looked upon justly as the great enemy (they themselves said the great persecutor) of the Puritans. Yet Whitgift was as extreme a Protestant as any who was ever made a bishop, and not only an extreme Protestant, but an extreme Calvinist; and in fact it was freely admitted on both sides, that Puritans and bishops alike were agreed to accept the Thirty-nine Articles as the true exponent of the doctrine of the Church of England.

There are certain occurrences which took place during the latter half of Elizabeth's reign which will serve so well to illustrate the position and progress of the Church of England, that it is well to state them in this place, although their relation to its position in the State is but indirect. The first of these has to do with the proposed deprivation of Mr. Whittingham, the Dean of Durham, and with the actual deprivation of Mr. Travers, the Afternoon Lecturer at the Temple. These two events, it is true, took place at intervals of several years, and the agents, both active and passive, were different, yet they are so closely connected in their causes and throw so much light upon one another that it is both easier and better to consider them together.

Almost from the beginning of his primacy at York

Archbishop Sandys had been dissatisfied with the condition of the Cathedral of Durham, and in 1578, at his instance, a commission was appointed to visit that body 'as well in its head as its members.'[1] 'Orders' are a special point to be investigated, and the commission is directed, 'if they find them' (*i.e.* the Dean or any of the Canons) 'insufficient in that behalf, to dismiss them from their offices and benefices.' The Archbishop's Chancellor expressly says that Dean Whittingham 'confessed that he was neither deacon nor minister according to the order and law of this realm,' but that he says 'he was ordered in Queen Mary's time in Geneva, according to the form there used.' This last statement is, however, expressly denied by the Archbishop himself, who says that Whittingham 'hath not proved that he was orderly made minister at Geneva, and as far as appears that he did not allege that he had received any imposition of hands.' The Chancellor also further quotes the words of the first certificate which Whittingham displayed to the Commission, saying that 'he was made a minister by *lot and election of the whole English congregation* at Geneva.' This certificate he afterwards attempted to amend, but to very little purpose. But there are two other letters quoted by Strype,[2] viz. one from the Archbishop of York to Lord Burghley, and the other from Lord Huntingdon, who was one of the commissioners in the case, to the same statesman. The Archbishop says: 'The Dean hath gotten more friends than the matter deserveth.' The discredit of the Church of Geneva is hotly alleged. 'Verily, my Lord, that Church is not touched. For he hath not received his ministry in that Church, or by any authority or order from that Church,

---

[1] Strype, *Annals*, vol. ii. pt. ii. p. 169.
[2] *Annals*, vol. ii. pt. ii. Appendix xiii. p. 620.

so far as yet can appear;' and Lord Huntingdon says that 'the commission would much differ in opinion for this matter' (viz. the deprivation of the Dean), and that 'for himself—he thought in conscience he might not agree to this sentence of deprivation for that cause only.' Further on in the same letter he goes on to suggest that the commission had better turn its attention to other matters, and put off this one of the Dean's deprivation indefinitely. As a fact, so it did; no further steps were taken in the matter, and Whittingham died some six months later, still in possession of his deanery. It is thus clear that Dean Whittingham was not deprived, that it is at least doubtful whether he would have been so, and, what is of far more importance than either, if he had been, it would have been not because he had Genevan orders instead of Anglican, but because he had them not.[1]

The case[2] of Travers occurred shortly after Whitgift's accession to the primacy. Walter Travers ranks second only to Cartwright as a leader of the Puritan party. He was confessedly a man of learning and ability, and apparently also of a disposition which attached many persons warmly to him. He had been a Fellow of Trinity, Cambridge, during Whitgift's mastership, and had then got into trouble by reason of his unbending Puritanism. He seems to have been thought well of by Lord Burghley and other great persons, and had many friends among the lawyers of the Temple. He was the author—though not confessedly—of the book

[1] For the Archbishop's letter plainly suggests that he would not have dreamed of questioning the sufficiency of orders duly conferred by the Church of Geneva, and in so doing accords with the tone universal throughout the correspondence between the Elizabethan divines and their friends in Geneva and Zurich.

[2] Strype, *Whitgift*, vol. i. pp. 342-6.

entitled 'De Disciplina Ecclesiastica,' which was and continued to be the acknowledged text-book of the Puritans, and was afterwards publicly adopted and authorised by the Parliament in 1644 as a Directory of Government. The Mastership of the Temple becoming vacant in 1584, Travers' name was mentioned as a candidate, and he was in the first instance supported by Lord Burghley. Whitgift not unnaturally objected, and wrote to Lord Burghley that 'unless he (Travers) would testify his conformity by subscription as all others did which now entered into ecclesiastical livings, and would also make proof unto him that he is a minister, ordered according to the laws of this Church of England (as he verily believed he was not, because he forsook his place in the college upon that occasion), he could by no means yield to consent to the placing him there, or elsewhere in any function of this Church.'

Travers on this also wrote a letter to Lord Burghley, in which he demurs to re-ordination, but expresses his readiness to subscribe the Articles, 'which most willingly and with all my heart I assent unto as agreeable to God's word.'[1] The appointment was given to Richard Hooker, but Travers remained for some time lecturer at the Temple, where he used to employ himself in controverting in the afternoon the statements made by Hooker in the morning. To this scandal, after some time, Whitgift put an end, by abruptly prohibiting Travers from preaching any more. Travers made an appeal to Lord Burghley and to the Privy Council, but without success. The document in which the appeal was made, or a copy thereof, was sent by Cecil to Whitgift, and has been preserved, together with Whitgift's annotations upon it. In this form it was published by Strype, and is of much

[1] See the whole letter in Strype, *Whitgift* (Appendix), vol. iii. pp. 115.

interest and some importance. It must be borne in mind in reading it that Lord Burghley was throughout far more favourable to Travers than Whitgift was, and that the latter was in these annotations making out his case to the best of his ability, in excuse for his somewhat sharp treatment of the former. On the whole, he makes out a good case. It was obvious that no discipline could be maintained at all if a man holding, as Travers did, the constituted authorities of his own Church in utter contempt, repudiating their discipline, and despising their orders, could go abroad on purpose to free himself from their authority, receive his commission there from the hands of a mere set of malcontents like himself, and then come back and claim that he held any office or cure in the Church of England which might fall to his lot, by as good a title as the best there. In the main, Whitgift's position was so strong that he had no difficulty in maintaining it, and Travers remained silenced, but he was shortly after called to Dublin by Archbishop Loftus and made Master of Trinity College.

There are, however, some incidental points touched by these disputants which are of value as showing the state of things in the English Church at the period. In the course of an argument that ordination in one Church was always held good in others, Travers says, 'Afore Mr. Whittingham's case there was never any question moved in this Church to the contrary,' and to this historical statement Whitgift takes no objection.[1] Travers proceeds: 'The question being moved about him, yet was neither the word of God nor the law of

---

[1] Any person who reads these papers, as given by Strype, will see that Whitgift is taking every point he can against Travers, and would have been most unlikely to let such a statement pass, had he been able to question it.

the land found to be against him. But notwithstanding that exception, he continued in his place and ministry after to his death.' Whitgift rejoins : 'This is untrue, for if Mr. Whittingham had lived he had been deprived, without special grace and dispensation.' Now, as we have just seen, Travers was right in this point, as to the fact : Whittingham was not condemned, and did retain his deanery for the few months he lived. Whether he would have been condemned is a matter of opinion, in which it is at least as likely that Lord Huntingdon, one of his judges, should have been right as Whitgift, who had nothing at all to do with the case.

These two cases, taken together, serve to show how the rise of Puritanism, together with Elizabeth's determination to give it no quarter, were gradually hardening Anglicanism, and while leaving it still in its old attitude of uncompromising opposition to Rome, were gradually compelling or inducing it to take up a position of exclusiveness towards other Protestant churches, to which, for nearly the first half-century of its existence, it was a stranger.[1]

Another important event belonging to this period was the publication of the famous Martin Marprelate tracts, which began to be secretly printed in the year 1590.[2] These tracts and the literature arising out of them serve very well to show both what the relative situation of the Bishop's party and the Puritans was at the time, and how far it had changed from what it had previously been. It is impossible to read any of them, for instance, the 'Epistle to the Terrible Priests,' or even

---

[1] The evidence of a great High Churchman of a later age, Dr. John Cosin, afterwards Bishop of Durham, may be taken to show what the practice of the Church of England in this matter had been and was. (See Appendix, note vi.)

[2] This was the year of the publication of Penry's *Appellation*.

the far more serious Puritan writings of the time such as Udall's 'Demonstration of the Truth,' without being struck at the same time by the bitter and cantankerous style adopted by the writers, and the perverse and impracticable character of the party whose spokesman they are. The hopeless narrowness with which they assume that opposition to Rome or Roman practice is of itself the test of right, and conformity to it an invariable proof of wrong, and that the mere words of the Bible—or more often their own conclusions as to the applicability of those words—are to settle every controverted point in their favour, without the shadow of an appeal, and the bitter and unsparing denunciation of every attempt at such appeal, as 'devilish practices against God his saints,' and of the bishops and others who thought better of the existing state of things, than they did, as 'impudent, shameless, and wainscote-faced bishops;'[1] all these are the marks of a bitter and unreasoning fanaticism, with which it is difficult if not impossible to deal, except with the strong hand. On the other hand, it appears certain that the bishops did use strong measures with these men, to an extent which to modern ideas appears harsh to an inexcusable degree. Mr. Arber, in his introduction, quotes contemporary documents showing twenty-five men in various prisons in London for ecclesiastical offences, many of whom appear to have been committed without warrants or kept in prison for months together without trial, and some beaten and 'cast in little ease,' and several to have died in prison, leaving their families destitute. To all this it must be added that printing was not permitted them; these very tracts were printed by stealth and under hiding, and the printers and authors hunted, im-

[1] See, *e.g.*, Martin's *Epistle*, Arber's edit. pp. 30-1.

prisoned, and sometimes, as in the case of John Penry, even executed. And the means used by the bishops were as unscrupulous and unfair as their acts were harsh and arbitrary.[1] In particular, what was called the 'oath ex officio' was a method of investigation worthy only of the Spanish Inquisition. Under it a man could be called before the Bishop or the Court of High Commission without a charge and without an accuser, and there have an oath administered to him to reveal whatsoever he knew, whether of himself or any-one else; and if he refused the oath he was sent to prison at once. What will strike any modern reader as at once the most remarkable, and from a moral point of view the most lamentable, feature in this bitter and important controversy, is that the points in dispute not only were really unimportant, but were admitted on both sides to be so. If we examine[2] Anthony Gilby's 'One Hundred Points of Poperie yet remaining which deform the English Reformation' (he enumerates in fact 151), omitting those concerning the administration of justice in the Bishop's Courts, which were only indirectly a religious question, we shall find that no one of the real doctrines of the Anglican Church is in question, but trifling matters of vestments or ceremonies, to which, as we have seen, the Anglican divines of that age attached no importance, and many of which they would willingly and even gladly have given up.[3] Yet neither party would yield an inch. The malcontents would not yield, for they had, as we have just seen,

---

[1] Arber's *Introductory Sketch*, p. 73.   [2] *Ibid.* p. 28.

[3] Mr. Mullinger (*University of Cambridge from the Royal Injunctions of* 1535 *to the Accession of Charles I.*, p. 263), quotes Travers himself as saying in his *Eccles. Discip. Explicatio*, 'The Universities are set on fire by causes most trivial in themselves,' and, as we have already seen, Travers professed himself entirely satisfied with the Thirty-nine Articles.

worked themselves up into a profound belief that every one of their own crotchets was directed by the infallible word of God ; and the bishops could not yield because to them to yield was to give up the cause altogether. They held their places simply on the condition that they maintained the state of Church doctrine and discipline which had been established by law and which Elizabeth was determined should not be changed. Many of them believed, and not unreasonably believed, that it was far better, in itself, than that which the Puritans would substitute for it, and even those who sympathised most strongly with the latter party, saw plainly that, if they proposed to yield, Elizabeth would simply get rid of them, and supply their places with any men she could find who would undertake to carry out her views, and such men, they might not unreasonably argue, were likely to be worse rather than better than themselves. And thus in the curious *mélange* of human motives the most disinterested anxiety for the safety of the Christian religion in England may have mingled in the most varying proportion, in the minds of the Elizabethan bishops, with a sordid and worldly care for their own personal profit and dignity.

That a moderate party did exist, and that it numbered, as may be expected, among its members many of the ablest and best men in the country, is evident. At Cambridge, where the influence of Cartwright and Travers had been greatest, we are told : ' We may clearly discern the existence of a not inconsiderable section whose retirement from the ranks of Puritanism was the result of a genuine and far from irrational conviction of the disastrous tendency of the consequences to which that movement was leading.'[1] Chaderton, the first Master of

[1] Mullinger, *op. cit.* p. 299.

the recently founded Emmanuel College, and Whitaker, Master of St. John's, both leading men in the University, are mentioned as examples of this moderate party. Like almost all the earlier Elizabethan bishops, they sympathised with the Puritans in the main, but were unwilling to accept the consequences of doing so openly, and they utterly condemned the violence, intemperance, and coarseness of the polemics; but in those days, as in all times in which party spirit, and especially religious party spirit, runs high, moderation is the unpardonable sin, and a theologian who ventures to suggest that a question has two sides, is consigned by both parties to the bottomless pit, as a hopeless example of Laodicean tepidity.

The Puritans insisted strongly on the absolute and divine right of their 'discipline' or form of Church government. It was, according to them, taken direct from Holy Scripture, and had an exclusive claim to the obedience of all Christian men.[1] Whitgift, and Hooker himself, in common with all the earlier defenders of the English Church against them, had insisted that the Church was free in these matters, as also in that of rites and ceremonies; and also on the necessity for some degrees of authority in the Church, and the consequent absurdity of requiring equality among all ministers. Now, for the first time, in February 1588, a sermon was preached by Dr. Bancroft (afterwards Archbishop) at Paul's Cross, in which he suggested, rather than asserted, the divine right of bishops in the Church of England, thus, as he supposed, making good its position against the asserted divine right of the Pope on the one hand and of the Puritan 'discipline' on

[1] See Hunt's *Religious Thought in England*, vol. i. pp. 54-60, for a short *résumé* of these arguments.

the other. This sermon of Bancroft's has attained to a fame out of all proportion to its intrinsic merits. It owes its immortality to the fact that in it for the first time, more than half a century after the separation from Rome, the above doctrine is maintained. It is put forward in a mild and scarcely more than suggestive tone, and to a modern reader appears scarcely noticeable as compared with the blast of unqualified asseveration with which the royal supremacy is asserted in its most unmitigated form; the preacher maintaining, almost in the words of Henry VIII.'s Act of Supremacy, that 'not only the title of supreme governor over all persons and in all causes, as well ecclesiastical as civil, did appertain and ought to be annexed to the Crown, but likewise all honours, dignities, pre-eminences, jurisdiction, privileges, authorities, immunities, profits and commodities, which by usurpation at any time did appertain to the Pope.'[1] Nevertheless, at the time when the sermon was preached, and for many years afterwards, it was the former and not the latter assertion which excited attention; because, while the latter was a mere every-day doctrine, with which mankind had been familiar since Cromwell's time, the former, at the time entirely novel, was a desertion of the ground hitherto held by Jewell, Whitgift, and Hooker, and appeared to have been enunciated simply, as one may say, in order to overtrump Cartwright's trick. A similar doctrine was, however, shortly after maintained in a much more serious work by Dr. Bilson, at that time Warden of Winchester College, and subsequently Bishop of Winchester. His treatise on the 'Perpetual Government of Christ's Church' is a careful and well-reasoned work, but the arguments, though familiar in

---

[1] *Perry*, vol. i. pp. 16, 19.

the present day, must, as applied to the Church of England, have been both new and startling in Elizabeth's reign, inasmuch as it was, if I mistake not, the first controversial work which dealt with the constitution of the Church, without specific reference to the points in dispute between the Reformed and the Roman Churches. The constant thesis of earlier works had been those differences—the consequent justification of the Reformation, and the substantial unity of the reformed communions in different countries. Here, for the first time, we have a work by a divine of the English Church, in which the Puritans are the avowed adversaries, Rome is practically left out of the account, and, by implication at least, the non-Episcopal Protestant Churches are rated as no Churches at all.[1] The work, as far as can be now judged, took its place for the moment simply as one among the many anti-Puritan polemics of the time; had it been looked on as anything more it could scarcely have failed to arouse the anger, not only of those against whom it was written, but also of the majority of the Churchmen whose cause it espoused.

The two controversies—that with the Romanists on the one hand and that with the Puritans on the other —continued with varying degrees of vigour during the rest of the reign and for long years afterwards. It has been held that the adversaries in both cases were persecuted, and that both persecutions were alike blots upon the credit of the English Church. In point of fact, however, so far as they were persecuted at all—

---

[1] The latest notice of Bilson that I have found—viz. that in the *Dictionary of National Biography*—speaks of his writing generally as 'halting in its logic and commonplace in its proofs.' His theory of Episcopacy, though not uncommon in the present day, was far too thoroughgoing, not only for Jewell and Whitgift before him, but for Andrewes afterwards. (See Appendix, note vi.)

and that they were so it seems impossible to deny—both were persecuted by the State rather than by the Church, and for reasons of State rather than for entertaining wrong opinions. Romanism, as has been already said, was constantly associated with the idea of treason, Puritanism with that of sedition; and not unreasonably. Not only did fanatical Romanists actually attempt the Queen's life, but Roman statesmen plotted and Roman theologians defended these attempted assassinations. Nor were the Puritans much less obnoxious to the State than these when we remember what the State proposed to do and to be in the sixteenth century.[1] They maintained the superiority of the clergy—*i.e.* of their elders and assemblies—over the civil power in ecclesiastical matters, to the extent of making the ministers the judges of what is law in all matters, and civil magistrates judges only of the facts, making the sovereign subject to the censures and excommunications of their elderships and assemblies, and establishing officers analogous to the Ephors at Sparta, with power to depose the sovereign if he seem to them to break the covenant, with many other similar extravagances. All these matters bore a vastly different appearance to the eye of a sovereign or a statesman in any State, in the sixteenth century, from that which they bear now; and in England we have to bear in mind that there was, as we have frequently had occasion to notice, a very special and close connection, almost an identification, of the Church with the State. The Sovereign had, as we have just seen stated in so many words by Dr. Bancroft, all the authority in

---

[1] See, *e.g.*, a paper (No. III.) in the Appendix to Strype, *Whitgift*, Book IV., entitled, 'The Doctrine with some of the Practices of sundry troublesome Ministers in England.'

the Church which 'by usurpation did ever at any time appertain to the Pope.'

Two other controversies arose in these closing years of Elizabeth's reign, both of which had certain relations, direct or indirect, with the governing powers of the State. One of these, viz. the predestinarian controversy, arose with a sermon by a Fellow of Caius College Cambridge, Barret by name, who called in question in the University pulpit some of the dogmas of the prevailing Calvinism of the period. This sermon, and the disputes which followed it, showed how completely these opinions were at the time in possession of the field in the English Church; Whitgift himself, Whitaker (the Regius Professor of Divinity), together with the great majority of the bishops and heads of houses, taking part against Barret. It showed also, at the same time, that there were, even then, especially among the younger divines, a few who were beginning to revolt against them, with one notable leader among the seniors in the person of Dr. Baro, the Margaret Professor. The point, however, with which we are concerned is this, that the controversy gave rise to a somewhat singular proceeding on the part of the archbishop, who seems to have assembled a meeting of bishops and clergy at Lambeth, which drew up a series of Calvinistic propositions since known as the 'Lambeth Articles.' It is impossible to read Strype's account of the proceeding, and especially the archbishop's letter [1] to the heads of houses at Cambridge, without a feeling that he must have been conscious that he was dealing with the whole matter in a perfunctory and irregular way, and endeavouring to keep matters quiet by a tacit assumption of an authority which he felt to be more than doubtful.

[1] Strype, *Whitgift*, vol. ii. p. 282.

In any case, however, he was reckoning without his host, and was brought up somewhat abruptly by a letter from Sir R. Cecil, written by the Queen's order, which completes the view of the situation so graphically that I give it at length as it is quoted by Strype:—

'That her Majesty had heard, as of Mr. Whitaker's death, so of some business that he came up about. And that she had commanded him to send unto his Grace to acquaint him that she misliked that any allowance had been given by his Grace and the rest of any such points to be disputed: being a matter tender and dangerous to weak, ignorant minds. And thereupon that she required of his Grace to suspend them. That he could not tell what to answer, but did this at Her Majesty's commandment and left the matter to his Grace, who, he knew, could best satisfy her in these things. And thus he humbly took his leave. From the Court, the 5th December, 1595.

'Your Grace's to command,
'Ro. Cecill.'

The sabbatarian controversy[1] also arose towards the close of this reign, certain preachers, more or less inclined to the Puritan party, having begun to preach in various parts of the country that the command to observe the Sabbath was moral and perpetual, and that infringements of it were to be put upon the same level with crimes such as murder and adultery. This doctrine was met by the archbishop and the Lord Chief Justice with their usual methods—viz., citations before the courts and prohibition of printing. The intervention of the latter functionary serves to show that in this, as in other cases, the Church and State were at

---

[1] Strype, *Whitgift*, vol. ii. p. 415.

one. As usual, however, the doctrine which was only now beginning to excite attention continued to spread, and led, as we know, in the following reign, to serious disorders and difficulties. And thus, with the constantly attempted suppression of her adversaries on the one side and the other, in these last years of Elizabeth's reign, the Church of England was more and more differentiating herself from the Roman Church on the one hand, and from the Churches of the Reformation on the other; but as she was forced into this position in the first instance mainly by the individual will of the sovereign, so she has maintained it ever since by close connection with and intimate dependence on the existing civil power for the time being. But the consideration of the total results of Elizabeth's reign may well require a chapter to itself.

CHAPTER XI

REIGN OF ELIZABETH (*continued*)

LET us endeavour now to sum up the results produced by the long and important reign of Elizabeth upon the relations between Church and State in England then and since her time. In so doing we must be careful to include in our record not only the effects produced, but also the means, and the power, and the authorities, by which they were brought about. No ruler of England has ever, since Elizabeth's day had opportunities similar to hers. At no time since has an equal amount of power rested in the hands of a single individual. Theoretically, no doubt, the power of the Crown was as great under James and Charles as under Elizabeth, but the Parliament in the one case was far less submissive, and in the other claimed and succeeded in establishing (for the moment) a power far greater than that of the Crown. And, again, the circumstances under which Elizabeth came to the throne were unusually favourable to a new departure. Mary's legislation had reduced the law and the constitution of England to a condition which practically gave her successor a liberty of action in ecclesiastical matters unexampled before or since. Not only had Mary, by two successive statutes, swept away the whole ecclesiastical legislation of the two previous reigns, but by further legislation, and by despotic acts of government unwarranted by any law, she had re-established the papal power in England to an extent unknown since the time of Henry III., and even then of at least doubtful legality. But Elizabeth was not, properly speaking, at liberty to inaugurate a great change : she was positively compelled to do so, and at liberty only to a limited degree as to the direction in which she made it. There is ample evidence that the disgust and discontent produced by Mary's government was by no means confined to the Protestant party alone, but was shared in to a great extent even by the Catholics, and was universal throughout that large portion of the nation which was neither bigotedly Catholic nor fanatically Protestant.

The first characteristic feature, then, of the whole relation of Church and State in Elizabeth's reign, is what would now be called its pure and undiluted Erastianism. From the beginning to the end of the reign the Church is subject to the State, and never pretends to be anything else. By far the greatest part of the ecclesiastical revolution was accomplished, as we have seen, in the first three years of her reign, not only altogether without the assistance of Convocation, but—so far as that body can be said to have acted at all—in the teeth of its unanimous opposition. Convocation apart, the only organ of the Church was its representatives in Parliament, the Bishops and Abbots in the Upper House; and their names—when they appear in the division list at all—appear constantly in Opposition, and as constantly in the minority. When—after the principal changes were effected, and, by means of them, the personality of the Upper House entirely changed, and both Houses effectually muzzled by the oath of Supremacy—Convocation was permitted to resume its functions, not only did it accept with meekness all the changes already made, but it appended to the results of its own labours the humble protestation already quoted.[1] There is, in point of fact, throughout the reign a unanimity amongst all parties (the Catholics always excepted) in exalting the royal power over the Church, and an entire agreement between theory and practice which it is difficult in the present day completely to realise. We find, first, the phraseology of the Act of Supremacy claiming authority in the most unmeasured terms; then we find this authority carried out avowedly under the sanction of that Act, at first by specially-appointed Commissions, and, after 1583, also by the constitution of the High Commission as a permanent court; and we find all sorts of functionaries, on all sorts of occasions, referring to that authority as a settled principle of the constitution. The whole ecclesiastical constitution of the country was revolutionised by the first two Acts of Elizabeth's first Parliament, and by the Commissions appointed under that first Act which carried out her visitation and enforced her famous 'injunctions.' All this was done in the year 1559, and entirely without either authority from, or reference to, any clerical or distinctively ecclesiastical authority whatsoever, other than that which belonged to the Crown itself. Indeed, as we have seen, Convocation was for all intents and purposes in abeyance, and had done nothing except express in a more or less informal, but in a perfectly unmistakable, manner its entire satisfaction with the state of things left by Mary, and its consequent disapproval of the whole of Elizabeth's ecclesiastical acts. And as the reign began so it continued to the end; the whole government of the Church was carried on by Commissions similar to the first one,

[1] See above, p. 201.

composed, like it, of mingled clerics and laymen; and deriving its authority direct from the Crown under the Great Seal, and, in fact, held responsible not to the Church in any sense, nor even to Parliament, but to the Privy Council. Thus, as far as law and practice could make it, the Church was completely subject to the State, and was, as I have said, incorporated with it; and how complete this subjection was, and how it was accepted in all good faith by the divines and functionaries of Elizabeth, may easily be seen by reference to contemporary records whether official or private.

Thus, in the instance given above, in which Calvin opened negotiations with Archbishop Parker for a union of all Protestant Churches, the latter, as we have seen, took instructions as to his reply, not from Convocation nor any assembly of bishops, but from the Privy Council.[1] It was by the Crown, again, that the congregations of foreign Protestants were permitted to organise themselves in London, Norwich, Canterbury, and elsewhere, and that the Bishop of London was set up as their official and acknowledged superintendent.[2] Later in the reign we find Whitgift writing to the heads of colleges in Cambridge,[3] and telling them, 'It is a most vain conceit to think that you have authority, in matters of controversy, to judge what is agreeable to the doctrines of the Church of England, what not—the law expressly laying that upon her Majesty and upon such as she shall by Commission appoint to that purpose'; and Bancroft,[4] in his famous sermon already quoted, claiming for the Crown 'all the authority and jurisdiction which by usurpation at any time did appertain to the Pope.'

[1] See above, p. 203.   [2] See above, p. 202.
[3] Strype, *Whitgift*, vol. ii. p. 252.
[4] Bancroft's sermon on trying the spirits (the very sermon in which divine authority was first claimed for the bishops).

Further still, as the quarrel between the Puritans and the bishops is becoming exacerbated, we find each party in turn charging the other with being disloyal to the supremacy.[1] Thus, one of the commonest charges against the former party is that 'they attribute in effect no more to her Majesty and all other civil magistrates in these causes than the Papists do, which is *potestatem facti non juris*; and, on the other hand, we find Sir Francis Knollys—who is holding a brief, as his manner was, for the Puritans—writing to Lord Burleigh[2] in complaint of the assumption of the bishops, 'Her Majesty is not supreme governor over the clergy if so be that our bishops be not under-governors to her Majesty, but superior governors by a higher claim than directly from her Majesty.' We see here how, during the latter part of the reign, each party was charged with putting forth claims which were felt to be incompatible with the old idea of the extent and character of the royal supremacy which, nevertheless, both parties represented as the undoubtedly orthodox and constitutional view. The explanation is probably to be found in the fact that thought upon every subject grows and ripens like a herb of the field, and, like that, its growth is favoured, checked, or altered, by the circumstances around it; and thus the ideas of these two parties developed by natural growth and were cramped and distorted by the different conditions in which they grew, by their opposition to one another and the different favour which they found with the Queen or with the people, until both of them arrived, sooner or later, by mere spontaneous development at the conclusion that, however much it might be the theory of the Tudor sovereignty that the will of the monarch for the time being was the standard of ortho-

---

[1] Bancroft, same sermon.   [2] Strype, *Annals*, vol. iv. p. 8.

doxy, it was yet impossible to build permanently on so uncertain a foundation. The result has been that the party which ultimately broke with the State, while it has shaken itself free from this impracticable theory, has gradually lost position and dignity by so doing, and that which adhered to it has maintained the theory as a theory, but has kept it carefully in the background, and studiously avoided bringing it into view, except on the rarest occasions; and in so doing, while retaining a position of dignity and importance, has lost its influence with the people, and is in danger, in its frantic efforts in our own day to reach a more defensible position, of breaking, in its turn, with the State, and losing its own *raison d'être* at the same moment.

The next fact which the history makes evident to us is that in this reign, at least, the supremacy really meant not any idea of State power in the abstract, but simply the concrete will—too often, indeed, the mere caprice— of the individual sovereign for the time being.

In this instance, again, we find theory and practice, in these early days of the Reformed Church, very much at one. The Elizabethan Act of Supremacy (1 Eliz. c. 1) provides for the government of the Church by the sovereign herself, by the machinery of Commissions under the Great Seal; and Elizabeth accordingly, and her next two successors after her, looked upon the government of the Church as their own individual prerogative, and invariably resented any attempt on the part of Parliament to interfere with it.[1] Proof of this has already been given in these pages in abundance, and if it were not, it lies on the surface of every document, public or private, which deals with the subject throughout the reign. In the beginning of the reign we find

[1] See above, p. 219.

Jewell stating that it is to the Queen's own determined dislike of change that the maintenance of the vestments and ceremonies objected to by the Puritans, and disliked only a little less by the bishops themselves, is due. Later on we have seen her personal objection to the 'prophesyings' leading to their prohibition by the bishops, and to the suspension of the archbishop himself, because he declined to acquiesce; and towards the end we have seen her rebuking Archbishop Whitgift for permitting the predestinarian controversy to emerge, and giving him an intimation which led at once to the virtual withdrawal of his Lambeth Articles, after he had already sent them down to the heads at Cambridge, as a sort of quasi-authoritative document: and throughout the reign we find any attempt on the part of Parliament to deal with ecclesiastical matters of any kind checked and rebuked in no measured terms, even in cases in which the Queen took the same view as the Commons themselves.

Since Elizabeth, then, was to so great an extent both in theory and practice Pope of England, it is of importance that we should consider, with the best light we can find, what kind of a Pope she was, what were the real acts which she did, and whether she deserves altogether the discredit of that deliberate and organised system of hypocrisy which Mr. Froude attributes to her. Elizabeth, then, we have to remember, besides being a woman of great natural abilities and quite exceptional force of character, and very wide culture, also had an experience of life almost unexampled. True, she was born in the purple, but it was purple in which were some very coarse threads; for at her birth Katherine of Arragon was still living, and, when she was but three years old, her own mother was attainted, divorced, and executed, and herself stigmatised as a bastard. That in essential and important matters she suffered less from this than we should expect, seems clear from the fact that her education was conducted with the most jealous care, and that she was at a later time included among the heirs to the throne appointed in her father's will; but, even so, it is incredible that she did not receive vastly different treatment, as the King's natural daughter, from that which had been her due as the heiress-apparent to the throne. Edward and his more important counsellors were all, either in fact or profession, Protestant bigots, and from them it is no secret that she received far more consideration than her sister; but this was counter-balanced in a great measure by the fact that Mary was before her in the order of succession, and, when the time came to attempt to set Mary aside, they seemed to feel no scruple in including Elizabeth in the same proscription. When the attempt failed, and Mary ascended the throne, Elizabeth, at the age of twenty, entered upon a term of trial, persecution, and actual danger, during which her individual liberty was constantly restrained, her personal attendants were appointed by others, and continually tampered with, and her own life was in such danger that she had no security from day to day that she might not be committed to the Tower or ordered for execution. Elizabeth was far from being destitute of religious feeling or of Christian belief. It was no mere acting that when Mary died, and the announcement was made to her that she was delivered from her thraldom and was herself a queen, she fell on her knees and exclaimed, 'It is the Lord's doing, and is marvellous in our eyes!' But while her life, with its rapid changes and constant danger, had been calculated to keep alive a sense of religion within her, yet she had lived through a time of the most exasperated religious controversy, and the controversialists of both sides had tried their skill upon her to the utmost. Moreover, if she had seen, and to some extent felt, the bitterness, cruelty, and relentless brutality of Mary's rule, not less had she also seen the selfish hypocrisy and unscrupulous greed of Edward's Protestant counsellors; and was in no danger of falling under the delusion that in the controversy of the times all the good was on one side and all the evil on the other.

Equally by nature and education Elizabeth was a woman of broad mind and clear understanding, but, like other people, her conduct was not always dictated by her understanding alone. She was biassed by her inordinate vanity, by her love of power, and not less by her self-will, her taste for display, and not unfrequently by mere feminine caprice and perversity. Added to all this, she stood constantly in most difficult situations, and was swayed by innumerable considerations of safety and policy. Considering the number and the force of the temptations to which she was exposed, the wonder is that her course was not even more erratic than it actually was. In regard to Church matters it was, in truth, singularly consistent. Having accepted the state of things established during the first years of her reign, which allowed a certain latitude of opinion in the more mysterious doctrines of the faith, while it maintained some outward decency and order in the worship of the Church, her constant endeavour afterwards, as we have seen, was to maintain uniformity in externals and to check controversy upon difficult and recondite questions. It is abundantly clear that it was to Elizabeth's personal opposition alone it is due that the demands of the earlier Puritans for the abolition of vestments and ceremonies were not conceded. That policy, as well as taste, may have conduced to this result is not unlikely, nor is it inconsistent with Elizabeth's habitual duplicity and dissimulation; but there is quite sufficient evidence to show that her apparent disposition towards the old religion was but skin deep, and that she was in the main a partisan of the Reformation.[1] In the early years of her reign, the terrible dangers by which the country was surrounded may well have made her hesitate to estrange and irritate her only ally, and not improbably add him to the already formidable number of her enemies, when, by merely talking in a vague manner to his ambassador, and leaving the cross standing in her private chapel, she might keep up in his constantly vacillating mind the idea of her possible conversion; but from the day when she published her famous Injunctions to that on which she spoke to the Privy Council about the Irish rebellion, of 'extirpating that monster who colours his traitorous ingratitude with a desire to plant the Romish superstition to the extirpation of God's true religion, wherein we will live and die,'[2] and to that further day when she actually did die, receiving her final consolation from the mouth of the Calvinist Whitgift, there is no reason to believe that Elizabeth was other than a Protestant in belief as well as in action. That times of great excitement, whether religious or political, lead many men to the adoption of extreme opinions, either on one side or the other, may be true; but it is not true, even in such times, that a man must of necessity be either a fanatic

---

[1] On these points further evidence from contemporary sources will be found in the Appendix, note vii.

[2] *State Papers*, vol. cclxxv. No. 10, June 20, 1600.

or an unbeliever: and a person with the intellect, the education, the experience, and, above all, the temperament, of Elizabeth, is predestined, by disposition and circumstances alike, to take the middle course, and does not deserve the stigma of hypocrisy for so doing.

If we now turn from Elizabeth's character to her work, we shall find that, whether good or bad—for on that point men will differ till the end of time—it was great and characteristic, it was of inestimable importance to the English nation, and it has been most wonderfully permanent—for it has not changed in any important feature since her time—and it was her own. That the Church of England as we now see it *is* as we now see it, is due to Elizabeth herself and to none other. The share of her counsellors was great, and amongst them in this matter, as in others, the foremost place must be assigned to Cecil; but it was not to her counsellors, and certainly not to Cecil, that it was due that the moderate and, at least theoretically, unobjectionable demands of the early Puritans were not conceded. The letters of Jewell and others of the early Elizabethan bishops, show plainly not only that there would have been no great opposition on their part, but that it was the Queen herself and the Queen only who stood between them and concession. To estimate the whole effect of such concession, had it been made, is of course impossible; but it seems clear that it must have changed the whole subsequent history of the Church of England. A large proportion of the nominal members of the English Church in the early part of Elizabeth's reign must have consisted of those more or less indifferent persons who had been brought up in childhood as Catholics, who had lacked ability or inclination to form opinions for themselves, and who complied more or less unwillingly with the law which compelled them to attend the English services. The loss of the vestments and ceremonies still retained, might no doubt have disgusted many of these, and have driven them back to the old faith; and of anything calculated to add strength to the Catholic party Elizabeth had throughout her reign a well-founded fear, and this fear came in aid of her own taste and feeling to prevent the concession. On the other hand, had the concession been made when first demanded, it would have conciliated the bulk of the early Puritans at the time, and it may doubtless be argued that it would have taken at once the brain and the heart out of the Puritan movement, would have enlisted the ablest and best of the Puritans on the side of the Church, and so prevented the formation of that great half-organised body of nonconformity which has played so considerable a part, for evil as well as for good, in the subsequent history of this country.[1] But it may be replied that it is by no means certain that all this would have happened.[2] It is at least as likely that the Puritan demands would have grown with the concession just as they did grow without it; that, having obtained the abolition of the vestments and ceremonies,

---

[1] It is argued, by no less a writer than Hallam, that up to the appearance of Cartwright as the leader of the Puritans, concessions to them would have been safe and judicious.

[2] Cartwright was not an isolated portent totally unconnected with other men, or with the circumstances of the times. Had he been so, he would have produced no effect; and the difficulty, or rather the impossibility, is to determine how far Cartwright was himself produced by Elizabeth's high-pressure system, or was the natural result of that very peculiar theology which her system had entirely failed to check; and with the example of the Scotch Church before us, we are naturally inclined to the latter explanation rather than the former.

they would have proceeded, as they actually did, to demand, one after another, the abolition of the liturgy, the establishment of lay elders, the abolition of bishops, and the equality of ministers; and thence to that complete exaltation of the ministry above the Parliament and the sovereign which, as we have seen, they proposed, and which a century or so later was actually realised to no slight degree in Scotland. All this could not, of course, be patent to the eyes of Elizabeth and her advisers, but they may well have felt that concession is often a two-edged weapon, and, in the act of disposing of one enemy, not unfrequently arouses others.

As we read the evidence in contemporary documents, it appears almost incredible that Elizabeth could have maintained as she did throughout her reign, with constantly increasing narrowness and rigidity, the system of universal repression which it displays to us. But the era of toleration had not yet dawned: none but a very few of the most enlightened minds had even dreamed of it: and the Puritans themselves insisted upon the universal obligation of their own system as strongly as did the Papists on theirs. Elizabeth's religious system, which was, in the first instance, merely a revival of Edward VI.'s, and is so spoken of constantly by those most intimately concerned in its establishment,[1] was treated from the first by the Papists as mere Protestantism, and was accepted as such by the foreign Protestants; but it retained a sufficient amount of the external forms and ceremonies of the old religion to maintain the decency and order of public worship, while the definitions of doctrine were elastic enough to admit

[1] *E.g.*, Parkhurst to Bullinger, *Zurich Letters*, p. 29; Jewell to the same, *ib.* p. 33.

considerable diversity of opinion and belief on points on which different minds can in general arrive at a similar conclusion only by a tacit agreement to accept words without too close inquiry as to their meaning. The bishops, though retaining their old position and dignity, and though permitted to revive many of their old courts and jurisdictions, nevertheless did so only as officers under the Crown, and the only one who ventured to oppose the Queen's views found himself, as we have seen, reduced to utter helplessness for the remainder of his life; and when, some quarter of a century later, the earliest attempt was made to claim Divine right for them, it was done under the pressure of controversy, and was guarded by a distinct claim of the whole Papal power for the Crown. The limitations on the Protestant side of the line, which occupy so prominent a position in the latter part of the reign, were in themselves nothing new. There was a heresy commission, in the days of Edward, against the Anabaptists, and Joan Bocher was put to death in the same reign; but in Elizabeth's time the extension of Puritan opinions among the ruling classes—Sir Francis Knollys, Leicester, and Burleigh himself being more or less affected by them—gave them more importance, and rendered her repressive policy more difficult.

Whatever moral criticisms we may make upon Queen Elizabeth's ecclesiastical policy, it must be admitted that she contrived to establish a system which has been in many respects wonderfully successful. If it satisfied the extreme of neither party, it has certainly continued, for three centuries and a half, so to conciliate to itself a large portion of the English people, that it has followed them to whatever parts of the world they have since spread, and now reckons among its members not only a larger number—for that it could not but do—but a larger proportion of professing Christians than it ever did before. In any case, it is certain that but for Elizabeth herself the subsequent history of the English Church must have been very different from what it has actually been.

CHAPTER XII

SUMMARY AND CONCLUSIONS

I HAVE now brought down a brief account of the history of the relations of Church and State during the earlier half of the Reformation period, to the end of the sixteenth century, and the almost simultaneous end of that wonderful dynasty which ruled England during the whole of that century and presided over the birth and youth of the Reformation. It has been my endeavour throughout to make no statement of fact which was not either admitted by a general consent of the best authorities, or at least supported by good contemporary evidence. Of the deductions which I have drawn or shall draw from these facts, my readers must judge for themselves how far they are or are not legitimate. I shall now attempt, in a concluding chapter, to sum up the results to which all these facts and deductions appear to lead us with as much impartiality as I can command, and without regard to any of those remote and ultimate consequences which so constantly tend to transform historical essays into mere party pamphlets.

The preliminary sketch which formed the necessary introduction to the proper subject of the book may serve to place in their fair light a few matters which are often forgotten or misrepresented in their bearing upon subsequent events.

It may serve to remind us how the Church was planted in England by the Roman missionary Augustine, and how, though possibly more than half the country was converted from an independent source, yet the whole deliberately submitted to the Roman Primacy, and from thenceforth became one with itself and with the rest of the Western Church: how the Norman conquest did but cement the union by eliminating much that was Saxon and insular in the law and the practice of the Church courts: and how the Papal power and influence, instead of being less in England than elsewhere, was in reality greater; and this not only in the times of Pope Innocent and King John, but generally throughout the whole period extending down to Henry VII. himself. It may serve also to place us on our guard against that peculiar second intention in which the word national is commonly used by English ecclesiastical historians, writing either with the general object of magnifying and glorifying everything English as such, or with the more specific intention of making out what they consider a more satisfactory pedigree for the modern English Church establishment. To an unsophisticated reader it might appear that the phrase National Church must at least imply the previous existence of a nation and a Church in the country of which it is used. Yet in the very last book which has been published on the subject[1] we find ourselves called upon to admire the specially national character of the English Church, at a time when there existed in England at least two Churches and no nation at all. Much has been made in this relation of the fact—or the alleged fact—already referred to, that a larger portion of England was converted by Scoto-Irish missionaries than by Roman. This appears difficult to

[1] *The English Church in the Middle Ages*, by W. Hunt, in Prof. Creighton's *Epochs of Church History*.

determine with certainty, and very unimportant when it is determined. Let it be admitted for the sake of the argument. It still remains true that the first primate, whose successor, after a sort, still sits at Canterbury, was a missionary sent direct from Pope Gregory the Great, in 597; that Theodore, the great reorganiser of the see, was also a papal missionary; that the Scoto-Irish converts in the North under Wilfrid's primacy formally submitted to Rome at the Synod of Whitby in 664, Colman, the leader on the other side, and those who would not submit, shaking off the dust from their feet and departing; and that Saxon England for the first time became a nation some 150 years later. These few facts alone—and there are others like them—serve to show plainly that national, in modern English ecclesiastical history, has often the same meaning as non-national elsewhere. Could we call the civil government of any country national, if its highest Court of Appeal was foreign, its highest officers were often appointed by a foreign power, and always paid tribute to it, and if its highest native judge,[1] when by indirect means he had succeeded in getting the final appeals mostly into his own hands, yet always gave his decisions avowedly as the delegate of a foreign potentate? Clearly, if we use the word national to describe such a state of things, we use it in a sense not only differing from, but contrary to, its common acceptation. The result, then, of our review of the history of the Church in England before the reign of Henry VIII. is, that we find that up to that time there was not, and indeed could not be, a National Church in any intelligible sense of the words.

Positively the only historical facts which tend

[1] Wolsey.

to support the now prevalent theory of the national character of the Church in England during the Middle Ages, are to be found in the series of antipapal statutes enacted under the Plantagenet and later kings. The true explanation of these is that quoted above from Bishop Stubbs, and amounts to the fact that they were intended to prevent the encroachment of the popes into the region of temporal government. Even in this, as we have seen, they were not remarkably successful. They were continually infringed by the kings themselves, and sometimes by their subjects; they had an incurable tendency to fall into abeyance; and moreover they were all passed at a time in which the Papacy was in a state of depression, and as soon as it revived, under Martin V., they were almost forgotten—to such an extent, at least, that when Henry VIII. suddenly revived the Statute of Præmunire, no one knew what it meant, and he was able to attach to it just what value pleased him.

Under Henry VIII. all this was completely changed. On the fall of Wolsey, he undertook on his own account a reform of the Church, which ended in nothing short of a revolution. By an ingenious application of the Statute of Præmunire he drove the clergy into a submission to himself which was practically unconditional, and he induced Parliament, by a series of measures culminating in the Act of Appeals and the Act of Supremacy, to simply transfer the whole of the papal power from the Pope to himself and his successors.

These Acts for the first time made the Church in England a National Church; but, at the same time, they incurred the excommunication of the Pope, and made it also, in ecclesiastical parlance, schismatical.[1] Here

---

[1] It is worthy of notice that Ranke used the words 'schism' and 'schis-

Henry would possibly have stopped. His immediate object had been to obtain his divorce from Katherine. That he could not obtain from the Pope, and therefore he abolished the Pope as far as his own domains extended, in order to get it. He was no Protestant, neither did he sympathise with Protestants; but Protestantism was at the moment on the rise, and it was difficult to break with the Pope without, in a greater or less degree, indirectly if not directly, encouraging Protestants. Again, he was sensible of the abuses of pilgrimages and shrines and magic images, things which had excited the anger of men like Colet and Erasmus and More, who were no more Protestants than he; and his appreciation of these matters was doubtless quickened by the further consideration that the cult of Thomas à Becket was a standing memorial of the victory of papal over regal power. It was therefore advisable that Becket should be abolished, as in truth a traitor rather than a saint; and, having proceeded so far, he found the gold and jewels of Becket's shrine so agreeable a remedy for his impecuniosity, that other saints, whose claims to reverence were in themselves not so obnoxious to royalty, had to share the same fate notwithstanding. The same mixture of motives—desire to depreciate the Pope in the eyes of his subjects, and desire to fill his own chronically empty exchequer—contributed in no small degree to produce his crusade against the monks and friars, who formed, as they have been often called, a kind of militia of the Papacy and possessed—even on the lowest computation—a vast amount of wealth. But

matical' in describing the events of the sixteenth century in England, though his translators have kindly modified it in the English edition into 'separation.'

Henry did not, or perhaps could not, stop short in his course at the precise point which he would have chosen. He seems to have proposed to himself to establish a Church which, though repudiating the Pope, and separating itself from the Catholic Church of which the Pope was the head, should yet remain orthodox in doctrine and Catholic in ritual. In this he found two obstacles—first that the Pope excommunicated him, and secondly that, as remarked by Marillac in a passage already quoted, it was far from an easy task to keep men orthodox apart from the Catholic Church; and thus he was led to carry his assumption of papal power further than at that time, or for long after, the popes themselves had carried it, and in his Ten Articles first, and his Six afterwards, began to prescribe the doctrines which his people were to believe, as well as the authority to which they were to defer. That those doctrines differed comparatively little from the Catholic standard of the time, is a matter of relatively small importance. They were the doctrines of the King, not of the Church, and were enforced upon the Church in England by the authority of the State alone. Convocation, bridled by the Submission and presided over by Cromwell or Cromwell's lay deputy, could be in no sense a legitimate organ of the Church. Thus when Henry died a complete revolution had been effected in the position of the Church. Instead of the Church *in* England, it had become in good truth the Church *of* England: instead, that is, of an integral part of that great Western province of Christendom to which it owed its first conversion, and with which it had been one ever since—for nearly a thousand years—it had become, for the first time in its history, a separate Christian community, of which little could be affirmed but that, for the time being at any rate, it agreed with no other, that it retained an anomalous and decapitated form of Catholicism, and that, in practice, if not in theory too, it owed its doctrine, as well as whatever of discipline it retained, to its lay supreme head.

This was the situation at the end of the reign; but the fact that its establishment coincided, in point of time, with the general rise of Protestantism throughout Europe and its extension into England, complicated it still further. Henry's death took off, in a great degree, the pressure which alone kept the two rival religious parties from flying at one another's throats; but the subjection of the Church to the State still continued, and, as circumstances now threw the power into the hands of the reforming party, the result was a revolution in the doctrines of the Church almost as complete as that which Henry had already brought about in its constitution: indeed, the prevalent idea on the subject at the time, and for long after, appears to have been that suggested in the passage already quoted from Archbishop Bramhall—that of the two great changes of which the Reformation consisted, that in the constitution of the Church was the work of Henry VIII., and that in its doctrine of Edward VI.'s Council. This, in the main, is a true account of the history; but it requires some modification, for Henry did not confine himself so entirely to matters of external constitution as this view suggests, and both these revolutionary changes were for the time entirely swept away by Mary; so that, in point of fact, Elizabeth began her government with a complete *tabula rasa* in the matter of religion; and the permanent importance of the constitutional changes of Henry's reign, and the doctrinal changes of Edward's, is limited to the degree in which they respectively served as models for the Elizabethan legislation. In thus speaking, I refer, of course, to the legal and constitutional position of the Church. No one could for a moment suppose that even such legislative somersaults as were performed in these successive reigns could do away with the political, social, or religious results of events like the suppression of the monasteries, or the Marian persecution, or the varying relations of England towards Spain, France, Scotland, and the Papacy.

On the accession of Edward VI., not yet ten years of age, the personal element of government, which, with Henry, had been everything, fell into abeyance—the national papacy which he had established was of necessity placed for the time in commission : the Council, in fact, reigned. Almost its first act was to reduce the bishops formally, as Henry had already done in fact, to the condition of mere State officials. The next result was an important change in the direction and course of the Reformation. Henry's personal views and personal action had hitherto pervaded every part of it, and the very Articles which expressed provisionally the doctrines of the English Church, were either his own work, or at least corrected by his hand. Edward's counsellors, for the most part, cared for none of these things, and were content to leave them in the hands of a knot of highly-placed divines, whose one qualification, from their point of view, was that they should belong to that Protestant faction with which their own interests were bound up. Hence, while Cranmer and Ridley, with the help of Peter Martyr and Bucer, compiled the Prayer-book and drew up the Articles, Gardiner and Bonner, and subsequently Heath and Day, went to prison or were deprived. That these men proceeded further as they went on—the second Prayer-book of Edward VI. showing a more advanced form of Protestantism than the first—Mr. Pocock attributes to deliberate dishonesty on their part; but, as it seems to me, it may be accounted for more naturally, as well as more charitably, by regarding it as the simple result of that natural progress of thought in their own minds, which is apt to be more rapid under the stimulus of party excitement than it is at other times. Something like this appears to be the rational interpretation of the facts of the Edwardian portion of the great religious revolution, if sentimental prepossessions and ecclesiastical theories be laid aside.

When Mary succeeded, in full age and in full possession of her powers, such as they were, and with the Tudor temper and more than the Tudor obstinacy, irritated by a life-long course of ill-treatment and annoyance, a furious reaction was the consequence. But what is of importance for us to notice in this place is that in Mary's government the personal element once more revived, and that the reaction, as we have seen, was almost entirely her own act and deed. Her methods were very much those employed by her father and Cromwell. She bribed the lay lords, deprived the Edwardian bishops, and packed the House of Commons; and when these vigorous methods proved insufficient for her purpose, she supplemented them by purely arbitrary acts of power: and finally she instituted that bloody persecution which filled all England at once with horror by its cruelty, and with disgust and contempt by the baseness with which it glutted itself upon poor, mean, harmless, and ignorant victims—tailors, peasants, cripples, and old women—while it left well-known and noble heretics in Parliament and at the council-board unimpeached and unassailed. The persecution was as fatal a mistake in policy as it was an immoral act in itself; but even had that mistake not been made, it is very doubtful whether Mary could ever have succeeded in her aim. Henry VIII.'s policy in destroying the monasteries and using their lands for the purpose of raising up a new territorial nobility, whether we believe it to have been deliberate and far-sighted or not, was that which made the successful re-establishment of the old Church system in England almost, if not altogether, impossible. The new families had risen to wealth and importance solely on the plunder of the Church; they could defend their own newly-acquired possessions only by a steady resistance to the claims of the Church, and the readiest means of making good that resistance was to take sides with the anti-Church or Protestant faction. Hence the new nobles—most of whom had probably first risen into importance by showing some useful abilities—formed, as a whole, the backbone of the Protestant party, and were pledged, by every consideration which ordinarily governs human actions, to oppose the rehabilitation of the old Church to the utmost.

With the accession of Elizabeth the Reformation entered upon a new phase. There was never any real doubt felt [1] by the nation in general but that she would take the Protestant side, while there was comparatively little danger of a re-establishment of the Protestant misrule which had existed in her brother's time; for with Elizabeth there was no lack of personal will or force of character. That she did not in every particular re-enact the whole of her brother's ecclesiastical legislation, is a fact which has been dwelt upon with no little insistance by many modern historians; but they have been less careful to observe to how great an extent she

[1] *De Feria*, quoted by Froude, vol. vii. pp. 13–14.

really did so, or how, in the main, her own contemporaries, friends and foes alike, constantly thought and spoke of religion as being restored to that form which it had in the time of Edward VI.[1] The supremacy was restored, and the Prayer-book—with but slight alteration—also; and both by authority of the State alone, not only without but against the strongly-declared wishes of the bishops and clergy.

The first of these measures, it should be observed, dropped nothing of Henry's claim except the title of supreme head, and, in fact, re-established to the full the national papacy of which I have spoken, and the claim to which, as we have seen, was put forward in the plainest terms by Dr. Bancroft towards the end of the reign, in the very same sermon in which he made a mild suggestion of some sort of Divine right in the bishops for the first time since the separation from Rome.

Another important feature in this reign also is the complete subjection of Convocation to the Queen and the Parliament. In the instance just referred to, it must be observed that the Convocation of 1559 was as much a Convocation as that of four years later, yet the Reformation was re-established in spite of its efforts to the contrary. From that time forth throughout the reign Convocation accepted its position, and confined itself strictly within the limits assigned to it. In 1563, indeed, a formal attempt was made by Bishop Sandys to obtain the concession of the whole of the early Puritan demands, which was defeated only, after counting proxies, by the narrow majority of one. When we consider the strong inducements to those in favour of such a measure to abstain from voting for it, arising

[1] *E.g.*, Grindal to Hubert in *Zurich Letters*, series 2, p. 19.

from the fact that the Queen was well known to be opposed to it, and that its passing would have involved the unsettlement of the law as established by Parliament only four years before, and after much debate and difficulty, such a majority can only be taken to represent a real minority. It constituted, nevertheless, a technical majority, and it is perhaps well that it did so, since that one shy and absent 'odd man' is all that stood between the maintenance of the system already established and a collision with the Crown, which could only have led to a second 'submission of the clergy,' entailing renewed loss of position and authority. A similar lesson is taught by almost every important ecclesiastical transaction of the reign.

Thus the revision of the Prayer-book at the beginning of the reign was carried through by a committee of divines appointed apparently by the Privy Council. Again, when De Quadra was negotiating with Elizabeth about receiving a papal nuncio and sending representatives to the Council of Trent, Elizabeth herself and Cecil appear to have managed the whole matter, and 'the Church' was in no way consulted. When Calvin reopened with Parker his previous negotiation for the unification of the Reformed Churches, Parker never once appears to have thought of taking Convocation or even his brother bishops into his confidence: and Whitgift, many years later, when he was anxious to settle the predestinarian controversy at Cambridge, first arranged the Lambeth Articles with the help of a few of his friends; and when compelled by the Queen's personal interference to withdraw them, informed the heads of colleges, as we have seen, that the final decision of what is or is not the doctrine of the Church of England lay with 'the Queen and those whom she has commissioned,' and not with them : that Convocation had anything to do with the matter it never once occurs to him to suggest. Lastly, the whole Puritan controversy arose, and was maintained throughout the reign, by the personal determination of Elizabeth to make no concessions, even in points which the majority of the bishops were quite willing to yield. But Elizabeth's bishops were no free agents. In the earlier part of her reign they had but little power : in the later, when Whitgift was primate, they obtained a great deal more ; but they obtained it by consenting to become simply the Queen's agents in her ecclesiastical policy, when she carried that personal power over the Church, which the Act of Supremacy had given her, to its full development under the Court of High Commission. Thus in this reign, almost as much as under Henry and Mary, the personal will of the sovereign was the chief agency in developing the ecclesiastical policy of the reign ; and it led under Elizabeth as directly and completely to the development of nonconformity, as under Henry to the separation from Rome, or under Mary to the persecution first and the reaction afterwards.

Thus from the date of the Submission of the Clergy, 1531, to the end of the Tudor dynasty with the death of Elizabeth, the relations of Church and State, which we have been following through all their vicissitudes, may be summed up in the two correlative words, dominion and subjection. Throughout the whole period, whatever may have been the variation of phraseology, the fact had been that the Church, as soon as it became emancipated from the Pope, became and remained the thrall of the sovereign. Under Henry its subjection had been thorough and undisguised ; under Mary it had been just as complete, only Mary had used her own arbitrary power for the purpose of installing the Pope in her place. Elizabeth's system had been more like her father's, but she had greater difficulties to contend with, and less absolutely submissive implements with which to work. A different state of things existed in Edward's reign, because his youth interfered with his personal action, and consequently the element of party was introduced to an extent otherwise unknown in the Tudor age: but it was essentially a transitory condition, and if it had not been brought to an end by his death, would have been so very little later by his majority; and there is every reason to believe that he would have displayed the Tudor self-will to the full as much as the other members of his house.

It is difficult to study the actual facts of sixteenth-century history, putting apart preconceived ecclesiastical theories, without arriving at the conclusion that the English National Church was as completely the creation of Henry VIII., Edward's Council, and Elizabeth, as Saxon Protestantism was of Luther, or Swiss of Calvin or of Zwingle. Obviously no man who sets forth a distinctive form of Christianity can proclaim himself the founder of a new religion or a new Church as such. So long as the new organisation claims to be Christian at all, it must go back for its foundation to Jesus Christ and His Apostles, and he himself can appear only as a reformer, a restorer of what professes, and must profess, to be the religion which they delivered to mankind. In this particular the claim of the English Reformers of the sixteenth century was the same as that of Luther and Calvin, or of Cartwright and Travers, and the whole question about what is to be recognised as 'primitive' or 'catholic' is one of interpretation and historical theory.

The history of the Church in England was continuous from the Mission of Augustine—or, if we prefer it, from the Synod of Whitby—to the time when Henry VIII., upon a disagreement with the Pope about his divorce, cast off his allegiance to the Papacy. From that time to the present, with the short interval between the reconciliation under Mary, and Elizabeth's first Parliament, it has been severed from and excommunicated by the great body of the Catholic Church: and as the latter was before precisely that which it has continued since, it is clear that the former must have been something not the same; and it is not the mere retention of a few names and titles, used in a kind of 'second intention,' and a few more or less maimed and amputated rites, which will ever make persons intelligently instructed believe that an establishment which obviously is the mere creature of a single State, is the legitimate and adequate representative of that imposing and magnificent Western Church, which is older than any existing State in Europe and grander than anything that the world has ever seen, and which has been picturesquely described by an old writer as 'the ghost of the old Roman Empire sitting robed and crowned upon the grave thereof.'[1] A fair consideration of the actual facts of the Tudor history serves further to show that a theory like that which prevails so widely at present—which represents the English Church in any other light than that of one (though it may, perhaps, be admitted, the greatest and the most dignified) of the many Protestant Churches which arose in the sixteenth century—is a novelty which took its very earliest rise some half-century or more after the separation from Rome, as a direct consequence of Elizabeth's determination to give no quarter to the

---

[1] See *Froude*, vol. vii. pp. 330-4.

earlier Puritans, and which made little or no progress for another half-century still. The evidence is simply overwhelming which shows, that during the whole period from 1552 onwards the English Church was considered, by friends and foes alike, to be for all intents and purposes one with the Swiss churches of Zurich and Geneva. The divines of the Church of England during the period in question differed, no doubt, among themselves on those minor points, which, as we have seen, were so nearly carried in favour of the Puritans in the Convocation of 1562; but their great anxieties were two only, viz., to shake themselves free from 'the tyranny of the Bishop of Rome and all his detestable enormities,' —to use words which once were sounded forth in all the churches in the land as one of the petitions in the Litany—and, secondly, to claim brotherhood and sympathy with the Protestant leaders in Switzerland and on the Upper Rhine. This remains true notwithstanding the equal truth of the fact that Henry VIII., who gave the first impulse to the Reformation in England, was no Protestant and no friend to Protestants. He had, as I have already suggested, been led on by circumstances to make further changes than he at first intended, and among them were those in parts of the Church Services from the use of the Latin to that of the English language, the arranging of which he committed to Cranmer in 1545. These were the beginnings of the English Liturgy, and since there was at that time little or no design of a change in doctrine, it was natural that they should be, as they were, mainly translations from the Roman Breviary. It is doubtless this natural history of the Liturgy which accounts, in part at least, for the discrepancies which have been discovered between it and the Articles of the Church of England.

Both were the work of the same master workman, though under different circumstances, and with the aid of different assistants. When Cranmer undertook the work at first, he was not yet a Protestant; when he finished it, in Edward's reign, he was a somewhat advanced one. In the latter years of his life, under the influence of Ridley and Peter Martyr, Cranmer's opinions had advanced rapidly, and he had become, as is shown in the Articles and the second Prayer-book of Edward, and as he himself tacitly admitted in his second examination at Oxford, Zwinglian in doctrine. Nevertheless he remained true to the conservative instincts characteristic of the English Reformation throughout, and altered as little as his new principles would permit. He may doubtless also have considered that a manual of devotion is one thing and a formula of doctrine another. The Liturgy he composed, as the beauty of its language and its reverential tone suggests, under the full influence of these feelings, retaining as much as possible of whatever was calculated to soothe the feelings and excite the devotion of the worshippers, and to suggest as little as might be the changes and controversies of the day; and without a thought that it also would one day be subjected to the torturing processes of controversial theologians and ecclesiastical lawyers, endeavouring to screw out of its rhetorical expressions and time-honoured metaphors, a constructive licence for holding doctrines which it was the one object of his later years to oppose and to denounce, and, if possible, to obliterate.

The Articles, on the other hand, he drew up distinctly as a formula of faith, intended to express the doctrines of the Church as accurately as was consistent with sufficient comprehensiveness to avoid splitting up the Protestant body into as many differing sects as there existed, or might exist, shades of opinion on obscure theological doctrines; and certainly without any foresight of those 'non-natural senses' to which the ingenuity of later times would compel them to submit, with the evident and even avowed object of forcing them to admit those very doctrines which the whole history, both of the documents and of their framers, shows that they were intended to exclude.[1] It was no doubt a stroke of genius on the part of those who, in after years, desired to undo Cranmer's work, when they claimed the right to interpret the Articles by the language of the Liturgy; but that the latter never was intended to be used for such a purpose may be considered to be historically proved by the following facts: (1) That while both were the work of the same hand, the Articles were the later composition of the two; (2) that a new edition of the Liturgy was published in the very same year with the Articles, in which the very few changes made were of such a kind as to bring it into accord with them in the one or two points which appeared to the compilers to be important; and (3) that, as just pointed out, the rhetorical and devotional tone of the older document, compared with the scholastic and argumentative style of the later, shows plainly which of the two was meant to serve a controversial or polemical purpose, and also which was not so intended. The final conclusions, then, at which we must arrive from the history of Church and State in England under the Tudor Dynasty appear to be as follows:—

(1.) That during the earlier part of the period—*i.e.*, during the whole reigns of Henry VII. and of Henry VIII.

---

[1] Compare Newman's *Apologia*, p. 242, and indeed the whole argument of Parts v. and vi. of that work.

until the fall of Wolsey, no change of importance took place, but there were many indications of the overbearing character of the clergy of the period, and of their unpopularity and evil repute among the laity, and of their generally corrupt condition.

(2.) That the primary motive of Henry VIII. in separating from Rome was his desire to obtain a divorce from Katherine, which the Pope refused.

(3.) That the separation was purely and simply the act of the King and the Parliament, the share of the clergy in it, such as it was, being entirely involuntary.

(4.) That the Act of Supremacy transferred the whole power—whatever that might have been—of the Pope, to the King, while the Submission of the Clergy bound them to entire dependence upon him.

(5.) That Henry thus for the first time created a National Church which was in truth schismatical, and of which he himself was, in all but name, Pope.

(6.) That he made some, but slight and few, changes in the doctrine and ritual of the Church thus established. Of these probably the most important, at least for the subsequent history of the Church, was the introduction, to some extent, of services in the English tongue.

(7.) That Henry, though he made the Church schismatical, did not make it in any appreciable degree Protestant.

(8.) That on Edward's accession the personal royal papacy fell of necessity into abeyance, and its powers were taken up by the predominant Protestant faction in the Council, which took a Zwinglian direction and retained it to the end of the reign.

(9.) That Mary, by two Acts of Parliament, swept away first the Protestant legislation of Edward's reign, and then the anti-Roman Acts of Henry's, and re-established the Roman Church in greater power than it had enjoyed since Henry III.; that she also, by setting up a violent persecution, gave occasion to a great and general reaction against that Church; and, further, she was unable to restore its wealth, which had been permanently taken from it by the abolition of the monastic system.

(10.) That Elizabeth, in the first year of her reign, restored the use of Edward's second Prayer-book with but two alterations, permitted the return of the Protestant divines who had gone into exile under Mary, and by means of the Act of Supremacy deprived all Mary's bishops with one only exception.

(11.) That the above Act, together with the Act of Uniformity, was passed by Elizabeth's first Parliament against the unanimous opposition of the Spiritual peers in the Upper House; and that Convocation took no part in the matter, except so far as the Lower House passed resolutions approving the whole of Mary's legislation.

(12.) That almost all the prominent Elizabethan bishops and divines were in doctrine Zwinglian or Calvinist, and were at much pains to declare themselves at one with the leading Swiss reformers, especially with Bullinger and Peter Martyr.

(13.) It was due to Elizabeth herself, and not to them, that the demands of the earlier Puritans were not complied with.

(14.) Bancroft in 1588, and Bilson some three years later, are the first writers who suggest any Divine right of bishops in the English Church, and of them the first accompanies his suggestion by a claim, in so many words, of the whole papal power for the Queen. It was plainly as a set-off against the Puritan claim of Divine right for their discipline that this counter-claim was made.

It may perhaps be said that some of these conclusions appertain to Church history exclusively and not to a history of the relations of Church and State. The reply is that, whatever may have happened later, up to the time with which we are now dealing, the distinction is trivial. From the time of Henry VIII.'s Acts of Supremacy and of Submission of the Clergy, the Church of England was, as its whole history shows, simply a department of the State. If, during that time, we wish to follow the history of an independent ecclesiastical organisation, we must look for it either in the proscribed Church of Rome, or among the unlicensed and persecuted Nonconformist sects, Anabaptists or other. It may further be objected that, in presenting this view, I have omitted many facts which seem to point in an opposite direction, such as the importance which has been attached in certain cases to the decisions of Convocation, the solemn form and language in which they have been framed, and the vast amount of learning and research which has been expended on the question of whether this, that, or the other important ecclesiastical act or document has or has not the authority of Convocation.

To this the answer is, that it has been a habit of governments generally to recommend every new ordinance by alleging every conceivable warrant in its defence, and that this habit never prevailed to a greater extent than in the Tudor age, when the civil government had taken upon itself a new set of functions, which it was endeavouring by every possible means to persuade men were but the natural developments of old ones, and consequently, wherever it could obtain, by whatever process of coercion, a colourable sanction from the clergy, for ecclesiastical enactments which, in former times, would have proceeded from the clergy themselves as a matter of course, it was glad enough to do so, but when it could not, it very simply, as we have seen, did without it. We have also seen that those early measures of Elizabeth, on which the permanent establishment of the Reformation hangs, were carried out in the teeth of the unanimous opposition of the clergy both in the House of Lords and in the Convocation—the only Convocation of the age which is above suspicion of having yielded to governmental pressure.

In the foregoing pages it has been my endeavour to confine myself as much as possible to facts, to what was actually done, said, or written by the actors in the great ecclesiastical revolution of the sixteenth century, and to what appear to be the necessary deductions from those facts. Except, perhaps, in the description of what their acts appear to me to show of the characters of some of the most important actors in the drama, I have as much as possible avoided both opinions and theories. How far the facts and the deductions hang together, and whether they accord best with the view of the whole transaction which was taken by contemporaries, and which remained general amongst Englishmen until our own days, or with those of that special party which arose in the seventeenth century, and all but expired with the non-jurors early in the eighteenth, but whose ideas have been revived and exaggerated within the last fifty years, it will be for my readers to determine for themselves. The earliest forms of those opinions we have seen arose about the year 1588 or '90. They were totally unknown before, and remained almost entirely inoperative for many years after—in fact, during nearly the whole of the period with which I have dealt.

In closing this work with what may fairly be considered to be the end of the first half of the Reformation period, I leave a state of things vastly different from that which existed at its beginning, and different also from that which it was to reach at its end. Nevertheless, the accession of a new dynasty brought many new things with it, and though the actual great changes which were to follow belong to the reign of Charles I. rather than to his father's, yet the reign of James was in many respects transitional: the causes which led to the great Rebellion became first plainly visible in that reign, and the characteristics of the Stuart dynasty stand in such marked contrast with those of the Tudors, that the time at which the monarchy passed from the one house to the other seems to afford a natural resting-place. If life and opportunity be given me, I shall hope one day to be able to trace the history of the relations of Church and State in England to the end of the period of great changes in their relations, towards the close of the seventeenth century.

APPENDIX

Note I. P. 62.

Chapuys, in one of his letters to Charles V., July 17, 1531, puts this question very shortly and forcibly, if somewhat coarsely, thus: 'The Queen has kept the articles sent from Rome &c. . . . On considering them, it seems to me that there has been omitted one deduction so necessary that without it conclusive proof cannot be obtained, because the point is to show that the Queen was not known by Prince Arthur, which is a general negative without restriction of time or place—a thing in law unprovable: and the presumption is against her, as she lay with the Prince several nights; and moreover they have brought testimony here that the Prince had several times boasted of having used her like a true and vigorous husband. For these reasons, even if all the Queen's allegations were proved as set forth in those articles, it would not amount to proof, except by the Queen's oath, which could not be admitted by law in opposition to the said proofs and presumptions.'

This is very strong evidence coming from whence it comes.

Note II. P. 68.

The following extracts from contemporary despatches will serve to illustrate four points maintained in the text—viz.:

(1) The close connection of the divorce with the separation from Rome;
(2) The complete coercion of the clergy, by means of the Præmunire;
(3) The unpopularity of the clergy; and
(4) The entire novelty of the Royal Supremacy.

1.

Chapuys to Charles V.

January 23, 1531.

Though the clergy know themselves innocent, seeing that it was determined to find fault with them, they offered of their own accord 160,000 ducats, which the King refused to accept, swearing that he will have 400,000 or will punish everyone with extreme rigour; so that they will be obliged to pass it, though it will compel them to sell their chalices and reliquaries. About five days ago it was agreed between the Nuncio and me that he should go to the said ecclesiastics in their congregation, and recommend them to support the immunity of the Church, and to inform themselves about the Queen's affairs, showing them the letter which the Pope has written thereupon, and offering to intercede for them with the King about the gift with which he wishes to charge them. On coming into the congregation, they were all utterly astounded and scandalised, and, without allowing him to open his mouth, they begged him to leave them in peace, for they had not the King's leave to speak with him; and if he came to execute any apostolic mandate, he ought to address himself to the Archbishop of Canterbury, their chief, who was not then present. The Nuncio accordingly returned without having public audience of them, and only explained his intention to the Bishop of London (Stokesley), their proctor, who said he would report it. But he will beware of doing so without having the King's command, for he is the principal promoter of these affairs.

2.

Chapuys to Charles V.

February 14, 1531.

Since my last letter the clergy have withdrawn the offer of money of which I wrote, because the King demanded that in case he or any of his allies made war, they should be bound to advance the said moneys without waiting the said five years; and also because the King would not grant them what had chiefly induced them to make the gift—viz., the restoration of their old liberties and exemption from Præmunire; and, thirdly, because the King declared to them the importance of the said law of Præmunire to guard himself from being misunderstood—which law no person in England can understand, and its interpretation lies solely in the King's head, who amplifies it and declares it at his pleasure, making it apply to any case he pleases, the penalty being confiscation of bodies and goods. At last, after a good deal of negotiation, the matter has been settled that the King shall not press them for payment before the expiration of the said five years, and that of the three demands of the clergy they should have that of the exemption and nothing more. . . . The thing that has been treated to the Pope's prejudice is that *the clergy have been compelled*, under pain of the said law of Præmunire, *to accept the King as head of the Church, which implies in effect as much as if they had declared him* POPE OF ENGLAND. It is true that the clergy have added to the declaration that they did so only so far as permitted by the law of God. But that is all the same, as far as the King is concerned, as if they had made no reservation, for no one will now be so bold as to contest with his lord the importance of the reservation. . . .

3.
Chapuys to Charles V.
February 21, 1531.

. . . And now the Act has been passed against the Pope which I wrote in my last. . . . By this his Holiness will perceive the truth of what I have always told the Nuncio and written to him—that his timidity and dissimulation would not only prejudice the Queen's interest but his own authority—and it seems to the Queen and her friends that the Pope has no great desire to settle the matter, and will justify what the Duke of Norfolk one day said to me, *that his Holiness was glad there should always be some discord* among the Princes, *fearing that if they were united they would reform the Church.* . .

If the Pope had ordered the lady to be separated from the King, the King would never have pretended to claim sovereignty over the Church; for, as far as I can understand, she and her father have been the principal cause of it. The latter, speaking of the affair a few days ago to the Bishop of Rochester, ventured to say he could prove by the Scripture that when God left this world, He left no successor nor vicar. *There is none who do not blame this usurpation*, except those who have promoted it. . . . The Nuncio has been with the King to-day. . . . The Nuncio then entered upon the subject *of this new papacy made here*, to which the King replied that it was nothing, and was not intended to infringe the authority of the Pope, provided his Holiness would pay due regard to him, *and otherwise he knew what to do.*

4.

Chapuys to Charles V.

March 8, 1531.

The clergy are more conscious every day of the great error they committed in acknowledging the King as sovereign of the Church, and they are urgent in Parliament to retract it. Otherwise they say they will not pay a penny of the 400,000 crowns. What will be the issue no one knows. . . .

5.

Chapuys to Charles V.

April 2, 1531.

. . . Since the ecclesiastics have obtained exemption from the Præmunire, the laity, understanding that the King would make his account to draw from them a large sum, insisted that the King should give them a similar exemption, showing that they had not incurred forfeiture; and if they had, that, in consideration of the large sums of money they had given him heretofore, they ought to be absolved. As the King would not listen to them for some days, there was great murmuring among them in the Chamber of the Commons, where it was publicly said, in the presence of some of the Privy Council, that the King had burdened and oppressed his kingdom with more imposts and exactions than any three or four of his predecessors, and he ought to consider that the strength of the King lay in the affections of his subjects. And many instances were alleged of the inconveniences which had happened to princes through ill-treatment of their subjects On learning this, the King granted the exemption, which was published in Parliament on Wednesday last, without any reservation. . . .

6.

Chapuys to Charles V.

May 22, 1531.

. . . Four days ago the clergy of York and Durham sent to the King a strong protestation against the supremacy which he pretended to have over them. The province of Canterbury have done the same, of which I send a copy to Granvelle. The King is greatly displeased. . . .

7.

Chapuys to Charles V.

June 6, 1531.

Giving an account of a visit of Henry VIII.'s Councillors to Katherine of Arragon to persuade her to give in. Katherine says incidentally : 'As to the *supremum caput*, she considered the King as her sovereign, and would therefore serve and obey him. He was also sovereign in his realm as regards temporal jurisdiction : but as to the spiritual, it was not pleasing to God either that the King should so intend, or that she should consent ; for the Pope was the only true sovereign and vicar of God who had power to judge of spiritual matters, of which marriage was one.'

8.

State Papers, June 13, 1531.—*Cranmer to the Earl of Wiltshire, concerning Reginald Pole's book against the divorce.*

Recapitulating Pole's arguments, he says, 'As to the people, he thinks it impossible to satisfy them by learning or preaching ; but as *they now begin to hate priests*, this will make them hate learned men all the more.'

9.

Spanish Despatches, 460.

October 15.

The King has called together the clergy and lawyers, to ascertain whether, in virtue of the privileges possessed by this kingdom, Parliament could and would enact that, notwithstanding the Pope's prohibition, the cause of the divorce be decided by the Archbishop of Canterbury. They have answered in the negative, and the King has prorogued Parliament to February. The King has told the Nuncio that, if the Pope would not show him more consideration, he would show the world that the Pope had no greater authority than Moses, and that every claim not grounded on Scripture was mere usurpation ; that the great concourse of people present had come solely and exclusively to request him to bastinado the clergy, who were hated by both nobles and people.

10.

Spanish Despatches, 492.

November 13.

The King has told the Ambassador that the Convocation of Councils, except on matters of faith, was the province of secular princes, not of the Pope ; and also that it would be doing God service to take away the temporalities from the clergy.

11.

Norfolk to Benet.

February 28, 1532.

... I spoke this day with his (the Pope's) ambassador here, who I doubt not will advertise him plainly of our conference, which the Pope must ponder if he wishes to retain the obedience of England to the See Apostolic. ... Notwithstanding the infinite clamour of the temporality here in Parliament against the misuse of the spiritual jurisdiction, the King will stop all evil effects if the Pope does not handle him unkindly. This realm did never grudge the tenth part against the abuses of the Church at no Parliament in my day as they do now. I hope we may before Easter finish our Parliament in good sort, but it must depend upon the good news from you. ...

NOTE III. P. 72.

State Papers, July 17, 1533.—*Cranmer to Hawkins.*

Giving an account of the Dunstable judgment and Anne Boleyn's coronation, he says: 'This coronation was not before her marriage, which took place *about St. Paul's Day last.*'

Mr. Pocock, reviewing Hamilton's edition of Wriothesley's Chronicle in the 'Academy,' July 10, 1875, quotes Nicholas Sanders as having given November 14 as the date of Anne Boleyn's marriage, and explains it by stating that the festival of St. Erkenwald's (November 14) was kept with great solemnity at St. Paul's in London, and was sometimes called Paul's Day. It was the day on which the remains of St. Erkenwald were removed from the centre of the church to the high altar in 1148; and, as he says, if the marriage took place on that day nothing can be more proper than the birth of Elizabeth in the following November. As neither Mr. Pocock himself nor Nicholas Sanders can be represented as partisans of Anne Boleyn, this testimony is of some value; though, to my own mind, the probabilities as stated in the text are sufficient without it.

NOTE IV. P. 116.

Mr. Pocock has some further remarks on Edward's Prayerbook in the 'English History Review,' No. 4, October 1886, in an article on the Reformation settlement. He says that under Henry VIII. there was 'the old form of belief minus the papal supremacy.' This appears to me, as I think I have shown in the text, to be not the whole truth on the subject, at least in Henry's later years.

He says further that the religion of Edward VI.'s reign is properly represented by his *second* Book, and that it was 'in the main Zwinglian, and characterised by a general disparagement of sacramental grace,' and that in Elizabeth's time the tendency was towards Calvinism. He disputes Archbishop Lawrence's view that the Articles of the Church of England are mainly Lutheran, by showing

(1) That the main difference between Luther and Calvin was in regard to the Sacraments.

(2) That much of what was afterwards known as Calvinism, was, in England, drawn from an earlier source, viz. : from Wycliffe.

(3) That the English Articles were always included among the Reformed, and not the Lutheran confessions.

This sort of Zwinglian Calvinism, he says, held its ground, and went on constantly progressing until the accession of James I., when the Hampton Court Conference was the first stage of a reaction against it, completed after the failure of the Savoy Conference. He maintains further that the two Prayer-books of Edward VI. were meant to be progressive and were so, and points out that the notes to the Geneva Bible and the *Reformatio Legum Ecclesiasticarum* all point in the same direction. He remarks also that the Elizabethan changes were slightly in the direction of conciliating those who were addicted to the old learning—*e.g.*, the restoration of the words used in the first Prayer-book of Edward VI. at the distribution of the consecrated elements—nevertheless they might have been adopted by Catholics, Lutherans, Zwinglians, or Calvinists. He maintains further, that the Geneva Bible, translated by Whittingham and other exiles, circulated generally in England, up to and beyond the publication of James I.'s authorised version, and had in its later editions, from 1579 to 1615, a Calvinistic catechism inserted into it, and marginal notes of a similar character. Similarly, that the University of Oxford in 1579 passed a statute requiring its junior members to study Calvin's catechism, or else the Heidelberg catechism, and afterwards Bullinger's catechism and Calvin's Institutes. He claims that the Hampton Court Conference was a first step in *the reaction from the principles of the Reformation*, and that Archbishop Laud, *by means of his Majesty's declaration, allowed a new sense of sub-*

scribing the Articles, and that the action which followed the failure of the Savoy Conference established a more Catholic tone than the formularies of the Church had countenanced for more than a century.

The fact that Elizabeth's divines were nearly all formed in the school of Zurich or Geneva, and that they (Grindal, for instance, as we have seen) looked upon Lutherans as 'semi-papists,' tends strongly to confirm these views.

NOTE V. P. 145 (from Burnet's collection, vol. v. p. 381).
Sent by the Queen's Majesty's commandment, in the month of March, Anno Domini 1553 (1554).

BY THE QUEEN.

A copy of a letter, with articles sent from the Queen's Majesty unto the Bishop of London ; and by him and his officers, at her grace's commandment, to be put in speedy execution with effect in the whole diocese, as well in places exempt as non-exempt whatsoever, according to the tenor and form of the same :—

'Right reverend father in God, right trusty and well-beloved, we greet you well. And whereas heretofore, in the time of the late reign of our most dearest brother, King Edward the Sixth (whose soul God pardon), divers notable crimes, excesses and faults, with sundry kinds of heresies, simony, advoutry, and other enormities, have been committed within this our realm, and other our dominions ; the same continuing yet hitherto in like disorder, since the beginning of our reign, without any correction or reformation at all ; and the people, both of the laity and also of the clergy, and chiefly of the clergy, have been given to much insolency and ungodly rule, greatly to the displeasure of Almighty God, and very much to our regret and evil contentation, and to no little slander of other Christian realms, and in manner, to the subversion and clean defacing of this our realm. And remembering our duty to Almighty God, to be, to foresee, as much as in us may be, that all virtue and godly living should be embraced, flourish and increase. And therewith also, that all vice and ungodly behaviour should be utterly banished and put away ; or at the least ways, so nigh as might be, so bridled and kept under, that godliness and honesty might have the over-hand : understanding, by very credible report, and public fame, to our no small heaviness and comfort (*sic*), that within your diocese, as well in not exempted as exempted places, the like disorder and evil behaviour hath been done and used; like also to continue and increase, unless due provision be had and made to reform the same (which earnestly in very deed we do mind and intend) to the uttermost all the ways we can possible, trusting of God's furtherance and help in that behalf.

'For these causes, and other most just considerations us moving, we send in to you certain articles of such special matter, as among other things be most necessary to be now put in execution by you and your officers, extending to the end by us desired, and the reformation aforesaid; wherein ye shall be charged with our special commandment, by these our letters, to the intent you and your officers may the more earnestly and boldly proceed thereunto, *without fear of any presumption to be noted on your part, or danger to be incurred of any such our laws, as by your doings, of that is in the said articles contained, might any wise grieve you, whatsoever be threatened in any such case;* and therefore we straitly charge and command you, and your said officers, to proceed to the execution of the said articles, without all tract and delay, as ye will answer to the contrary. Given under our own signet, at our palace of Westminster, the fourth day of March, the first year of our reign.'

Here follow the articles referred to.

A commission to turn out some of the reformed bishops.

Id. p. 386.

'Regina dei gratiâ, &c., perdilectis et fidelibus consiliariis suis, Stephano Wintoniensi episcopo, summo suo Angliæ cancelario, et Cuthberto Dunelmensi episcopo, necnon reverendis et dilectis sibi in Christo Edmundo Londoniensi episcopo, Roberto Assavensi episcopo, Georgio Cicestrensi episcopo, et Anthonio Landavensi episcopo salutem.

'Quia omne animi vicium tanto conspectius in se crimen habet, quanto qui peccat major habetur, et quoniam certis et indubitatis testimoniis, una cum facti notorietate et famâ publicâ referente, luculenter intelleximus et manifeste comperimus Robertum archiepiscopum Eboracensem, Robertum Menevensem, Joannem Cestrensem, et Paulum Bristoliensem episcopos, aut certe pro talibus se gerentes, Dei et animarum suarum salutis immemores, valde gravia et enormia dudum commisisse et perpetrâsse scelera atque peccata, et inter cætera quod dolenter certe, et magnâ cum amaritudine animæ nostræ proferimus, post expressam professionem castitatis, expresse, rite et legitime emissam, cum quibusdam mulieribus nuptias de facto, cum de jure non deberent, in Dei contemptum et animarum suarum peccatum manifestum necnon in grave omnium ordinum, tam clericorum quam laicorum scandalum ; denique cæterorum omnium Christi fidelium perniciosissimum exemplum contraxisse et cum illis tanquam cum uxoribus cohabitâsse.

'Ne igitur tantum scelus remaneat impunitum ac multos alios pertrahat in ruinam, vobis tenore præsentium committimus et mandamus, quatenus vos omnes, aut tres saltem vestrûm qui præsentes literas commissionales duxerint exequendas, dictos archiepiscopum Eboracensem, episcopum Menevensem, episcopum Cestrensem, et episcopum Bristoliensem, diebus, horis et locis, vestro, aut trium vestrum arbitrio, eligendis et assignandis ad comparendum coram vobis, ceu tribus vestrûm, vocetis aut vocari faciatis, vocent, aut vocari faciant, tres vestrûm : (ceu saltem) si ita vobis aut tribus vestrûm videatur, eosdem archiepiscopum et episcopos prædictos adeatis, aut tres vestrûm adeant, et negocio illis summarie et de plano sine ullo strepitu et figurâ judicii exposito et declarato, si per summariam examinationem et discussionem negotii per vos aut tres vestrûm fiendam, eundem archiepiscopum et episcopos prædictos sic contraxisse, aut fecisse constiterit ; eosdem a dignitatibus suis prædictis, cum suis juribus pertinentibus universis, omnino amoviatis, deprivetis et perpetuo excludetis, ceu tres vestrûm sic amoveant, deprivent, perpetuo excludant : pœnitentiam salutarem et congruam pro modo culpæ vestro aut trium vestrûm arbitrio imponendam eisdem injungentis, cæteraque in prædictis cum eorum incidentibus emergentiis annexis et connexis quibuscumque, facientes quæ necessaria fuerint, ceu quomodolibet oportuna.

'Ad quæ omnia et singula facienda expedienda et finienda, nos tam auctoritate nostrâ ordinariâ, quam absolutâ, ex mero motu certâque scientiâ nostrâ, vobis et tribus vestrûm postestatem, auctoritatem et licenciam concedimus, et impertimur per præsentes cum cujuslibet cohercionis et castigationis severitate et potestate in contrarium facientes, non obstantibus quibuscumque.

'In cujus rei, &c. Teste Reginâ apud Westmonasterium 13. die Martii.'

Another commission to turn out the rest of them.

Id. p. 388.

'Mary by the grace of God, &c., to the right reverend fathers in God, our right trusty and right well-beloved councillors,

Stephine, Bishop of Winchester, our Chancellor of England; Cuthbert, Bishop of Duresme; Edmond, Bishop of London; Robert, Bishop of Sainte Asaphe; George, Bishop of Chichester, our almoner; and Anthonye, Bishop of Landaff, greeting. Where John Taylor, Doctor of Divinity, naming himself Bishop of Lincolne; John Hoper, naming himself Bishop of Worcester and Glocester; John Harley, Bishop of Hereford; having their said several pretensed bishoprics given to them, by the letters patents of our late deceased brother, King Edward the Sixte, to have and to hold the same during their good behaviours, with the express clause (quamdiu se bene gesserint) have sithence, as hath been credibly brought to our knowledge, both by preaching, teaching, and setting forth of erroneous doctrine, and also by inordinate life and conversation, contrary both to the laws of Almighty God, and use of the universal Christian Church, declared themselves very unworthy of that vocation and dignity in the Church.

'We minding to have their several cases duly heard and considered, and thereupon such order taken with them, as may stand with justice, and the laws, have, for the special trust we have conceived of your wisdoms, learning and integrity of life, appointed you four, three, or two of you, to be our commissioners in this behalf: giving unto you four, three, or two of you, full power and authority to call before you, if you shall think so good, the said John Taylor, John Hoper, John Harley, and every of them; and thereupon, either by order of the ecclesiastical laws, or of the laws of our realm, or of both, proceed to the declaring of the said bishoprics to be void, as they be already indeed void. To the intent some such other meet personages may be elected thereunto, as for their godly life, learning, and sobriety, may be thought worthy the places.

'In witness, &c. Teste Reginâ apud Westm. 15 die Martii.'

Note VI. P. 233.

Orders in the Church of England.

It can be proved beyond reasonable doubt, that Episcopal orders were not insisted upon in practice, in the Church of England, as an indispensable condition to ministry, down to the great rebellion, or in one or two instances even after it.

(1.) In the answers of the Commission in the year 1540 to the questions raised in preparation for the issuing of the 'Erudition of a Christian man,' on the special subject of orders, the rest of the commissioners are unanimous in considering that the Apostles had Divine authority to ordain, three only going so far as to say that had there been Christian princes at the time, their licence would have been required—a manifest complaisance on their part to Henry's recent legislation. Cranmer in his answers plainly treats ordination as a matter of indifference, as does also Barlow.[1]

The latter also states in a sermon :[2] 'If the King's Grace, being supreme head of the Church of England, did choose denominate and elect any lay man (being learned) to be a bishop, that he so chosen (without mention being made of any orders), should be as good a bishop as he is or the best in England.'

2. Edward VI. assumed the power of dispensing with orders at his pleasure. Thus he writes [3] to the Bishop of Exeter in December 1552, that 'the King's pleasure is to dispense with Dr. Haddon for taking of any other orders than he had already. What his orders were does not appear, but they must have been irregular, otherwise dispensation would have been needless.

3. The real difficulty—as far as one exists—in proving the point of the employment of non-episcopally ordained ministers, in the earlier part of the period referred to, arises from the fact that contemporaries do not notice it in individual cases, because there was no real question about it. It is simply inconceivable, from the general history of the times, that all the hot-gospellers and volunteers of the Reformation, and all the foreign allies who came from Germany, Holland, and elsewhere, were in every case either re-ordained by the English bishops, or were prohibited from ministering in the churches, and that in no single case should any record of the fact exist. The cases of Whittingham and Travers have been sufficiently referred to in the text. Travers, I may repeat, expressly states that 'afore Mr. Whittingham's case (*i.e.*, 1578) there was never any question moved to the contrary,' and Whitgift finds no fault with his statement.

As has been frequently pointed out—most recently and very clearly by the Dean of Peterborough [4]—the Church of England, though she requires her own ministers to be episcopally ordained, nowhere asserts that non-episcopal orders are invalid. Indeed, we may go further than this, and say that the requirement is to be

[1] *Burnet*, vol. i. p. 461, and vol. iv. p. 471.
[2] Quoted in Hunt, *Religious Thought in England*, vol. i. p. 43, *note*.
[3] Strype, *Memorials*, vol. ii. pt. ii. pp. 275-6.
[4] *Lippincott's Monthly Magazine*, January 1890, p. 146.

found only in the preface to the Ordinal—where it was apparently in the first edition—and that the language used in this, as in the Articles, seems carefully to avoid deciding the question, when obviously it would have been more natural to have used more definite expressions.

4. Two further points call for remark in this matter, viz., (1) As the Dean further notices, the Church of England has not in practice always insisted upon the above requirement. (2) Has this non-insistance been lawful or otherwise? I will take the latter question first.

The words of the Act of the 13 Eliz. c. 12, s. 6, are given in the note above, p. 219. It is quite clear that those words contemplate that there are or may be persons who 'shall pretend to be priests, &c.,' and shall 'have ecclesiastical living' in some diocese 'by reason of some other form of consecration or ordering' than the one contained in the Book of Common Prayer, and to such persons the Act prescribes, not re-ordaining, but that they shall, in the presence of the ordinary, declare and subscribe their assent to the Articles.

It has been alleged, no doubt, that this Act was *intended* to take security, so to speak, of the old incumbents who had continued in their livings since Mary's reign, and not to admit irregularly-ordained Protestants. The answer is obvious—viz., that the words, however they might have been intended, *did* admit both; and, further, that a strong presumption exists that they were intended to do so, from the practice to be shortly referred to, and from the following passage of Bishop Cosin, written in the year 1650.[1] This letter is now well known. He is writing to a person named Cordel, who, while residing in France during the Great Rebellion, scrupled about communicating with the French Protestants. Cosin, who was, or had been, as may be remembered, a Laudian High Churchman, advises him to do so, under protest as to the irregularity of their orders, 'considering that there is no prohibition of our Church against it, as there is against our communicating with Papists, and that well founded upon Scripture and the will of God.' Upon the immediate point before us he says—after objecting to the 'irregularity' of the orders of the French Protestants, 'If at any time a minister so ordained (*i.e.*, unepiscopally) in their French churches came to incorporate himself in ours, and to receive a public charge or cure of souls among us in the Church of England (as I have known some of them to have so done of late, and can instance in *many*

[1] Cosin's *Works*, vol. iv. p. 403.

others before my time), our bishops *did not re-ordain him* before they admitted him to his charge, as they would have done if his former ordination here in France had been void. Nor did *our laws* require more of him than to declare his public consent to the religion received among us and to subscribe the Articles established.' This one quotation might suffice for both my present points. No better authority could be imagined than Bishop Cosin. He had been secretary to Bishop Overall, at Norwich, more than thirty years before, and was greatly esteemed as a churchman and a man of learning.[1] Baxter says of him that 'he was excellently well versed in canons, councils, and fathers,' and he was one of the principal speakers at the Savoy Conference.

But the question of the practice of the Church of England needs not to depend on any one authority however eminent. On the contrary, we may trace a perfect 'tradition' in the English Church, to the effect of the validity of non-episcopal orders, through a whole line of bishops, from Jewell in the commencement of Elizabeth's reign, through Whitgift, Bancroft, Andrews, Overall, Morton, and Cosin, who died some twelve years after the passing of the last Act of Uniformity : thus Whitgift—besides the negative evidence given in the text in reference to the Travers case—says plainly, in a letter to Sir Francis Knollys,[2] 'If it had pleased her Majesty, with the wisdom of the realm, to have used no bishops at all, we could not have complained justly of any defect in our Church'; and again, 'If it had pleased her Majesty to have assigned the imposition of hands to the deans of every cathedral church, or some other number of ministers which in no sort were bishops, but as they be pastors, there had been no wrong done to their persons that I can conceive.'

Andrews, as is well known, took part in the consecration of three bishops for Scotland who had never been ordained priests, and in so doing was supported by Bancroft. There are two somewhat different accounts of this transaction in which both Andrews and Bancroft are implicated. Thus Canon Perry (vol i. p. 184) says that Bancroft removed Andrews's scruple —viz., that the Presbyterians to be consecrated bishops had not received episcopal ordination—by the argument that episcopal orders might be conferred at once even on a layman, and that it contained in itself the lower functions of deacon and priest, alleging the cases of Ambrose and Nectarius as examples. He

---

[1] Quoted in Hunt's *Religious Thought in England*, vol. i. p. 298.
[2] Strype, *Whitgift*, vol. iii. pp. 222-3.

refers to Collier (vol. vii. p. 362) as his authority. But Spotswoode's 'History of the Church of Scotland,' vol. iii. p. 29, has the following account : ' A question in the meantime was moved by Dr. Andrews, Bishop of Ely, touching the consecration of the Scottish bishops, who, as he said, must first be ordained presbyters, as having received no ordination from a bishop. The Archbishop of Canterbury (Dr. Bancroft), who was by, maintained "that thereof there was no necessity, seeing where bishops could not be had, the ordination given by presbyters must be esteemed lawful, otherwise that it might be doubted if there were any lawful vocation in most of the Reformed Churches." This, applauded to by the other bishops, Ely acquiesced, and on the day and in the place appointed, the three Scottish bishops were consecrated.' Collier quotes Heylin as his authority for putting the other reasons into Bancroft's mouth. The difference of value of the two authorities appears to be that whereas Spotswoode was one of the Scottish bishops then and there consecrated, Heylin was at the time a boy of ten years old.

Further than this, in carrying on a correspondence with the well-known Peter du Moulin, Andrews says, in comparing the Anglican with the French Huguenot Church : 'Though our government be by Divine right, it follows not that there is no salvation, or that a Church cannot stand, without it. He must needs be stone blind that sees not Churches standing without it. He must needs be made of iron and hard-hearted, that denies them salvation. . . . Somewhat may be wanting that is of Divine right (at least in external government), and yet salvation may be had.'[1]

In another letter while speaking of Calvin and Beza, he writes : 'To what purpose is it to abolish the name and to retain the thing (for even you retain the thing without the title), as they two, whom you named, while they lived, what were they but bishops in deed, though not in name ?'[2] Now it must be observed that Calvin had received no orders in the Catholic Church above those of sub-deacon, and Beza none at all.

With regard to Bishop Overall, we have the authority of Cosin, who was at one time his secretary, in a letter quoted by Birch in his life of Tillotson[3]—and which letter Birch says he had before him when he wrote—which is so circumstantial that the passage is worth quoting in full. He says : ' Dr. de Laune, who translated the English Liturgy into French, being presented to a

[1] *Letters*, ii. p. 24.   [2] *Ibid.* i. p. 16.
[3] Birch, *Life of Tillotson*, prefixed to his works (1820), p. cxxii.

living, and coming to the bishop then at Norwich with his presentation, his lordship asked him where he had his orders. He answered that he was ordained by the presbytery at Leyden. The bishop, upon this, advised him to take the opinion of council (*sic*) whether by the laws of England he was capable of a benefice without being ordained by a bishop. The doctor replied that he thought his lordship would be unwilling to re-ordain him if his council should say that he was not otherwise capable of the living by law. The Bishop rejoined: "*Re-ordination we must not admit, no more than a re-baptisation*; but in case you find it doubtful whether you be a priest capable to receive a benefice among us or no, I will do the same office for you, if you desire it, that I should do for one who doubts of his baptism, when all things belonging essentially unto it have not been duly observed in the administration of it, according to the rule in the Book of Common Prayer, 'If thou hast not already,' &c. Yet, *for mine own part, if you will adventure the orders that you have, I will admit your presentation, and give you institution into the living howsoever.*" But the title which this presentation had from the patron proving not good, there were no further proceedings in it; yet afterwards Dr. de Laune *was admitted into another benefice without any new ordination.*'

The evidence in regard to Morton comes from two opponents in a controversy—viz., the once celebrated John Durel, author of the 'Sanctæ Ecclesiæ Anglicanæ vindicia,' and Mr. Hickman, a nonconformist fellow of Magdalen ejected at the Restoration. These both tell pretty much the same story, though the latter adds the fullest particulars. He says that 'the Archbishop of Spalato (Antonio di Dominis), while living in England, asked Morton, Bishop of Durham, to do someone who had been ordained beyond the seas the favour of re-ordaining him presbyter, in order that he might have freer access to ecclesiastical benefices. Morton wrote back to say that such a thing could not be done without very great offence to the Reformed Churches, a scandal of which he did not choose to be the originator. My witness is . . . Calendrin, pastor of the Anglo-Belgian Church in Essex, who has in his possession the original letter in Morton's own handwriting.' The above quotation I make at second hand from an anonymous pamphlet (by 'Cantab,' a Cambridge man who has joined the Church of Rome) entitled 'Apostolical Succession Not a Doctrine of the Church of England,'[1] p. 65. But I am now able to give the original quotation from Hickman's

[1] Longmans, 1870.

book 'Apologia pro ministris &c.,' 2nd edit. p. 18, Eleutheropoli, anno æræ Bartholomeæ, as follows :—

'Petiit e Mortono Episcopo Dunelmensi Spalatensis dum apud nos ageret, ut dignaretur quendam in Ecclesiis transmarinis ordinatum denuo ordinare presbyterum, quo liberior esset ei aditus ad beneficia ecclesiastica. Rescripsit Mortonus, non posse illud fieri, sine gravissimo ecclesiarum reformatarum scandalo, cujus ipse autor esse noluit . . . testem habeo Dominum Calendrinum ecclesiæ Anglo-Belgicæ apud Trinobantes pastorem, in cujus manibus est ipsum autographum literarum Mortoniarum.'

I may add that there is independent evidence that Mr. Calendrin was a friend of Bishop Morton.

Cosins' own view upon the subject, as well as his evidence (or some of it) in regard to the usage of the English Church up to the time of the Commonwealth, has been already given. There is, however, a further letter of his[1] to a Mr. Gunning, wherein he speaks of the re-ordination of Presbyterian ministers as a thing 'which was never yet done in the Church of England' (except in an individual case to which he refers apparently with disapproval); but he says, 'it has rather admitted them and employed them at several times in the public administration of the Sacraments'; and he quotes Bishop Overall to the same effect.

To this series of bishops I am now enabled to add the name[2] of Joseph Hall. He says: 'The sticking at the admission of our brethren returning from the Reformed Churches was not in the case of ordination, but of institution; they had been acknowledged ministers of Christ without any other hands laid upon them. . . . I know those more than one, who by virtue only of that ordination which they have brought with them from other Reformed Churches have enjoyed spiritual promotion and livings without any exception against the lawfulness of their calling.'

There is also a vast array of individual instances in which men of more or less distinction have been admitted to various offices in the English Church, where no notice can be found of their re-ordination, when they were undoubtedly ordained first in one of the foreign Protestant Churches, and when the presumption is so strong against it, especially when taken in connection with the distinct statements of Overall, Morton, Cosin, and Hall already quoted, that it seems pure quibbling to insist on the probability, or even possibility, of their having been so. The

[1] *Works*, vol. iv. pp. 449-50.
[2] Dean Perowne, in article above quoted, p. 150.

case of several of these who were admitted to canonries is attempted to be got over by the statement that these and other such dignities have no cure of souls attached to them, and so might possibly be held by laymen. I will therefore adduce but very few, and those shall be such as had cure of souls in some shape or another. The well-known Dr. Saravia is the first instance I will mention. Saravia was made a minister in Holland and was employed in Guernsey in 1564. Afterwards he became a schoolmaster at Southampton, and then Professor of Divinity at Leyden. Later than this he received preferment in the Church of England—not only a canonry of Canterbury, and afterwards of Westminster, but also the rectory of Great Chart in Kent, to which he was presented by Archbishop Bancroft. Now, there is no reason whatever to believe, but a total absence of any, that Saravia was ever re-ordained by any English bishop. No proof, no record of any such proceeding is produced, and had it been so, it would have invalidated entirely the statements of Overall, Morton, and Cosin already quoted. This is the more remarkable since Saravia himself preferred the Anglican to the Presbyterian discipline, and even wrote a work in defence of the three orders of the ministry, and also urged upon the unepiscopally-ordained ministers of Guernsey the propriety of taking episcopal orders, if they were natives of the island. In the last years of Richard Hooker's life, Saravia was his near neighbour and intimate friend, and is specially mentioned by Walton as having administered the Communion to him and his friends on the day before his death.[1] This and his incumbency of Great Chart seem to settle the question so often raised of whether the privileges of an unepiscopally-ordained person in the Church of England did not stop short of the 'cure of souls.'

In the same way Peter du Moulin the elder, who was a very distinguished French Protestant pastor, became chaplain to King James I., and frequently administered the Communion to him, and was preferred to a canonry of Canterbury. He returned to France, and presided over a synod at Alaix which confirmed the decrees of Dort. Afterwards he came back to England, and was presented to a sinecure rectory in Wales, but on the death of James I. he once more returned to France, and became Professor of Divinity at Sedan, where he died at a great age in 1658. There is of course, in this as in the last case, not the smallest evidence, nor the least reason to believe, that Du Moulin was ever re-

---

[1] Keble, *Hooker*, vol. i. p. 85.

ordained ; and, at any rate, he alternately performed the duties of a French Protestant pastor and an Anglican clergyman, in a way which goes far to show that the two positions were not looked upon in his day as in any way incompatible.

I will give but one other instance in the case of the son [1] of the above, another Peter du Moulin, born at Paris in 1600, and who took his degree of D.D. at Leyden. He was instituted Rector of Adisham and Staple, in Kent, 1662. The curious part of this is, that this Presbyterian minister was so instituted in succession to one Charles Nichols, who was also a Presbyterian, and was ejected as such ! The difference between the two was that Nichols was an Englishman ordained by presbyters in England, Du Moulin a Frenchman ordained equally by presbyters abroad. Thus then, within a few months of the passing of the Act of Uniformity, did Charles II. take advantage of the saving clause which was, and still is in it, 'That the penalties in this Act shall not extend to the foreigners or aliens of the foreign Reformed Churches allowed or to be allowed by the King's Majesty, his heirs or successors, in England.' The same transaction also shows that the objection to Presbyterian orders in the English Church was still in 1662 what it was when Whitgift silenced Travers in 1584, namely not a theological or ecclesiastical, but purely a legal objection. I shall not refer at length to the case of the Channel Islands, in which, though they were a part of the diocese of Winchester, many of the ministers had no more than Presbyterian ordination until the year 1820, as the fact is now well known ; but it seems to prove that the Bishops of Winchester, either deliberately left some hundreds of the people committed to their charge without valid Sacraments, or else did not believe in the doctrine of Apostolic succession : and this from generation to generation for a matter of 250 years.

As a commentary on some of the above, I may refer to the diary of Philip Henry, one of the ministers expelled in 1662. He says (p. 247) : 'All or most of the Conformity have said they could not deny us ministers, but not ministers of the Church of England, without episcopal ordination. . . . Now suppose a Dutch or French Protestant minister to come into England to preach, he is not re-ordained but only licensed ' ; and further, in referring to the transaction which I have commented upon, he

---

[1] For the particulars above given in the case of Peter du Moulin the younger, and partly also of those of his father and of Saravia, I am indebted to 'Cantab's' pamphlet above referred to.

says: 'In King James's time when four (*sic*) Scotch presbyters were to be consecrated bishops at Lambeth, 'twas moved they might be first ordained presbyters again, but overruled—'twas without need.'

Lord Bacon's[1] remarks on the subject are worth quoting also, as those of a man of the very highest intellect of his time, and also from his position and occupation likely to be well informed as to the actual state of the facts. He wrote 'an Advertisement touching the controversies of the Church of England,' according to Mr. Spedding, about 1589, occasioned by the 'Martin Marprelate' tracts. In it he says of the controversies themselves that 'they are not touching the high mysteries of the faith, . . . neither are they concerning the great parts of the worship of God of which it is true that "non servatur unitas in credendo, nisi eadem est in colendo," such as were the controversies of the East and West Churches touching images, and such as are many of those between the Church of Rome and us, as about the adoration of the Sacrament and the like. But we contend about ceremonies and things indifferent, about the external policy of government of the Church.' Again (pp. 86-7), he points out the growth of extreme views on both sides thus : ' It may be remembered that on their part who call for reformation ' (*i.e.*, the Puritan party) ' was first propounded some dislike of certain ceremonies supposed to be superstitious ; some complaint of dumb ministers who possess rich benefices, and some invectives against the idle and monastical continuance within the Universities by those who had livings to be resided upon, and such-like abuses. Thence they went on to condemn the government of bishops as an hierarchy remaining to us of the corruptions of the Roman Church, and to except to sundry institutions as not sufficiently delivered from the pollution of former times. And lastly they advanced to define of an only and perpetual form of policy in the Church, which without consideration of possibility or foresight of peril or perturbation of the Church and State must be erected and planted of the magistrate. Here *they* stay. Others, not able to keep footing in so steep a ground, descend further. That the same must be entered into and accepted of the people at their peril, without the attending of the establishment of authority ; and so in the meantime they refuse to communicate with us, as reputing us to have no Church. This hath been the progression on that side—I mean the generality, for I know some persons (being of the nature not

---

[1] Bacon, *Ellis and Spedding*, vol. viii. p. 75.

only to love extremities, but also to fall to them without degrees) were at the highest strain at the first. The other part' (*i.e.*, the Church party), 'which maintaineth the present government of the Church, hath not kept one tenor neither. First those ceremonies which were pretended to be corrupt they maintained to be things indifferent, opposed the examples of the good times of the Church to the challenge that was made to them because they were used in the later superstitious times. Then were they also content mildly to acknowledge many imperfections in the Church as tares come up among the corn which yet (according to the wisdom taught by our Saviour) were not with strife to be pulled up lest it might spoil and supplant the good corn, but to grow on together until the harvest. After they grew to a more absolute defence and maintenance of the orders of the Church, and stiffly to hold that nothing was to be innovated partly because it needed not, partly because it would make a breach upon the rest. Thence (exasperate through contentions) they are fallen into a direct condemnation of the contrary part as of a sect. Yea, and some indiscreet persons have been bold in open preaching *to use dishonourable and derogative speech and censure of the Churches abroad; and that so far as some of our men (as I have heard) ordained in foreign parts have been pronounced to be no lawful ministers.* Thus we see the beginnings were modest but the extremes are violent ; so as there is almost as great a distance now of either side from itself as was at first from one to the other.'

These remarks seem to be valuable on other grounds besides the main intention of the writer, in showing the progressive character of differences originally small, as proving also—(1) That there was no doubt in the minds of the men of that time as to the trifling character of the original differences between the Church party and the Puritans, nor yet of the important and essential differences between the Roman and English Churches ; (2) the respect in which the foreign Protestant Churches were at first held in the English Church, of which there is also ample proof in the other writings and correspondence of the time ; (3) that the idea of questioning foreign Protestant orders was looked upon by Bacon (fifty years after the separation from Rome) as not only a novelty, but also an outrageous novelty.

The above extracts are very far from exhausting the subject, but they seem difficult to reconcile with any continuous adhesion to a strict view of the necessity of episcopal ordination, whether in theory or in practice.

Since the above Note was in print I have seen two other papers which require notice. One is a letter addressed by Dr. Hammond to Lord Burleigh, Nov. 4, 1588, on the Divine Authority of Bishops, published in the 'Hatfield Calendar,' Pt. III. No. 754, in which he expressly denies it, and concludes his paper almost in the same words as does Archbishop Whitgift, above (p. 296) :—
'The bishops of our realm do not (so far as I ever yet heard), nor may not, claim to themselves any other authority than is given them by the statute of the 25th of King Henry the Eighth, recited in the first year of her Majesty's reign, or by other statutes of this land : neither is it reasonable they should make other claims, for, if it had pleased her Majesty, with the wisdom of the realm, to have used no bishops at all, we could not have complained justly of any defect in our Church ; or if it had liked them to limit the authority of bishops to shorter terms, they might not have said they had any wrong. But sith it hath pleased her Majesty to use the ministry of bishops, and to assign them this authority, it must be to me, that am a subject, as God's ordinance, and therefore to be obeyed according to St. Paul's rule.'

The other is an answer (?), published in the 'Newbery House Magazine,' by the Rev. J. Hancock, to the Dean of Peterborough's paper quoted above. To this it must be objected—(1) That it quite fails to answer any one of Dean Perowne's facts. It fails to show how men like Bishop Cosin could have either stated what was not true, or failed to know what had happened in their own days and in those of older men, like Bishop Overall, with whom they had been associated. (2) That it falls into the somewhat fashionable error of treating the Reformation as an event of the seventeenth century alone, and almost entirely ignoring the occurrences of the sixteenth. The position which all the advocates on this side of the question fail to touch is, shortly, this— that for almost two generations after the separation from Rome, neither the practice nor the theory of the Church of England even suggested a belief in the modern doctrine of Apostolical succession, while many instances occur, as I have already shown, in which it was both neglected in practice and repudiated in theory.

Note VII. P. 253.

As to the Protestantism of Elizabeth and her advisers:

(1.) Letter of Sandys, afterwards Bishop of Worcester and Archbishop of York, to Bullinger, from Strasburg, December 20, 1558.

He reports as part of Elizabeth's reply to Queen Mary's last request that she would make no change in religion: 'I will not change it provided only it can be proved by the Word of God, which shall be the only foundation and rule of my religion.'[1] This can, of course, only be a report, and goes therefore for little but a proof that such reports were about at the time.

(2.) There is a letter from Cecil to one Mr. Herd, about a commonplace book and some notes of Cranmer's, in which he says that the Queen thinks such a rare and precious treasure should not be hid in secret, and commands him to send up without delay the precious documents for perusal.[2]

(3.) In the Queen's declaration after the suppression of the rebellion in the north, she sets forth 'her determination to continue in support of the *true Christian religion.*' This being also a good instance of the use of *true Christian religion* in contradistinction to the Roman Church.[3]

(4.) The Queen, in a letter urging the sending of contributions towards the relief of *those of the religion* in the town of Montpelier suffering from an earthquake, speaks of her own subjects as 'fellow members' with the Montpelier people, and 'such as do make profession of one religion with them.' She thus treats the French Huguenots as of one religion with the Church of England.[4]

(5.) A private letter from one Herll to Sir Edward Horsey speaks of the Queen as 'sharply set against the Papists.'[5]

(6.) The Queen's instructions to Lord Huntingdon, President of the Council of the North. There were thirty members of this Council, of which five were clerics—viz., Edmund Grindal, Archbishop of York; James Pilkington, Bishop of Durham; Richard Barnes, Bishop of Carlisle; Mathew Hutton, Dean of York; and William Whittingham, Dean of Durham. Amongst their duties were that whenever they sit they shall enforce observance of laws, ordinances, &c., made by the Privy Council, the Ecclesiastical

---

[1] *Zurich Letters*, ser. i. p. 4.
[2] *State Papers*, April 14, 1563, vol. xxviii. 30.
[3] *Ibid.* Feb. 1570, vol. lxvi. 54.
[4] *Ibid.* May 1580, vol. cxxxviii. 37.
[5] *Ibid.* Dec. 12, 1580, vol. cxliv. 49.

Commissioners, or Parliament, touching religion and Divine service, and aid the archbishop and bishops therein also. Not a word of Convocation or the Church as distinct from the State.[1]

What was thought of the matter by the authorities of the Roman Church is sufficiently proved—by the refusal of all but one of the Marian bishops to crown Elizabeth, by the unanimous adhesion of Convocation to the arrangements of Mary by the equally unanimous opposition of the bishops in the Upper House to the Acts of Restoration and Uniformity (1 Eliz. c. 1 and 2), by the excommunication of Pope Pius V., and by the innumerable plots against the Queen's life sanctioned, as we have seen, by popes, cardinals, and princes.

It is certain also that Elizabeth's adhesion to Protestantism was taken as a matter of course before her accession, by both friends and foes, and further, as her earliest biographer Camden points out, that it would have been impossible for her to acknowledge the Roman Church without declaring Mary Stuart's title to the throne better than her own, inasmuch as two popes had declared her illegitimate.

The fact is that in the early times of the Reformation there was no thought of, and no room for, a *via media*, and it is this very fact which constitutes the difficulty in showing clearly that it did not exist. There is absolutely nothing to suggest its existence, and much that is incompatible with it; but the actual proof of a negative is, of course, an impossible task.

The first suggestion of a Divine right of bishops was made, as we have seen, some fifty years after the separation from Rome, and early in the latter half of Elizabeth's reign. How it was then received may be seen from a letter of Sir Francis Knollys to Burleigh, in the State Papers, vol. ccxxxiii. 62, in which he suggests that Whitgift (whom he uniformly accuses of it) had incurred the penalty of a præmunire (!) by claiming it. Henry VIII.'s *via media* broke down as soon as his hand ceased to support it, and had even before that given indications that it would have to advance further in the direction of Protestantism if it was to hold its own.

I have said enough in the text to show that it is difficult to exaggerate the Erastianism of the whole of this period; but I may give one more instance of it[2] which is almost comic when we observe the quarter from whence it comes. It is amusing to find the very Dr. Bancroft whose claim of Divine right for

---

[1] *State Papers* (Dom., Addenda Elizabeth), May 1574, vol. xxiii. 59.
[2] *Ibid.* Eliz. cclxxiii. 55.

bishops had made such a sensation in 1588, a few years after—having himself become Bishop of London in the interval—writing to Sir J. Stanhope in 1599 as follows, in evident tribulation at having fallen into disgrace with the Queen : 'Those things that I do well in are either kept from her or depraved, and every omission or want of foresight has been aggravated ever since I was bishop; so that I rather marvel at her clemency, that she has not either cast me into prison, or *thrust me from my bishoprick*, than to hear of her great displeasure towards me.' This seems to show that he felt no great confidence that the 'Divine right,' which he had so mildly suggested in his sermon, would avail much against the papal power which he had so boldly claimed for the Queen in the same sermon.

There is a very curious paper which is anonymous,[1] in which it is argued that the Queen in her recent general pardon could not have intended to include offences, such as adultery, &c., punishable by ecclesiastical law, because though *she has the power of the Pope* (and, the writer seems to imply, even more, inasmuch as she has it *de jure* as well as *de facto*, which the Pope had not), yet as the Pope '*non potest dispensare contra jus divinum aut naturale*,' neither can the Queen. This was the very question which was argued in regard to Katherine of Arragon's divorce.

Lord Huntingdon, when first made President of the North, began his instructions to the Justices of the Peace thus: 'You are first to inquire and certify to us the names and addresses of all known and suspected Papists within your rule, *the enemies of God* and of good order.'[2]

Another anonymous paper[3] says : 'The realm is divided into three parties, the Papist, the Atheist, and the Protestant. All these are alike favoured : the first and second being many, we dare not displease them ; the third because, having religion, we fear to displease God in them. All three are blamed : the Papist as a traitor, the Atheist as godless, the Protestant as a precisian. The last should not be feared, as he obeys in God's fear ; the other two know no obedience, and Government must either tread down the bad, or let them devour the godly,' &c. This appears to be a Puritan production, but it shows something of the contemporary view of the Church of Rome.

In another paper[4] we have a letter from one Copley,

---

[1] *State Papers*, Eliz. Addenda, vol. xix. 54.
[2] *Ibid.* Eliz. Addenda, vol. xxi. 111.
[3] *Ibid.* Eliz. Addenda, vol. xxi. 121.
[4] *Ibid.* Eliz. Addenda, vol. xxiii. 9.

apparently a Catholic exile, to Burleigh, in which he defends his own position, and speaks of the Catholic Church as 'a surer pillar to lean unto than the changeable, confused doctrine of contrary teachers; yea, or any Act of Parliament which has not long used to judge causes of faith, or prescribe ecclesiastical laws:' showing how the Catholics at that day, as ever since, looked upon the Anglican Church as the creation of Parliament—*i.e.*, of the State.

Again, we have some notes by Lord Burleigh,[1] in which he speaks of 'the sacrifice of the Mass as a thing to be rooted out of the Church as altogether evil,' with answers thereto arguing that it should be tolerated in those who think the Mass to be the service of God, as Christ kept company with Pharisees, and meat offered to idols was not forbidden to be eaten.

Bishop Cooper in his 'Admonition,'[2] answering one of the Martin Marprelate libels, and in particular a charge of committing simony *like the Pope*, says that 'there ought to be great difference between Christian preachers and writers inveighing against Antichrist and his members, and ministers of the Gospel and zealous professors blaming and reproving the faults of their own bishop and clergy, in the estate of a Church by authority settled. The one part is handled with an earnest zeal and detestation of the obstinate patrons of error and idolatry; the other should be moved only with a charitable sorrow and grief to see preachers of the truth not to declare in life that which they utter to other in doctrine.'

The Bishops, in answering Barrow's (the Puritan's) demand for a conference, say : 'It is no reason that all *the Reformed Churches in Europe (acknowledging our Church of England for a sister)*, the same should be now brought into question at the will and request of a few sectaries.'[3]

Whitgift also, in a letter to Beza,[4] when in the act of remonstrating with him for his interference in favour of the Puritans, says : 'If the labour of some had been employed, not against their brethren that professed one and the same substance of true doctrine, but to the throwing down and beating back the kingdom of the common enemy, the Roman antichrist, it would now have fared better and happier, in his judgment, with the Church of Christ'; and this letter he addresses : 'Ornatissimo atque eruditissimo viro, D. Theodoro Bezæ, *fratri et symmistæ suo in Christo* charissimo, &c.

[1] *State Papers*, Eliz. Addenda, vol. xxv. 65.
[2] Arber's edition, p. 75. [3] Strype, *Annals*, vol. iv. p. 241.
[4] Strype, *Whitgift*, vol. ii. pp. 160, 173.

It would be equally tedious and needless to multiply instances of similar expressions. The correspondence of the greater number of the Elizabethan bishops is full of them; and they seem to establish plainly these propositions—viz., (1) That these men were throughout intensely—nay, many of them bitterly—Protestant: *e.g.*, Jewell, who, writing to Peter Martyr (without a date, but apparently in 1559) from London,[1] says: 'Our Papists oppose us most spitefully, and none more obstinately than those who have abandoned us. This it is to have once tasted of the Mass! He who drinks of it is mad. Depart from it all ye who value a sound mind: he who drinks of it is mad.' (2) That they themselves looked upon Elizabeth's reform as a restoration of Edward's— *e.g.*, Cox, writing to Weidner, in May 1559,[2] says: 'The sincere religion of Christ is therefore established among us in all parts of the kingdom, just in the same manner as it was formerly promulgated under our Edward of most blessed memory.' (3) That they looked upon themselves as of the same faith as the Swiss Churches, and as absolutely contrary to the Roman, I have already sufficiently shown. (4) That the claim of Divine right for bishops was a novelty introduced mainly as a weapon against the Puritans, and was not well received even then, the last note has sufficiently established; as also (5) That the whole Papal power was claimed for the Crown.

In her answer to the petition of the Puritans in Parliament for the adoption of the new model, in 1586, Elizabeth expressly claims *for herself*, as part of her prerogative, that the full power, authority, jurisdiction, and supremacy in Church causes, which heretofore the Popes usurped and took to themselves, should be united and annexed to the imperial crown of this realm. (Strype, 'Whitgift,' vol. i. p. 494, where the authority quoted is the Lambeth MSS.)

I am not concerned to argue for or against these propositions in themselves: all I assert is that they were the prevailing views of the divines and the statesmen of Elizabeth's reign, and, in a great degree at least, of the Queen herself.

Of evidence on the other side I find little or none. One curious document there is among the State Papers which I have taken some pains to investigate. It is in volume vii. No. 46, and is entered under date of November 1559, and called 'List of Bishops who returned into England on Queen Elizabeth's Acces-

---

[1] Jewell to Peter Martyr, *Zurich Letters*, series i. p. 34.

[2] Cox to Weidner, *Zurich Letters*, series i. p. 28. Parkhurst also to Bullinger, on the next page.

sion, and the Bishops present in her first Parliament. Progress of Convocation in framing the Book of Common Prayer':—

'That returned to England upon Queen Mary's death that had been bishops in King Edward's time :—

    1. Coverdale.   3. Cheyne (*sic*).
    2. Scory.   4. Barlowe.

'That remained bishops for some time that were bishops in Queen Mary's time:—

    1. Oglethorp, Bishop of Carlisle, who crowned Queen Elizabeth.
    2. Kitchin, Bishop of Landaff.

'There were bishops in the Parliament holden *primo Eliz.*, and in Convocation holden at the same time:—

    Edmund, Bishop of London.
    John, Bishop of Winton.
    Richard, Bishop of Worcester.
    Ralph, Bishop of Coventry and Lichfield.
    Thomas (*sic*), Bishop of Lincoln.
    James, Bishop of Exeter.

'The Book of Common Prayer published *primo Eliz.* was first resolved upon and established in the Church in the time of King Edward VI. It was re-examined, with some small alterations, by the Convocation, consisting of the said bishops and the rest of the clergy, in *primo Eliz.*, which being done by the Convocation and published under the great seal of England, there was an Act of Parliament for the same book, which is ordinarily printed in the beginning of the book ; not that the book was ever subjected to the censure of the Parliament, but, being agreed upon and published as aforesaid, a law was made by the Parliament for the inflicting of penalty upon all such as should refuse to use and observe the same : for the authority therefor is not in the Parliament, neither hath been in former times yielded to the Parliament, in things of that nature, but the judgment and determination thereof hath ever been in the Church, thereto authorised by the King, which is that which is yielded to Henry VIII. by the Statute 25 of his reign.'

The style of this paper is at once sufficient to show that it is not contemporary, and what struck me first on reading it was that the ideas and opinions it contains were not invented at the date to which it refers; they belong to the epoch of Laud, and not that of the early part of Elizabeth's reign. There are, it should be mentioned, two copies of the paper, in different hands, of which one is endorsed by Sir Joseph Williamson, with the words 'In Sir Th. Wilson's hand.' Sir Thomas Wilson was appointed Keeper of the State Papers in James I.'s reign, and therefore, unless the other copy be the older, which I have been unable to ascertain with certainty, it would appear that my conjecture is right. The contents of the paper are of no value whatsoever except as showing the ignorance or dishonesty, or both, of the Laudians in their dealings with history. Thus, as will be seen, the writer reckons Cheney as one of the 'bishops who returned into England upon Queen Mary's death that had been bishops in King Edward's time,' whereas Cheney was first made a bishop in 1562. The account of Elizabeth's Prayer-book is entirely mythical. The Convocation '*primo Elizabethæ*' certainly had nothing to do with it whatever, and the fictitious history of it here given seems to have been made to suit the Laudian theory, and to be entirely independent of facts. What the meaning of the last list of bishops may be, it is difficult to discover, unless the writer supposed that there were but eight Marian bishops remaining, and that *they* were responsible for Elizabeth's Prayer-book! or that the members of all these three lists sat in Parliament together!

One other point is worthy of notice as remarkable. In the same vol. vii. No. 68 is entered as 'Relation of the Rites and Ceremonies observed at the Consecration and Installation of Archbishop Parker.' The original is in Latin, and contains two curious points. One is a statement which appears almost incidentally introduced, 'Nullum Archiepiscopo tradens pastorale baculum'; the other that the prayers, &c., used are stated to be 'juxta formam libri auctoritate parliamenti editi.' This appears under date of December 17, 1559. It is singular that in a previous paper, vol. v. No. 25, entitled 'Order for the Consecration of an Archbishop of Canterbury; the Mode to be Pursued,' with marginal notes by Cecil, the text (which is not very legible) concludes with a statement that the order of King Edward's book is to be observed, for that there is none other special made in this last session of Parliament; to which Cecil annotates, 'This book is not established by Parliament.'

Note VIII.

The alleged corruption of the clergy in the sixteenth century.

The ecclesiastical reaction of the last half-century, together with the vastly-increased accessibility of innumerable original sources of information in State Papers and other archives which has come about during the same period, has produced a vast number of calls upon us to reconsider the evidence upon which our fathers believed in the intense and almost universal corruption of the late pre-Reformation clergy, and in more than one instance a demand that the old verdict of condemnation should be reversed.

I may take two recent writers as at once thorough-going and at the same time well-informed advocates on the side of the reversal—viz., Canon Dixon and Father Gasquet. The former says[1] very plainly that 'no general charge of corruption has ever been made good against the English clergy.' The latter, in a voluminous and special work dealing with the whole question of Henry VIII. and the English monasteries, says that 'the voices raised against the monks were those of Cromwell's agents, of the cliques of new men, and of his hireling scribes, who formed a crew of as truculent and filthy libellers as ever disgraced a revolutionary cause.' I shall confine myself in this discussion to two questions: (1) Are we in fairness entitled to dismiss the evidence of Cromwell's visitors as entirely worthless? and (2) Is there, or is there not, sufficient evidence, independent of theirs, of the general corruption of the monasteries? The first question is one which need not detain us long. If there were no further evidence in the case than that of Cromwell's commissioners, it would closely resemble one of those cases so common in our inferior courts in which the only evidence against the prisoner is the evidence of policemen: and then, if doubts were thrown upon the individual policemen's character—as they often are—it would be the duty of the magistrate to consider what the value of those doubts was, from what quarter and with what probable motives they were suggested; and if he thought that they were justified, it would no doubt largely modify the importance that he attached to the police evidence, and might in some cases induce him, if no untainted evidence against the prisoner were adduced, to dismiss the case. On the other hand, if further evidence, though but slight, were produced, he would not entirely reject that of the

---

[1] *History of the Church of England*, vol. i. p. 23.

constables, but would estimate it in a great degree according to the support, or the reverse, which it received from that which was entirely unconnected with it. He would in scarcely any case be justified in rejecting the evidence altogether, without a previous consideration of how far it looked in itself like a truthful account of the particular transactions which it professed to describe.

Unless we are prepared to pronounce very rash judgment, and fall into a great number of errors and inaccuracies, we must not lay down a hard-and-fast rule that because a man is not what is ordinarily considered a respectable member of society, therefore his evidence on no subject whatever is to be held as entitled to any weight. That this is the rational view of such matters is sufficiently proved by the fact that we constantly see criminals brought up from gaol itself in order to give evidence in court, and that their evidence is considered necessary for the purpose of enabling the court to arrive at a correct decision. If, then, we apply these principles to the case before us, there can, I think, be no doubt but that we ought not to dismiss the whole evidence of Cromwell's commissioners as unworthy of credit, but to examine, in the first place, the character of the evidence itself, and, in the second, to see how far it is corroborated, or the reverse, by independent evidence gathered from other sources. If Cromwell's commissioners were commonly indebted, as Father Gasquet is constantly suggesting, mainly 'to their imaginations for their facts,' why did their accounts of different houses differ so widely from one another?[1] Why did they show so much favour to Catesby and Godstow, to Ramsey and Woolstrope, and various other houses, both of monks and nuns? They speak here of the abbot as an honest man, with some very disorderly monks under him; elsewhere of the abbot being the worst offender, or of but one or two monks being bad.

The various charges brought against the commissioners and their employers are to a great extent mutually destructive. If it be true that Henry and Cromwell had made up their minds for the general suppression of the religious houses, and sent these

---

[1] A good example is to be found in the *State Papers*, Sept. 27, 1535, in which Tregonwell writes to Cromwell his account of the visitation of nine religious houses—viz., Godstow, Eynsham, Bruern, Wroxton, Clattercot, Catesby, Canons Ashby, Chacombe, and Bicester. He gives very scanty particulars, but some are commended, some the reverse. The whole letter has a genuine look, not at all as if the visitor went with a ready-formed intention of only finding fault.

men down, not to inquire but to condemn, and that they themselves knew the purpose for which they were sent and were indifferent as to the truth of the facts they alleged, so that they lent support to their employers' purpose, why did they send good reports when they knew that evil would be more acceptable? and why did they make out a case against a comparatively small minority of the thousands of 'religious' inhabiting the houses?[1]

The fact to which I have just referred is the point upon which the whole question really turns. It was, after all, to but a minority of the clergy that gross vice was really brought home; and that fact has been used equally by their apologists and their detractors for more than it is really worth. Apologists have said in effect: 'You cannot make men in large bodies perfect. There were of course a few bad men among the monks, as there are and always will be amongst any numerous body of men; but they were the rare exception, and the rest were what they professed to be—men who had forsaken the world and its pleasures and gains, and given up their time to devotion or to pastoral work: and to condemn the body as a body is as unreasonable as it is unjust.' The detractors reply somewhat as follows: '"*Ex uno disce omnes.*" Here were a set of men who were nothing if not better than the rest of the world—who had severed themselves from the world because it was not good enough for them—and yet you find them wallowing in sensual vice which would have disgraced a body of brigands or free-lances, and using the opportunities afforded by their sacred calling to make others twofold more children of hell than themselves; and since they were all one united body, and all trying to make out the best case they could for themselves, and possessed every advantage for successful combination, there can be no doubt that the evil which we know of them was all well established, and was, in fact, far wider spread among them than was ever suffered to appear. Their whole *raison d'être* was to be the light of the world, and their own light was darker than the outer darkness itself.' In each instance the case is overstated, but there is no room for real doubt that the second is nearer to the facts than the first.

Still, it may be admitted that, if the reports of Cromwell's commissioners were all the evidence we have, it would not go for much. Their stories, if taken together, as they ought in fairness to be, do not, it is true, look as if they were 'cooked': but, on the other hand, the character of at least some of the men, and the

[1] *Gasquet*, vol. i. p. 352.

evident hostility of their employers towards the monks, would be enough to discredit them as witnesses; and if their evidence stood alone, the utmost it could do would be to leave an uncomfortable doubt on a reader's mind as to whether or not monasteries were all that they should have been or professed to be. But the case is in fact the very reverse of the one here supposed. There is ample proof of the corruption of the monasteries, quite apart from the evidence of Cromwell's commissioners; and it is just the coincidence of their evidence with that of other witnesses, untainted by the suspicion which attaches to them, which alone gives value to it. Into this evidence I do not propose to go at length, for reasons many and obvious. I will but classify it here; but I will claim, and do claim, that those who call for a reversal of the sentence pronounced more than three centuries ago, and persisted in by all English historians of credit down to the time of Lingard, shall meet this evidence fully and fairly before their demand can be even listened to. There is, then, first, and of least importance, the evidence of the satirists and lampooners from Walter de Map and Piers the Ploughman down to Simon Fish. Depreciate these men as you will, say that they romanced, and even lied boldly and unscrupulously, and I admit at once of them, as of Cromwell's commissioners, that their evidence standing alone might be worthless. It is its coincidence in the main with other and worthier writers which gives it value. There is, secondly, the evidence to which I have referred in the text—viz., the records of the law courts, as seen in the Ripon Chapter-book and the excerpts from Consistory Court of London. These belong to a quite different category from the above, and the effect which they produce on a mind like that of Bishop Stubbs I have already quoted. Finally, there is evidence supplied by the visitations of Archbishops Morton, Wareham, and Wolsey. Of these, if I mistake not, only a portion of the first has been published. Every effort has been made to minimise its effect, and not without reason; for it establishes in every particular against the most magnificent of all monasteries, the very charges which the commissioners subsequently made against so many others: and this on the authority, not of a rapacious Minister or an unscrupulous commissioner, but of the orthodox episcopal Minister of the most orthodox of fifteenth-century kings, duly authorised by the Pope himself. It has been pleaded that it was half a century before Cromwell's visitation, and there had been ample time for amendment since; and that it applied to one monastery, and that it is unfair to extend its conclusions to others. These allegations have been met beforehand by Mr. Froude, who states of Morton's visitation, after quoting a portion only of his account of St. Albans, 'Offences similar in kind, and scarcely less gross, were exposed at Waltham, at S. Andrew's, Northampton, at Calais, and at other places'; and further that 'in 1511 a second visitation was attempted by Archbishop Warham. This inquiry was more partial than the first, yet similar practices were brought to light. . . . A third effort was made by Wolsey twelve years later; again exposure followed, and again no remedy was found.'

These statements are definite; they can but be either true or false If the apologists of the monks really believe in their own case, why do they not publish these registers, or at least those parts of them which contain the account of these visitations ? If they do so, and can show that little or no scandalous matter is contained in them, they will not only refute Mr. Froude, but they will do more by that one publication to rehabilitate the monks than by all the thousands of pages of special pleading which have been, and no doubt will be, expended upon their defence; but unless or until they can do that, they will fail to reverse what is, in the main, the verdict of history for more than three hundred years, and in almost every country in Europe.

In fact, the evidence of Cromwell's commissioners, which these writers treat as if it were the sole evidence against the moral condition of the monasteries, is the very best that can be used in their favour, inasmuch as it shows, on the testimony of witnesses certainly not favourable to them, that a certain considerable proportion of them still led decent and regular, if not very useful, lives—a fact which might have fallen out of sight if we had only the strictures of episcopal visitors like Morton, or the records of courts of justice, wherewith to correct the scurrility of lampooners and the declamation of moralists.

When we compare the particulars, for example, charged against the abbot and monks of S. Alban's in Morton's visitation with those contained in many of the visitors' letters in regard to other places, we find that they are of so exactly similar a character, and so precisely like those brought in vague and general terms against the clergy in the lampoons and satires of the time, that it is quite impossible to avoid the conclusion that these were the actual faults of monasteries generally, and that they were and had been very prevalent in them for some generations before the suppression. Mr. Froude states, as we have seen, supporting his statement by reference to the MS. registers of Warham and Wolsey, that they also make similar charges. These registers I do not profess to have examined myself, but it obviously lies with the apologists of the monks to show that they fail to support the charges which are founded upon them, if, indeed, they do so fail. At present these gentlemen seem to rest their case mainly upon the allegations which they are enabled to make against the personal character of some of Cromwell's commissioners. These allegations are many of them probably true, but they are not always relevant, and at the best they serve to remind us of the Old Bailey practice on certain occasions of 'abusing the plaintiff's attorney,' and, like it, to suggest that the advocate who resorts to it has in reality 'no case.' And in truth the advocates of the pre-Reformation clergy have no case. The evidence comes thick and from every source imaginable, from the grave records of Morton and his successors, from the fierce denunciations of Colet and other preachers, from the unimpassioned entries in Court records and law-books, no less than from the perpetual and constantly-repeated libels of the poets and lampooners from Walter de Map to Chaucer, from Chaucer to Simon Fish; and yet even the latter productions, little as they may be worth as evidence, cannot go for nothing. Our forefathers can hardly have listened, generation after generation, to an endless repetition of the same jokes and the same scurrilities, if in very deed they never had any point; and it is the coincidence of the reports of Cromwell's commissioners with, not one of the above, but with all of them, which serves to vindicate the truth and even the moderation of their statements, notwithstanding the occasional holes which a critic can pick in the individual characters of some of them.

There is one somewhat minute point which may not be unworthy of notice. The commissioners are constantly referring to the fact that they can get no evidence, though they are sure that irregularities exist; and this is naturally pointed to by the advocates of the monks as showing the determination of the visitors to find the evils which they were sent to seek. It may be so to some extent, but it is surely as well explained by the very simple facts that, as these visitors had no commission from any authority whom the monks acknowledged, the latter had every facility—and, as they might themselves fairly consider, every right, over and above the natural instinct of self-preservation—to conceal as much as they could; and the case of St. Alban's [1] rather suggests the probability of this explanation, since there the commissioners 'found little,' though, as we know, in the very same monastery,

[1] *Gasquet*, vol. i. p. 328.

Cardinal Morton, fifty years before, being armed with an authority which the monks could not gainsay, 'found' a good deal.

I have admitted above, possibly without clear proof, that it was but a minority of the pre-Reformation clergy who deserved the denunciations which Colet put in such general and trenchant terms. Indeed, we may believe, and be thankful to believe, that Chaucer's good and humble and gentle 'parson' was ever to be found more frequently than the opposite characters; but what are we to think of times in which the latter could exist in appreciable numbers at all? and what of the political effect which their existence must have had in an age when, after a slumber of many generations, a general uprising was at hand in which no belief, no institution, no class of men, could escape being called in question? To put the question in a practical shape, what would happen in the present day if an archbishop could state officially of any imaginable ecclesiastical institution one quarter of what Cardinal Morton stated against the greatest monastery of the fifteenth century?

One further question in conclusion. If the clergy were as immaculate as Canon Dixon and Father Gasquet will have them, how was it that they were so bitterly hated by the people, as is evidenced by the letter of Bishop Fitz-James's, and the despatches of Chapuy referred to in the text? It must be admitted that the tone of morality in the sixteenth century was, on the whole, low, and there is certainly evidence enough that among the clergy it was not higher than among the laity.

Over and above that which is contained in the authorities referred to above, I may cite a letter [1] from Foxe, Bishop of Winchester, to Wolsey, dated January 2, 1520-1. He expresses satisfaction at Wolsey's proposed reformation of the clergy, 'the day of which he had desired to see as Simeon desired to see the Messiah. As for himself, though within his own small jurisdiction he had given nearly all his study to the work for nearly three years, yet whenever he had to correct and punish, he found *the clergy* and particularly (what he did not at first suspect) *the monks*, so *depraved*, so *licentious and corrupt*, that he despaired of any proper reformation till the work was undertaken on a more general scale, and with a stronger arm.'

Again, in 1561 there are letters [2] from John Scory, Bishop of Hereford, to Cecil, in which he requests to have power to nominate

---

[1] In the *National Biography,* article 'Foxe,' by the President of C. C. C., Oxford.

[2] *State Papers,* Eliz. vol. xvii. 82.

impartial persons to survey his bishopric, and complains that he finds great disorder in his cathedral church, which he says is 'a very nursery of blasphemy, whoredom, pryde, superstition, and ignorance.'

Another bishop, John Best, of Carlisle, reporting [1] the state of his diocese, also to Cecil, a month later, says that the priests are 'wicked imps of antichrist, for the most part very ignorant and stubborn, past measure false and subtle.' The use of the word antichrist, and the general terms in which the accusation is couched, raises a doubt in this last case whether it may not be a mere charge of addiction to Popish practices, which, considering the date, and that many of the men so charged must have held their cures through Henry, Edward, and Mary's reigns, would hardly be surprising; but Bishop Scory's case cannot admit of the doubt—the charges are too specific.

Finally, the case of Nicholas Udal already referred to (see p. 54, above—note) shows that the general tone of morality of the period was a very low one.

That the low tone was not confined to the Catholic clergy is unhappily proved by Latimer's reproofs of it, by the history of Bishop Ponet, and by the constant complaints of the covetousness of the Elizabethan bishops, and their unscrupulous dealing with the property of their sees.

In this, as in the last two notes, I do not profess more than to have given a few samples of the prevailing opinion of the times on the subject with which they deal.

[1] *State Papers*, Eliz. vol. xviii. 21.

APPENDIX OF STATUTES

23 HENRY VIII.
Cap. XX.

An act concerning restraint of payment of Annates *to the see of* Rome.

<small>Not in the printed *stats.* Co:lex, Tit. 5. c. 1.
Great sums of money have been conveyed out of the realm, &c. for first-fruits of archbishopricks and bishopricks,</small>

Forasmuch as it is well perceived, by long approved experience, that great and inestimable sums of money have been daily conveyed out of this realm, to the impoverishment of the same; and especially such sums of money as the Pope's holiness, his predecessors, and the court of Rome, by long time have heretofore taken of all and singular those spiritual persons which have been named, elected, presented, or postulated to be archbishops or bishops within this realm of England, under the title of Annates, *otherwise called first-fruits: which* Annates, *or first-fruits, have been taken of every archbishoprick, or bishoprick, within this realm, by restraint of the Pope's bulls, for confirmations, elections, admissions, postulations, provisions, collations, dispositions, institutions, installations, investitures, orders, holy benedictions, palles, or other things*

<small>(without which dispatch could not be had at the see of Rome) to the impoverishing of the nation, and sometimes the ruin of the friends of the persons promoted,</small>

requisite and necessary to the attaining of those their promotions; and have been compelled to pay, before they could attain the same, great sums of money, before they might receive any part of the fruits of the said archbishoprick, or bishoprick, whereunto they were named, elected, presented, or postulated; by occasion whereof, not only the treasure of this realm hath been greatly conveighed out of the same, but also it hath happened many times, by occasion of death, unto such archbishops, and bishops, so newly promoted, within two or three years after his or their consecration, that his or their friends, by whom he or they have been holpen to advance and make payment of the said Annates, *or first-fruits, have been thereby utterly undone and impoverished: and for because the said* Annates *have risen, grown, and encreased, by an uncharitable custom, grounded upon no just or good title, and the payments thereof obtained by restraint of bulls, until the same* Annates, *or first-fruits, have been paid, or surety made for the same; which declareth the said payments to be exacted, and taken by constraint, against all equity and justice: the noblemen therefore of the realm, and the wise, sage, politick commons of the same, assembled in this present parliament, considering that the court of* Rome *ceaseth not to tax, take, and exact the said great sums of money, under the title of* Annates, *or first-fruits, as is aforesaid, to the great damage of the said prelates, and this realm; which* Annates, *or first-fruits, were first suffered to be taken within the same realm, for the only defence of christian people against the infidels, and now they be claimed and demanded as mere duty, only for lucre, against all right and conscience: insomuch that it is evidently known, that there hath passed out of this realm unto the court of* Rome, *sithen the second year of the reign of the most noble Prince, of famous memory, King* Henry *the Seventh, unto this present time, under the name of* Annates, *or first-fruits, payed for the expedition of bulls of archbishopricks, and bishopricks, the sum of eight hundred thousand ducats, amounting in sterling money, at the least, to eight score thousand pounds, besides other great and intolerable sums which have yearly been conveighed to the said court of* Rome, *by many other ways and means, to the great impoverishment of this realm: and albeit, that our said sovereign the King, and all his natural subjects, as well spiritual as temporal, been as obedient, devout, catholick and humble children of God, and holy church, as any people be within any realm christned; yet the said exactions of* Annates, *or first-fruits, be so intolerable and importable to this realm, that it is considered and declared, by the whole body of this realm now represented by all the estates of the same assembled in this present parliament, that the King's Highness before Almighty God, is bound, as by the duty of a good christian prince, for the conservation and preservation of the good estate and commonwealth of this his realm, to do all that in him is to obviate, repress and redress the said abusions and exactions of* Annates, *or first-fruits: and because that divers prelates of this realm, being now in extream age, and in other debilities of their bodies, so that of likelihood, bodily death in short time shall or may succeed unto them; by reason whereof great sums of money shall shortly after their deaths be conveighed unto the court of* Rome, *for the unreasonable and uncharitable causes abovesaid, to the universal damage, prejudice, and impoverishment of this realm, if speedy remedy be not in due time provided:*

which demands though made without any just title,

yet from the second H. 7. 160,000l. hath been paid for first-fruits,

besides other great sums;

and though the King and his subjects are obedient children of holy church,

yet the said exactions being intolerable, the estates have represented, that the King is bound to repress them; especially now when divers prelates are in extream age.

Y

II. It is therefore ordained, established, and enacted, by authority of this present parliament, That the unlawful payment of *Annates*, or first-fruits, and all manner contributions for the same, for any archbishoprick, or bishoprick, or for any bulls hereafter to be obtained from the court of *Rome*, to or for the aforesaid purpose and intent, shall from henceforth utterly cease, and no such hereafter to be paid for any archbishoprick, or bishoprick, within this realm, other or otherwise than hereafter in this present act is declared; and that no manner person, nor persons hereafter to be named, elected, presented, or postulated to any archbishoprick, or bishoprick, within this realm, shall pay the said *Annates*, or first-fruits, for the said archbishoprick, or bishoprick, nor any other manner of sum or sums of money, pensions or *Annates* for the same, or for any other like exaction, or cause, upon pain to forfeit to our said sovereign lord the King, his heirs and successors, all manner his goods and chattels for ever, and all the temporal lands and possessions of the same archbishoprick, or bishoprick, during the time that he or they which shall offend, contrary to this present act, shall have, possess, or enjoy the archbishoprick, or bishoprick, wherefore he shall so offend contrary to the form aforesaid. And furthermore it is enacted, by authority of this present parliament, That if any person hereafter named and presented to the court of *Rome* by the King, or any of his heirs or successors, to be bishop of any see or diocese within this realm hereafter, shall be letted, deferred, or delayed at the court of *Rome* from any such bishoprick, whereunto he shall be so represented, by means of restraint of bulls apostolick, and other things requisite to the same; or shall be denied at the court of *Rome*, upon convenient suit made, any manner bulls requisite for any of the causes aforesaid, any such person or persons so presented, may be, and shall be consecrated here in *England* by the archbishop, in whose province the said bishoprick shall be, so alway that the same person shall be named and presented by the King for the time being to the same archbishop: and if any persons being named and presented, as aforesaid, to any archbishoprick of this realm, making convenient suit, as is aforesaid, shall happen to be letted, deferred, delayed or otherwise disturbed from the same archbishoprick, for lack of pall, bulls, or other to him requisite, to be obtained in the court of *Rome* in that behalf, that then every such person named and presented to be archbishop, may be, and shall be, consecrated and invested, after presentation made, as is aforesaid, by any other two bishops within this realm, whom the King's highness, or any of his heirs or successors, Kings of *England*, for the time being, will assign and appoint for the same, according and in like manner as divers other archbishops and bishops have been heretofore, in antient time, by sundry the King's most noble progenitors, made, consecrated, and invested within this realm: and that every archbishop and bishop hereafter, being named and presented by the King's highness, his heirs or successors, Kings of *England*, and being consecrated and invested, as is aforesaid, shall be installed accordingly, and shall be accepted, taken, reputed, used, and obeyed, as an archbishop or bishop of the dignity, see or place whereunto he so shall be named, presented, and consecrated, requireth ; and as other like prelates of that province, see, or diocese, have been used, accepted, taken, and obeyed, which have had, and obtained compleatly, their bulls, and other things requisite in that behalf from the court of *Rome*. And also shall fully and entirely have and enjoy all the spiritualities and temporalities of the said archbishoprick or bishoprick, in as large, ample, and beneficial manner, as any of his or their predecessors had, or enjoyed in the said archbishoprick, or bishoprick, satisfying and yielding unto the King our sovereign lord, and to his heirs and successors, Kings of *England*, all such duties, rights, and interests, as before this time had been accustomed to be paid for any such archbishoprick, or bishoprick, according to the antient laws and customs of this realm, and the King's prerogative royal. *(as divers heretofore have been) after which, he shall be installed, and be archbishop and bishop of the see, and shall enjoy all spiritualities and temporalities yielding unto the King all duties, rights, &c.*

III. And to the intent our said holy father the Pope, and the court of *Rome*, shall not think that the pains and labours taken, and hereafter to be taken, about the writing, sealing, obtaining, and other businesses sustained, and hereafter to be sustained, by the offices of the said court of *Rome*, for and about the expedition of any bulls hereafter to be obtained or had for any such archbishoprick, or bishoprick, shall be irremunerated, or shall not be sufficiently and condignly recompensed in that behalf ; and for their more ready expedition to be had therein ; it is therefore enacted by the authority aforesaid, That every spiritual person of this realm, hereafter to be named, presented, or postulated, to any archbishoprick or bishoprick of this realm, shall and may lawfully pay for the writing and obtaining of his or their said bulls, at the court of *Rome*, and ensealing the same with lead, to be had without payment of any *Annates*, or firstfruits, or other charge or exaction by him or them to be made, yielded, or paid for the same, five pounds *Sterling*, for and after the rate of the clear and whole yearly value of every hundred *and that due reward may be allowed for the expedition of bulls, every person presented to archbishoprick, or bishoprick, shall pay 5l. for every hundred that the promotion is of clear yearly value.*

pounds *Sterling*, above all charges of any such archbishoprick, or bishoprick, or other money, to the value of the said five pounds, for the clear yearly value of every hundredth pounds of every such archbishoprick, or bishoprick, and not above, nor in any otherwise, any thing in this present act before written notwithstanding. And forasmuch as the King's highness, and this his high court of parliament, neither have, nor do intend to use in this, or any other like cause, any manner of extremity or violence, before gentle courtesie or friendship, ways and means first approved and attempted, and without a very great urgent cause and occasion given to the contrary, but principally coveting to disburthen this realm of the said great exactions, and intolerable charges of *Annates*, and first-fruits, have therefore thought convenient to commit the final order and determination of the premisses, in all things, unto the King's highness. So that if it may seem to his high wisdom, and most prudent discretion, meet to move the Pope's holiness, and the court of *Rome*, amicably, charitably, and reasonably, to compound, other to extinct and make frustrate the payments of the said *Annates*, or first-fruits, or else by some friendly, loving, and tolerable composition to moderate the same in such wise as may be by this realm easily borne and sustained; that then those ways and compositions taken, concluded, and agreed, between the Pope's holiness and the King's highness, shall stand in strength, force and effect of law, inviolably to be observed. And it is also further ordained, and enacted by the authority of this present parliament, That the King's highness at any time, or times, on this side the feast of *Easter*, which shall be in the year of our Lord God, one thousand five hundred and three and thirty, or at any time on this side the beginning of the next parliament, by his letters patents under his great seal, to be made, and to be entred of record in the roll of this present parliament, may and shall have full power and liberty to declare, by the said letters patents, whether that the premisses, or any part, clause, or matter thereof, shall be observed, obeyed, executed, and take place and effect, as an act and statute of this present parliament, or not. So that if his highness, by his said letters patents, before the expiration of the times above limited, thereby do declare his pleasure to be, that the premisses, or any part, clause, or matter thereof, shall not be put in execution, observed, continued, nor obeyed, in that case all the said premisses, or such part, clause, or matter, as the King's highness so shall refuse, disaffirm, or not ratify, shall stand and be from henceforth uttely void and of none effect.

[Marginal notes:]
The parliament not willing to use extremity without urgent cause

have committed this matter to the King (to compound it with the court of Rome)

whose compositions shall be inviolably observed,

and who shall have power to declare, by letters patents, whether this shall be a statute or not,

so as, what he shall refuse in whole or in part shall be void,

And in case that the King's highness, before the expiration of the times afore prefixed, do declare by his said letters patents, his pleasure and determination to be, that the said premisses, or every clause, sentence, and part thereof, that is to say, the whole, or such part thereof as the King's highness so shall affirm, accept, and ratify, shall in all points stand, remain, abide, and be put in due and effectual execution, according to the purport, tenor, effect, and true meaning of the same; and to stand and be from henceforth for ever after, as firm, stedfast, and available in the law, as the same had been fully and perfectly established, enacted and confirmed, to be in every part thereof, immediately, wholly, and entirely executed, in like manner, form, and effect, as other acts and laws; the which being fully and determinately made, ordained, and enacted in this present parliament. And if that upon the aforesaid reasonable, amicable and charitable ways and means, by the King's highness to be experimented, moved, or compounded, or otherwise approved, it shall and may appear, or be seen unto his grace, that this realm shall be continually burdened and charged with this, and such other intolerable exactions and demands, as heretofore it hath been; and that thereupon, for continuance of the same, our said holy father the Pope, or any of his successors, or the court of *Rome*, will, or do, or cause to be done at any time hereafter, so as is above rehearsed, unjustly, uncharitably, and unreasonably, vex, inquiet, molest, trouble, or grieve our said sovereign lord, his heirs or successors, Kings of *England*, or any of his or their spiritual or lay subjects, or this his realm, by excommunication, excomengement, interdiction, or by any other process, censures, compulsories, ways or means; be it enacted by the authority aforesaid, That the King's highness, his heirs and successors Kings of *England*, and all his spiritual and lay subjects of the same, without any scruples of conscience, shall and may lawfully, to the honour of almighty God, the encrease and continuance of virtue and good example within this realm, the said censures, excommunications, interdictions, compulsories, or any of them notwithstanding, minister, or cause to be ministred, throughout this said realm, and all other the dominions or territories belonging or appertaining thereunto, all and all manner of sacraments, sacramentals, ceremonies, or other divine services of the holy church, or any other thing or things necessary for the health of the soul of mankind, as they heretofore at any time or times have been virtuously used or accustomed to do within the same; and that no manner such censures, excommunications,

Marginalia: and what he shall accept shall be put in execution. and be as available in law, as any other acts. If no redress may be had by these amicable means, but the court of Rome shall enforce the continuance of those exactions, by excommunications, interdicts, &c. In such case, all sacraments and divine services shall continue to be ministred, notwithstanding, and the excommunications, interdicts, &c. shall not be executed.

interdictions, or any other process or compulsories, shall be by any of the prelates, or other spiritual fathers of this region, nor by any of their ministers or substitutes, be at any time or times hereafter published, executed, nor divulged, nor suffered to be published, executed, or divulged in any manner of ways.

<small>Rol. Parl.</small>

Memorand. *Quod nono die Julii, anno regni regis Henrici vicesimo quinto, idem dominus rex per literas suas patentes sub magno sigillo suo sigillat. Actum predictum ratificavit & confirmavit, et actui illi assensum suum regium dedit, prout per easdem literas patentes, cujus tenor sequitur in hæc verba, magis apertè constat.*

<small>Ratified and confirmed by 25 H. 8. c. 20. f. 2.</small>

Then follows the ratification in form, with the act recited at large.

24 HENRY VIII.

Cap. XII.

For the restraint of appeals.

<small>The power, pre-eminence and authority of the King of England.</small>

Where by divers sundry old authentick histories and chronicles, it is manifestly declared and expressed, that this realm of England, *is an empire, and so hath been accepted in the world, governed by one supreme head and King, having the dignity and royal estate of the imperial crown of the same;* (2) *unto whom a body politick, compact of all sorts and degrees of people, divided in terms, and by names of spiritualty and temporalty, been bounden and owen to bear, next to God, a natural and humble obedience;* (3) *he being also institute and furnished, by the goodness and sufferance of Almighty God, with plenary, whole, and entire power, pre-eminence, authority, prerogative and jurisdiction, to render and yield justice, and final determination to all manner of folk, resiants, or subjects within this his realm, in all causes, matters, debates and contentions, happening to occur, insurge, or begin within the limits thereof, without restraint, or provocation to any foreign princes or potentates of the world;* (4) *the body spiritual whereof having power, when any cause of the law divine happened to come in question, or of spiritual learning, then it was declared, interpreted, and shewed by that part of the said body politick, called the spiritualty, now being usually called the* English *church, which always hath been reputed, and also found of that sort, that both for knowledge, integrity and sufficiency of number, it hath been always thought, and is also at this hour, sufficient and meet of it self, without the intermeddling of any exterior person or persons, to declare and determine all such doubts, and to administer all such*

<small>The power, learning and wisdom of the body spiritual.</small>

offices and duties, as to their rooms, spiritual doth appertain; (5) *for the due administration whereof, and to keep them from corruption and sinister affection, the King's most noble progenitors, and the antecessors of the nobles of this realm, have sufficiently endowed the said church, both with honour and possessions;* (6) *and the laws temporal, for trial of property of lands and goods, and for the conservation of the people of this realm in unity and peace, without rapine or spoil, was and yet is administred, adjudged and executed by sundry judges and ministers of the other part of the said body politick, called the temporalty;* (7) *and both their authorities and jurisdictions do conjoin together in the due administration of justice, the one to help the other.* The form and manner of government of the estate temporal.

II. *And whereas the King his most noble progenitors, and the nobility and commons of this said realm, at divers and sundry parliaments, as well in the time of King* Edward *the First,* Edward *the Third,* Richard *the Second,* Henry *the Fourth, and other noble Kings of this realm, made sundry ordinances, laws, statutes, and provisions for the entire and sure conservation of the prerogatives, liberties and pre-eminences of the said imperial crown of this realm, and of the jurisdiction spiritual and temporal of the same, to keep it from the annoyance as well of the see of* Rome, *as from the authority of other foreign potentates, attempting the diminution or violation thereof, as often, and from time to time, as any such annoyance or attempt might be known or espied:* (2) *and notwithstanding the said good statutes and ordinances made in the time of the King's most noble progenitors, in preservation of the authority and prerogative of the said imperial crown, as is aforesaid; yet nevertheless sithen the making of the said good statutes and ordinances divers and sundry inconveniencies and dangers, not provided for plainly by the said former acts, statutes and ordinances, have arisen and sprung by reason of appeals sued out of this realm to the see of* Rome, *in causes testamentary, causes of matrimony and divorces, right of tithes, oblations and obventions, not only to the great inquietation, vexation, trouble, cost and charges of the King's highness, and many of his subjects and resiants of this his realm, but also to the great delay and let to the true and speedy determination of the said causes, for so much as the parties appealing to the said court of* Rome *most commonly do the same for the delay of justice.* (3) *And forasmuch as the great distance of way is so far out of this realm, so that the necessary proofs, nor the true knowledge of the cause, can neither there be so well known, ne the witnesses there so well examined, as within this realm, so that the parties grieved by means of the said appeals be*

No appeals shall be used, but within this realm.

The several inconveniencies in suing of appeals to Rome.

most times without remedy: (4) in consideration whereof, the King's highness, his nobles and commons, considering the great enormities, dangers, long delays and hurts, that as well to his highness, as to his said nobles, subjects, commons, and resiants of this his realm, in the said causes testamentary, causes of matrimony and divorces, tithes, oblations and obventions, do daily ensue, doth therefore by his royal assent, and by the assent of the lords spiritual and temporal, and the commons, in this present parliament assembled, and by authority of the same, enact, establish and ordain, That all causes testamentary, causes of matrimony and divorces, rights of tithes, oblations and obventions (the knowledge whereof by the goodness of princes of this realm, and by the laws and customs of the same, appertaineth to the spiritual jurisdiction of this realm) already commenced, moved, depending, being, happening, or hereafter coming in contention, debate or question within this realm, or within any the King's dominions, or marches of the same, or elsewhere, whether they concern the King our sovereign lord, his heirs and successors, or any other subjects or resiants within the same, of what degree soever they be, shall be from henceforth heard, examined, discussed, clearly, finally, and definitively adjudged and determined within the King's jurisdiction and authority, and not elsewhere, in such courts spiritual and temporal of the same, as the natures, conditions, and qualities of the cases and matters aforesaid in contention, or hereafter happening in contention, shall require, without having any respect to any custom, use, or sufferance, in hindrance, let, or prejudice of the same, or to any other thing used or suffered to the contrary thereof by any other manner of person or persons in any manner of wise; any foreign inhibitions, appeals, sentences, summons, citations, suspensions, interdictions, excommunications, restraints, judgments, or any other process or impediments, of what natures, names, qualities, or conditions soever they be, from the see of *Rome*, or any other foreign courts or potentates of the world, or from and out of this realm, or any other the King's dominions, or marches of the same, to the see of *Rome*, or to any other foreign courts or potentates, to the let or impediment thereof in any wise notwithstanding. (5) And that it shall be lawful to the King our sovereign lord, and to his heirs and successors, and to all other subjects or resiants within this realm, or within any of the King's dominions or marches of the same, notwithstanding that hereafter it should happen any excommengement, excommunications, interdictions, citations, or any other censures, or foreign process out of any outward parts,

Marginal note: All causes determinable by any spiritual jurisdiction shall be adjudged within the King's authority.

to be fulminate, promulged, declared, or put in execution within this said realm, or in any other place or places, for any of the causes before rehearsed, in prejudice, derogation, or contempt of this said act, and the very true meaning and execution thereof, may and shall nevertheless as well pursue, execute, have and enjoy the effects, profits, benefits and commodities of all such processes, sentences, judgments and determinations done, or hereafter to be done, in any of the said courts spiritual or temporal, as the cases shall require, within the limits, power and authority of this the King's said realm, and dominions and marches of the same, and those only, and none other to take place, and to be firmly observed and obeyed within the same. (6) As also, that all the spiritual prelates, pastors, ministers and curates within this realm, and the dominions of the same, shall and may use, minister, execute and do, or cause to be used, executed, ministred and done, all sacraments, sacramentals, divine services, and all other things within the said realm and dominions, unto all the subjects of the same, as catholick and christian men owen to do; any former citations, processes, inhibitions, suspensions, interdictions, excommunications, or appeals, for or touching the causes aforesaid, from or to the see of *Rome*, or any other foreign prince or foreign courts, to the let or contrary thereof in any wise notwithstanding. *The prelates of this realm may execute all sacraments and divine service to the subjects of this realm.*

III. And if any of the said spiritual persons, by the occasion of the said fulminations of any of the same interdictions, censures, inhibitions, excommunications, appeals, suspensions, summons, or other foreign citations for the causes beforesaid, or for any of them, do at any time hereafter refuse to minister, or cause to be ministred, the said sacraments and sacramentals, and other divine services, in form as is aforesaid, shall for every such time or times that they or any of them do refuse so to do, or cause to be done, have one year's imprisonment, and to make fine and ransom at the King's pleasure. *The penalty of them who omit to do their duty.*

IV. And it is further enacted by the authority aforesaid, That if any person or persons inhabiting or resiant within this realm, or within any of the King's said dominions, or marches of the same, or any other person or persons, of what estate, condition or degree soever he or they be, at any time hereafter, for or in any the causes aforesaid, do attempt, move, purchase, or procure, from or to the see of *Rome*, or from or to any other foreign court or courts out of this realm, any manner foreign process, inhibitions, appeals, sentences, summons, citations, suspensions, interdictions, excommunications, restraints, or judgments, of *Whosoever procureth from the see of Rome, &c. any appeals, process, sentences, &c. incur the forfeiture of premunire.*

what nature, kind or quality soever they may be, or execute any of the same process, or do any act or acts to the let, impediment, hindrance or derogation of any process, sentence, judgment or determination had, made, done, or hereafter to be had, done or made, in any courts of this realm, or the King's said dominions, or marches of the same, for any of the causes aforesaid, contrary to the true meaning of this present act, and the execution of the same, that then every such person or persons so doing, and their fautors, comforters, abettors, procurers, executors, and counsellors, and every of them, being convict of the same, for every such default shall incur and run in the same pains, penalties and forfeitures, ordained and provided by the statute of provision and *Præmunire*, made in the sixteenth year of the reign of the right noble prince King *Richard* the Second, against such as attempt, procure, or make provision to the see of *Rome*, or elsewhere, for any thing, or things, to the derogation, or contrary to the prerogative or jurisdiction of the crown and dignity of this realm.

16 R. 2. c. 5.

V. And furthermore, in eschewing the said great enormities, inquietations, delays, charges and expences hereafter to be sustained in pursuing of such appeals, and foreign process, for and concerning the causes aforesaid, or any of them, do therefore by authority aforesaid, ordain and enact, That in such cases where heretofore any of the King's subjects or resiants have used to pursue, provoke, or procure any appeal to the see of *Rome*, and in all other cases of appeals, in or for any of the causes aforesaid, they may and shall from henceforth take, have and use their appeals within this realm, and not elsewhere, in manner and form as hereafter ensueth, and not otherwise ; that is to say, first from the archdeacon, or his official, if the matter or cause be there begun, to the bishop diocesan of the said see, if in case any of the parties be grieved.

Before whom, and in what courts appeals shall be sued within this realm.
4 Mod. 116, 117.
Dyer 209.

VI. And in like wise if it be commenced before the bishop diocesan, or his commissary, from the bishop diocesan, or his commissary, within fifteen days next ensuing the judgment or sentence thereof there given, to the archbishop of the province of *Canterbury*, if it be within his province ; and if it be within the province of *York*, then to the archbishop of *York* ; and so likewise to all other archbishops in other the King's dominions, as the case by order of justice shall require ; and there to be definitely and finally ordered, decreed, and adjudged, according to justice, without any other appellation or provocation to any other person or persons, court or courts.

Appeals ought to be

VII. And if the matter or contention for any of the causes

aforesaid be or shall be commenced, by any of the King's subjects or resiants, before the archdeacon of any archbishop, or his commissary, then the party grieved shall or may take his appeal within fifteen days next after judgment or sentence there given, to the court of the arches, or audience, of the same archbishop or archbishops; (2) and from the said court of the arches or audience, within fifteen days then next ensuing after judgment or sentence there given, to the archbishop of the same province, there to be definitively and finally determined, without any other or further process or appeal thereupon to be had or sued. *within 15 days.*

VIII. And it is further enacted by the authority aforesaid, that all and every matter, cause and contention now depending, or that hereafter shall be commenced by any of the King's subjects or resiants for any of the causes aforesaid, before any of the said archbishops, that then the same matter or matters, contention or contentions, shall be before the same archbishop where the said matter, cause or process shall be so commenced, definitively determined, decreed, or adjudged, without any other appeal, provocation, or any other foreign process out of this realm, to be sued to the let or derogation of the said judgment, sentence or decree, otherwise than is by this act limited and appointed; (2) saving always the prerogative of the archbishop and church of *Canterbury*, in all the foresaid causes of appeals, to him and to his successors to be sued within this realm, in such and like wise as they have been accustomed and used to have heretofore. *Suits commenced before an archbishop shall be determined by him without any further appeal. The prerogative of the archbishop of Canterbury saved.*

IX. And in case any cause, matter or contention, now depending for the causes before rehearsed, or any of them, or that hereafter shall come in contention for any of the same causes, in any of the foresaid courts, which hath, doth, shall or may touch the King, his heirs or successors, Kings of this realm; that in all and every such case or cases the party grieved, as before is said, shall or may appeal from any of the said courts of this realm, where the said matter, now being in contention, or hereafter shall come in contention, touching the King, his heirs, or successors (as is aforesaid) shall happen to be ventilate, commenced or begun, to the spiritual prelates and other abbots and priors of the upper house, assembled and convocate by the King's writ in the convocation being, or next ensuing within the province or provinces where the same matter of contention is or shall be begun; (2) so that every such appeal be taken by the party grieved within fifteen days next after the judgment or sentence thereupon given or to be given; (3) and that whatsoever be done, or shall be done and affirmed, determined, de- *Before whom an appeal shall be sued in any cause touching the King.*

creed and adjudged by the foresaid prelates, abbots and priors of the upper house of the said convocation, as is aforesaid, appertaining, concerning, or belonging to the King, his heirs, and successors, in any of these foresaid causes of appeals, shall stand and be taken for a final decree, sentence, judgment, definition and determination, and the same matter, so determined, never after to come in question and debate, to be examined in any other court or courts.

X. And if it shall happen any person or persons hereafter to pursue or provoke any appeal contrary to the effect of this act, or refuse to obey execute and observe all things comprised within the same, concerning the said appeals, provocations and other foreign processes to be sued out of this realm, for any the causes aforesaid, that then every such person or persons so doing, refusing, or offending contrary to the true meaning of this act, their procurers, fautors, advocates, counsellors, and abettors, and every of them, shall incur into the pains forfeitures and penalties ordained and provided in the said statute made in the said sixteenth year of King *Richard* the Second, and with like process to be made against the said offenders, as in the same statute made in the said sixteenth year more plainly appeareth.

<small>16 R. 2. c. 5.
28 H. 8. c. 10.
Rep. 1 & 2
Ph. & M. c. 8.
and revived
by 1 El. c. 1.</small>

25 HENRY VIII.

Cap. XIX.

The submission of the Clergy, and restraint of appeals.

Where the King's humble and obedient subjects, the clergy of this realm of England, *have not only knowledged according to the truth, that the convocations of the same clergy, is, always hath been, and ought to be assembled only by the King's writ, but also submitting themselves to the King's majesty, have promised* in Verbo Sacerdotii, *that they will never from henceforth presume to attempt, allege, claim or put in ure, or enact, promulge or execute any new canons, constitutions, ordinance provincial, or other, or by whatsoever other name they shall be called, in the convocation, unless the King's most royal assent and licence may to them be had, to make, promulge and execute the same; and that his Majesty do give his most royal assent and authority in that behalf:* (2) *and where divers constitutions, ordinances and canons provincial or synodal, which heretofore have been enacted, and be thought not only to be much prejudicial to the King's prerogative royal, and*

<small>Several canons have been prejudicial to the King's prerogative.</small>

repugnant to the laws and statutes of this realm, but also overmuch onerous to his Highness and his subjects; the said clergy hath most humbly besought the King's highness, that the said constitutions and canons may be committed to the examination and judgment of his Highness, and of two and thirty persons of the King's subjects, whereof sixteen to be of the upper and nether house of the parliament of the temporalty, and the other sixteen to be of the clergy of this realm; and all the said two and thirty persons to be chosen and appointed by the King's majesty; (3) and that such of the said constitutions and canons, as shall be thought and determined by the said two and thirty persons, or the more part of them, worthy to be abrogated and adnulled, shall be abolite and made of no value accordingly; (4) and such other of the same constitutions and canons, as by the said two and thirty, or the more part of them, shall be approved to stand with the laws of God, and consonant to the laws of this realm, shall stand in their full strength and power, the King's most royal assent first had and obtained to the same; (5) be it therefore now enacted by authority of this present parliament, according to the said submission and petition of the said clergy, That they ne any of them from henceforth shall presume to attempt, allege, claim or put in ure any constitutions or ordinances provincial or synodal, or any other canons; nor shall enact, promulge or execute any such canons, constitutions or ordinances provincial, by whatsoever name or names they may be called, in their convocations in time coming (which alway shall be assembled by authority of the King's writ) unless the same clergy may have the King's most royal assent and licence to make, promulge and execute such canons, constitutions and ordinances provincial or synodal, (6) upon pain of every one of the said clergy doing contrary to this act, and being thereof convict, to suffer imprisonment, and make fine at the King's will.

II. *And forasmuch as such canons, constitutions and ordinances, as heretofore have been made by the clergy of this realm, cannot now at the session of this present parliament, by reason of shortness of time, be viewed, examined and determined by the King's highness, and thirty-two persons to be chosen and appointed according to the petition of the said clergy in form above rehearsed:* be it therefore enacted by authority aforesaid, That the King's highness shall have power and authority to nominate and assign, at his pleasure, the said two and thirty persons of his subjects, whereof sixteen to be of the clergy, and sixteen to be of the temporalty of the upper and nether house of the parliament; and if any of the said two and thirty persons so chosen shall happen to die before their full determination, then his Highness to nominate other from time to time of the said two houses of the parliament, to supply the number of the said two and thirty ; (2) and that the same two and thirty, by his highness so to be named, shall have power and authority to view, search and examine the said canons, constitutions and ordinances provincial and synodal heretofore made, and such of them as the King's highness and the said two and thirty, or the more part of them, shall deem and adjudge worthy to be continued, kept and obeyed, shall be from thenceforth kept, obeyed and executed within this realm, so that the King's most royal assent under his great seal be first had to the same ; (3) and the residue of the said canons, constitutions and ordinances provincial, which the King's highness, and the said two and thirty persons or the more part of them, shall not approve, or deem and judge worthy to be abolite, abrogate and made frustrate, shall from thenceforth be void and of none effect, and never be put in execution within this realm. (4) Provided alway, That no canons, constitutions or ordinances shall be made or put in execution within this realm by authority of the convocation of the clergy, which shall be contrariant or repugnant to the King's prerogative royal, or the customs, laws or statutes of this realm ; any thing contained in this act to the contrary hereof notwithstanding.

35 H. 8. c. 16.
3 & 4 Ed. 6. c. 11.
3 Inst. 39. Hob. 148.
13 Co. 47.
2 Roll. 481.
2 Lev. 222.

No canons shall be executed which be contrary to the King's prerogative, or to the laws.

III. And be it further enacted by authority aforesaid, That from the feast of *Easter*, which shall be in the year of our Lord God 1534, no manner of appeals shall be had, provoked, or made out of this realm, or out of any the King's dominions, to the bishop of *Rome*, nor to the see of *Rome*, in any causes or matters happening to be in contention, and having their commencement and beginning in any of the courts within this realm, or within any the King's dominions, of what nature, condition or quality soever they be of ; but that all manner of appeals, of what nature or condition soever they be of, or what cause or matter soever they concern, shall be made and had by the parties grieved, or having cause of appeal, after such manner, form and condition, as is limited for appeals to be had and prosecuted within this realm in causes of matrimony, tythes, oblations and obventions, by a statute thereof made and established sithen the beginning of this present parliament, and according to the form and effect of the said estatute ; any usage, custom, prescription, or any thing or things to the contrary hereof notwithstanding.

3 Inst. 178.
There shall be no appeals to Rome, but appeals shall be according to the statute made 24 H. 8. c. 12.

IV. And for lack of justice at or in any the courts of the archbishops of this realm, or in any the King's dominions, it shall

Appeals from the archbishop's

be lawful to the parties grieved to appeal to the King's majesty in the King's court of chancery; (2) and that upon every such appeal, a commission shall be directed under the great seal to such persons as shall be named by the King's highness, his heirs or successors, like as in case of appeal from the admiral's court, to hear and definitively determine such appeals, and the causes concerning the same. (3) Which commissioners, so by the King's highness, his heirs or successors, to be named or appointed, shall have full power and authority to hear and definitively determine every such appeal, with the causes and all circumstances concerning the same; and that such judgment and sentence, as the said commissioners shall make and decree, in and upon any such appeal, shall be good and effectual, and also definitive; and no further appeals to be had or made from the said commissioners for the same.

<small>court into the chancery. 4 Mod. 117. Dyer, 209.</small>

V. And if any person or persons, at any time after the said feast of *Easter*, provoke or sue any manner of appeals, of what nature or condition soever they be of, to the said bishop of *Rome*, or to the see of *Rome*, or do procure or execute any manner of process from the see of *Rome*, or by authority thereof, to the derogation or let of the due execution of this act, or contrary to the same, that then every such person or persons so doing, their aiders, counsellors and abettors, shall incur and run into the dangers, pains and penalties contained and limited in the act of provision and *Præmunire* made in the sixteenth year of the King's most noble progenitor, King *Richard* the Second, against such as sue to the court of *Rome* against the King's crown and prerogative royal.

<small>Præmunire for suing of appeal to Rome, or executing any process from thence. 16 R. 2. c. 5.</small>

VI. Provided always, That all manner of provocations and appeals hereafter to be had, made or taken from the jurisdiction of any abbots, priors, or other heads and governors of monasteries, abbeys, priories and other houses and places exempt, in such cases as they were wont or might afore the making of this act, by reason of grants or liberties of such places exempt, to have or make immediately any appeal or provocation to the bishop of *Rome*, otherwise called Pope, or to the see of *Rome*, that in all these cases every person and persons, having cause of appeal or provocation, shall and may take and make their appeals and provocations immediately to the King's majesty of this realm, into the court of chancery, in like manner and form as they used afore to do to the see of *Rome*; (2) which appeals and provocations so made, shall be definitively determined by authority of the King's commission, in such manner and form as in this act

<small>Appeals from places exempt which were to the see of Rome, shall now be into the chancery.</small>

is abovementioned; (3) so that no archbishop or bishop of this realm shall intermit or meddle with any such appeals, otherwise or in any other manner than they might have done afore the making of this act; any thing in this act to the contrary thereof notwithstanding.

<small>What canons, &c. are still in force.
27 H. 8. c. 20.
37 H. 8. c. 17. f. 2.
Repealed by 1 & 2 Ph. & M. c. 8. and revived by 1 El. c. 1. f. 10.</small>

VII. Provided also, That such canons, constitutions, ordinances and synodals provincial being already made, which be not contrariant or repugnant to the laws, statutes and customs of this realm, nor to the damage or hurt of the King's prerogative royal, shall now still be used and executed as they were afore the making of this act, till such time as they be viewed, searched, or otherwise ordered and determined by the said two and thirty persons, or the more part of them, according to the tenor, form and effect of this present act.

CAP. XX.

An act for the non-payment of first-fruits to the bishop of Rome.

<small>No first-fruits shall be paid to bishop of Rome; and within what time a bishop shall be chosen, invested and consecrated.
Vide stat. 23 H. 8. c. 20. not in the printed statutes before. Vid. Codex Tit. 5. c. 1.</small>

Where sithen the beginning of this present parliament, for repress of the exaction of annates and first-fruits of archbishopricks and bishopricks of this realm wrongfully taken by the bishop of Rome, otherwise called the pope, and the see of Rome, it is ordained and established by an act, among other things, That the payments of the annates or first-fruits, and all manner contributions for the same, for any such archbishoprick or bishoprick, or for any bulls to be obtained from the see of Rome, to or for the said purpose or intent, should utterly cease, and no such to be paid for any archbishoprick or bishoprick within this realm, otherwise than in the same act is expressed: (2) *and that no manner of person or persons to be named, elected, presented or postulated to any archbishoprick or bishoprick within this realm, should pay the said annates or first-fruits, nor any other manner of sum or sums of money, pensions or annuities for the same, or for any other like exaction or cause,* (3) *upon pain to forfeit to our sovereign lord the King, his heirs and successors, all manner his goods and chattels for ever, and all the temporal lands and possessions of the said archbishoprick or bishoprick during the time that he or they that should offend contrary to the said act, should have, possess and enjoy the said archbishoprick or bishoprick.* (4) *And it is further enacted, That if any person*

<small>If any presented by the King to the see of Rome to a</small>

named or presented to the see of Rome by the King's highness, or his heirs or successors, to be bishop of any see or diocese within this

APPENDIX

realm, should happen to be letted, delayed or deferred at the see of Rome *from* any such bishoprick whereunto he should be so presented, by mean of restraint of bulls of the said bishop of Rome, otherwise called the Pope, and other things requisite to the same, or should be denied at the see of Rome, upon convenient suit made, for any bulls requisite for any such cause, that then every person so presented might or should be consecrated here in England by the archbishop in whose province the said bishoprick shall be; so always, that the same person should be named and presented by the King for the time being to the said archbishop. (5) And if any person being named and presented (as is before said) to any archbishoprick of this realm, making convenient suit, as is aforesaid, should happen to be letted, delayed, deferred or otherwise disturbed from the said archbishoprick, for lack of pall, bulls, or other things to him requisite to be obtained at the see of Rome, that then every such person so named and presented to the archbishop, might and should be consecrated and invested, after presentation made as is aforesaid, by any other two bishops within this realm, whom the King's highness, or any his heirs or successors, Kings of England, would appoint and assign for the same, according and after like manner as divers archbishops and bishops have been heretofore in ancient time by sundry the King's most noble progenitors made, consecrated and invested within this realm. (6) And it is further enacted by the said act, That every archbishop and bishop, being named and presented by the King's highness, his heirs and successors, Kings of England, and being consecrated and invested, as is aforesaid, should be installed accordingly, and should be accepted, taken and reputed, used and obeyed as an archbishop or bishop of the dignity, see or place whereunto he shall be so named, presented and consecrated, and as other like prelates of that province, see or diocese, have been used, accepted, taken and obeyed, which have had and obtained compleatly their bulls and other things requisite in that behalf from the see of Rome, (7) and also should fully and entirely have and enjoy all the spiritualties and temporalties of the said archbishoprick or bishoprick, in as large, ample and beneficial manner, as any of his or their predecessors had or enjoyed in the said archbishoprick or bishoprick, satisfying and yielding unto the King's highness, and to his heirs and successors, all such duties, rights and invests as beforetime hath been accustomed to be paid for any such archbishoprick or bishoprick, according to the ancient laws and customs of this realm and the King's prerogative royal, as in the said act amongst other things is more at large mentioned.

bishoprick in England be there delayed, he may be consecrated by an archbishop in England.

One presented to the see of Rome to an archbishoprick, and there letted, may be consecrated by two bishops of England.

II. And albeit the said bishop of Rome, otherwise called the

Pope, hath been informed and certified of the effectual contents of the said act, to the intent that by some gentle ways the said exactions might have been redressed and reformed, yet nevertheless the said bishop of Rome *hitherto hath made none answer of his mind therein to the King's highness, nor devised nor required any reasonable ways to and with our said sovereign lord for the same :*

<small>The King's consent to the foresaid statute.</small>

(2) wherefore his most royal majesty of his most excellent goodness, for the wealth and profit of this his realm and subjects of the same, hath not only put his most gracious and royal assent to the foresaid act, but also hath ratified and confirmed the same, and every clause and article therein contained, as by his letters patents under his great seal inrolled in the parliament roll of this present parliament more at large is contained.

III. *And forasmuch as in the said act it is not plainly and certainly expressed in what manner and fashion archbishops and bishops shall be elected, presented, invested and consecrated within this realm, and in all other the King's dominions,* (2) be it now

<small>No man shall be presented to the see of Rome for the dignity of an archbishop or bishop, nor annates or first-fruits shall be paid to the same see.</small>

therefore enacted by the King our sovereign lord, by the assent of the lords spiritual and temporal, and the commons, in this present parliament assembled, and by the authority of the same, That the said act and every thing therein contained shall be and stand in strength, virtue and effect; except only, that no person or persons hereafter shall be presented, nominated or commended to the said bishop of *Rome*, otherwise called the Pope, or to the see of *Rome*, to or for the dignity or office of any archbishop or bishop within this realm, or in any other the King's dominions, nor shall send nor procure there for any manner of bulls, breeves, palls or other things requisite for an archbishop or bishop, nor shall pay any sums of money for annates, first-fruits nor otherwise, for expedition of any such bulls, breeves, or palls; but that by the authority of this act, such presenting, nominating or commending to the said bishop of *Rome*, or to the see of *Rome*, and such bulls, breeves, palls, annates, first-fruits, and every other sums of money heretofore limited, accustomed or used to be paid at the said see of *Rome*, for procuration or expedition of any such bulls, breeves or palls, or other thing concerning the same, shall utterly cease and no longer be used within this realm, or within any the King's dominions; any thing contained in the said act aforementioned, or any use, custom or prescription to the contrary thereof notwithstanding.

<small>The manner of electing an archbishop or bishop.</small>

IV. And furthermore be it ordained and established by the authority aforesaid, That at every avoidance of every archbishoprick or bishoprick within this realm, or in any other the King's dominions, the King our sovereign lord, his heirs and successors, may grant to the prior and convent, or the dean and chapiter of the cathedral churches or monasteries where the see of such archbishoprick or bishoprick shall happen to be void, a licence under the great seal, as of old time hath been accustomed, to proceed to election of an archbishop or bishop of the see so being void, with a letter missive, containing the name of the person which they shall elect and choose : (2) by virtue of which licence the said dean and chapiter, or prior or convent, to whom any such licence and letters missive shall be directed, shall with all speed and celerity in due form elect and choose the same person named in the said letters missive, to the dignity and office of the archbishoprick or bishoprick so being void, and none other. (3) And if they do defer or delay their election above twelve days next after such licence or letters missive to them delivered, that then for every such default the King's highness, his heirs and successors, at their liberty and pleasure shall nominate and present, by their letters patents under their great seal, such a person to the said office and dignity so being void, as they shall think able and convenient for the same ; (4) and that every such nomination and presentment to be made by the King's highness, his heirs and successors, if it be to the office and dignity of a bishop, shall be made to the archbishop and metropolitan of the province where the see of the same bishoprick is void, if the see of the said archbishoprick be then full, and not void ; and if it be void, then to be made to such archbishop or metropolitan within this realm, or in any the King's dominions, as shall please the King's highness, his heirs or successors : (5) and if any such nomination or presentment shall happen to be made for default of such election to the dignity or office of any archbishop, then the King's highness, his heirs and successors by his letters patents under his great seal, shall nominate and present such person as they will dispose to have the said office and dignity of archbishoprick being void, to one such archbishop and two such bishops, or else to four such bishops within this realm, or in any of the King's dominions, as shall be assigned by our said sovereign lord, his heirs or successors.

For default of election by the dean and chapiter, the King shall nominate a bishop by his letters patent.

V. And be it enacted by the authority aforesaid, That whensoever any such presentment or nomination shall be made by the King's highness, his heirs or successors, by virtue and authority of this act, and according to the tenor of the same ; that then every archbishop and bishop, to whose hands any such presentment and nomination shall be directed, shall with all speed and

Consecration of a bishop.

celerity invest and consecrate the person nominate and presented by the King's highness, his heirs or successors, to the office and dignity that such person shall be so presented unto, and give and use to him pall, and all other benedictions, ceremonies and things requisite for the same, without suing, procuring or obtaining hereafter any bulls or other things at the see of *Rome*, for any such office or dignity in any behalf. (2) And if the said dean and chapiter, or prior and convent, after such licence and letters missive to them directed, within the said twelve days do elect and choose the said person mentioned in the said letters missive, according to the request of the King's highness, his heirs or successors, thereof to be made by the said letters missive in that behalf, then their election shall stand good and effectual to all intents ; (3) and that the person so elected, after certification made of the same election under the common and covent seal of the electors, to the King's highness, his heirs or successors, shall be reputed and taken by the name of lord elected of the said dignity and office that he shall be elected unto ; (4) and then making such oath and fealty only to the King's majesty, his heirs and successors, as shall be appointed for the same, the King's highness, by his letters patents under his great seal, shall signify the said election, if it be to the dignity of a bishop, to the archbishop and metropolitan of the province where the see of the said bishoprick was void, if the see of the said archbishop be full and not void ; and if it be void, then to any other archbishop within this realm, or in any other the King's dominions ; requiring and commanding such archbishop, to whom any such signification shall be made, to confirm the said election, and to invest and consecrate the said person so elected to the office and dignity that he is elected unto, and to give and use to him all such benedictions, ceremonies, and other things requisite for the same, without any suing, procuring or obtaining any bulls, letters or other things from the see of *Rome* for the same in any behalf. (5) And if the person be elected to the office and dignity of an archbishop, according to the tenor of this act, then after such election certified to the King's highness in form aforesaid, the same person so elected to the office and dignity of an archbishop, shall be reputed and taken lord elect to the said office and dignity of an archbishop, whereunto he shall be so elected ; (6) and then after he hath made such oath and fealty only to the King's majesty, his heirs and successors, as shall be limited for the same, the King's highness, by his letters patents under his great seal, shall signify the said election to one archbishop and two other bishops, or else

The name of a bishop newly chosen, viz. a lord elect.

The King's signification of a bishop or archbishop elect.

to four bishops within this realm, or within any other the King's dominions, to be assigned by the King's highness, his heirs or successors, requiring and commanding the said archbishop and bishops, with all speed and celerity, to confirm the said election, and to invest and consecrate the said person so elected to the office and dignity that he is elected unto, and to give and use to him such pall, benedictions, ceremonies and all other things requisite for the same, without suing, procuring or obtaining any bulls, briefs or other things at the said see of *Rome*, or by the authority thereof in any behalf.

VI. And be it further enacted by authority aforesaid, That every person and persons being hereafter chosen, elected, nominate, presented, invested and consecrated to the dignity or office of any archbishop or bishop within this realm, or within any other the King's dominions, according to the form, tenor and effect of this present act, and suing their temporalties out of the King's hands, his heirs or successors, as hath been accustomed, and making a corporal oath to the King's highness, and to none other, in form as is afore rehearsed, shall and may from henceforth be thrononised or installed, as the case shall require, (2) and shall have and take their only restitution out of the King's hands, of all the possessions and profits spiritual and temporal, belonging to the said archbishoprick or bishoprick whereunto they shall be so elected or presented, and shall be obeyed in all manner of things, according to the name, title, degree, and dignity that they shall be so chosen or presented unto, and do and execute in every thing and things touching the same, as any archbishop or bishop of this realm, without offending the prerogative royal of the crown and the laws and customs of this realm, might at any time heretofore do. *This election of a bishop shall be lawful.*

VII. And be it further enacted by the authority aforesaid, That if the prior and covent of any monastery, or dean and chapter of any cathedral church, where the see of an archbishop or bishop is within any the King's dominions, after such licence as is afore rehearsed, shall be delivered to them, proceed not to election, and signify the same according to the tenor of this act, within the space of twenty days next after such licence shall come to their hands; (2) or else if any archbishop or bishop, within any the King's dominions, after any such election, nomination or presentation shall be signified unto them by the King's letters patents, shall refuse, and do not confirm, invest and consecrate with all due circumstance as is aforesaid, every such person as shall be so elected, nominate or presented, and to them signi- *The penalty for not electing or not consecrating a bishop named.*

fied as is above mentioned, within twenty days next after the King's letters patents of such signification or presentation shall come to their hands; (3) or else if any of them, or any other person or persons, admit, maintain, allow, obey, do or execute any censures, excommunications, interdictions, inhibitions, or any other process or act, of what nature, name or quality soever it be, to the contrary, or let of due execution of this act; (4) that then every prior and particular person of his convent, and every dean and particular person of the chapiter, and every archbishop and bishop, and all other persons, so offending and doing contrary to this act, or any part thereof, and their aiders, counsellers and abetters, shall run into the dangers, pains and penalties of the estatute of the provision and *præmunire* made in the five and twentieth year of the reign of King Edward the Third, and in the sixteenth year of King Richard the Second.

25 Ed. 3. stat. 5. c. 22.
16 R. 2. c. 5.
26 H. 8. c. 14.
31 H. 8. c. 9
8 El. c. 1.
Rep. 1 & 2 Ph. and M. c. 8. and revived by 1 El. c. 1.

31 HENRY VIII.

CAP. IX.

REP. by
1 & 2 Ph. &
M. c. 8.
8 El. c. 1

An act authorizing the King's highness to make bishops by his letters patents.

CAP. XIV.

An act for abolishing of diversity of opinions in certain articles concerning christian religion.

Where the King's most excellent majesty is by God's law supreme head immediately under him of this whole church and congregation of England, *intending the conservation of the same church and congregation in a true, sincere and uniform doctrine of Christ's religion, calling also to his blessed and most gracious remembrance, as well the great and quiet assurance, prosperous increase, and other innumerable commodities, which have ever insued, come and followed of concord, agreement and unity in opinions, as also the manifold perils, dangers and inconveniencies, which have heretofore, in many places and regions, grown, sprung and arisen of the diversities of minds and opinions, especially of matters of christian religion, and therefore desiring that such an unity might and should be charitably established in all things touching and concerning the same, as the same so being established might chiefly be to the honour of Almighty God, the very author and fountain of all true unity and sincere concord, and consequently redound to the common wealth of this his Highness most noble realm, and of all his loving subjects, and other resiants and inhabitants of or in the same; hath therefore caused and commanded this his most high court of parliament, for sundry and many urgent causes and considerations, to be at this time summoned, and also a synod and convocation of all the archbishops, bishops and other learned men of the clergy of this his realm, to be in like manner assembled.*

And forasmuch as in the said parliament, synod and convocation, there were certain articles, matters, and questions proponed and set forth touching christian religion, that is to say:

First, Whether in the most blessed sacrament of the altar remaineth, after the consecration, the substance of bread and wine or no.

Secondly, Whether it be necessary by God's law, that all men should be communicate with both kinds, or no.

Thirdly, Whether priests, that is to say, men dedicate to God by priesthood, may by the law of God marry after, or no.

Fourthly, Whether vow of chastity or widowhood, made to God advisedly by man or woman, be by the law of God to be observed, or no.

Fifthly, Whether private masses stand with the law of God, and be to be used and continued in the church and congregation of *England,* as things whereby good christian people may and do receive both godly consolation and wholesome benefits, or no.

Sixthly, Whether auricular confession is necessary to be retained, continued, used and frequented in the church, or no.

The King's most royal majesty, most prudently pondering and considering, that by occasion of variable and sundry opinions and judgments of the said articles, great discord and variance hath arisen, as well amongst the clergy of this his realm, as amongst a great number of vulgar people, his loving subjects of the same; and being in a full hope and trust, that a full and perfect resolution of the said articles should make a perfect concord and unity generally amongst all his loving and obedient subjects; of his most excellent goodness not only commanded, that the said articles should deliberately and advisedly, by his said archbishops, bishops and other learned men of his clergy, be debated, argued and reasoned, and their opinions therein to be understood, declared and known, but also most graciously vouchsafed, in his own princely person, to descend and come into his said high court of parliament and counsel, and there, like a prince of most high prudence, and no less learning, opened and declared many things of high learning and great knowledge, touching the said articles, matters, and questions, for an unity to be had in the same; whereupon, after a great and long, deliberate and advised disputation and consultation, had and made concerning the said articles, as well by the consent of the King's highness, as by the assent of the lords spiritual, and temporal, and other learned men of his clergy in their convocations, and by the consent of the commons, in this present parliament assembled, it was and is finally resolved, accorded and agreed in manner and form following, that is to say,

First, That in the most blessed sacrament of the altar, by the strength and efficacy of Christ's mighty word (it being spoken by the priest) is present really, under the form of bread and wine, the natural body and blood of our Saviour Jesus Christ, conceived of the Virgin *Mary;* and that after the consecration there remaineth no substance of bread or wine, nor any other substance: but the substance of Christ, God and man.

Secondly, That communion in both kinds is not necessary *ad salutem*, by the law of God, to all persons; and that it is to be believed, and not doubted of, but that in the flesh, under the form of bread, is the very blood; and with the blood, under the form of wine, is the very flesh; as well apart, as though they were both together.

Thirdly, That priests after the order of priesthood received, as afore, may not marry by the law of God.

Fourthly, That vows of chastity or widowhood, by man or woman made to God advisedly, ought to be observed by the law of God; and that it exempteth them from other liberties of christian people, which without that they might enjoy.

Fifthly, That it is meet and necessary, that private masses be continued and admitted in this the King's *English* church and congregation, as whereby good christian people, ordering themselves accordingly, do receive both godly and goodly consolations and benefits; and it is agreeable also to God's law.

Sixthly, That auricular confession is expedient and necessary to be retained and continued, used and frequented in the church of God.

For the which most godly study, pain, and travel of his Majesty, and determination and resolution of the premisses, his most humble

and obedient subjects, the lords spiritual and temporal, and the commons, in this present parliament assembled, not only render and give unto his Highness their most high and hearty thanks, and think themselves most bound to pray for the long continuance of his Grace's most royal estate, but also being desirous that his most godly enterprise may be well accomplished, and brought to a full end and perfection, and so established, that the same might be to the honour of God, and after to the common quiet, unity and concord to be had in the whole body of this realm for ever, most humbly beseechen his royal Majesty, that the resolution and determination above written of the said articles may be established, and perpetually perfected by authority of this present parliament, &c.

* 1 If any person by word, writing, printing, cyphering, or any otherwise, do preach, teach, dispute, or hold opinion that in the blessed sacrament of the altar, under form of bread and wine, (after the consecration thereof) there is not present really the natural body and blood of our Saviour Jesus Christ conceived of the Virgin *Mary.* Or that after the said consecration, there remaineth any substance of bread or wine, or any other substance, but the substance of Christ, God and man: Or that in the flesh under form of bread, is not the very blood of Christ: Or that with the blood under the form of wine, is not the very flesh of Christ, as well apart, as though they were both together: Or affirm the said sacrament to be of other substance than is aforesaid: Or deprave the said blessed sacrament: then he shall be adjudged an heretick, and suffer death by burning, and shall forfeit to the King all his lands, tenements, hereditaments, goods and chattels, as in case of high treason.

* Ex Edit. Rastal.

2 And if any person preach in any sermon, or collation openly made, or teach in any common school or congregation, or obstinately affirm or defend, that the communion of the blessed sacrament in both kinds is necessary for the health of man's soul, or ought or should be ministered in both kinds: Or that it is necessary to be received by any person (other than by priests) being at mass, and consecrating the same.

3 Or that any man after the order of priesthood received, may marry or contract matrimony.

4 Or that any man or woman which advisedly hath vowed or professed, or should vow or profess chastity or widowhood, may marry, or contract marriage.

5 Or that private masses be not lawful, or not laudable, or should not be used, or be not agreeable to the laws of God.

6 Or that auricular confession is not expedient, and necessary to be used in the church of God, he shall be adjudged, suffer death, and forfeit lands and goods, as a felon. If any priest or other man or woman, which advisedly hath vowed chastity, or widowhood, do actually marry or contract matrimony with another: Or any man which is or hath been a priest, do carnally use any woman, to whom he is, or hath been married, or with whom he hath contracted matrimony, or openly be conversant or familiar with any such woman; both the man and the woman shall be adjudged felons. Commissions shall be awarded to the bishop of the diocese, his chancellor, commissary, and others, to enquire of the heresies, felonies, and offences aforesaid. And also justices of peace in their sessions, and every steward, under-steward, and deputy of stewards in their leet, or lawday, by the oaths of twelve men have authority to enquire of all the heresies, felonies, and offences aforesaid.

32 H. 8. c. 10.
35 H. 8. c. 5.
Repealed
1 Ed. 6, c. 12.
1 Eliz. c. 1. s. 18.

32 HENRY VIII.

Cap. XXVI.

All decrees and ordinances, which according to God's word, and Christ's gospel, by the King's advice and confirmation by his letters patents, shall be made and ordained by the archbishops, bishops and doctors appointed, or to be appointed, in and upon the matter of Christian religion and Christian faith, and the lawful rites, ceremonies and observations of the same, shall be in every point thereof believed, obeyed and performed to all intents and purposes, upon the pains therein comprised. Provided, that nothing shall be ordained or desired, which shall be repugnant to the laws and statutes of this realm.

Rep. 1 Ed. 6. c. 12.

35 HENRY VIII.

Cap. III.

An act for the ratification of the King's majesty's stile.

The King's stiles and titles.

Where our most dread natural and gracious sovereign liege lord the King hath heretofore been, and is justly lawfully and notoriously known, named, published and declared to be, King of England, France and Ireland, defender of the faith, and of the church of England, and also of Ireland, in earth supreme head; and hath justly and lawfully used the title and name thereof, as to his grace appertaineth: be it enacted by the King our sovereign lord, with the assent of the lords spiritual and temporal, and

the commons, in this present parliament assembled, and by the
authority of the same, That all and singular his Grace's subjects
and resiants, of or within this his realm of *England, Ireland,*
and elsewhere within other his Majesty's dominions, shall from
henceforth accept and take the same his Majesty's stile, as it is
declared and set forth in manner and form following, that is to
say, in the *Latin* tongue by these words, *Henricus Octavus Dei
Gratia, Angliæ, Franciæ & Hiberniæ Rex, fidei defensor, & in
terra ecclesiæ Anglicanæ & Hibernicæ supremum caput;* and in
the *English* tongue by these words, *Henry the Eighth, by the
grace of God King of* England, France *and* Ireland, *defender of
the faith, and of the church of* England, *and also of* Ireland, *in
earth the supreme head:* and that the said stile, declared and set
forth by this act, in manner and form as is above-mentioned,
shall be from henceforth, by the authority aforesaid, united and
annexed for ever to the imperial crown of his Highness realm of
England.

 II. It shall be high treason to attempt to deprive the King of
this stile. *Rep.* 1 *M. st.* 1. *c.* 1. *s.* 3.

Repealed 1 & 2 Ph. & M. c. 8. and revived by 1 El. c. 1. Dyer 98.

---

1 EDWARD VI.
Cap. I.

An act against such as shall unreverently speak against the sacrament of the altar, and of the receiving thereof under both kinds.

 The King's most excellent Majesty minding the governance and
order of his most loving subjects to be in most perfect unity and
concord in all things, and in especial in the true faith and religion
of God, and wishing the same to be brought to pass with all clemency
and mercy on his Highness part towards them, as his most princely
serenity and Majesty hath already declared by evident proof, to the
intent that his most loving subjects provoked by clemency and goodness of their prince and King, shall study rather for love than for
fear to do their duties, first to Almighty God, and then to his
Highness and the common wealth, nourishing concord and love
amongst themselves; (2) yet considereth and perceiveth that in a
multitude all be not on that sort, that reason and the knowledge of
their duties can move them from offence, but many which had need
have some bridle of fear, and that the same be men most contentious
and arrogant for the most part, or else most blind and ignorant:
(3) by the means of which sort of men, many things well and

The penalty for unreverent speaking against the sacrament of the body and blood of Christ, or against the receiving thereof in both kinds.

The King mindeth to have unity in religion by clemency.

godly instituted, and to the edification of many, be perverted and abused, and turned to their own and others great loss and hindrance, and sometime to extreme destruction: the which doth appear in nothing more or sooner, than in matters of religion, and in the great and high mysteries thereof, as in the most comfortable sacrament of the body and blood of our Saviour Jesus Christ, commonly called the sacrament of the altar, and in scripture, the (a) supper (b) table of the lord, the (c) communion and (d) partaking of the body and blood of Christ: (4) Which sacrament was instituted of no less author than of our Saviour, both God and man, when at his last supper amongst his apostles, he did take the bread into his holy hands, and did say, (e) Take you and eat, this is my body which is (f) given and (g) broken for you. And taking up the (h) chalice or cup, did give thanks and say, (i) This is my blood of the new testament, which is shed for (k) you, and for (l) many, for the (m) remission of sins, that (n) whensoever we should do the same, we should do it in the remembrance of him, and to declare and set forth his death and most glorious passion, until his coming. Of the which (o) bread whosoever eateth, or of the which cup whosoever drinketh unworthily, (p) eateth and drinketh condemnation and judgment to himself, making no difference of the Lord's body. (5) The institution of which sacrament being ordained by Christ, as is beforesaid, and the said words spoken of it here before rehearsed, being of eternal, infallible and undoubted truth: yet the said sacrament (all this notwithstanding) hath been of late marvellously abused by such manner of men before rehearsed, who of wickedness, or else of ignorance and want of learning, for certain abuses heretofore committed of some, in misusing thereof, have condemned in their hearts and speech the whole thing, and contemptuously depraved, despised or reviled the same most holy and blessed sacrament, and not only disputed and reasoned unreverently and ungodly of that most high mystery, but also in their sermons, preachings, readings, lectures, communications, arguments, talks, rhimes, songs, plays or jests, name or call it by such vile and unseemly words, as christian ears do abhor to hear rehearsed: (6) for reformation whereof, be it enacted by the King's highness, with the assent of the lords spiritual and temporal, and of the commons, in this present parliament assembled, and by the authority of the same, That whatsoever person or persons, from and after the first day of *May* next coming, shall deprave, despise or contemn the said most blessed sacrament, in contempt thereof, by any contemptuous words, or by any words of depraving, despising or reviling; or what person or persons shall advisedly in

---

Marginal notes:

The blessed sacrament instituted by Christ himself, and by what words of his. (a) 2 Cor. 11. 20. (b) 1 Cor. 10. 21. (c) 1 Cor. 10. 16. (d) 1 Cor. 10. 16, 17. (e) Mat. 26. 26. (f) Luke 22. 19. (g) 1 Cor. 11. 24. (h) Mat. 26. 27. (i) Mar. 14. 23. (k) Mar. 14. 24. (l) Luke 28. 19. (m) Mar. 14. 24. (n) Mat. 26. 28. (o) 1 Cor. 11. 29. (p) 1 Cor. 11. 26.

The causes of the abuse of the blessed sacrament.

The penalty for speaking unreverently of the most blessed sacrament.

any otherwise contemn, despise or revile the said most blessed sacrament, contrary to the effects and declaration abovesaid : that then he or they shall suffer imprisonment of his or their bodies, and make fine and ransom at the King's will and pleasure. (7) and for full and effectual execution of the premises before devised, ordained and enacted by this act, be it furthermore enacted by the authority of this present parliament, That immediately after the first day of *May* next coming, the justices of peace, or three of them at the least, whereof one of them to be of the *quorum*, in every shire of this realm, and *Wales*, and all other places within the King's dominions shall have full power and authority by virtue of this act, as well to take information and accusation by the oaths and depositions of two able, honest and lawful persons at the least, (8) and after such accusation or information so had, to inquire by the oaths of xii. men, in every of their four quarter-sessions yearly to be holden, of all and singular such accusations or informations to be had or made of any of the offences abovesaid, to be committed or done after the said first day of *May*, within the limits of their commission : (9) and that upon every such accusation and information, the offender and offenders shall be enquired of, and indicted before the said justices of peace, or three of them at the least, as is aforesaid, of the said contempts and offences, by the verdict of twelve honest and indifferent men, if the matter of the said accusation and information shall seem to the said jury good and true. Justices of peace may enquire of offenders.

II. And it is also further enacted by the authority aforesaid, That the said justices of peace, or three of them at the least, as is aforesaid, before whom any such presentment, information and accusation shall be made or taken as is aforesaid, shall examine the accusers, what other witness were by and present at the time of the doing and committing of the offence, whereof the information, accusation and presentment shall be made, and how many others than the accusers have knowledge thereof, (2) and shall have full power and authority by their discretions to bind by recognizance to be taken before them, as well the said accusers, as all such other persons whom the said accusers shall declare to have knowledge of the offences by them presented and informed, every of them in five pounds to the King, to appear before the said justices of peace, before whom the offender or offenders shall be tried at the day of trial and deliverance of such offenders. Examination of the accusers.

III. And it is further enacted by the authority aforesaid, That the said justices of peace or three of them at the least, as is abovesaid, by virtue of this act, shall have full power and authority to 12 Co. 103. What process shall be awarded make process against every person and persons so indicted, by two *capias* and an exigent, and by *capias utlagatum*, as well within the limits of their commission, as into all other shires and places of this realm, *Wales* and other the King's dominions, as well within liberties as without, and the same process to be good and effectual in the law to all intents, constructions and purposes ; (2) and upon the appearance of any of the offenders, shall have full power and authority by virtue of this act and the commission of peace to determine the contempts and offences aforesaid according to the laws of this realm and the effects of this act : (3) and that the said justices of peace, or three of them at the least, as is abovesaid, shall have full power and authority to let any such person or persons so indicted upon sufficient sureties, by their discretions, to bail for their appearance to be tried, according to the tenor, form and effect of this act.

IV. Provided always, and be it enacted, That the said justices of peace, or three of them at the least, at their quarter-sessions, where any offender or offenders shall be or stand indicted of any of the contempts or offences abovesaid, shall direct and award one writ in the King's name to the bishop of the diocese where the said offence or offences be supposed to be committed or done willing and requiring the said bishop to be in his own person or by his chancellor, or other his sufficient deputy learned, at the quarter-sessions in the said county to be holden, when and where the said offender shall be arraigned and tried, appointing to them in the said writ the day and place of the said arraignment ; (2) which writ shall be of this form : *Rex &c. Episcopo L. salutem. Præcipimus tibi quod tu, Cancellarius tuus, vel alius deputat' tuus sufficienter eruditus, sitis cum justic. nostris ad pacem in com. nostro B. conservand. assignat. apud D. tali die, ad sessionem nostram, ad tunc et ibm. tenend. ad dand. consilium et advisament. eisdem justiciariis nostris ad pacem, super arranament. et deliberationem offendent. contra form. Statutic oncernen. sacrosanct' sacramentum altaris.*

V. Provided always, and be it enacted by the authority aforesaid, That no person or persons shall be indicted of any of the contempts or offences abovesaid, but only of such contempts or offences as shall be done or perpetrated within three months next after the said offence or offences so committed or done.*

VI. And be it further enacted by the authority aforesaid, That in all trials, for any such offenders before the said justices, as is aforesaid, the person or persons being complained on and arraigned, shall be admitted to purge or try his or their innocency, by as many or more witnesses in number, and of as good honesty and credence, as the witnesses be which deposed against him or them or any of them.

VII. *And forasmuch as it is more agreeable, both to the first institution of the said sacrament of the most precious body and blood of our Saviour Jesus Christ, and also more conformable to the common use and practice both of the apostles and of the primitive church by the space of 500 years and more after Christ's ascension, that the said blessed sacrament should be ministered to all christian people under both the kinds of bread and wine, than under the form of bread only:* (2) *and also it is more agreeable to the first institution of Christ, and to the usage of the apostles, and the primitive church, that the people being present should receive the same with the priest, than that the priest should receive it alone:* (3) Therefore be it enacted by our said sovereign lord the King, with the consent of the lords spiritual and temporal, and the commons, in this present parliament assembled, and by the authority of the same, That the said most blessed sacrament be hereafter commonly delivered and ministered unto the people within the church of *England* and *Ireland*, and other the King's dominions, under both the kinds, that is to say, of bread and wine, except necessity otherwise require: (4) And also that the priest which shall minister the same, shall, at the least one day before, exhort all persons which shall be present likewise to resort and prepare themselves to receive the same. (5) And when the day prefixed cometh, after a godly exhortation by the minister made, (wherein shall be further expressed the benefit and comfort promised to them which worthily receive the said holy sacrament, and the danger and indignation of God threatned to them which shall presume to receive the same unworthily, to the end that every man may try and examine his own conscience before he shall receive the same) (6) the said minister shall not without a lawful cause deny the same to any person that will devoutly and humbly desire it; any law, statute, ordinance or custom contrary thereunto in any wise notwithstanding, not condemning hereby the usage of any church out of the King's majesty's dominions. 5 & 6 *Edw.* 6. *c.* 1. *repealed by* 1 *Ma. sess.* 2. *c.* 2. *and revived by* 1 *Eliz. c.* 1. *s.* 14.

The blessed sacrament shall be delivered unto the people under both kinds of bread and wine.

The usage of other churches not condemned.

Cap. II.

An act for the election of bishops.

Forasmuch as the elections of archbishops and bishops by the deans and chapters within the King's majesty's realms of England

25 H. 8. c. 20.
31 H. 8. c. 9.
1 M. stat. 2.
c. 2.

8 Eliz. c. 1.
1 Jac. 1. c. 25. s. 48.
Elections of bishops belong only to the King.
None but the King shall collate to a bishoprick.
A bishop col'ated by the King shall pay the usual fees.
All processes

and Ireland, *at this present time, be as well to the long delay, as to the great costs and charges of such persons, as the King's majesty giveth any archbishoprick or bishopric unto:* (2) *and whereas the said elections be in very deed no elections, but only by a writ of* Conge d'eslire, *have colours, shadows or pretences of elections, serving nevertheless to no purpose, and seeming also derogatory and prejudicial to the King's prerogative royal, to whom only appertaineth the collation and gift of all archbishopricks and bishopricks, and suffragan bishops within his Highness said realms of* England *and* Ireland, Wales, *and other his dominions and marches, &c.* ecclesiastical shall be in the King's name, but the teste in the bishop's name. Every bishop's, &c. seal of office shall have the King's arms engraven upon it. Usual fees shall be taken. The archbishop of Canterbury may use his own seal. In what cases other bishops may use their own seals. 32 H. 8. c. 45. Certificates into a court of record shall be in the King's name, teste the bishop. *Repealed by* 1 Eliz. c. 1. and 8 Eliz. c. 1, *which revive* 25 H. 8. c. 20.

2 & 3 EDWARD VI.

Cap. I.

An act for uniformity of service and administration of the sacraments throughout the realm.

Revived by 1 Eliz. c. 1. s. 14.

The penalty for not using uniformity of service, and administration of sacraments, &c.

Innovators not punished, for that they did it upon good zeal.

Where of long time there hath been had in this realm of England *and in* Wales *divers forms of common prayer, commonly called the service of the church; that is to say, the use of* Sarum, *of* York, *of* Bangor, *and of* Lincoln; *and besides the same now of late much more divers and sundry forms and fashions have been used in the cathedral and parish churches of* England *and* Wales, *as well concerning the mattens or morning prayer and the evensong, as also concerning the holy communion, commonly called the mass, with divers and sundry rites and ceremonies concerning the same, and in the administration of other sacraments of the church:* (2) *and as the doers and executors of the said rites and ceremonies, in other form than of late years they have been used, were pleased therewith: So other not using the same rites and ceremonies were thereby greatly offended:* (3) *and albeit the King's majesty, with the advice of his most entirely beloved uncle the lord protector and other of his Highness council, hath heretofore divers times assayed to stay innovations or new rites concerning the premisses; yet the same hath not had such good success as his Highness required in that behalf; whereupon his Highness by the most prudent advice aforesaid, being pleased to bear with the frailty and weakness of his subjects in that behalf, of his great clemency hath not been only content to abstain from punishment of those that have offended in that behalf, for that his Highness taketh that they did it of a good zeal; but also to the intent a uniform quiet and godly order should* be had concerning the premisses, hath appointed the archbishop of Canterbury, and certain of the most learned and discreet bishops, and other learned men of this realm, to consider and ponder the premisses; (4) and thereupon having as well eye and respect to the most sincere and pure christian religion taught by the scripture, as to the usages in the primitive church, should draw and make one convenient and meet order, rite and fashion of common and open prayer and administration of the sacraments, to be had and used in his Majesty's realm of England and in Wales; the which at this time, by the aid of the Holy Ghost, with one uniform agreement is of them concluded, set forth and delivered to his Highness, to his great comfort and quietness of mind, in a book intituled The book of the common prayer and administration of the sacraments, and other rites and ceremonies of the church, after the use of the church of *England*. (5) *Wherefore the lords spiritual and temporal, and the commons, in this present parliament assembled, considering as well the most godly travel of the King's highness, of the lord protector, and of other his Highness council, in gathering and collecting the said archbishop, bishops and learned men together, as the godly prayers, orders, rites and ceremonies in the said book mentioned, and the considerations of altering those things which be altered, and retaining those things which be retained in the said book, but also the honour of God and great quietness, which by the grace of God shall ensue upon the one and uniform rite and order in such common prayer and rights and external ceremonies to be used throughout* England *and in* Wales, *at* Calais *and the marches of the same, do give to his Highness most hearty and lowly thanks for the same:* (6) and humbly prayen, that it may be ordained and enacted by his Majesty, with the assent of the lords and commons in this present parliament assembled, and by the authority of the same, That all and singular person and persons that have offended concerning the premisses, other than such person and persons as now be and remain in ward in the Tower of *London*, or in the Fleet, may be pardoned thereof; (7) and that all and singular ministers in any cathedral or parish church or other place within this realm of *England*, *Wales*, *Calais*, and the marches of the same or other the King's dominions, shall, from and after the feast of *Pentecost* next coming, be bounden to say and use the mattens, evensong, celebration of the Lord's Supper, commonly called the mass, and administration of each of the sacraments, and all their common and open prayer, in such order and form as is mentioned in the same book, and none other or otherwise.

The book of common prayer by the aid of the Holy Ghost, is set forth by the bishops and learned men of the realm.

Cap. XXI.

An act to take away all positive laws made against marriage of priests.

<small>All laws prohibiting spiritual persons to marry, who by God's law may marry, shall be void. The benefits which would ensue if priests and ministers did live chaste, sole, and unmarried.</small>

Although it were not only better for the estimation of priests, and other ministers in the church of God, to live chaste, sole and separate from the company of women, and the bond of marriage, but also thereby they might the better intend to the administration of the gospel, and be less intricated and troubled with the charge of household, being free and unburdened from the care and cost of finding wife and children, and that it were most to be wished, that they would willingly and of their selves endeavour themselves to a perpetual chastity and abstinence from the use of women: (2) *Yet forasmuch as the contrary hath rather been seen, and such uncleanness of living, and other great inconveniencies, not meet to be rehearsed, have followed of compelled chastity, and of such laws as have prohibited those (such persons) the godly use of marriage: It were better and rather to be suffered in the common wealth, that those which could not contain, should after the counsel of scripture live in holy marriage, than feignedly abuse with worse enormity outward chastity or single life:*

II. Be it therefore enacted by our sovereign lord the King, with the assent of the lords spiritual and temporal, and the commons in this present parliament assembled, and by the authority of the same, That all and every law and laws positive, canons, constitutions and ordinances heretofore made by authority of man only, which do prohibit or forbid marriage to any ecclesiastical or spiritual person or persons, of what estate, condition or degree they be, or by what name or names soever they be called, which by God's law may lawfully marry, in all and every article, branch and sentence, concerning only the prohibition for the marriage of the persons aforesaid, shall be utterly void and of none effect: (2) And that all manner of forfeitures, pains, penalties, crimes or actions which were in the said laws contained, and of the same did follow concerning the prohibitions for the marriage of the persons aforesaid, be clearly and utterly void, frustrate and of none effect, to all intents, constructions and purposes, as well concerning marriages heretofore made by any of the ecclesiastical or spiritual persons aforesaid, as also such which hereafter shall be duly and lawfully had, celebrate and made, betwixt the persons which by the laws of God may lawfully marry.

III. Provided alway, and be it enacted by the authority aforesaid, That this act, or anything therein contained, shall not extend to give any liberty to any person to marry without asking in the church, or without any ceremony being appointed by the order prescribed and set forth in the book intituled, *The Book of Common Prayer and administration of the sacraments, &c.* any thing above mentioned to the contrary in any wise notwithstanding. 2 & 3 *Ed.* 6. *c.* 1. No marriage without asking in the church.

IV. Provided also, and be it enacted by the authority aforesaid, That this act, or any thing therein contained, shall not extend to alter, change, revoke, repeal, or otherwise to disannul any decree, judgment, sentence or divorce heretofore had or made, but that all and every such decree, judgment, sentence and divorce, shall remain and be of such like force, effect, strength and degree, to all intents, constructions and purposes, as they were in before the making of this act, and as though this act had never been had ne made; this act, or any thing therein contained to the contrary in any wise notwithstanding. *Enforced by* 5 & 6 *Ed.* 6. *c.* 12. *Repealed by* 1 *M. Sess.* 2. *c.* 2. *and made perpetual by* 1 *Jac.* 1. *c.* 25. § 50. Decrees and divorces heretofore made.

5 & 6 EDWARD VI.

CAP. I.

An act for the uniformity of service and administration of sacraments throughout the realm.

Where there hath been a very godly order set forth by the authority of parliament, for common prayer and administration of the sacraments to be used in the mother tongue within the church of England, agreeable to the word of God, and the primitive church, very comfortable to all good people, desiring to live in christian conversation, and most profitable to the estate of this realm, upon the which the mercy, favour and blessing of Almighty God is in no wise so readily and plenteously poured as by common prayers, due using of the sacraments, and often preaching of the gospel, with the devotion of the hearers: (2) *and yet this notwithstanding, a great number of people in divers parts of this realm, following their own sensuality, and living either without knowledge or due fear of God, do wilfully and damnably before Almighty God abstain and refuse to come to their parish churches and other places where common prayer, administration of the sacraments, and preaching of the word of God, is used upon* Sundays, *and other days ordained to be holydays.* Uniformity of prayer and administration of sacraments shall be used in the church.

356 CHURCH AND STATE UNDER THE TUDORS

March 95.

II. For reformation hereof, be it enacted by the King our sovereign lord, with the assent of the lords and commons in this present parliament assembled, and by the authority of the same, That from and after the feast of *All Saints* next coming all and every person and persons inhabiting within this realm, or any other the King's majesty's dominions, shall diligently and faithfully (having no lawful or reasonable excuse to be absent) endeavour themselves to resort to their parish church or chapel accustomed; (2) or upon reasonable lett thereof, to some usual place where common prayer and such service of God shall be used in such time of lett, (3) upon every *Sunday*, and other days ordained and used to be kept as holydays, (4) and then and thereto abide orderly and soberly during the time of the common prayer, preachings or other service of God there to be used and ministred; (5) upon pain of punishment by the censures of the church.

Every person shall resort to his parish church or chapel upon Sundays and holidays.

III. And for the due execution hereof, the King's most excellent Majesty, the lords temporal, and all the commons, in this present parliament assembled, doth in God's name earnestly require and charge all the archbishops, bishops and other ordinaries, that they shall endeavour themselves to the uttermost of their knowledges, that the due and true execution thereof may be had throughout their dioceses and charges, as they will answer before God for such evils and plagues wherewith Almighty God may justly punish his people for neglecting this good and wholesome law.

They which come not to church may be punished by the censures of the church.

IV. And for their authority in this behalf, be it further likewise enacted by the authority aforesaid, That all and singular the same archbishops, bishops and all other their officers exercising ecclesiastical jurisdiction, as well in place exempt as not exempt, within their dioceses, shall have full power and authority by this act to reform, correct and punish by censures of the church, all and singular persons which shall offend within any their jurisdictions or diocesses, after the said feast of *All Saints* next coming, against this act and statute; any other law, statute, privilege, liberty or provision heretofore made, had or suffered to the contrary notwithstanding.

V. *And because there hath arisen in the use and exercise of the aforesaid common service in the church, heretofore set forth, divers doubts for the fashion and manner of the ministration of the same, rather by the curiosity of the minister and mistakers, than of any other worthy cause; (2) therefore as well for the more plain and manifest explanation hereof, as for the more perfection of the said order of common service, in some places where it is necessary to make the same prayers and fashion of service more earnest and fit to stir christian people to the true honouring of Almighty God;* (3) the King's most excellent Majesty, with the assent of the lords and commons in this present parliament assembled, and by the authority of the same, hath caused the aforesaid order of common service, entituled, *The book of common prayer,* to be faithfully and godly perused, explained and made fully perfect, and by the aforesaid authority hath annexed and joined it, so explained and perfected, to this present statute: (4) adding also a form and manner of making and consecrating of archbishops, bishops, priests and deacons, to be of like force, authority and value as the same like foresaid book entituled, *The book of common prayer,* was before, and to be accepted, received, used and esteemed in like sort and manner, and with the same clauses of provisions and exceptions, to all intents, constructions and purposes, as by the act of parliament made in the second year of the King's majesty's reign was ordained, limited, expressed and appointed for the uniformity of service and administration of the sacraments throughout the realm, upon such several pains as in the said act of parliament is expressed. (5) And the said former act to stand in full force and strength, to all intents and constructions, and to be applied, practised and put in ure, to and for the establishing of the book of common prayer, now explained and hereunto annexed, and also the said form of making of archbishops, bishops, priests and deacons hereunto annexed, as it was for the former book.

The book of common prayer, with the form of consecrating bishops, priests, deacons. 1 Ed. 6. c. 2.

2 & 3 Ed. 6. c. 1.

VI. And by the authority aforesaid it is now further enacted, That if any manner of person or persons inhabiting and being within this realm, or any other the King's majesty's dominions, shall after the said feast of *All Saints* willingly and wittingly hear and be present at any other manner or form of common prayer, of administration of the sacraments, of making of ministers in the churches, or of any other rites contained in the book annexed to this act, than is mentioned and set forth in the said book, or that is contrary to the form of sundry provisions and exceptions contained in the foresaid former statute, and shall be thereof convicted according to the laws of this realm, before the justices of assise, justices of *oyer* and *determiner,* justices of peace in their sessions, or any of them, by the verdict of twelve men or by his or their own confession or otherwise, shall for the first offence suffer imprisonment for six months, without bail or mainprise; (2) and for the second offence, being likewise convicted as is abovesaid, imprisonment for one whole year; and for the third

The penalties for being present at any other common prayer or sacraments. Altered as to the penalty by 1 El. c. 2. s. 7, 8.

offence in like manner, imprisonment during his or their lives. (3) And for the more knowledge to be given hereof, and better observation of this law, be it enacted by the authority aforesaid, That all and singular curates shall upon one *Sunday* every quarter of the year during one whole year next following the aforesaid feast of *All Saints* next coming, read this present act in the church at the time of the most assembly, and likewise once in every year following; at the same time declaring unto the people by the authority of the scripture, how the mercy and goodness of God hath in all ages been shewed to his people in their necessities and extremities, by means of hearty and faithful prayers made to Almighty God, especially where people be gathered together with one faith and mind, to offer up their hearts by prayer, as the best sacrifices that christian men can yield. (*This act is repealed by* 1 *Ma. Sess.* 2. *c.* 2. *which is repealed by* 1 *El. c.* 2. *&* 1 *Jac.* 1. *c.* 28. *s.* 48. *And this act is now made perpetual by* 5 *Ann. c.* 5. *as to the establishment of the church.*)

CAP. XII.

An act touching the declaration of a statute made for the marriage of priests, and for the legitimation of their children.

<small>The marriage of priests and other spiritual persons shall be adjudged lawful. 2 & 3 Ed. 6. c. 21.</small>

Albeit that at the session of this parliament holden by prorogation at Westminster *the fourth day of* November *in the second year of the reign of the King's majesty that now is, it was ordained and enacted by the authority of the same parliament, That all and every law and laws positive, canons, constitutions and ordinances before that made by the authority of man only, which then did prohibit and forbid marriage to any ecclesiastical and spiritual person or persons, of what estate, condition, or degree they then were, or by what name or names soever they then were called, which by God's law might lawfully marry, and all and every article, branch and sentence concerning only the prohibition for the marriage of the persons aforesaid, should be utterly void and of none effect:* (2) *and that all manner of forfeitures, pains, penalties, crimes or actions, which were in the said laws contained, or of the same did follow, concerning the prohibition for the marriage of the persons aforesaid, should be clearly and utterly void, frustrate and of none effect, to all intents, constructions and purposes, as well concerning marriage afore that time made by any of the ecclesiastical or spiritual persons aforesaid, as also such which thereafter should be duly and lawfully had, celebrated and made betwixt the persons which by the laws of*

God might lawfully marry: (3) yet since the making of the said act, divers evil disposed persons perversely taking occasion of certain words and sentences in the same act comprised, have and do untruly and very slanderously report of priests matrimony, saying that the same statute is but a permission of priests matrimony, as usury and other unlawful things be now permitted, for the eschewing of greater inconvenience and evils, so that thereby the lawful matrimony of priests, in the opinion of many, and the children procreate and born in such lawful matrimony rather be of a greater number of the King's subjects accounted as bastards, than lawfully born, to the great slander, peril and disherison of such children: (4) which untrue slanderous reproach of holy matrimony doth not only redound to the high dishonour of Almighty God, but also to the King's majesty's dishonour, and his high court of parliament, and the learned clergy of this realm, who have determined the same to be most lawful by the law of God in their convocation, as well by their common assent, as by the subscription of their hands: (5) and that most of all is to be lamented, through such uncomly railings of matrimony and slanderous reproaches of the clergy, the word of God is not heard with reverence, followed with diligence, the godly proceedings of the King's majesty not received with due obedience, and thereby the wealthy men of this realm discouraged to nourish and bring up their children in learning, so as it is to be feared, lest in place of good learning and knowledge shall creep in ignorance, and for learned men, unlearned ambitious men and flatterers, to the great displeasure of Almighty God, and to the peril of the whole state of God's true religion within this realm, if speedy remedy be not provided herein:*

II. Therefore it is enacted by the King our sovereign lord, with the assent of the lords spiritual and temporal; and the commons, in this present parliament assembled, and by the authority of the same parliament, That the matrimony of all and every priest and other ecclesiastical and spiritual person and persons heretofore had, celebrated and made, and the matrimony of every priest and other ecclesiastical and spiritual person, which shall hereafter duly be had, celebrated and made, shall be adjudged, deemed and taken for true, just and lawful matrimony, to all intents, constructions and purposes: (2) and that all and every children and child born in any such matrimony, shall be deemed, judged, reputed and taken to all intents, constructions and purposes, to be born in lawful matrimony, and to be legitimate and inheritable to lands, tenements and other hereditaments, from and by any of their fathers, mothers and other ancestors, in like

Priests children shall be legitimate, and inherit their ancestors lands.

manner and form, to all intents, constructions and purposes, as any other children born in lawful matrimony betwixt any of the King's lay-subjects be inheritable : (3) and that by the authority aforesaid, as well all and every priest and other ecclesiastical and spiritual person and persons be and shall be enabled to be tenants by the curtesy, after the death of their wives, of such lands, tenements and other hereditaments as their wives shall happen to be seised of, of estate in fee-simple or estate in fee-tail general, during the spousals ; (4) as also every wife of every such priest and other ecclesiastical person, shall be enabled to claim, demand, have and enjoy dower of the lands, tenements and other hereditaments, whereof her husband during the espousals between them was seised, of estate in fee-simple or fee-tail general in his own right, in like manner and form, to all intents, constructions and purposes, as any other husband or wife may or might claim, demand, have or enjoy ; any law, statute, ordinance, canon, constitution, prescription or custom had, made, exercised or used in this realm, to the contrary in any wise notwithstanding.

Priests shall be tenants by the courtesy, and their wives endowable of their lands.

III. Provided alway, That this act, nor any thing therein contained, shall extend to give liberty to any person to marry without asking in the church, or without the ceremonies according to the book of common prayer and administration of the sacraments, (2) nor shall make any such matrimony already made, or hereafter to be made, good, which are prohibited by the law of God for any other cause.

Asking in the church.

IV. Provided also, That this act, nor any thing therein contained, shall extend to alter, change, revoke, repeal or otherwise to disannul any decree, judgment or sentence of divorce heretofore had or made, or to change or alter the possession or inheritance of any lands or tenements already descended ; but that they and every of them shall remain, continue and be of such like force, effect, strength and degree, to all intents, constructions and purposes, as they were before the making of this act ; this act or any thing therein contained to the contrary in any wise notwithstanding. REP. 1 *M. sess.* 2. *c.* 2. *and made perpetual by* 1 *Jac.* 1. *c.* 25. *s.* 50.

Divorces already made.

1 SESS. 1 MARY.

Cap. I.

An act repealing and taking away certain treasons, felonies and cases of premunire.

Forasmuch as the state of every King, ruler and governor of any realm, dominion or commonalty, standeth and consisteth more assured by the love and favour of the subject toward their sovereign ruler and governor, than in the dread and fear of laws made with rigorous pains and extreme punishment for not obeying of their sovereign ruler and governor: (2) *and laws also justly made for the preservation of the commonweal, without extreme punishment or great penalty, are more often for the most part obeyed and kept, than laws and statutes made with great and extreme punishments, and in special such laws and statutes so made, whereby not only the ignorant and rude unlearned people, but also learned and expert people, minding honesty, are often and many times trapped and snared, yea many times for words only, without other fact or deed done or perpetrated:* The state of a King standeth more assuredly by the love of his subjects than in fear of laws.

II. *The Queen's most excellent Majesty, calling to remembrance that many, as well honourable and noble persons, as other of good reputation within this her Grace's realm of* England, *have of late (for words only, without other opinion, fact or deed) suffered shameful death not accustomed to nobles; her Highness therefore of her accustomed clemency and mercy, minding to avoid and put away the occasion and cause of like chances hereafter to ensue, trusting her loving subjects will, for her clemency to them shewed, love, serve, and obey her Grace the more heartily and faithfully, than for dread or fear of pains of body, is contented and pleased that the severity of such like extreme, dangerous and painful laws, shall be abolished, annulled and made frustrate and void.*

III. Be it therefore ordained and enacted by the Queen our sovereign lady, with the assent of the lords spiritual and temporal, and of the commons, in this present parliament assembled, and by the authority of the same, That from henceforth none act, deed or offence, being by act of parliament or statute made treason, petty treason or misprision of treason, by words, writing, ciphering, deeds or otherwise whatsoever, shall be taken, had, deemed or adjudged to be high treason, petty treason or misprision of treason, but only such as be declared and expressed to be treason, petty treason or misprision of treason, in or by the act of No act or offence shall be treason, petty treason or misprision, but such as be declared by the stat. of 25 Ed. 3. stat. 5. c. 2.

parliament or statute made in the xxv. year of the reign of the most noble King of famous memory, King *Edward* the Third, touching or concerning treason or the declarations of treasons, and none other; (2) nor that any pains of death, penalty or forfeiture in any wise ensue or be to any offender or offenders, for the doing or committing any treason, petty treason or misprision of treason, other than such as be in the said estatute made in the said xxv. year of the reign of the said King *Edward* the Third, ordained and provided; any act or acts of parliament, statute or statutes, had or made at any time heretofore, or after the said xxv. year of the reign of the said late King *Edward* the Third, or any other declaration or matter to the contrary in any wise notwithstanding.

<small>Certain persons exempted out of the benefit of this statute.</small>

IV. Provided always, and be it ordained and enacted by the authority aforesaid, That this act of parliament, or any thing therein mentioned, shall not in any wise extend to give any manner of benefit, advantage or commodity to any person or persons, being the last day of *September* last past arrested or imprisoned for treason, petty treason or misprision of treason, or to any person or persons heretofore being indicted of treason, petty treason or misprision of treason, or being outlawed or attainted of treason, petty treason or misprision of treason, before the said last day of *September* last past, or being commanded to keep his or their house or houses, or other men's houses, or otherwise excepted out of the Queen's highness most gracious pardon given the day of her coronation, but that they and every of them, for any the offences before mentioned perpetrated, committed or done by them or any of them, before the said last day of *September*, shall suffer such pains of death, losses and forfeitures of lands and goods, as in cases of treason, as though this act had never been had ne made; any thing in this act to the contrary in any wise notwithstanding.

<small>All offences made felony or in the case of premunire, since anno 1 H. 8. repealed.</small>

V. And be it further ordained and enacted by the authority aforesaid, That all offences made felony, or limited or appointed to be within the case of *premunire*, by any act or acts of parliament, statute or statutes, made sithence the first day of the first year of the reign of the late King of famous memory, King *Henry* the Eighth, not being felony before, nor within the case of *premunire*, and also all and every branch, article and clause mentioned or in any wise declared in any of the same estatutes, concerning the making of any offence or offences to be felony, or within the case of *premunire*, not being felony nor within the case of *premunire* before, and all pains and forfeitures concerning the same, or any of them, shall from henceforth be repealed, and utterly void and of none effect.

2 SESS. 1 MARY.
Cap. II.

A repeal of the stat. of 1 Ed. 6. c. 1. made against such as shall speak unreverently of the body and blood of Christ, and of the stat. of 1 Ed. 6. c. 2. touching the election of bishops, and the stat. of 2 Ed. 6. c. 1. concerning the uniformity of service, and administration of the sacraments, and of the stat. of 2 & 3 Ed. 6. c. 21. made to take away all positive laws ordained against the marriage of priests, and of the stat. of 3 & 4 Ed. 6. c. 10. made for the abolishing of divers books and images, and the stat. of 3 & 4 Ed. 6. c. 12. made for the ordering of ecclesiastical ministers, and of the stat. of 5 & 6 Ed. 6. c. 1. made for the uniformity of common prayer and administration of the sacraments, and of the stat. of 5 & 6 Ed. 6. c. 3. made for the keeping of holy-days and fasting-days, and of the stat. of 5 & 6 Ed. 6. c. 12. touching the marriage of priests and legitimation of their children. All such divine service and administration of sacraments as were most commonly used in England in the last year of Hen. 8. shall be used through the realm, after the 20th day of December, *Anno Dom.* 1553. and no other kind of service nor administration of sacraments. 1 El. c. 2. Repealed by 1 Jac. 1. c. 25. s. 48.

1 & 2 PHILIP AND MARY.
Cap. VI.

A reviver of the statute of 5 R. 2. stat. 2. c. 5. concerning arresting of heretical preachers, and of the statute of 2 H. 4. c. 15. touching repressing of heresies and punishment of hereticks, and of the statute of 2 H. 5. c. 7. concerning the enormity of heresy and lollardy, and the suppression thereof. Repealed by 1 El. c. 1. s. 15.

Cap. VIII.

An act repealing all articles and provisions made against the see apostolick of Rome, *since the twentieth year of King* Henry *the Eighth, and for the establishment of all spiritual and ecclesiastical possessions and hereditaments conveyed to the laity.*

Whereas since the twentieth year of King Henry *the Eighth of famous memory, father unto your Majesty our most natural*

All statutes against the see of Rome repealed.

sovereign, and gracious lady and Queen, much false and erroneous doctrine hath been taught, preached and written, partly by divers the natural born subjects of this realm, and partly being brought in hither from sundry other foreign countries, hath been sowen and spread abroad within the same: (2) by reason whereof, as well the spiritualty as the temporalty of your Highness realms and dominions have swerved from the obedience of the see apostolick, and declined from the unity of Christ's church, and so have continued, until such time as your Majesty being first raised up by God, and set in the seat royal over us, and then by his divine and gracious providence, knit in marriage with the most noble and virtuous prince the King our sovereign lord your husband, the pope's holiness and the see apostolick sent hither unto your majesties (as unto persons undefiled, and by God's goodness preserved from the common infection aforesaid) and to the whole realm, the most reverend father in God the lord cardinal Pool, *legate* de latere, *to call us home again into the right way from whence we have all this long while wandered and strayed abroad; (3) and we, after sundry long and grievous plagues and calamities, seeing by the goodness of God our own errors, have knowledged the same unto the said most reverend father, and by him have been and are the rather at the contemplation of your Majesties received and embraced into the unity and bosom of Christ's church, and upon our humble submission and promise made for a declaration of our repentance, to repeal and abrogate such acts and statutes as have been made in parliament since the said twentieth year of the said King Henry the Eighth, against the supremacy of the see apostolick, as in our submission exhibited to the said most reverend father in God by your Majesties appeareth: the tenor whereof ensueth.*

[Margin: Much false doctrine hath been preached and written since the xx. year of King Hen. 8. Cardinal Pool sent from Rome to call the realm into the right way from whence it hath strayed.]

II. *We the lords spiritual and temporal and the commons, assembled in this present parliament, representing the whole body of the realm of* England, *and the dominions of the same, in the name of our selves particularly, and also of the said body universally, in this our supplication directed to your Majesties, with most humble suit, that it may by your Grace's intercession and mean be exhibited to the most reverend father in God, the lord cardinal* Pool, *legate, sent specially hither from our most holy father pope* July the Third, *and the see apostolick of* Rome, *do declare ourselves very sorry and repentant of the schism and disobedience committed in this realm and dominions aforesaid against the said see apostolick, either by making, agreeing or executing any laws, ordinances or commandments, against the supremacy of the said see, or otherwise doing or speaking, that might impugne the same: (2) offering ourselves and*

[Margin: The suplication of the parliament to the King and Queen to be a mean to reduce them into the catholick church.]

promising by this our supplication, that for a token and knowledge of our said repentance, we be and shall be always ready, under and with the authorities of your Majesties, to the uttermost of our powers, to do that shall lie in us for the abrogation and repealing of the said laws and ordinances in this present parliament, as well for ourselves as for the whole body whom we represent : (3) *whereupon we most humbly desire your Majesties, as personages undefiled in the offence of this body towards the said see, which nevertheless God by his providence hath made subject to you, so to set forth this our most humble suit, that we may obtain from the see apostolick, by the said most reverend father, as well particularly and generally, absolution, release and discharge from all danger of such censures and sentences, as by the laws of the church we be fallen into ;* (4) *and that we may as children repentant be received into the bosom and unity of Christ's church, so as this noble realm, with all the members thereof, may in this unity and perfect obedience to the see apostolick and popes for the time being, serve God and your Majesties, to the furtherance and advancement of his honour and glory.* (5) *We are at the intercession of your Majesties, by the authority of our holy father pope* July the Third *and of the see apostolick, assoiled, discharged and delivered from excommunications, interdictions and other censures ecclesiastical, which hath hanged over our heads for our said defaults since the time of the said schism mentioned in our supplication :* (6) *it may now like your Majesties, that for the accomplishment of our promise made in the said supplication, that is, to repeal all laws and statutes made contrary to the said supremacy and see apostolick, during the said schism, the which is to be understood since the xx. year of the reign of the said late King* Henry *the Eighth, and so the said lord legate doth accept and recognise the same.*

A repeal of all statutes made against the supremacy and see apostolick since the time of the schism.

III. *Where in the Parliament begun and holden at* Westminster *in the xxi. year of the reign of the late King of famous memory, King* Henry *the Eighth, one act was then and there made against pluralities of benefices, for taking of ferms by spiritual men and for non-residence, in the which act, amongst other things, it was ordained and enacted, That if any person or persons, at any time after the first day of* April *in the year of our Lord God one thousand five hundred and thirty, contrary to the same act, should procure and obtain at the court of* Rome, *or elsewhere, any licence or licences, union, toleration, or dispensation, to receive and take any more benefices with cure than was limited and appointed by the same act, or else at any time after the said day should put in execution any such licence toleration or dispensation before that*

The statute of 21 H. 8. c. 13. made against pluralities of benefices, taking of ferms by spiritual men, and non-residence.

time obtained contrary to the said act, that then every such person or persons so after the said day suing for himself, or receiving and taking such benefice by force of such licence or licences, union, toleration or dispensation, that is to say, the same person or persons only, and no other, should for every such default incur the danger, pain and penalty of twenty pound sterling, and should also lose the whole profits of every such benefice or benefices, as he receiveth or taketh by force of any such licence or licences, union, toleration or dispensation: (2) and where also in the said act it was ordained and enacted, That if any person or persons did procure or obtain at the court of Rome, or elsewhere any manner of licence or dispensation to be non-resident at their dignities, prebend or benefices, contrary to the said act, that then every such person or persons putting in execution any such dispensation or licence for himself, from the said first day of April in the year of our Lord God MDXXX, should run and incur the penalty, damage and pain of xx. l. sterling for every time so doing, to be forfeited and recovered as by the said act is declared, and yet such licence or dispensation so procured, or to be put in execution, to be void and of none effect, as by the same act more plainly it doth and may appear.

A repeal of so much of the statute of 21 H. 8. c. 13, as is abovementioned.

IV. Be it enacted by the authority of this present parliament, That as much only of the said act as concerneth the articles and clauses aforesaid, and all and every the words and sentences contained in the said act, concerning the said articles and clauses, and every of them, shall from henceforth be repealed, adnulled, revoked, annihilated and utterly made void for ever; any thing in the said act to the contrary in any wise notwithstanding.

23 H. 8. c. 9.

V. And where also at the session of the same parliament holden upon prorogation in the xxiii. year of the reign of the said late King Henry the Eighth, one act entituled, The act that no person shall be cited out of the diocese where he or she dwelleth, except in certain cases;

24 H. 8. c. 12.

VI. And where also at the said parliament, in the session holden at Westminster upon prorogation in the xxiv. year of the reign of the said late King Henry the Eighth, one act was made, that appeals in such cases as hath been used to be pursued to the see of Rome, should not from henceforth be had or used, but within this realm;

21 H. 8. c. 20.

VII. And where also at the said parliament holden at Westminster in the xxi. year of the reign of the said late King Henry the Eighth, and there continued by divers prorogations until the xiv. day of April in the xxvii. year of his reign, one act was made

APPENDIX

concerning restraints of payments of annates and first-fruits of archbishopricks and bishopricks to the see of Rome.

VIII. *And where at a session of the said parliament holden in the five and twentieth year of the reign of the said late King, there was also one act made, entituled, The submission of the clergy to the King's majesty.* 25 H. 8. c. 19.

IX. *And one other act, entituled, one act restraining the said payments of annates or first-fruits to the bishop of* Rome, *and of the electing and consecrating of the archbishops and bishops within this realm.* 25 H. 8. c. 20.

X. *And one other act was then and there made, entituled, An act concerning the exoneration of the King's subjects from exactions and impositions before that time payed to the see of* Rome, *and for having licences and dispensations within this realm, without suing further for the same.* 25 H. 8. c. 21.

XI. Be it enacted by the authority of this present parliament, That the said several acts made for the restraint of payments of the said annates and first-fruits, and all other the said acts made in the said twenty-fourth and twenty-fifth years of the reign of the said late King, and every of them, and all and every branch, article, matter and sentence in them and every of them contained, shall be by authority of this present parliament from henceforth utterly void, made frustrate and repealed to all intents, constructions and purposes. A repeal of the before recited statutes.

XII. And be it further enacted by the authority of this present parliament, That all and every these acts following, that is to say, one act made at the session of the said parliament holden upon prorogation at *Westminster* in the xxvi. year of the reign of the said late King *Henry* the Eighth, entituled, An act concerning the King's highness to be supreme head of the church of *England*, and to have authority to reform and redress all errors, heresies and abuses in the same; 26 H. 8. c. 1.

XIII. And one other act made in the same session of the same parliament, entituled, An act for nomination and consecration of suffragans within this realm; 26 H. 8. c. 14.

XIV. And one other act made in the xxvii. year of the reign of the said late King *Henry* the Eighth, entituled, An act whereby the King should have power to nominate thirty-two persons of his clergy and lay-fee for the making of ecclesiastical laws. 27 H. 8. c. 15.

XV. And also one other act made at the parliament holden at *Westminster* in the eight and twentieth year of the reign of the said late King *Henry* the Eighth, entituled, An act extinguishing the authority of the bishop of Rome; 28 H. 8. c. 10.

28 H. 8. c. 16.	XVI. And also one other act made in the same parliament, entituled, An act for the release of such as then had obtained pretended licences and dispensations from the see of *Rome*;
28 H. 8. c. 7.	XVII. And also all that part of the act made in the said eight and twentieth year of the said King, entituled, An act for the establishment of the succession of the imperial crown of the realm, that concerneth a prohibition to marry within the degrees expressed in the said act;
31 H. 8. c. 9.	XVIII. And also one other act made at the parliament holden at *Westminster* in the one and thirtieth year of the reign of the said late King *Henry* the Eighth, entituled, An act authorising the King's highness to make bishops by his letters patents;
32 H. 8. c. 38.	XIX. And one other act made in the session of the same parliament, begun in the said one and thirtieth year, holden upon prorogation the two and thirtieth year of the reign of the said King *Henry* the Eighth, entituled, An act concerning pre-contracts of marriages, and touching degrees of consanguinity;
35 H. 8. c. 3.	XX. And one other act made in the parliament holden at *Westminster* in the xxxv. year of the reign of the said late King *Henry* the Eighth, entituled, an act for the ratification of the King's majesty's style; (2) shall henceforth be repealed, made frustrate, void and of none effect;
35 H. 8. c. 1.	XXI. *And where also at the said parliament holden at Westminster in the five and thirtieth year of the reign of the said late King Henry the Eighth, one other act was made, entituled, An act concerning the stablishment of the succession of the said King in the imperial crown of this realm: in the which act there is a form of a corporal oath devised and set forth, that every subject of this realm should be bound to take, against the power, authority and jurisdiction of the see of* Rome: (2) be it enacted by the authority of this present parliament, That so much of the said act as toucheth the said oath against the supremacy, and all oaths thereupon had, made and given, shall be from henceforth utterly void, repealed and of none effect.
37 H.8.c.17. A repeal of the statute last before recited.	XXII. And where also one other act was made in the seven and thirtieth year of the reign of the said late King Henry the Eighth, entituled, An act that doctors of the civil law, being married, might exercise ecclesiastical jurisdiction: (2) be it enacted by the authority of this present parliament, That the said act last before mentioned, and all and every branch, article, sentence and matter contained in the same, shall from henceforth be repealed and utterly made void and of none effect.

XXIII. *And where one other act was made at the first session of the parliament holden at* Westminster *in the first year of the reign of King* Edward *the sixth, entituled, An act for the repeal of certain statutes concerning treasons, felonies, &c. In which act, amongst other things, there is contained certain provisions, pains, penalties and forfeitures, for and against such as should by open preachings, express words, sayings, writing, printing, overt-deed or act, affirm or set forth, that the King of this realm, for the time being, is not or ought not to be the supream head on earth of the churches of* England *and* Ireland, *ne of any of them, or that the bishop of* Rome *or any other person or persons, other than the King of* England *for the time being, is or ought to be supream head of the same churches, or any of them, as in the same act last before rehearsed more at large is contained and may appear:* (2) be it enacted by the authority of this present parliament, That these clauses before rehearsed, and other of the said act concerning the supremacy, and all and every branch, article words and sentences in the same, sounding or tending to the derogation of the supremacy of the pope's holiness, or the see of *Rome*, and all pains, penalties and forfeitures made against them that should by any means set forth and extol the said supremacy, shall be from henceforth utterly void, and of none effect.

<small>A repeal of part of the statute of 1 Ed. 6. c. 12. s. 7. hereafter specified.</small>

XXIV. And be it further enacted by the authority aforesaid, That all clauses, sentences and articles of every other statute or act of parliament, made sithence the said twentieth year of the reign of King *Henry* the Eighth, against the supream authority of the pope's holiness, or see apostolick of *Rome*, or containing any other matter of the same effect only, that is repealed in any of the statutes aforesaid, shall be also by authority hereof from henceforth utterly void, frustrate and of none effect.

<small>A repeal of all statutes made against the supremacy of the pope or see apostolick.</small>

(2) *And where we your most humble subjects, the lords spiritual and temporal, and commons, in this present parliament assembled, have exhibited to your Majesties one other supplication in form following:*

XXV. *We the lords spiritual and temporal, and the commons, in this present parliament assembled, representing the whole body of this realm, reduced and received by your Majesties intercession to the unity of Christ's church, and the obedience of the see apostolick of* Rome, *and the pope's holiness governing the same, make most humble suit unto your Majesties to be likewise means and intercessors, that all occasions of contention, hatred, grudge, suspicion and trouble, both outwardly and inwardly in mens con-*

<small>A supplication by the parliament that these articles may be confirmed.</small>

sciences, which might arise amongst us by reason of disobedience, may by authority of the pope's holiness, and by ministration of the same unto us by the most reverend father in God the lord Cardinal Pool, by dispensation, toleration or permission respectively, as the case shall require, be abolished and taken away, and by authority sufficient these articles following, and generally all others, when any occasion shall require, may be provided for and confirmed.

<small>Ecclesiastical foundations made sithence the schism shall continue.</small>

XXVI. *First, That all bishopricks, cathedral churches, hospitals, colleges, schools and other such foundations now continuing, made by authority of parliament, or otherwise established according to the order of the laws of this realm, sithence the schism, may be confirmed and continued for ever.*

<small>Marriages.</small>

XXVII. *Item, That marriages made* infra gradus prohibitos consanguinitatis, affinitatis, cognationis spiritualis, *or which might be made void* propter impedimentum publicæ honestatis, justitiæ, *or for any other cause prohibited by the canons only, may be confirmed, and children born of those marriages declared legitimate, so as those marriages were made according to the laws of the realm for the time being, and be not directly against the laws of God, nor in such case as the see apostolick hath not used to dispence withal.*

<small>Institutions of benefices and dispensations.</small>

XXVIII. *That institutions of benefices, and other promotions ecclesiastical, and dispensations made according to the form of the act of parliament, may be likewise confirmed.*

<small>Judicial processes made upon appeals.</small>

XXIX. *That all judicial process made before any ordinaries of this realm, or before any delegates upon any appeals, according to the order of the laws of this realm, may be likewise ratified and confirmed.*

<small>The lands and goods of bishopricks, monasteries, chantries, dispersed, shall so continue.</small>

XXX. *And finally, where certain acts and statutes have been made in the time of the late schism, concerning the lands and hereditaments of archbishopricks and bishopricks, the suppression and dissolution of monasteries, abbeys, priories, chantries, colleges, and all other the goods and chattels of religious houses; since the which time the right and dominion of certain lands and hereditaments, goods and chattels, belonging to the same, be dispersed abroad, and come to the hands and possessions of divers and sundry persons, who by gift, purchase, exchange, and other means, according to the order of the laws and statutes of this realm for the time being, have the same:* (2) *for the avoiding all scruples that might grow by any the occasions aforesaid, or by any other ways or means whatsoever, it may please your Majesties to be intercessors and mediators to the said most reverend father Cardinal Pool, that all such causes and quarrels, as by pretence of the said schism, or by any other occasion or mean whatsoever might be moved by the pope's holiness or see apostolick, or by any other jurisdiction ecclesiastical, may be utterly removed and taken away; (3) so as all persons having sufficient conveyance of the said lands and hereditaments, goods and chattels as is aforesaid, by the common laws, acts or statutes of this realm, may without scruple of conscience enjoy them without impeachment or trouble by pretence of any general council, canons or ecclesiastical laws, and clear from all dangers of the censures of the church.*

XXXI. *And conformably hereunto, the bishops and clergy of the province of* Canterbury *have presented to your Majesties a supplication in this tenor that followeth.*

(2) Nos episcopi & clerus Cantuariensis provinciæ in hac synodo more nostro solito, dum Regni parliamentum celebratur, congregati, cum omni debita humilitate & reverentia, exponimus Majestatibus vestris, quod licet ecclesiarum quibus in episcopos, decanos, archidiaconos, rectores & vicarios præfecti sumus, & animarum, quæ & nobis curæ nostræ subjectæ sunt, & earundum bonorum, jurisdictionum & jurium, ex sacrorum canonum dispositione, defensores & curatores constituti sumus, & propterea ipsarum bona, jurisdictiones, & jura in pernicioso hujus Regni præterito schismate deperdita & amissa, omni studio, & totis nostris viribus recuperare, & ad pristinum ecclesiarum jus revocare, juris remediis niti demeremus: (3) nihilominus tamen habito prius per nos super hac re maturo consilio, & deliberatione, ingenue fatemur nos optime cognoscere quam hæc bonorum ecclesiasticorum difficilis & quasi impossibilis esset recuperatio, propter multiplices ac pene inextricabiles super his habitos contractus & dispositiones, & quod si ea tentaretur, quies & tranquillitas Regni facile perturbaretur, & unitas ecclesiæ catholicæ, quæ jam pietate & authoritate Majestatum vestrarum, hoc in regno introducta est, cum maxima difficultate suum debitum progressum & finem sortiri posset: (4) Ideo nos bonum & quietem publicam privatis commoditatibus, & salutem tot animarum pretioso *Christi* sanguine redemptarum terrenis bonis anteponentes, & non quæ nostra sed quæ *Jesu Christi* sunt quærentes, Majestates vestras enixe rogamus, easque humiliter supplicamus, ut reverendissimo in *Christo* patri domino *Reginaldo* Cardinali *Polo*, ad ipsas & universum hoc *Angliæ* regnum sanctissimi domini nostri, domini *Julii* papæ tertii, & apostolicæ sedis de latere legato, hæc nomine nostro insinuari, & apud eum intercedere dignentur, ut in his bonis ecclesiasticis, in parte vel in toto, arbitrio suo juxta facultates

<small>The clergy's petition that the lands and goods of the clergy, late dispersed amongst the temporalty, might so remain.</small>

<small>The clergy do prefer the publick peace before their private commodity.</small>

sibi ab eodem sanctissimo domino nostro papa concessas, eorundem bonorum detentoribus, elargiendis & relaxandis, publicum bonum privato, pacem & tranquillitatem dissidiis & perturbationibus, atque animarum salutem bonis terrenis præferre & anteponere velit. (5) Nos enim in omnibus quæ ab ipso legato statuta & ordinata circa hæc bona fuerint, exnunc, prout extunc, & econtra consensum nostrum præstamus, imo etiam & in præmissis se difficilem aut restrictum reddere non velit, Majestates vestræ nostro nomine eum hortari, & rogare dignabuntur. (6) Insuper Majestatibus vestris supplicamus ut pro sua pietate efficere dignentur, ut ea quæ ad jurisdictionem nostram et libertatem ecclesiasticam pertinent, sine quibus debitum nostri pastoralis officii & curæ animarum nobis commissæ exercere non possumus, nobis superiorum temporum injuria ablata, restituantur, & ea nobis & ecclesiæ perpetuo illæsa & salvum permaneant, & ut omnes leges, quæ hanc nostram jurisdictionem & libertatem ecclesiasticam tollunt, seu quovis modo impediunt, abrogentur, ad honorem Dei & Majestatum vestrarum, & universi hujus regni spirituale & temporale commodum & salutem ; (7) certam spem etiam habentes, Majestates vestras, pro sua singulari in ipsum Deum pietate, proque multis & insignibus, ab ipsius Dei bonitate acceptis beneficiis, necessitatibus, & incommodis hujus sui regni ecclesiarum, maxime curam animarum habentium, nunquam defuturas esse, sed prout opus fuerit, consulturas atque provisuras.

The clergy's suit that ecclesiastical jurisdiction may be restored unto them, and that all laws which do hinder it may be abrogated.

XXXII. *Forasmuch as the said most reverend father the lord legate, at the intercession of your Majesties, hath by the authority of the see apostolick sufficiently dispensed in the matters specified in the said several supplications, as in his said letters of dispensation is contained more at large : The tenor whereof ensueth.*

[Here follows the dispensation.]

(23) We the said lords spiritual and temporal, and the commons in this present parliament assembled, rendring most humble thanks to your Majesties, by whose intercession and means we have obtained the said dispensations of the pope's holiness, by the said most reverend father in God, his legate, most humbly beseech the same, that it may be ordained as followeth :

The cardinal's dispensation confirmed by parliament.

XXXIII. And therefore be it enacted by the authority of this present parliament, That all and singular articles and clauses contained in the said dispensation, as well touching the establishment of bishopricks and cathedral churches, (2) as also the confirmation of marriages in degrees prohibited by the canons of the church, the legitimation of children, (3) and the ratification of

APPENDIX 373

process, and of sentences in matters ecclesiastical, touching
the invalidity of them for want of jurisdiction, (4) and the institutions and destitutions of and in benefices and promotions
ecclesiastical, dispensations and graces given by such order as
the publick laws of the realm then approved, (5) and all other
things before contained in the said letters of dispensations, (6)
shall remain and be reputed and taken to all intents and constructions in the laws of this realm, lawful, good and effectual,
to be alledged and pleaded in all courts ecclesiastical and temporal, for good and sufficient matter, either for the plaintiff or
defendant, without any allegation or objection to be made
against the validity of them, by pretence of any general council,
canon or decree to the contrary made or to be made in that behalf.

XXXIV. *And whereas divers and sundry late monasteries,* Monasteries, and all their lands and heredita-ments were given to King Hen. 8. by the statutes made 27 H. 8. c. 28. and 31 H. 8. c. 13.
priories, commandries, nunneries, deanaries, prebends, colleges,
hospitals, houses of friers, chantries, and other religious and
ecclesiastical houses and places, and the manors, granges, messuages,
lands, tenements, rectories, tithes, pensions, portions, vicarages,
churches, chapels, advowsons, nominations, patronages, annuities,
rents, reversions, services, and other possessions and hereditaments
to the said late monasteries, priories, nunneries, commandries,
deanaries, chantries, prebends, houses of friers, colleges, hospitals,
and other religious and ecclesiastical houses and places, and sundry
archbishopricks and bishopricks within this realm, late appertaining
and belonging, came as well to the hands and possessions of the
said King of famous memory, Henry *the Eighth, father unto your*
Majesty our said sovereign Lady, by dissolution, gift, grant,
surrender, attainder or otherwise, as also to the hands and possession
of divers and sundry other persons, and bodies politick and cor-
porate, by sundry means, conveyances and assurances, according to
the order of the laws and statutes of this realm.

XXXV. *And where also divers manors, lands, tenements and* Chantries, colleges, free chapels and their lands, given to King Ed. 6. The statute of 1 Ed. 6. c. 14.
hereditaments, parcel of the possessions of archbishopricks and
bishopricks, and many and sundry late deanaries, colleges, chantries,
rectories, prebends, free chapels, guilds and fraternities, manors,
houses, granges, lands, tenements, rents, services, and other ecclesi-
astical possessions and hereditaments, goods and chattels to the said
archbishopricks, bishopricks, deanaries, colleges, chantries, free
chapels, rectories, guilds and fraternities, late appertaining and
belonging, or appointed to and for the finding of priests, obits,
lights, or other like purpose, came as well to the hands and possessions
of the said late noble King Edward *the Sixth, brother unto your*
Majesty our sovereign Lady, by virtue of an act of parliament

thereof made, or otherwise; as also to the hands and possession of divers and sundry other persons, and bodies politick and corporate, by sundry means, conveyances and assurances, according to the order of the laws of this realm; (2) a great number of which said late monasteries, priories, nunneries, commandries, deanaries, colleges, hospitals, prebends, chantries, free chapels, guilds and fraternities, and the manors, granges, messuages, lands, tenements, rents, reversions, services, tithes, pensions, portions, vicarages, churches, chapels, advowsons, nominations, patronages, annuities and hereditaments, goods and chattels, to the said monasteries, priories, nunneries, commandries, deanaries, colleges, hospitals, chantries, free chapels, guilds, fraternities and other ecclesiastical houses, archbishopricks and bishopricks belonging, as well for great sums of money, as for other good and reasonable causes and considerations, have been conveyed and assured to divers the subjects and bodies politick of this realm, as well by the said King Henry the Eighth, the said King Edward the Sixth, and by your Highness our sovereign Lady, and jointly by both your Majesties, as also by divers the owners of the said ecclesiastical possessions; which said conveyances and assurances by their sundry letters patents and other writings more plainly do and may appear. (3) Forasmuch as the said most reverend father hath also by the said dispensations removed and taken away all matter of impeachment, trouble and danger, which by occasion of any general council, canon or decree ecclesiastical, might touch and disquiet the possessions of such goods moveable lands, tenements, possessions and hereditaments, as were of late belonging to any of the said archbishopricks, bishopricks, monasteries, priories, nunneries, commandries, deanaries, colleges, chantries, prebends, rectories, hospitals, houses of friers, or other religious and ecclesiastical houses and places, of what nature, name, kind, or quality soever they be of; (4) Yet for that the title of all lands, possessions and hereditaments, in this your Majesties realm and dominions, is grounded in the laws, statutes and customs of the same, and by your high jurisdiction, authority royal, and crown imperial, and in your courts only, to be impleaded, ordered, tried and judged, and none otherwise; (5) and understanding that the whole, full, and most gracious intents, mind and determination of your most excellent Majesties be, That all and every person and persons, bodies politick and corporate, their heirs, successors and assigns, and every of them, shall have, keep, retain and enjoy all and every their estates, rights, possessions and interests that they and every of them now have, or hereafter shall have, of and in all and every the manors, granges, messuages, lands, tenements, tithes,

The cardinal's dispensations have only removed all trouble which by any ecclesiastical decree might disquiet the possessions of lands or goods.

The title of all lands is grounded upon the laws of the realm, and to be impleaded and tried only in the King's courts.

pensions, portions, advowsons, nominations, patronages, annuities, rents, reversions, services, hundreds, wapentakes, liberties, franchises, and other the possessions and hereditaments of the said monasteries, abbies, priories, nunneries, commandries, deanaries, colleges, prebends, hospitals, houses of friers, chantries, rectories, vicarages, churches, chapels, archbishopricks, bishopricks, and other religious or ecclesiastical houses or places, or of any of them, within this realm or the dominions of the same, by such laws and statutes as were in force before the first day of this present parliament, and by other lawful conveyance to them thereof made.

XXXVI. That it may be enacted by the authority of this present parliament, That as well your Majesty, sovereign Lady, your heirs and successors, and also all and every other person and persons, bodies politick and corporate, their heirs, successors and assigns, now having, or that hereafter shall have, hold or enjoy any of the scites of the said late monasteries, and other the religious or ecclesiastical houses or places, and all the said manors, granges, messuages, lands, tenements, tithes, pensions, portions, glebe lands, advowsons, nominations, patronages, annuities, rents, reversions, services, hundreds, wapentakes, liberties, franchises, profits, commodities, and other the possessions and hereditaments of the said late monasteries, abbies, priories, nunneries, commandries, deanaries, colleges, prebends, hospitals, houses of friers, rectories, vicarages, chantries, churches, chapels, archbishopricks, bishopricks, and other religious and ecclesiastical houses and places, or of any of them, of what name, nature or kind soever they be, shall have, hold, possess, retain, keep and enjoy all and every the said scites, manors, granges, messuages, lands, tenements, possessions, profits, commodities, and other hereditaments, according to such interests and estates, as they and every of them now have or hold, or hereafter shall have or hold, of and in the same, by the due order, and course of the laws and statutes of this realm, which now be, or were standing in force before the first day of this present parliament, in manner and form as they should have done, if this act had never been had ne made; this act or any thing herein contained to the contrary in any wise notwithstanding.

The Queen and all other shall enjoy such sites of monasteries, &c. and their lands, as they now have or shall have.

XXXVII. Saving to you our said sovereign Lady, your heirs and successors and every of them, and to all and every other person or persons subjects of this realm, and bodies politick and corporate, and to their heirs and successors, and to the heirs and successors of all and every of them (other than such whose right, title or interest is bounded or taken away, undone or extinct by

Other mens titles saved.

any act of parliament heretofore made or otherwise (2) all such right, title, claim, possession, interests, rents, annuities, commodities, commons, offices, fees, leases, liveries, livings, pensions, portions, debts, duties and other profits, which they or any of them lawfully have, or of right ought to have, or might have had, in, of, or to any of the premises, or in, of, or to any part or parcel thereof, in such like manner and form, and condition, to all intents, respects, constructions and purposes, as if this act had never been had ne made.

<small>A confirmation of all statutes concerning the assurance of abbey lands or chantries, &c. of King Hen. 8, King Ed. 6.</small>

XXXVIII. And that it may be further enacted by the authority aforesaid, That all and every article, clause, sentence and proviso, contained or specified in any act or acts of parliament concerning or touching the assurance or conveyance of any the said monasteries, priories, nunneries, commandries, deaneries, prebends, colleges, chantries, hospitals, houses of friers, rectories, vicarages, churches, chapels, archbishopricks, bishopricks and other religious and ecclesiastical houses and places or any of them, or in any wise concerning any manors, lands, tenements, profits, commodities, hereditaments, or other the things before specified to the said King *Henry* the Eighth, or King *Edward* the Sixth or either o them, or any other person or persons, or body politick or corporate and every of them, and all and every writing, deed and instrument concerning the assurance of any the same, shall stand, remain and be in as good force, effect and strength, and shall be pleaded and taken advantage of, to all intents, constructions and purposes, as the same should, might or could have been, by the laws and statutes of this realm, in case this present act had never been had ne made.

<small>A confirmation of assurances to K. Hen. 8. Ed. 6. and all other persons of abbey lands.</small>

XXXIX. And that all feoffments, fines, surrenders, forfeitures, assurances, conveyances, estates and interests in any wise conveyed, had or made to our said late sovereign lord King *Henry* the Eighth, or to our said late sovereign lord King *Edward* the Sixth or either of them, or to any other person or persons, bodies politick or corporate or to any of them, by deed or deeds, act or acts of parliament or otherwise, of any the scites, manors, lands, tenements, possessions, profits, commodities or hereditaments of any of the said archbishopricks, bishopricks, late monasteries, priories, nunneries, commandries, deaneries, houses of friers, colleges, chantries, hospitals, prebends, free chapels, or of any manors, lands, tenements, reversions, services, tithes, pensions, portions, annuities, or of any other hereditaments, of, by or from any ecclesiastical or spiritual person or persons, or by or from any spiritual or ecclesiastical corporation or body politick, shall be as good and available in the law, to all intents, constructions and purposes, as they were by the laws and statutes of this realm standing in force before the first day of this present parliament : (2) and that the same may and shall be pleaded, alledged or taken advantage of, in such sort, and to such effect, as they should, could or might have been by the laws and statutes of this realm standing in force before the said first day of this present parliament ; (3) and that all and every clause and article of saving, contained in all and every the said acts and statutes, shall stand, remain and be in such force, strength and effect, as they were before the said first day of this present parliament ; any thing contained in this present act to the contrary in any wise notwithstanding.

XL. And that it may be in like manner enacted by authority aforesaid, That whosoever shall by any process obtained out of any ecclesiastical court within this realm or without or by pretence of any spiritual jurisdiction or otherwise, contrary to the laws of this realm, inquiet or molest any person or persons or body politick, for any of the said manors, lands, tenements, hereditaments or things above specified, contrary to the words, sentences and meaning of this act, shall incur the danger of the act of *Præmunire*, made the xvi. year of King *Richard* the Second, and shall suffer and incur the forfeitures and pains contained in the same. *The penalty for molesting any person for any abbey lands. This clause is not repealed 16 R. 2. c. 5. 1 El. c. 1. s. 32.*

XLI. Provided alway, That it shall and may be lawful to any person or persons, body politick and corporate, to sue in any competent ecclesiastical or spiritual court within this realm, for tithes, rights and duties that they or any of them shall pretend to have of or out of any the said manors, lands, tenements and other the premisses, and to have full and perfect remedy for the same, in such manner and form as they or any of them might or ought to have done, or had by the laws and statutes of this realm, before the making of this act, and as though this act had never been had or made. *Proviso for suits for tithes of abbey lands.*

XLII. And that it may be further provided and enacted by the authority aforesaid, That albeit the title or stile of supremacy, or supreme head of the church of *England* and of *Ireland*, or either of them, never was, ne could be justly or lawfully attributed or acknowledged to any king and sovereign governor of this realm, nor in any wise could or might rightfully, justly or lawfully by any king or sovereign governor of this realm, be claimed, challenged or used ; (2) yet forasmuch as the said title and stile, sithence the third day of *November* in the xxvi. year of *The title of supreme head of the church never could be justly attributed to any King or governor.*

the reign of the said King *Henry* the Eighth hath been used, and is mentioned and contained in divers and sundry writs, letters patents, records, exemplifications, court-rolls, charters, deeds, instruments, evidences, books and writings; (3) it shall be lawful as well to and for your Majesties and your sovereign Lady's heirs and successors, as to and for every other person and persons, and bodies politick and corporate, at all time and times hereafter, to have, retain and keep the said writs, letters patents, records, exemplifications, court-rolls, charters, deeds, instruments, evidences, books and writings, and them to shew, exhibit, use, alledge and plead, in all times and places requisite or needful, without any danger, penalty, loss, forfeiture, trouble, vexation or impeachment for the same; any thing in this act, or in any other act or acts to the contrary thereof, in any wise notwithstanding.

Writs, letters patents and other writings with the title of supreme head, may be kept and pleaded.

XLIII. *And where your Highness, sovereign lady, since your coming to the crown of this realm, of a good and christian conscience, omitted to write the said stile of supremacy, specified in one act made in the parliament holden at* Westminster *by prorogation in the* xxxv. *year of the reign of your late father King* Henry *the Eighth, as well in gifts, grants, letters patents, as in commissions and other writings, and also other have in their writings done the same, as well in your time as before:* (2) *and forasmuch as notwithstanding any law made concerning the said stile of supremacy, it was in the free choice, liberty and pleasure of the King of this realm, and of your Highness, whether you would express the same in the said stile or not:*

35 H. 8. c. 3.

XLIV. Be it therefore declared and enacted by the authority of this present parliament, That all grants, letters patents, commissions, indictments, records and writings made in your our sovereign Lady's name, or in the names of your sovereign Lord and Lady, or any other wherein the said stile of supremacy is omitted, is and shall be to all intents and purposes, as good and effectual, as if the same had been therein expressed, and may be detained, kept, pleaded and alledged, without any danger, pain, penalty or forfeiture to ensue to any person or persons or body politick, for or concerning the omission of the same stile, or any part thereof, in any such writings; and that no person ne persons shall be impeached, molested or damnified, for or by reason of any such omission.

Writings wherein the Queen's stile of the church is omitted.

XLV. *And where in an act of parliament, made since the said twentieth year of King* Henry *the Eighth, all bulls, dispensations and writings, which were before that time obtained from the*

28 H. 8. c. 16.

see of Rome, should be void, abolished and extinguished, with a clause nevertheless, that the matter of them, by virtue of letters patents from the King then being, should and might be alledged, pleaded and allowed, as if the same had not been so abolished and extinguished; forasmuch as the said act is here before amongst other repealed and made void:

XLVI. Be it therefore enacted by the authority of this present parliament, That all bulls, dispensations and privileges, obtained before the said twentieth year, or at any time sithence, or which shall hereafter be obtained of the see of *Rome*, not containing matter contrary or prejudicial to the authority, dignity or preheminence royal or imperial of the realm, or to the laws of this realm now being in force, and not in this parliament repealed, may be put in execution, used and alledged in any court within this realm or elsewhere, whether the same remain yet whole, or can appear to have been cancelled, in as available and effectual manner, to all intents and purposes, as if the said act had never been had or made; any objection by pretence of extinguishment, or cancelling of the said bulls, dispensations or privileges, or of any other matter or cause by the pretence of the laws of this realm whatsoever, in any wise notwithstanding.

What bulls, dispensations and licences obtained from Rome, may be put in execution.

XLVII. *And whereas by dissolution of monasteries and other religious houses, certain parish churches and chapels which were before exempt from the jurisdiction of the archbishop and bishop of the diocese, and by special exemption and privilege from* Rome *were under the government and order of the abbots and priors of those religious houses; which said churches by colour of the said exemptions, be now of special grant from King* Henry *and King* Edward, *under the rule and government and jurisdiction of temporal and lay-men, who can no more enjoy that supremacy, over those particular churches, than the King might over the whole realm:*

XLVIII. Be it therefore enacted, That all archbishops and bishops in their diocese, and all other spiritual person and persons having jurisdiction, and their ministers and officers, and no lay person or persons, in every church and place within the precinct of the same, being exempt, or not exempt, may freely, and without impediment, execute their spiritual jurisdiction in all points and articles, as though no such exemption or grant had never been made.

Who shall have the jurisdiction of churches and chapels exempt from bishops, &c.

XLIX. Provided alway, and be it enacted, That this act extend not to take away or diminish the privileges of the universities of *Cambridge* and *Oxford*, (2) ne the privileges or pre-

The privileges of certain persons and places reserved.

rogatives granted heretofore to the churches of *Westminster* and *Windsor*, (3) ne the tower of *London*, (4) ne prejudicial to such temporal lords and possessioners in this realm, as by ancient custom have enjoyed probate of testaments of their tenants or other.

<small>By the reconciliation of the realm to God's church, devotion is hoped for.</small>

L. *And forasmuch as after this reconciliation and unity of this noble realm to the body of christ's church, it is to be trusted that by the abundance of God's mercy and grace devotion shall increase and grow in the hearts of many the subjects of this realm, with desire to give and bestow their worldly possessions, for the resuscitating of alms, prayer, and example of good life in this realm, to the intent such godly motions and purposes should be advanced:*

LI. Be it therefore enacted by authority of this present parliament, That it shall be lawful to such as shall be seised of any manors, lands, tenements, parsonages, tithes, pensions, portions or other hereditaments whatsoever, in fee-simple, in possession, reversion or remainder, in their own rights, not being copyhold, may thereof make feoffments, grants or any other assurances, or by his last will and testament in writing may bequeath and give in fee-simple, all and every the said manors, lands, tenements, parsonages, tithes, pensions, portions or other hereditaments, to any spiritual body politick or corporate in this realm, or dominions of the same, now erected or founded, or hereafter to be erected or founded, without any licence of *Mortmain* therein to be obtained, or any writ of ad quod damnum to be sued out for the same; the acts de terris ad manum mortuam non ponendis, or any other act or statute heretofore had or made, in any wise notwithstanding; saving to the lords of the fee all rents services due or going out of any of the said lands, tenements, or hereditaments, so to be amortized as is aforesaid.

<small>Lands may be given to spiritual bodies politick or corporate. Dyer, 255. 11 Co. 72. Hob. 123. 1 Roll. 166, 418.</small>

LII. Provided always, That this clause of this act, for giving the liberty of or for the amortizing of lands or tenements, shall continue for and during the space of twenty years next and immediately following, and no longer.

LIII. *And forasmuch as we your Majesty's humble and obedient subjects, the lords spiritual and temporal, and commons, in this present parliament assembled, neither by the making or delivering of either the supplications aforesaid, nor by any clause, article or sentence thereof, or of any other clause, article or sentence of this or any other statute, or any of the preambles of the same, made or agreed upon in this session of this present parliament, by any manner of interpretation, construction, implication or otherwise, intend to derogate, impair or diminish any of the preroga-*

tives, *liberties, franchises, preheminences or jurisdictions of your crown imperial of this realm, and other the dominions to the same belonging;* (2) we do most humbly beseech your Majesties, that it may be declared and ordained, and be it enacted and declared by authority of this present parliament, That neither the making, exhibiting or inserting in this present statute, or in the preambles of the same, of the supplication or promise aforesaid or either of them, nor any other thing or things, words, sentences, clauses or articles in the preambles or body of the acts aforesaid, shall be construed, understood or expounded, to derogate, diminish or take away any liberties, privileges, prerogatives, preheminences, authorities or jurisdictions, or any part or parcel thereof, which were in your imperial crown of this realm, or did belong to your said imperial crown the twentieth year of the reign of yours, the Queen's majesty's most noble father, or any other of your most noble progenitors, before the said twentieth year; (3) and the pope's holiness and see apostolick to be restored, and to have and enjoy such authority, preheminence and jurisdiction, as his holiness used and exercised, or might lawfully have used and exercised, by authority of his supremacy, the said twentieth year of the reign of the King your father, within this your realm of *England*, and other your dominions, without diminution or inlargement of the same, and none other; (4) and the ecclesiastical jurisdictions of the archbishops, bishops and ordinaries, to be in the same state for process of suits, punishment of crimes, and execution of censures of the church, with knowledge of causes belonging to the same, and as large in these points as the said jurisdictions was the said twentieth year.

Nothing in this statute shall be prejudicial to the liberties of the crown.

The pope and see apostolick restored to the authority that they had.

The jurisdiction of the bishops of this realm.

LIV. Provided always, and be it enacted by the authority aforesaid, That in and upon every such gifts and devises to be made to such spiritual corporations or persons as is aforesaid, the donor, feoffor, or devisor thereof, may reserve to him and to his heirs for ever, a tenure in *frank almoigne,* or a tenure by divine service, and to have all remedies and actions for and upon the said gifts or devises, and tenures, in like manner and form as was used before the estatute of *Westminster* third, commonly called *Quia emptores terrarum;* the said estatute or any law or custom now being to the contrary in any wise notwithstanding.

What tenure shall be reserved upon gifts to be made to spiritual corporations.

LV. Provided always, and be it enacted, That all and every person and persons, and bodies politick and corporate, which now have or hereafter shall have any estate of inheritance, freehold, term or interest, of, in or to any portion, pension, tithes, glebe-lands, or other ecclesiastical or spiritual profit, which by

The remedy to recover any pension, tithes, glebe-lands.

this act and letters of dispensation rehearsed in the same, be permitted and suffered to remain and continue in lay mens possessions, shall and may have like remedy for the recovery of the same, and every part thereof, as they and every of them might have had before the first day of this present parliament; any thing in this act contained to the contrary in any wise notwithstanding.

<small>In part repealed by 1 El. c. 1. s. 2.</small>

2 & 3 PHILIP AND MARY.

CAP. IV.

The payment of the first-fruits of spiritual livings to the Queen shall cease. The yearly tenths heretofore paid to the Queen by the statute of 26 H. 8. c. 3. shall be employed to other godly uses. Parsonages impropriate, tithes, glebe-lands, and other ecclesiastical livings, renounced by the Queen. But this act shall not extend to tenths reserved upon letters patents. Rep. 1 Eliz. c. 4.

---

1 ELIZABETH.

CAP. I.

An act to restore to the crown the ancient jurisdiction over the estate ecclesiastical and spiritual, and abolishing all foreign powers repugnant to the same.

<small>All ancient jurisdiction restored to the crown.</small>

Most humbly beseech your most excellent Majesty, your faithful and obedient subjects, the lords spiritual and temporal, and the commons, in this your present parliament assembled, That where in time of the reign of your most dear father, of worthy memory, King Henry the Eighth, divers good laws and statutes were made and established, as well for the utter extinguishment and putting away of all usurped and foreign powers and authorities out of this your realm, and other your Highness dominions and countries, as also for the restoring and uniting to the imperial crown of this realm, the ancient jurisdictions, authorities, superiorities and pre-eminences to the same of right belonging or appertaining, by reason whereof we your most humble and obedient subjects, from the xxv. year of the reign of your said dear father, were continually kept in good order, and were disburdened of divers great and intolerable charges and exactions before that time unlawfully taken and exacted by such foreign power and authority as before that was usurped, until such time as all the said good laws and statutes by

<small>A repeal of divers statutes, and revivor of others, and all foreign power abolished. 1 & 2 Ph. & M. c. 8.</small>

one act of parliament made in the first and second years of the reigns of the late King Philip *and Queen* Mary, *your Highness sister, intituled an act repealing all statutes, articles and provisions made against the see apostolick of* Rome *since the twentieth year of King* Henry *the Eighth, and also for the establishment of all spiritual and ecclesiastical possessions and hereditaments conveyed to the laity, were all clearly repealed and made void, as by the same act of repeal more at large doth and may appear; by reason of which act of repeal, your said humble subjects were eftsoons brought under an usurped foreign power and authority, and do yet remain in that bondage, to the intolerable charges of your loving subjects, if some redress (by the authority of this your high court of parliament, with the assent of your Highness) be not had and provided:* 1. Roll. 162. Hct 121.

II. May it therefore please your Highness, for the repressing of the said usurped foreign power, and the restoring of the rites, jurisdictions and preheminences appertaining to the imperial crown of this your realm, that it may be enacted by authority of this present parliament, That the said act made in the said first and second years of the reigns of the said late King *Philip* and Queen *Mary*, and all and every branches, clauses and articles therein contained (other than such branches, clauses and sentences, as hereafter shall be excepted) may from the last day of this session of parliament, by authority of this present parliament, be repealed, and shall from thenceforth be utterly void and of none effect: A repeal of the stat. of 1 & 2 Ph. & M. c. 8.

III. And that also for the reviving of divers of the said good laws and statutes made in the time of your said dear father, it may also please your Highness, That one act and statute made in the xxiij. year of the reign of the said late King *Henry* the Eighth, intituled, An act, That no person shall be cited out of the diocess wherein he or she dwelleth, except in certain cases. A revivor of the statutes hereafter specified, viz. 23 H. 8. c. 9.

IV. And one other act made in the xxiv. year of the reign of the said late King, intituled, An act, That appeals in such cases as hath been used to be pursued to the see of *Rome*, shall not be from henceforth had ne used, but within this realm: 24 H. 8. c. 12.

V. And one other act made the xxv. year of the said late King, concerning restraint of payment of annates and first-fruits of archbishopricks and bishopricks to the see of *Rome*: 25 H. 8. c. 20. not printed in the former editions.

VI. And one other act in the said xxv. year, intituled, An act concerning the submission of the clergy to the King's majesty: 25 H. 8. c. 19.

25 H. 8. c. 20.   VII. And also one act made in the said xxv. year, intituled, An act restraining the payment of annates or first-fruits to the bishop of *Rome*, and of the electing and consecrating of archbishops and bishops within this realm:

25 H. 8. c. 21.   VIII. And one other act made in the said xxv. year, intituled, An act concerning the exoneration of the King's subjects from exactions and impositions heretofore paid to the see of *Rome*, and for having licences and dispensations within this realm, without suing further for the same:

26 H. 8. c. 14.   IX. And one other act made in the xxvi. year of the said late King, intituled, An act for nomination and consecration of suffragans within this realm:

28 H. 8. c. 16.   X. And also one other act made in the xxviij. year of the reign of the said late King, intituled, An act for the release of such as have obtained pretended licences and dispensations from the see of *Rome*; (2) and all and every branches, words and sentences in the said several acts and statutes contained, by the authority of this present parliament, from and at all times after the last day of this session of parliament, shall be revived, and shall stand and be in full force and strength, to all intents, constructions and purposes: (3) And that the branches, sentences and words of the said several acts, and every of them, from thenceforth shall and may be judged, deemed and taken to extend to your Highness, your heirs and successors, as fully and largely as ever the same acts, or any of them, did extend to the said late King *Henry* the Eighth, your Highness father.

The sentences and branches in the aforesaid statutes shall extend to the Queen.

32 H. 8. c. 38.   XI. And that it may also please your Highness, that it may be enacted by the authority of this present parliament, That so much of one act or statute made in the xxxij. year of the reign of your said dear father King *Henry* the Eighth, intituled, An act concerning precontracts of marriages, and touching degrees of consanguinity, as in the time of the late King *Edward* the Sixth, your Highness most dear brother, by one other act or statute, was not repealed.

2 & 3 Ed. 6. c. 23.

37 H. 8. c. 17.   XII. And also one act made in the xxxvij. year of the reign of the said late King *Henry* the Eighth, intituled, An act that doctors of the civil law, being married, may exercise ecclesiastical jurisdiction; (2) and all and every branches and articles in the said two acts last mentioned, and not repealed in the time of the said late King *Edward* the Sixth, may from henceforth likewise stand and be revived, and remain in their full force and strength, to all intents and purposes; any thing contained in the said act or

repeal before mentioned, or any other matter or cause to the contrary notwithstanding.

XIII. And that it may also please your Highness, that it may further be enacted by the authority aforesaid, That all other laws and statutes, and the branches and clauses of any act or statute, repealed and made void by the said act of repeal, made in the time of the said late King *Philip* and Queen *Mary*, and not in this present act specially mentioned and revived, shall stand, remain, and be repealed and void, in such like manner and form as they were before the making of this act; any thing herein contained to the contrary notwithstanding. *What statutes repealed by the statute of 1 & 2 Ph. & M. c. 8. shall continue repealed.*

XIV. And that it may also please your Highness, that it may be enacted by the authority aforesaid, That one act and statute made in the first year of the reign of the late King *Edward* the Sixth, your majesty's most dear brother, intituled, An act against such persons as shall unreverently speak against the sacrament of the body and blood of Christ, commonly called the Sacrament of the Altar, and for the receiving thereof under both kinds, and all and every branches, clauses and sentences therein contained, shall and may likewise from the last day of this session of parliament be revived, and from thenceforth shall and may stand, remain and be in full force, strength and effect, to all intents, constructions and purposes, in such like manner and form as the same was at any time in the first year of the reign of the said late King *Edward* the Sixth; any law, statute, or other matter to the contrary in any wise notwithstanding. *A revivor of the statute 1 Ed. 6. c. 1.*

XV. And that also it may please your Highness, that it may be further established and enacted by the authority aforesaid, That one act and statute made in the first and second years of the said late King *Philip* and Queen *Mary*, intituled, An act for the reviving of three statutes made for the punishment of heresies; and also the said three statutes mentioned in the said act, and by the same act revived, (2) and all and every branches, articles, clauses and sentences contained in the said several acts and statutes, and every of them, shall be from the last day of this session of parliament deemed and remain utterly repealed, void and of none effect, to all intents and purposes; any thing in the said several acts, or any of them contained, or any other matter or cause to the contrary notwithstanding. *A repeal of the statute of 1 & 2 Ph. & M. c. 6. 5 R. 2. stat. 2. c. 5. 2 H. 4. c. 15. 2 H. 5. c. 7.*

XVI. And to the intent that all usurped and foreign power and authority spiritual and temporal, may for ever be clearly extinguished, and never to be used or obeyed within this realm, or any other your Majesty's dominions or countries; (2) may it *The abolishing of foreign authority.*

please your Highness that it may be further enacted by the authority aforesaid, That no foreign prince, person, prelate, state or potentate spiritual or temporal, shall at any time after the last day of this session of parliament use, enjoy or exercise any manner of power, jurisdiction, superiority, authority, preheminence or privilege spiritual or ecclesiastical, within this realm, or within any other your Majesty's dominions or countries that now be, or hereafter shall be, but from henceforth the same shall be clearly abolished out of this realm, and all other your Highness dominions for ever; any statute, ordinance, custom, constitutions, or any other matter or cause whatsoever to the contrary in any wise notwithstanding.

Co. pla. fol. 465, 487. Ecclesiastical jurisdiction annexed to the crown. 1 Leonard 176.

XVII. And that also it may likewise please your Highness, that it may be established and enacted by the authority aforesaid, That such jurisdictions, privileges, superiorities and preheminences, spiritual and ecclesiastical, as by any spiritual or ecclesiastical power or authority hath heretofore been, or may lawfully be exercised or used for the visitation of the ecclesiastical state and persons, and for reformation, order and correction of the same, and of all manner of errors, heresies, schisms, abuses, offences, contempts and enormities, shall for ever by authority of this present parliament be united and annexed to the imperial crown of this realm.

The Queen may assign commissioners to exercise ecclesiastical jurisdiction. Repealed 16 Car. I. c. 11. f. 3.

XVIII. And that your Highness, your heirs and successors, Kings or Queens of this realm, shall have full power and authority by virtue of this act, by letters patents under the great seal of *England*, to assign, name and authorize, when and as often as your Highness, your heirs or successors shall think meet and convenient, and for such and so long time as shall please your Highness, your heirs or successors, such person or persons being natural-born subjects to your Highness, your heirs or successors, as your Majesty, your heirs or successors shall think meet, to exercise, use, occupy and execute under your Highness, your heirs and successors, all manner of jurisdictions, privileges and preheminences, in any wise touching or concerning any spiritual or ecclesiastical jurisdiction, within these your realms of *England* and *Ireland*, or any other your Highness dominions and countries: (2) and to visit, reform, redress, order, correct and amend all such errors, heresies, schisms, abuses, offences, contempts and enormities whatsoever, which by any manner of spiritual or ecclesiastical power, authority or jurisdiction, can or may lawfully be reformed, ordered, redressed, corrected, restrained or amended, to the pleasure of Almighty God, the increase of virtue, and the conservation of the peace and unity of this realm; (3)

and that such person or persons so to be named, assigned, authorized and appointed by your Highness, your heirs or successors after the said letters patents to him or them made and delivered, as is aforesaid, shall have full power and authority by virtue of this act, and of the said letters patents under your Highness, your heirs and successors, to exercise, use, and execute all the premisses, according to the tenour and effect of the said letters patents; any matter or cause to the contrary in any wise notwithstanding.

XIX. And for the better observation and maintenance of this act, may it please your Highness that it may be further enacted by the authority aforesaid, That all and every archbishop, bishop, and all and every other ecclesiastical person, and other ecclesiastical officer and minister, of what estate, dignity, preheminence or degree soever he or they be or shall be, (2) and all and every temporal judge, justice, mayor and other lay or temporal officer and minister, and every other person having your Highness fee or wages, (3) within this realm, or any your Highness dominions, shall make, take and receive a corporal oath upon the evangelist, before such person or persons as shall please your Highness, your heirs or successors, under the great seal of *England* to assign and name, to accept and to take the same according to the tenour and effect hereafter following; that is to say, *Who are compellable to take the oath. Ecclesiastical persons and officers. Judge. Justice. Mayor. Temporal officer. He that hath the Queen's fee.*

I *A. B.* do utterly testify and declare in my conscience, That the Queen's highness is the only supreme governor of this realm, and of all other her Highness dominions and countries, as well in all spiritual or ecclesiastical things or causes, as temporal; and that no foreign prince, person, prelate, state or potentate, hath or ought to have any jurisdiction, power, superiority, preheminence, or authority ecclesiastical or spiritual, within this realm; and therefore I do utterly renounce and forsake all foreign jurisdictions, powers, superiorities and authorities, and do promise, that from henceforth I shall bear faith and true allegiance to the Queen's Highness, her heirs and lawful successors, and to my power shall assist and defend all jurisdictions, preheminences, privileges and authorities granted or belonging to the Queen's highness, her heirs and successors, or united and annexed to the imperial crown of this realm. So help me God, and by the contents of this book. *The Oath of the Queen's supremacy. Repealed by 1 W. & M. sess. 1. c. 8. s. 2. 1 Bulst. 199.*

XX. And that it may also be enacted, That if any such archbishop, bishop or any other ecclesiastical officer or minister, or any of the said temporal judges, justiciaries, or other lay officer or minister, shall peremptorily or obstinately refuse to take or *The penalty for refusing the oath.*

receive the said oath; that then he so refusing shall forfeit and lose only during his life all and every ecclesiastical and spiritual promotion, benefice and office, and every temporal and lay promotion and office, which he hath solely at the time of such refusal made; and that the whole title, interest, and incumbency, in every such promotion, benefice, and other office, as against such person only so refusing, during his life, shall clearly cease and be void, as though the party so refusing were dead.

XXI. And that also all and every such person and persons so refusing to take the said oath, shall immediately after such refusal, be from thenceforth, during his life, disabled to retain or exercise any office or other promotion which he at the time of such refusal hath jointly, or in common, with any other person or persons.

<small>All things touching the præmunire in 1 & 2 Ph. & M. c. 8. s. 40. do continue in force.</small>

XXXII. Provided always and be it enacted by the authority aforesaid, That this act, or any thing therein contained, shall not in any wise extend to repeal any clause, matter or sentence contained or specified in the said act of repeal made in the said first and second years of the reigns of the said late King *Philip* and Queen *Mary*, as doth in any wise touch or concern any matter or cause of *Præmunire*, or that doth make or ordain any matter or cause to be within the case of *Præmunire* ; (2) but that the same, for so much only as toucheth or concerneth any case, or matter of *Præmunire*, shall stand and remain in such force and effect, as the same was before the making of this act ; any thing in this act contained to the contrary in any wise notwithstanding.

<small>Commissioners may adjudge such things to be heresy as are so declared by the scripture, the first four general councils, or the parliament, with the convocation.
1 Hale's H. P. c. 404.</small>

XXXVI. Provided always, and be it enacted by the authority aforesaid, That such person or persons to whom your Highness, your heirs or successors, shall hereafter by letters patents, under the great seal of *England*, give authority to have or execute any jurisdiction, power or authority spiritual, or to visit, reform, order or correct any errors, heresies, schisms, abuses or enormities by virtue of this act, shall not in any wise have authority or power to order, determine or adjudge any matter or cause to be heresy, but only such as heretofore have been determined, ordered or adjudged to be heresy, by the authority of the canonical scriptures, or by the first four general councils, or any of them, or by any other general council wherein the same was declared heresy by the express and plain words of the said canonical scriptures, or such as hereafter shall be ordered, judged or determined to be heresy by the high court of parliament of this realm, with the assent of the clergy in their convocation ; anything in this act contained to the contrary notwithstanding.

XXXVII. And be it further enacted by the authority aforesaid, That no person or persons shall be hereafter indicted or arraigned for any of the offences made, ordained, revived or adjudged by this act, unless there be two sufficient witnesses or more, to testify and declare the said offences whereof he shall be indicted or arraigned: (2) and that the said witnesses, or so many of them as shall be living and within this realm at the time of the arraignment of such person so indicted, shall be brought forth in person face to face before the party so arraigned, and there shall testify and declare what they can say against the party so arraigned, if he require the same. *None shall be indicted or arraigned but by two witnesses.*

Cap. II.

An act for the uniformity of common prayer and service in the church, and administration of the sacraments.

Where at the death of our late sovereign lord King Edward the Sixth there remained one uniform order of common service and prayer, and of the administration of sacraments, rites and ceremonies in the church of England, which was set forth in one book, intituled, The book of common prayer, and administration of sacraments, and other rites and ceremonies in the church of England; authorized by act of parliament holden in the fifth and sixth years of our said late sovereign lord King Edward the Sixth, intituled, An act for the uniformity of common prayer, and administration of the sacraments; the which was repealed and taken away by act of parliament in the first year of the reign of our late sovereign lady Queen Mary, to the great decay of the due honour of God, and discomfort to the professors of the truth of Christ's religion: *13 & 14 Car. 2. c. 4. Stat. 5 & 6 Ed. 6. c. 1. A repeal of the statute of 1 M. sess. 2. c. 2.*

II. Be it therefore enacted by the authority of this present parliament, That the said estatute of repeal, and every thing therein contained, only concerning the said book, and the service, administration of the sacraments, rites and ceremonies, contained or appointed in or by the said book, shall be void and of none effect, from and after the feast of the nativity of St. *John Baptist* next coming; (2) and that the said book, with the order of service, and of the administration of sacraments, rites and ceremonies, with the alterations and additions therein added and appointed by this estatute, shall stand and be, from and after the said feast of the nativity of St. *John Baptist*, in full force and effect, according to the tenor and effect of this estatute; any thing in the aforesaid estatute of repeal to the contrary notwithstanding. *And the book of common prayer shall be of effect. 1 Leon. 295.*

III. And further be it enacted by the Queen's highness, with the assent of the lords and commons in this present parliament assembled, and by the authority of the same, That all and singular ministers in any cathedral or parish church, or other place within this realm of *England, Wales*, and the marches of the same, or other the Queen's dominions, shall from and after the feast of the nativity of St. *John Baptist* next coming be bounden to say and use the mattens, even-song, celebration of the Lord's supper and administration of each of the sacraments, and all the common and open prayer, in such order and form as is mentioned in the said book, so authorized by parliament in the said fifth and sixth years of the reign of King *Edward* the Sixth, with one alteration or addition of certain lessons to be used on every Sunday in the year, and the form of the litany altered and corrected, and two sentences only added in the delivery of the sacrament to the communicants, and none other or otherwise.

IV. And that if any manner of parson, vicar or other whatsoever minister, that ought or should sing or say common prayer mentioned in the said book, or minister the sacraments, from and after the feast of the nativity of St. *John Baptist* next coming, refuse to use the said common prayers, or to minister the sacraments in such cathedral or parish church, or other places as he should use to minister the same, in such order and form as they be mentioned and set forth in the said book ; (2) or shall wilfully or obstinately, standing in the same, use any other rite, ceremony, order, form or manner of celebrating of the Lord's supper, openly or privily, or mattens, even-song, administration of the sacraments, or other open prayers, than is mentioned and set forth in the said book, (3) (open prayer in and throughout this act, is meant that prayer which is for others to come unto, or hear, either in common churches, or private chapels or oratories, commonly called, the service of the church.) (4) or shall preach, declare or speak any thing in the derogation or depraving of the said book, or any thing therein contained, or of any part thereof, (5) and shall be thereof lawfully convicted, according to the laws of this realm, by verdict of twelve men, or by his own confession, or by the notorious evidence of the fact, shall lose and forfeit to the Queen's highness, her heirs and successors, for his first offence, the profit of all his spiritual benefices or promotions coming or arising in one whole year next after his conviction : (6) and also that the person so convicted shall for the same offence suffer imprisonment for the space of six months, without bail or mainprise.

XIV. And that from and after the said feast of the nativity

of St. *John Baptist* next coming, all and every person and persons inhabiting within this realm, or any other the Queen's majesty's dominions, shall diligently and faithfully, having no lawful or reasonable excuse to be absent, endeavour themselves to resort to their parish church or chapel accustomed, or upon reasonable let thereof, to some usual place where common prayer and such service of God shall be used in such time of let, upon every Sunday, and other days ordained and used to be kept as holy days, and then and there to abide orderly and soberly during the time of the common prayer, preaching or other service of God there to be used and ministred; (2) upon pain of punishment by the censures of the church, and also upon pain that every person so offending shall forfeit for every such offence twelve pence, to be levied by the churchwardens of the parish where such offence shall be done, to the use of the poor of the same parish, of the goods, lands and tenements of such offender, by way of distress. resort to the church upon the holy days. Godbolt 148 pl. 191. One justice may convict the offender, &c. by 3 Jac. 1. c. 4. s. 27. 2 Roll 438, 455. March 93. The forfeiture for not coming to church. 23 Eliz. c. 1. 11 Co. 56. 1 Roll. 89.

XVI. And for their authority in this behalf, be it further enacted by the authority aforesaid, That all and singular the said archbishops, bishops, and all other their officers exercising ecclesiastical jurisdiction, as well in place exempt as not exempt, within their diocese, shall have full power and authority by this act to reform, correct and punish by censures of the church, all and singular persons which shall offend within any their jurisdictions or diocese, after the said feast of the nativity of St. *John Baptist* next coming, against this act and statute; any other law, statute, privilege, liberty or provision heretofore made, had or suffered, to the contrary notwithstanding. The ordinary may punish offenders by the censures of the church.

XXII. Provided also, and be it ordained and enacted by the authority aforesaid, That the mayor of *London*, and all other mayors, bailiffs and other head officers of all and singular cities, boroughs and towns corporate within this realm, *Wales*, and the marches of the same, to the which justices of assize do not commonly repair, shall have full power and authority by virtue of this act to enquire, hear and determine the offences abovesaid and every of them, yearly within fifteen days after the feast of *Easter*, and St. *Michael* the archangel, in like manner and form as justices of assize and *oyer* and *determiner* may do. Chief officers of cities and boroughs shall enquire of offenders

XXIII. Provided always, and be it ordained and enacted by the authority aforesaid, That all and singular archbishops and bishops, and every of their chancellors, commissaries, archdeacons and other ordinaries, having any peculiar ecclesiastical jurisdiction, shall have full power and authority by virtue of this act, The ordinary's jurisdiction in these cases.

as well to enquire in their visitation, synods, and elsewhere within their jurisdiction at any other time and place, to take accusations and informations of all and every the things above-mentioned, done, committed or perpetrated within the limits of their jurisdictions and authority, and to punish the same by admonition, excommunication, sequestration or deprivation, and other censures and process, in like form as heretofore hath been used in like cases by the Queen's ecclesiastical laws.

<small>None shall be punished above once for one offence.</small>

XXIV. Provided always, and be it enacted, That whatsoever persons offending in the premises shall for their offences first receive punishment of the ordinary, having a testimonial thereof under the said ordinary's seal, shall not for the same offence eftsoons be convicted before the justices: (2) and likewise receiving for the said offence punishment first by the justices, shall not for the same offence, eftsoons receive punishment of the ordinary; any thing contained in this act to the contrary notwithstanding.

<small>Ornaments of the church and ministers.</small>

XXV. Provided always, and be it enacted, That such ornaments of the church and of the ministers thereof, shall be retained and be in use, as was in this church of *England* by authority of parliament, in the second year of the reign of King *Edward* the Sixth, until other order shall be therein taken by the authority of the Queen's majesty, with the advice of her commissioners appointed and authorized under the great seal of *England* for causes ecclesiastical, or of the metropolitan of this realm.

XXVI. And also, That if there shall happen any contempt or irreverence to be used in the ceremonies or rites of the church, by the mis-using of the orders appointed in this book, the Queen's majesty may, by the like advice of the said commissioners or metropolitan, ordain and publish such further ceremonies or rites, as may be most for the advancement of God's glory, the edifying of his church, and the due reverence of Christ's holy mysteries and sacraments.

<small>All laws and ordinances made for other service shall be void.</small>

XXVII. And be it further enacted by the authority aforesaid, That all laws, statutes and ordinances, wherein or whereby any other service, administration of sacraments or common prayer, is limited, established or set forth to be used within this realm, or any other the Queen's dominions or countries, shall from henceforth be utterly void and of none effect. *Made perpetual by 5 Ann. c. 5. as to the establishment of the church.*

5 ELIZABETH.

CAP. I.

An act for the assurance of the Queen's royal power over all estates and subjects within her dominions.

For preservation of the Queen's most excellent highness, her heirs and successors, and the dignity of the imperial crown of this realm of England, and for avoiding both of such hurts, perils, dishonours and inconveniencies, as have before-time befallen, as well to the Queen's majesty's noble progenitors, Kings of this realm, as for the whole estate thereof; by means of the jurisdiction and power of the see of Rome, unjustly claimed and usurped within this realm and the dominions thereof, and also of the dangers by the fautors of the said usurped power, at this time grown to marvellous outrage and licentious boldness, and now requiring more sharp restraint and correction of laws, than hitherto in the time of the Queen's majesty's most mild and merciful reign have been had, used or established:

II. Be it therefore enacted, ordained and established by the Queen our sovereign lady, and the lords spiritual and temporal, and the commons, in this present parliament assembled, and by authority of the same, That if any person and persons, dwelling, inhabiting, or resiant within this realm, or within any other the Queen's dominions, seigniories, or countries, or in the marches of the same, or elsewhere within or under her obeysance and power, of what estate, dignity, preheminence, order, degree or condition soever he or they be, after the first day of *April* which be in the year of our Lord God one thousand five hundred sixty-three, shall by writing, cyphering, printing, preaching or teaching, deed or act, advisedly and wittingly hold or stand with, to extol, set forth, maintain or defend the authority, jurisdiction or power of the bishop of *Rome*, or of his see, heretofore claimed, used or usurped within this realm, or in any dominion or country, being of, within or under the Queen's power or obeysance; (2) or by any speech, open deed or act, advisedly and wittingly attribute any such manner of jurisdiction, authority or preheminence to the said see of *Rome*, or to any bishop of the same see for the time being, within this realm, or in any the Queen's dominions or countries: (3) that then every such person or persons so doing or offending, their abetters, procurers and counsellers, and also their aiders, assistants and comforters, upon purpose, and to the intent to set forth, further and extol the said usurped power, authority or jurisdiction of any of the said bishop or bishops of *Rome* and

The penalty for maintaining the authority of the bishop or see of Rome. 28 H. 8. c. 10. 13 El. c. 2.

every of them, being thereof lawfully indicted or presented within one year next after any such offences by him or them committed, and being lawfully convicted or attainted at any time after, according to the laws of this realm, for every such default and offence, shall incur into the dangers, penalties, pains and forfeitures ordained and provided by the statute of provision and *Præmunire*, made in the sixteenth year of the reign of King *Richard* the Second.

16 R. 2. c. 5.

The bishop may tender the oath to any spiritual person.
VI. And also be it enacted by the authority of this present parliament, That every archbishop and bishop within this realm, and dominions of the same, shall have full power and authority by virtue of this act, to tender or minister the oath aforesaid, to every or any spiritual or ecclesiastical person within their proper diocese, as well in places and jurisdictions exempt, as elsewhere.

The lord chancellor may direct a commission to take the oath of any person.
VII. And be it enacted by the authority aforesaid, That the lord chancellor or keeper of the great seal of *England* for the time being, shall and may at all times hereafter, by virtue of this act, without further warrant, make and direct a commission or commissions under the great seal of *England*, to any person or persons, giving them or some of them thereby authority to tender and minister the oath aforesaid, to such person or persons, as by the aforesaid commission or commissions the said commissioners shall be authorized to tender the same oath unto.

The penalty for the first refusal of the oath.
VIII. And be it also further enacted by the authority of this present parliament, That if any person or persons appointed or compellable by this act, or by the said act made in the said first year, to take the said oath; or if any person or persons to whom the said oath by any such commission or commissions shall be limited and appointed to be tendred, as is aforesaid, do or shall, at the time of the said oath so tendred, refuse to take or pronounce the said oath in manner and form aforesaid, that then the party so refusing, and being thereof lawfully indicted or presented within one year next after any such refusal, and convicted or attainted at any time after, according to the laws of this realm, shall suffer and incur the dangers, penalties, pains and forfeitures, ordained and provided by the statute of provision and *præmunire* aforesaid, made in the sixteenth year of the reign of King *Richard* the Second.

16 R. 2. c. 5.

X. And for stronger defence and maintenance of this act, it is further ordained, enacted and established by the authority aforesaid, That if any such offender or offenders, as is aforesaid, of the first part or branch of this estatute, that is to say, by writing, cyphering, printing, preaching or teaching, deed or act, advisedly and wittingly hold or stand with, to extol, set forth, maintain or defend the authority, jurisdiction or power of the bishop of *Rome*, or of his see, heretofore claimed, used or usurped within this realm, or in any dominion or country, being of, within or under the Queen's power and obeysance : (2) or by any speech, open deed or act, advisedly and wittingly attribute any such manner of jurisdiction, authority or preheminence to the said see of *Rome*, or to any bishop of the same see for the time being, within this realm, or in any the Queen's dominions or countries ; (3) or be to any such offender or offenders abetting, procuring or counselling, or aiding, assisting or comforting, upon purpose, and to the intent to set forth, further and extol the said usurped power, authority or jurisdiction, after such conviction and attainder as is aforesaid, do eftsoons commit or do the said offences or any of them, in manner and form aforesaid, and be thereof duly convicted and attainted as is aforesaid :

XI. And also, That if any the persons above named and appointed by this act to take the oath aforesaid, do after the space of three months next after the first tender thereof, the second time refuse to take and pronounce, or do not take and pronounce the same, in form aforesaid to be tendered, that then every such offender or offenders, for the same second offence and offences, shall forfeit, lose and suffer such like and the same pains, forfeitures, judgment and execution, as is used in cases of high treason. It shall be treason the second time to maintain the authority of the bishop or see of Rome, or to refuse the oath.

XIV. Provided also, That the oath expressed in the said act made in the said first year, shall be taken and expounded in such form as is set forth in an admonition annexed to the Queen's majesty's injunctions, published in the first year of her Majesty's reign ; that is to say, to confess and acknowledge in her Majesty, her heirs and successors, none other authority than that was challenged and lately used by the noble King *Henry* the Eighth and King *Edward* the Sixth ; as in the said admonition more plainly may appear. How the oath expressed anno 1 El. c. 1. shall be expounded.

XXIII. Provided always, and be it enacted by the authority aforesaid, That no person or persons shall hereafter be indicted for assisting, aiding, maintaining, comforting or abetting of any person or persons for any the said offences, in extolling, setting forth or defending of the usurped power and authority of the bishop of *Rome*, unless he or they be thereof lawfully accused by such good and sufficient testimony or proof, as by the jury by whom he shall so be indicted, shall be thought good, lawful and sufficient, to prove him or them guilty of the said offences. 23 *El.* c. 1. Upon what proof only any person may be indicted.

8 ELIZABETH.

Cap. I.

An act declaring the making and consecrating of the archbishops and bishops of this realm to be good, lawful and perfect.

<small>Acts made since 1 El. for the consecrating, investing, &c. of any archbishop or bishop, shall be good.
Dyer 234. A question whether the making of bishops were duly and orderly done.</small>

Forasmuch as divers questions, by overmuch boldness of speech and talk amongst many of the common sort of people being unlearned, hath lately grown upon the making and consecrating of archbishops and bishops within this realm, whether the same were and be duly and orderly done according to the law or not, which is much tending to the slander of all the state of the clergy, being one of the great states of this realm: (2) *therefore for the avoiding of such slanderous speech, and to the intent that every man that is willing to know the truth, may plainly understand that the same evil speech and talk is not grounded upon any just matter or cause, it is thought convenient hereby partly to touch such authorities as do allow and approve the making and consecrating of the same archbishops and bishops to be duly and orderly done, according to the laws of this realm, and thereupon further to provide for the more surety thereof, as hereafter shall be expressed.*

<small>26 H. 8. c. 1.</small>

II. *First, it is very well known to all degrees of this realm, that the late King of most famous memory, King* Henry *the Eighth, as well by all the clergy then of this realm in their several convocations, as also by all the lords spiritual and temporal, and commons, assembled in divers of his parliaments, was justly and rightfully recognized and knowledged to have the supreme power, jurisdiction, order, rule and authority over all the estate ecclesiastical of the same, and the same power, jurisdiction and authority did use accordingly:*

<small>25 H. 8. c. 20.</small>

(2) *and that also the said late King, in the five and twentieth year of his reign, did by authority of parliament, amongst other things, set forth a certain order of the manner and form how archbishops and bishops, within this realm and other his dominions, should be elected and made, as by the same more plainly appeareth:* (3) *and that also the late King of worthy memory, King* Edward *the Sixth, did lawfully succeed the said late King* Henry *his father, in the imperial crown of this realm, and did justly possess and enjoy all the same power, jurisdiction and authority beforemention'd, as a thing to him descended with the same imperial crown, and so used*

<small>5 & 6 Ed. 6. c. 1.</small>

the same during his life: (4) *and that also the said late King* Edward *the Sixth, in his time by authority of parliament caused a godly and virtuous book, intituled,* The book of common prayer, and administration of sacraments, and other rites and ceremonies in the church of England, *to be made and set forth, not only for one uniform order of service, common prayer, and the administration of sacraments, to be used within all this realm and other his dominions, but also did add and put to the same book a very good and godly order of the manner and form how archbishops, bishops, priests, deacons and ministers, should from time to time be consecrated, made and ordered within this realm and other his dominions, as by the same more plainly will and may appear:* (5) *and although* 1 & 2 Ph. & M. c. 8. *in the time of the late Queen Mary, as well the said act and statute made in the five and twentieth year of the reign of the said late King* Henry *the Eighth, as also the several acts and statutes made in the second, third, fourth, fifth and sixth years of the reign of the said late King* Edward, *for the authorising and allowing of the said book of common prayer, and other the premises, amongst divers other acts and statutes touching the said supream authority, were repealed: yet nevertheless, at the parliament holden at* West- 1 El. c. 1. *minster in the first year of the reign of our sovereign lady the Queen's majesty that now is, by one other act and statute there made, all such jurisdictions, privileges, superiorities and preheminences spiritual and ecclesiastical, as by any spiritual or ecclesiastical power or authority hath heretofore been, or may lawfully be used over the ecclesiastical estate of this realm, and the order, reformation and correction of the same, is fully and absolutely by the authority of the same parliament, united and annexed to the imperial crown of this realm:* (6) *and by the same act and statute there is also given to the Queen's highness, her heirs and successors, Kings and Queens of this realm, full power and authority, by letters patents under the great seal of* England, *from time to time to assign, name and authorise such person or persons as she or they shall think meet and convenient, to exercise, use, occupy and execute under her Highness, all manner of jurisdiction, privileges, preheminences and authorities, in any wise touching or concerning any spiritual or ecclesiastical power or jurisdiction within this realm, or any other her Highness dominions or countries:* (7) *and also by the same act and statute, the said act made in the five and twentieth year of the reign of the said late King* Henry *the Eighth, for the order and form of the electing and making of the said archbishops and bishops, together with divers other statutes touching the jurisdiction over the state ecclesiastical, is revived and made in full force and effect, as by the same act and statute more plainly appeareth:* (8) *and that also by another act and statute made in the said* 1 El. c. 2. *parliament in the first year of the reign of our said sovereign Lady, intituled,* An act for the uniformity of common prayer, and service in the church, and the administration of sacraments, *the said book of common prayer, and the administration of sacra-*

ments, and other the said orders, rites and ceremonies before-mentioned, and all things therein contained, with certain additions therein newly added and appointed by the said estatute, is fully established and authorised to be used in all places within this realm, and all other the Queen's majesty's dominions and countries; as by the said act, amongst other things, more plainly appeareth: (9) whereupon our said sovereign lady the Queen's most excellent majesty, being most justly and lawfully invested in the imperial crown of this realm, with all authorities, preheminences and dignities thereunto appertaining, and thereby having in her majesty's order and disposition all the said jurisdictions, power and authorities over the state ecclesiastical and temporal, as well in causes ecclesiastical as temporal, within this realm and other her Majesty's dominions and countries, hath by her supream authority, at divers times sithence the beginning of her Majesty's reign, caused divers and sundry grave and well learned men to be duly elected, made and consecrated archbishops and bishops of divers arch-bishopricks and bishopricks within this realm, and other her Majesty's dominions and countries, according to such order and form, and with such ceremonies in and about their consecrations, as were allowed and set forth by the said acts, statutes and orders annexed to the said book of common prayer before-mentioned:

The Queen by her supream authority caused divers persons to be elected and consecrated archbishops and bishops.

(10) and further, for the avoiding of all ambiguities and questions that might be objected against the lawful confirmations, investing and consecrations of the said archbishops and bishops, her Highness in her letters patents under the great seal of England, directed to any archbishop, bishop or others, for the confirming, investing and consecrating of any person elected to the office or dignity of any archbishop or bishop, hath not only used such words and sentences as were accustomed to be used by the said late King Henry and King Edward, her Majesty's father and brother, in their like letters patents made for such causes, but also hath used and put in her Majesty's said letters patents divers other general words and sentences, whereby her Highness, by her supream power and authority, hath dispensed with all causes or doubts of any imperfection or disability that can or may in any wise be objected against the same, as by her Majesty's said letters patents remaining of record more plainly will appear:

The Queen's dispensation of all doubts of imperfections or disability of electing bishops.

(11) so that to all those that will well consider of the effect and true intent of the said laws and statutes, and of the supream and absolute authority of the Queen's highness, and which she by her Majesty's said letters patents hath used and put in ure in and about the making and consecrating of the said archbishops and bishops, it is and may be very evident and

apparent, that no cause of scruple, ambiguity or doubt, can or may justly be objected against the said elections, confirmations or consecrations, or any other material thing meet to be used or had in or about the same; but that every thing requisite and material for that purpose hath been made and done as precisely, and with as great a care and diligence, or rather more, as ever the like was done before her Majesty's time, as the records of her Majesty's said father and brother's time, and also of her own time, will more plainly testify and declare:

III. Wherefore for the plain declaration of all the premisses, and to the intent that the same may the better be known to every of the Queen's majesty's subjects, whereby such evil speech as heretofore hath been used against the high state of prelacy may hereafter cease, (2) be it now declared and enacted by the authority of this present parliament, That the said act and statute made in the first year of the reign of our said sovereign lady the Queen's majesty, whereby the said book of common prayer and the administration of sacraments, with other rites and ceremonies, is authorized and allowed to be used, shall stand and remain good and perfect, to all respects and purposes : (3) and that such order and form for the consecrating of archbishops and bishops, and for the making of priests, deacons and ministers, as was set forth in the time of the said late King *Edward* the Sixth, and added to the said book of common prayer, and authorized by parliament in the fifth and sixth years of the said late King, shall stand and be in full force and effect, and shall from henceforth be used and observed in all places within this realm, and other the Queen's majesty's dominions and countries : _{A confirmation of the statute of 1 El. c. 2. touching the book of common prayer and administration of the sacraments.}

_{A confirmation of the statute of 5 & 6 Ed. 6. c. 1. touching the form of consecrating archbishops, &c.}

IV. And that all acts and things heretofore had, made or done by any person or persons in or about any consecration, confirmation or investing of any person or persons elected to the office or dignity of any archbishop or bishop within this realm, or within any other the Queen's majesty's dominions or countries, by virtue of the Queen's majesty's letters patents or commission sithence the beginning of her Majesty's reign, be and shall be by authority of this present parliament declared, judged and deemed at and from every of the several times of the doing thereof, good and perfect to all respects and purposes ; any matter or thing that can or may be objected to the contrary thereof in any wise notwithstanding. _{All acts done by any person about consecration or investing any person elected to be bishop by virtue of the Queen's letters patents sithence the beginning of her reign, shall be good.}

V. And that all persons that have been or shall be made, ordered or consecrated archbishops, bishops, priests, ministers of God's holy word and sacraments, or deacons, after the form and _{All persons made and to be made bishops, priests,}

order prescribed in the said order and form how archbishops, bishops, priests, deacons and ministers should be consecrated, made and ordered, be in very deed, and also by authority hereof declared and enacted to be, and shall be archbishops, bishops, priests, ministers and deacons, and rightly made, ordered and consecrated; any statute, law, canon or other thing to the contrary notwithstanding.

ministers, &c. according to the stat. of 5 & 6 Ed. 6. c. 1. be rightly made. 39 El. c. 8.

VI. Provided always and nevertheless be it enacted by the authority aforesaid, That no person or persons shall at any time hereafter be impeached or molested, in body, lands, livings or goods, by occasion or mean of any certificate by any archbishop or bishop heretofore made, or before the last day of this present session of parliament to be made, by virtue of any act made in the first session of this present parliament, touching or concerning the refusal of the oath declared and set forth by act of parliament in the first year of the reign of our said sovereign lady Queen *Elizabeth;* any thing in this act, or any other act or statute heretofore made to the contrary notwithstanding.

No person shall be impeached by any certificate of any bishop heretofore made, touching the oath of supremacy made 1 El. c. 1.

VII. And that all tenders of the said oath, made by any archbishop or bishop aforesaid, or before the last day of this present session to be made by authority of any act established in the first session of this present parliament, and all refusals of the same oath so tendred, or before the last day of this present session to be tendred, by any archbishop or bishop, by authority of any act established in the first session of this present parliament, shall be void and of none effect or validity in the law.

13 ELIZABETH.

Cap. I.

It shall be high treason to intend destruction or bodily harm to the Queen, or to levy war, or to move others to war against her, or to affirm, That the Queen ought not to enjoy the crown, but some other person; or to publish, That the Queen is an heretick, schismatick, tyrant, infidel or usurper of the crown; or to claim right to the crown, or to usurp the same during the Queen's life; or to affirm the right in succession of the crown in some other than the Queen; or to affirm, That the laws and statutes do not bind the right of the crown, and the descent, limitation, inheritance, or governance thereof.

Treason. 3 Inst. 6, 10, 12, 14. 4 Inst. 36. Poph. 122.

II. Whosoever shall during the Queen's life, by any book, or work written or printed, expresly affirm, (before the same be established by parliament) That any one particular person

APPENDIX 401

is or ought to be heir or successor to the Queen, except the
same be the natural issue of her body: or shall wilfully set
up in open place, or spread any books or scrowls to that
effect; or shall print, bind or put to sale, or utter, cause, &c.,
any such book or writing, he, his abettors and counsellers
shall for the first offence be a whole year imprisoned, and
forfeit half his goods; and for the second offence shall incur
the penalty of a præmunire. EXP. 26 H. 8. c. 13. 1 Ed. 6.
c. 12. 1 & 2 Ph. & M. c. 10. 1 El. c. 5.

CAP. II.

*An act against the bringing in, and putting in execution of bulls,
writings or instruments and other superstitious things from the
see of* Rome.

Where in the parliament holden at Westminster *in the fifth
year of the reign of our sovereign lady the Queen's majesty that
now is, by one act and statute then and there made, intituled,* An
act for the assurance of the Queen's majesty's royal power over
all states and subjects within her Highness dominions, *it is
among other things very well ordained and provided for the
abolishing of the usurped power and jurisdiction of the bishop of*
Rome *and of the see of* Rome, *heretofore unlawfully claimed and
usurped within this realm and other the dominions to the Queen's
majesty belonging, That no person or persons shall hold or stand
with, to set forth, maintain, defend or extol the same usurped
power, or attribute any manner of jurisdiction, authority or preheminence, to the same, to be had or used within this realm or any
the said dominions, upon pain to incur the danger, penalties and
forfeitures ordained and provided by the statute of provision and
præmunire, made in the sixteenth year of the reign of King*
Richard *the Second, as by the same act more at large it doth and
may appear:* (2) *and yet nevertheless divers seditious and very evil-
disposed people, without the respect of their duty to Almighty GOD,
or of the faith and allegiance which they ought to bear and have to
our said sovereign lady the Queen, and without all fear and regard
had to the said good law and statute, or the pains therein limited,
but minding, as it should seem, very seditiously and unnaturally,
not only to bring this realm and the imperial crown thereof (being
in very deed of itself most free) into the thraldom and subjection
of that foreign, usurped and unlawful jurisdiction, preheminence
and authority claimed by the said see of* Rome; (3) *but also to*

A rehearsal of the statute of 5 El. c. 1. touching the abolishing of the autho- rity of the bishop and see of Rome.

16 R. 2. c. 5.

D D

estrange and alienate the minds and hearts of sundry her Majesty's subjects from their dutiful obedience, and to raise and stir sedition and rebellion within this realm, to the disturbance of the most happy peace thereof; (4) have lately procured and obtained to themselves from the said bishop of *Rome* and his said see, divers bulls and writings, the effect whereof hath been, and is, to absolve and reconcile all those that will be contented to forsake their due obedience to our most gracious sovereign lady the Queen's majesty, and to yield and subject themselves to the said feigned, unlawful and usurped authority; (5) and by colour of the said bulls and writings, the said wicked persons very secretly, and most seditiously, in such parts of this realm where the people for want of good instruction are most weak, simple and ignorant, and thereby farthest from the good understanding of their duties toward GOD and the Queen's majesty, have by their lewd and subtil practices and perswasions so far forth wrought, that sundry simple and ignorant persons have been contented to be reconciled to the said usurped authority of the see of *Rome*, and to take absolution at the hands of the said naughty and subtil practisers; (6) whereby hath grown great disobedience and boldness in many, not only to withdraw and absent themselves from all divine service, now most godly set forth and used within this realm, but also have thought themselves discharged of and from all obedience, duty and allegiance to her Majesty, whereby most wicked and unnatural rebellion hath ensued, and to the further danger of this realm is hereafter very like to be renewed, if the ungodly and wicked attempts in that behalf be not by severity of laws in time restrained and bridled :

The effect of bulls brought from Rome.

Putting in ure any bull of absolution or reconciliation from the bishop of Rome.

II. For remedy and redress whereof, and to prevent the great mischiefs and inconveniences that thereby may ensue, be it enacted by the Queen's most excellent majesty, with the assent of the lords spiritual and temporal, and the commons, in this present parliament assembled, and by the authority of the same, That if any person or persons, after the first day of *July* next coming, shall use or put in ure in any place within this realm, or in any the Queen's dominions, any such bull, writing or instrument written or printed, of absolution or reconciliation, at any time heretofore obtained and gotten, or at any time hereafter to be obtained or gotten from the said bishop of *Rome* or any his successors, or from any other person or persons authorized or claiming authority by or from the said Bishop of *Rome*, his predecessors or successors, or see of *Rome*; (2) or if any person or persons after the said first day of *July* shall take upon him or them, by colour of any such bull, writing instrument or authority,

Absolving or reconciling of any person, and

to absolve or reconcile any person or persons, or to grant or promise to any person or persons within this realm, or any other the Queen's majesty's dominions any such absolution or reconciliation, by any speech, preaching, teaching, writing or any other open deed ; (3) or if any person or persons within this realm or any the Queen's dominions after the said first day of *July* shall willingly receive and take any such absolution or reconciliation : being absolved or reconciled.

III. Or else if any person or persons have obtained or gotten since the last day of the parliament holden in the first year of the Queen's majesty's reign, or after the said first day of *July* shall obtain or get, from the said bishop of *Rome*, or any his successors or see of *Rome*, any manner of bull writing or instrument, written or printed, containing any thing, matter or cause whatsoever ; (2) or shall publish, or by any ways or means put in ure any such bull, writing or instrument ; (3) that then all and every such act and acts, offence and offences shall be deemed and adjudged by the authority of this act to be high treason ; (4) and the offender and offenders therein, their procurers, abetters and counsellors to the fact and committing of the said offence or offences, shall be deemed and adjudged high traitors to the Queen and the realm ; (5) and being thereof lawfully indicted and attainted according to the course of the laws of this realm, shall suffer pains of death, and also lose and forfeit all their lands, tenements, hereditaments, goods and chattels, as in cases of high treason by the laws of this realm ought to be lost and forfeited. Getting of any bull from Rome containing any matter whatsoever, or publishing or putting in ure the same. 3 Inst. 101, 106.

IV. And be it further enacted by the authority aforesaid, That all and every aiders, comforters or maintainers of any the said offender or offenders, after the committing of any the said acts or offences, to the intent to set forth, uphold or allow the doing or execution of the said usurped power, jurisdiction or authority, touching or concerning the premises, or any part thereof, shall incur the pains and penalties contained in the statute of *præmunire* made in the sixteenth year of the reign of King *Richard* the Second. Aiders, comforters and maintainers of offenders after the offence. 16 R. 2. c. 5.

V. Provided always, and be it further enacted by the authority aforesaid, That if any person or persons, to whom any such absolution, reconciliation, bull, writing or instrument as is aforesaid, shall after the said first day of *July* be offered, moved or perswaded to be used, put in ure or executed, shall conceal the same offer, motion or perswasion, and not disclose and signify the same by writing or otherwise, within six weeks then next following, to some of the Queen's majesty's privy council, or else to the Concealing or not disclosing a bull or reconciliation offered.

president or vice-president of the Queen's majesty's council established in the north parts, or in the marches of *Wales*, for the time being, that then the same person or persons so concealing and not disclosing, or not signifying the said offer, motion or perswasion, shall incur the loss, danger, penalty and forfeiture of misprision of high treason:

VI. And that no person or persons shall at any time hereafter be impeached, molested or troubled in or for misprision of treason, for any offence or offences made treason by this act, other than such as by this act are before declared to be in case of misprision of high treason.

<small>Bringing into the realm, or using of agnus dei, pictures, crosses, &c.</small>

VII. And be it further enacted by the authority aforesaid, That if any persons or persons shall at any time after the said first day of *July* bring into this realm of *England*, or any the dominions of the same, any token or tokens, thing or things, called or named by the name of *agnus dei*, or any crosses, pictures, beads or such like vain and superstitious things, from the bishop or see of *Rome*, or from any person or persons authorized or claiming authority by or from the said bishop or see of *Rome*, to consecrate or hallow the same; (which said *agnus dei* is used to be specially hallowed and consecrated, as it is termed, by the said bishop in his own person, and the said crosses, pictures, beads and such like superstitious things been also hallowed either by the same bishop, or by others having power or pretending to have power for the same by or from him or his said see; and divers pardons, immunities and exemptions granted by the authority of the said see to such as shall receive and use the same:) (2) and that if the same person or persons so bringing in, as is aforesaid, such *agnus dei* and other like things as have been before specified, shall deliver, or cause or offer to be delivered the same, or any of them, to any subject of this realm, or of any the dominions of the same, to be worn or used in any wise: (3) that then as well the same person and persons so doing, as also all and every other person or persons which shall receive and take the same, to the intent to use or wear the same, being thereof lawfully convicted and attainted by the order of the common laws of this realm, shall incur the dangers, penalties, pains and forfeitures ordained and provided by the statute of *præmunire* and provision made in the sixteenth

<small>16 R. 2. c. 5.</small> year of the reign of King *Richard* the Second.

<small>Apprehending an offender, or disclosing his name.</small>

VIII. Provided nevertheless, and be it further enacted by the authority aforesaid, That if any person or persons, to whom any such *agnus dei* or other the things aforesaid shall be tendred and offered to be delivered, shall apprehend the party so offering the same, and bring him to the next justice of peace of that shire where such tender shall be made, if he shall be of power and able so to do, or for lack of such ability, shall within the space of three days next after such offer made as is aforesaid, disclose the name and names of such person or persons as so shall make the same offer, and the dwelling-places, or place of resort of the same person or persons (which he shall endeavour himself to know by all the ways and means he can) to the ordinary of that diocese, or to any justice of peace of that shire where such person or persons to whom such offer shall be made, as is aforesaid, shall be resiant: (2) and also if such person or persons to whom such offer shall be made, shall happen to receive any such *agnus dei* or other thing above-remembred, and shall within the space of one day next after such receipt deliver the same to any justice of peace within the same shire where the party so receiving shall be then resiant, or shall happen to be; (3) that then every such person or persons doing any the acts or things in this provision above-mentioned, in form above declared, shall not by force of this statute incur any danger or penalty appointed by this statute, or any other pain or penalty; this act, or any thing therein contained to the contrary in any wise notwithstanding. *Delivering an agnus dei to the ordinary, or a justice of peace.*

IX. And be it further enacted by the authority aforesaid, That all and every person and persons, which at any time since the beginning of the first year of the Queen's majesty's reign that now is, have brought or caused to be brought into this realm any such bulls, writings or instruments of reconciliation only as are above-mentioned, and now have any of the same bulls, writings or instruments in his or their hands or custody, and shall and do within the space of three months next after the end of any session or dissolution of this present parliament, bring and deliver all such bulls, writings and instruments which they or any of them now have in his or their custody, to the bishop of the diocese where such absolution hath been given and received, to the intent that the same bulls, writings or instruments may be cancelled and defaced, and shall openly and publickly before such bishop confess and acknowledge his or their offence therein, and humbly desire to be received, restored and admitted to the church of *England*, shall stand and be clearly pardoned and discharged of all and every offence and offences done or committed in any matter or cause concerning any of the said bulls, writings or instruments, for or touching such absolution *A pardon to them that shall bring in to be cancelled those bulls which before they received.*

or reconciliation only. (2) And that all and every person or persons which have received or taken any absolution from the said bishop of *Rome*, or his said see of *Rome*, of any reconciliation unto the said bishop of *Rome*, or to the said see of *Rome*, sithence the said first year of the reign of our said sovereign lady the Queen, and shall within the said space of three months next after any session or dissolution of this present parliament come before the bishop of the diocese of such place where such absolution or reconciliation was had or made, and shall publickly and openly before the same bishop confess and acknowledge his or their offence therein, and humbly desire to be received, restored and admitted to the church of *England*, shall likewise stand and be clearly pardoned and discharged of all and every offence and offences done or committed in any matter or cause concerning the said bulls, writings or instruments, for or touching only receiving of such absolution or reconciliation, and for and concerning all absolution or reconciliation had or received by colour of any the said bulls, writings or instruments only.

X. Provided also, and be it further enacted by the authority aforesaid, That if any justice of peace, to whom any matter or offence before-mentioned shall be uttered, shewed, or declared, as is aforesaid, do not within the space of fourteen days next after it shall be to him shewed or uttered, signify or declare the same to some one of the Queen's majesty's privy council, that then the same justice of peace shall incur the danger, pain and forfeiture provided by the said statute made in the said sixteenth year of King *Richard* the Second.

XI. Provided also, and be it further enacted by the authority aforesaid, That if any nobleman, being a peer of this realm, shall at any time hereafter happen to be indicted for any the offence or offences aforesaid, that then every such nobleman and peer of this realm shall have his trial by his peers, as in cases of high treason and misprision of treason hath heretofore been accustomed or used.

XII. Saving to all and every person and persons, bodies politick and corporate, their heirs and successors, and the heirs and successors of every of them, other than the said offenders and their heirs claiming only as heir or heirs to any such offenders, and such person and persons as claim to any their uses, (2) all such rights, titles, interests, possessions, leases, rents, reversions, remainders, offices, fees and all other profits, commodities and hereditaments, as they or any of them shall have at the day of the committing of such offence or offences, or at any time before, in as large and ample manner to all intents and purposes, as if this act had never been had nor made; any thing herein contained to the contrary thereof notwithstanding. 23 *El. c.* 1.

CAP. XII.

An act for the ministers of the church to be of sound religion.

That the churches of the Queen's majesty's dominions may be served with pastors of sound religion, (2) be it enacted by the authority of this present parliament, That every person under the degree of a bishop, which doth or shall pretend to be a priest or minister of God's holy word and sacraments, by reason of any other form of institution, consecration or ordering, than the form set forth by parliament in the time of the late King of most worthy memory, King *Edward* the Sixth, or now used in the reign of our most gracious sovereign Lady, before the feast of the nativity of Christ next following, (3) shall in the presence of the bishop or guardian of the spiritualities of some one diocese where he hath or shall have ecclesiastical living, declare his assent, and subscribe to all the articles of religion, which only concern the confession of the true christian faith and the doctrine of the sacraments, comprised in a book imprinted, intituled, *Articles, whereupon it was agreed by the archbishops and bishops of both provinces, and the whole clergy in the convocation holden at* London *in the year of our Lord God one thousand five hundred sixty and two, according to the computation of the church of* England, *for the avoiding of the diversities of opinions, and for the establishing of consent touching true religion put forth by the Queen's authority;* (4) and shall bring from such bishop or guardian of spiritualities in writing, under his seal authentick, a testimonial of such assent and subscription; (5) and openly on some sunday in the time of the publick service afore noon, in every church where by reason of any ecclesiastical living he ought to attend, read both the said testimonial and the said articles; (6) upon pain that every such person which shall not before the said feast do as is above appointed, shall be *ipso facto* deprived, and all his ecclesiastical promotions shall be void, as if he then were naturally dead.

II. And that if any person ecclesiastical, or which shall have ecclesiastical living, shall advisedly maintain or affirm any doctrine directly contrary or repugnant to any of the said articles, and being convented before the bishop of the diocese or the ordinary, or before the Queen's highness commissioners in causes ecclesiastical, shall persist therein, or not revoke his error, or after such revocation eftsoon affirm such untrue doctrine, such maintaining or affirming and persisting, or such eftsoon affirming, shall be just cause to deprive such person of his ecclesiastical promotions; (2) and it shall be lawful to the bishop of the diocese or the ordinary, or the said commissioners, to deprive such person so persisting, or lawfully convicted of such eftsoons affirming, and upon such sentence of deprivation pronounced he shall be indeed deprived.

<small>Several things required in him who shall be admitted to a benefice.
1 Leon. 230.
1 And. 62.</small>

III. And that no person shall hereafter be admitted to any benefice with cure, except he then be of the age of three and twenty years at the least and a deacon, and shall first have subscribed the said articles in presence of the ordinary, and publickly read the same in the parish church of that benefice, with declaration of his unfeigned assent to the same: (2) and that every person after the end of this session of parliament, to be admitted to a benefice with cure, except that within two months after his induction he do publickly read the said articles in the same church whereof he shall have cure, in the time of common prayer there, with declaration of his unfeigned assent thereunto, and be admitted to minister the sacraments within one year after his induction, if he be not so admitted before, shall be upon every such default, *ipso facto*, immediately deprived.

IV. And that no person now permitted by any dispensation or otherwise, shall retain any benefice with cure, being under the age of one and twenty years, or not being deacon at the least, or which shall not be admitted as is aforesaid, within one year next after the making of this act, or within six months after he shall accomplish the age of four and twenty years, on pain that such his dispensation shall be meerly void.

<small>The age of a minister or preacher, and his testimonials.
3 Bulstr. 90.
3 Mod. 67.
4 Mod. 135, 136.
2 Salk. 539.</small>

V. And that none shall be made minister, or admitted to preach or administer the sacraments, being under the age of four and twenty years; (2) nor unless he first bring to the bishop of that diocese, from men known to the bishop to be of sound religion, a testimonial both of his honest life and of his professing the doctrine expressed in the said articles: (3) nor unless he be able to answer, and render to the ordinary an account of his faith, in *latin* according to the said articles, or have special gift or ability to be a preacher: (4) nor shall be admitted to the order of deacon or ministry, unless he shall first subscribe to the said articles.

<small>Who may have a</small>

VI. And that none hereafter shall be admitted to any benefice with cure of or above the value of thirty pounds yearly in the Queen's books, unless he shall then be a batchelour of divinity, or a preacher lawfully allowed by some bishop within this realm, or by one of the universities of *Cambridge* or *Oxford*.

<small>benefice of the yearly value of 30 l.</small>

VII. And that all admissions to benefices, institutions and inductions, to be made of any person contrary to the form or any provision of this act, and all tolerations, dispensations, qualifications and licences whatsoever to be made to the contrary hereof, shall be meerly void in law, as if they never were.

<small>Admissions, inductions, tolerations.</small>

VIII. Provided alway, That no title to confer or present by lapse, shall accrue upon any deprivation *ipso facto*, but after six months after notice of such deprivation given by the ordinary to the patron. 1 Roll. 155.

<small>No lapse upon deprivation, but after notice. Dyer 377.</small>

23 ELIZABETH.

Cap. I.

An act to retain the Queen's majesty's subjects in their due obedience.

Where sithence the statute made in the thirteenth year of the reign of the Queen our sovereign lady, intituled, An act against the bringing in, and putting in execution of bulls, writings and instruments, and other superstitious things from the see of *Rome*, *divers evil-affected persons have practised, contrary to the meaning of the said statute, by other means than by bulls or instruments written or printed, to withdraw divers the Queen's majesty's subjects from their natural obedience to her Majesty, to obey the said usurped authority of* Rome, *and in respect of the same to perswade great numbers to withdraw their due obedience from her Majesty's laws, established for the due service of Almighty God.*

<small>13 Eliz. c. 2. 3 Inst. 193.</small>

II. For reformation whereof, and to declare the true meaning of the said law, be it declared and enacted by the authority of this present parliament, That all persons whatsoever, which have or shall have, or shall pretend to have power, or shall by any ways or means put in practice to absolve, perswade or withdraw any of the Queen's majesty's subjects, or any within her Highness realms and dominions, from their natural obedience to her Majesty : (2) or to withdraw them for that intent from the religion now by her Highness authority established within her Highness dominions, to the *Romish* religion, (3) or to move them or any of them to promise any obedience to any pretended autho-

<small>Treason to withdraw any from the religion established to the Romish religion. 1 Leon, 239.</small>

rity of the see of *Rome*, or of any other prince, state or potentate, to be had or used within her dominions, (4) or shall do any overt act to that intent or purpose ; and every of them shall be to all intents adjudged to be traitors, and being thereof lawfully convicted shall have judgment, suffer and forfeit, as in case of high treason. (5) And if any person shall after the end of this session of parliament, by any means be willingly absolved or withdrawn as aforesaid, or willingly be reconciled, or shall promise any obedience to any such pretended authority, prince, state or potentate, as is aforesaid, that then every such person, their procurers and counsellors thereunto, being thereof lawfully convicted, shall be taken, tried and judged, and shall suffer and forfeit, as in cases of high treason.

It shall be treason to be reconciled or withdrawn to the Romish religion.

III. And be it likewise enacted and declared, That all and every person and persons that shall wittingly be aiders or maintainers of such persons so offending as is above expressed, or any of them, knowing the same, or which shall conceal any offence as aforesaid, and shall not within twenty days at the furthest, after such persons knowledge of such offence, disclose the same to some justice of peace or other higher officer, shall be taken, tried and judged, and shall suffer and forfeit, as offenders in misprision of treason.

The penalty of aiders, maintainers and concealers.

IV. And be it likewise enacted, That every person which shall say or sing mass, being thereof lawfully convicted, shall forfeit the sum of two hundred marks, and be committed to prison in the next gaol, there to remain by the space of one year, and from thenceforth till he have paid the said sum of two hundred marks : (2) and that every person which shall willingly hear mass, shall forfeit the sum of one hundred marks, and suffer imprisonment for a year.

The forfeiture for saying or hearing of mass.

V. Be it also further enacted by the authority aforesaid, That every person above the age of sixteen years, which shall not repair to some church, chapel or usual place of common prayer but forbear the same, contrary to the tenor of a statute made in the first year of her Majesty's reign, for uniformity of common prayer, and being thereof lawfully convicted, shall forfeit to the Queen's majesty for every month, after the end of this session of parliament, which he or she shall so forbear, twenty pounds of lawful *English* money ; (2) and that over and besides the said forfeitures, every person so forbearing by the space of twelve months as aforesaid, shall for his or her obstinacy, after certificate thereof in writing made into the court commonly called the King's bench, by the ordinary of the diocese, a justice

The penalty of not coming to the church by the space of a month, according to the stat. 1 Eliz. c. 2. The King may seize two parts of the offenders lands, &c. in lieu of the twenty pounds. 3 Jac. 1. c. 4. s. 11. Hob. 127. 1 Leon. 241. 2 Leon. 5. 1 Anders. 138.

APPENDIX 411

of assise and gaol-delivery, or a justice of peace of the county where such offender shall dwell or be, be bound with two sufficient sureties in the sum of two hundred pounds at least, to the good behaviour, (3) and so to continue bound, until such time as the persons so bound do conform themselves and come to the church, according to the true meaning of the said statute made in the said first year of the Queen's majesty's reign.

<small>Hob. 205.
11 Co. 66.
Cro. Jac. 480.
1 Roll. 89, 92.
Lane 60, 91.
Bridg. 120.
2 Bulstr. 324.
3 Bulstr. 87.</small>

VI. And be it further enacted, That if any person or persons, body politick or corporate, after the feast of *Pentecost* next coming, shall keep or maintain any school-master which shall not repair to church as is aforesaid, or be allowed by the bishop or ordinary of the diocese where such school-master shall be so kept, shall forfeit and lose for every month so keeping him, ten pounds.

<small>The forfeiture for keeping of a school-master not repairing to the church, or not allowed by the ordinary.</small>

VII. (Provided that no such ordinary or their ministers shall take any thing for the said allowance.) (2) And such school-master or teacher, presuming to teach contrary to this act, and being thereof lawfully convicted, shall be disabled to be a teacher of youth, and shall suffer imprisonment without bail or mainprise for one year.

XV. Provided also, That neither this act, nor any thing therein contained, shall extend to take away or abridge the authority or jurisdiction of the ecclesiastical censures for any cause or matter, but that the archbishops and bishops and other ecclesiastical judges may do and proceed, as before the making of this act they lawfully did or might have done; any thing in this act to the contrary notwithstanding. 1 *W. & M. stat.* 1. *c.* 18.

<small>Ecclesiastical censures.</small>

27 ELIZABETH.

Cap. II.

An act against jesuits, seminary priests, and other such like disobedient persons.

Where divers persons called or professed jesuits, seminary priests and other priests, which have been, and from time to time are made in the parts beyond the seas, by or according to the order and rites of the Romish Church, have of late years comen and been sent, and daily do come and are sent, into this realm of England and other the Queen's majesty's dominions, (2) of purpose (as it hath

<small>Jesuits and priests in England shall depart, and none shall come into this realm. The penalty for relieving of them, &c.</small>

appeared, *as well by sundry of their own examinations and confessions, as by divers other manifest means and proofs*) not only to withdraw her Highness subjects from their due obedience to her Majesty, but also to stir up and move sedition, rebellion and open hostility within the same her Highness realms and dominions, (3) to the great endangering of the safety of her most royal person, and to the utter ruin, desolation and overthrow of the whole realm, if the same be not the sooner by some good means foreseen and prevented:

<small>The causes why jesuits and priests do come into this realm.</small>

II. For reformation whereof be it ordained, established and enacted by the Queen's most excellent majesty, and the lords spiritual and temporal, and the commons, in this present parliament assembled, and by the authority of the same parliament, That all and every jesuits, seminary priests, and other priests whatsoever made or ordained out of the realm of *England* or other her Highness dominions, or within any of her Majesty's realms or dominions, by any authority, power or jurisdiction derived, challenged or pretended from the see of *Rome*, since the feast of the nativity of St. *John Baptist* in the first year of her Highness reign, shall within forty days next after the end of this present session of parliament depart out of this realm of *England*, and out of all other her Highness realms and dominions, if the wind, weather and passage shall serve for the same, or else so soon after the end of the said forty days as the wind, weather and passage shall so serve.

<small>All jesuits and priests shall depart forth of the realm. Poph. 93.</small>

III. And be it further enacted by the authority aforesaid, That it shall not be lawful to or for any jesuit, seminary priest, or other such priest, deacon, or religious or ecclesiastical person whatsoever, being born within this realm, or any other her Highness dominions, and heretofore since the said feast of the nativity of St. *John Baptist*, in the first year of her Majesty's reign, made, ordained or professed, or hereafter to be made, ordained or professed by any authority or jurisdiction derived, challenged or pretended from the see of *Rome*, by or of what name, title or degree soever the same shall be called or known, to come into, be or remain in any part of this realm, or any other her Highness dominions, after the end of the same forty days, other than in such special cases, and upon such special occasions only, and for such time only, as is expressed in this act; and if he do, that then every such offence shall be taken and adjudged to be high treason; and every person so offending shall for his offence be adjudged a traitor, and shall suffer, lose and forfeit, as in case of high treason.

<small>No jesuits or priests shall come into, or remain in this realm.</small>

<small>Receiving or relieving</small>

IV. And every person which after the end of the same forty

days, and after such time of departure as is before limited and appointed, shall wittingly and willingly receive, relieve, comfort, aid or maintain any such jesuit, seminary priest or other priest, deacon or religious or ecclesiastical person, as is aforesaid, being at liberty, or out of hold, knowing him to be a jesuit, seminary priest or other such priest, deacon, or religious or ecclesiastical person, as is aforesaid, shall also for such offence be adjudged a felon, without benefit of clergy, and suffer death, lose and forfeit, as in case of one attainted of felony. *a jesuit or priest shall be felony.*

V. And be it further enacted by the authority aforesaid, If any of her Majesty's subjects (not being a jesuit, a seminary priest, or other such priest, deacon, or religious or ecclesiastical person, as is before-mentioned) now being, or which hereafter shall be of, or brought up in, any college of jesuits, or seminary already erected and ordained, or hereafter to be erected or ordained, in the parts beyond the seas, or out of this realm in any foreign parts shall not within six months next after proclamation in that behalf to be made in the city of *London*, under the great seal of *England*, return into this realm, and thereupon within two days next after such return, before the bishop of the diocese, or two justices of peace of the county where he shall arrive, submit himself to her Majesty and her laws, and take the oath set forth by act in the first year of her reign; that then every such person which shall otherwise return, come into, or be in this realm or any other her Highness dominions, for such offence of returning or being in this realm or any other her Highness dominions, without submission, as aforesaid, shall also be adjudged a traitor, and suffer, lose and forfeit, as in case of high treason. *They who be in seminaries shall after proclamation return and take the oath.*

VI. And be it further enacted by the authority aforesaid, If any person under her Majesty's subjection or obedience shall at any time after the end of the said forty days, by way of exchange, or by any other shift, way or means whatsoever, wittingly and willingly, either directly or indirectly, convey, deliver or send, or cause or procure to be conveyed or delivered, to be sent over the seas, or out of this realm, or out of any other her Majesty's dominions or territories, into any foreign parts, (2) or shall wittingly or willingly yield, give or contribute any money or other relief to or for any jesuit, seminary priest, or such other priest, deacon, or religious or ecclesiastical person, as is aforesaid; (3) or to or for the maintenance or relief of any college of jesuits, or seminary already erected or ordained, or hereafter to be erected or ordained, in any the parts beyond the seas, or out of this realm in any foreign parts, or of any person then being of or in *Sending relief to any jesuit, priest or other person abiding in a seminary.*

any the same colleges or seminaries, and not returned into this realm with submission, as in this act is expressed, and continuing in the same realm : (5) That then every such person so offending, for the same offence shall incur the danger and penalty of a *præmunire*, mentioned in the statute of *præmunire*, made in the sixteenth year of the reign of King *Richard* the Second.

16 R. 2. c. 5.

None shall send his child or other beyond the seas without licence. EXP. 3 Jac. 1. c. 5.

VII. And be it further enacted by the authority aforesaid, That it shall not be lawful for any person of or under her Highness obedience, at any time after the said forty days, during her Majesty's life (which God long preserve) to send his or her child, or other person, being under his or her government, into any the parts beyond the seas out of her Highness obedience, without the special licence of her Majesty, or of four of her Highness privy council, under their hands in that behalf first had or obtained (except merchants, for such only as they or any of them shall send over the seas only for or about his, her or their trade of merchandize, or to serve as mariners, and not otherwise) upon pain to forfeit and lose for every such their offence the sum of one hundred pounds.

Where the offences committed against this act shall be enquired of and determined.

VIII. And be it also enacted by the authority aforesaid, That every offence to be committed or done against the tenor of this act shall and may be inquired of, heard and determined, as well in the court commonly called the King's bench in the county where the same court shall for the time be, as also in any other county within this realm, or any other her Highness dominions where the offence is or shall be committed, or where the offender shall be apprehended and taken.

Transporting of jesuits, priests, &c.

IX. Provided also, and be it enacted by the authority aforesaid, That it shall and may be lawful for and to every owner and master of any ship, bark or boat, at any time within the said forty days, or other time before limited for their departure, to transport into any the parts beyond the seas any such jesuit, seminary priest, or other priest aforesaid, so as the same jesuit, seminary priest, or other priest aforesaid so to be transported, do deliver unto the mayor or other chief officer of the town, port or place, where he shall be taken in to be transported, his name, and in what place he received such order, and how long he hath remained in this realm, or in any other her Highness dominions, being under her obedience.

A jesuit or priest submitting himself, and taking the oath, and obeying the laws.

X. Provided also, That this act, or any thing therein contained, shall not in any wise extend to any such jesuit, seminary priest, or other such priest, deacon, or religious or ecclesiastical person as is before-mentioned, as shall at any time within the said forty days, or within three days after that he shall hereafter come into this realm, or any other her Highness dominions, submit himself to some archbishop or bishop of this realm, or to some justice of peace within the county where he shall arrive or land, and do thereupon truly and sincerely, before the same archbishop, bishop, or such justice of peace, take the said oath set forth in *anno primo*, and by writing under his hand confess and acknowledge, and from thenceforth continue, his due obedience unto her Highness laws, statutes and ordinances, made and provided or to be made or provided in causes of religion.

_{1 El. 1. c. 1.}

XI. Provided always, if it happen at any time hereafter any peer of this realm to be indicted of any offence made treason, felony or *præmunire*, by this act, that he shall have his trial by his peers, as in other cases of treason, felony or *præmunire*, is accustomed.

XII. Provided nevertheless, and it is declared by authority aforesaid, That if any such jesuit, seminary priest, or other priest abovesaid, shall fortune to be so weak or infirm of body, that he or they may not pass out of this realm by the time herein limited without imminent danger of life, and this understood as well by the corporal oath of the party as by other good means, unto the bishop of the diocese and two justices of peace of the same county where such person or persons do dwell or abide; that then, and upon good and sufficient bond of the person or persons, with sureties, of the sum of two hundred pounds at the least, with condition that he or they shall be of good behaviour towards our sovereign lady the Queen and all her liege people, then he or they so licenced and doing as is aforesaid, shall and may remain and be still within this realm, without any loss or danger to fall on him or them by this act, for so long time as by the same bishop and justices shall be limited and appointed, so as the same time of abode exceed not the space of six months at the most: (2) And that no person or persons shall sustain any loss, or incur any danger by this act, for the receiving or maintaining of any such person or persons so licenced as is aforesaid, for and during such time only as such person or persons shall be so licenced to tarry within this realm; any thing contained in this act to the contrary notwithstanding.

XIII. And be it also further enacted by authority aforesaid, That every person or persons, being subjects of this realm, which after the said forty days shall know and understand that any such jesuit, seminary priest, or other priest abovesaid, shall abide, stay, tarry or be within this realm or other the Queen's dominions

_{One knowing a jesuit or priest to remain in the realm, and not discovering it to a justice of peace.}

and countries, contrary to the true meaning of this act, and shall not discover the same unto some justice of peace or other higher officer, within twelve days next after his said knowledge, but willingly conceal his knowledge therein; That every such offender shall make fine, and be imprisoned at the Queen's pleasure: (2) and that if such justice of peace, or other such officer to whom such matter shall be so discovered, do not within eight and twenty days then next following give information thereof to some of the Queen's privy council, or to the president or vice-president of the Queen's council established in the north, or in the marches of *Wales*, for the time being; That then he or they so offending shall for every such offence forfeit the sum of two hundred marks.

<small>Skinner 369.</small>

XIV. And be it likewise enacted by the authority aforesaid, That such of the privy council, president or vice-president, to whom such information shall be made, shall thereupon deliver a note in writing, subscribed with his own hand, to the party by whom he shall receive such information, testifying that such information was made unto him.

<small>All oaths, bonds and submissions, certified into the chancery.</small>

XV. And be it also enacted, That all such oaths, bonds and submissions, as shall be made by force of this act, as aforesaid, shall be certified into the chancery by such parties before whom the same shall be made, within three months next after such submission; (2) upon pain to forfeit and lose for every such offence one hundred pounds of lawful *English* money; the said forfeiture to be to the Queen, her heirs and successors:

<small>None submitting himself shall come within ten miles of the Queen.</small>

XVI. And that if any person so submitting himself, as aforesaid, do at any time within the space of ten years after such submission made, come within ten miles of such place where her Majesty shall be, without especial licence from her Majesty in that behalf to be obtained in writing under her hand; That then and from thenceforth such person shall take no benefit of his said submission, but that the same submission shall be void as if the same had never been. 1 *Jac.* 1. *c.* 4. 3 *Jac.* 1. *c.* 5.

29 ELIZABETH.

Cap. VI.

An act for the more speedy and due execution of certain branches of the statute made in the twenty-third year of the Queen's majesty's reign, intituled, An act to retain the Queen's majesty's subjects in their due obedience.

<small>Certain assurances of lands</small>

For avoiding of all frauds and delays heretofore practised, or hereafter to be put in ure, to the hindrance of the due and

APPENDIX. 417

speedy execution of the statute made in the session of parliament
holden by prorogation at *Westminster* the sixteenth day of
January in the three and twentieth year of the reign of our
most gracious sovereign lady the Queen's majesty, intituled, *An
act to retain the Queen's majesty's subjects in their due obedience*,
(2) be it enacted by the authority of this present parliament,
That every feoffment, gift, grant, conveyance, alienation, estate,
lease, incumbrance and limitation of use, of or out of any lands,
tenements or hereditaments whatsoever, had or made at any time
since the beginning of the Queen's majesty's reign, or at any time
hereafter to be had or made, by any person which hath not
repaired or shall not repair to some church, chapel or usual place
of common prayer, but hath forborn or shall forbear the same,
contrary to the tenor of the said statute, (3) and which is or
shall be revokable at the pleasure of such offender, (4) or in any
wise directly or indirectly meant or intended, to or for the behoof,
relief or maintenance, or at the disposition of any such offender,
(5) or wherewith or whereby, or in consideration whereof, such
offender or his family shall be maintained, relieved or kept;
(6) shall be deemed and taken to be utterly frustrate and void,
as against the Queen's majesty, for or concerning the levying and
paying of such sums of money as any such person by the laws or
statutes of the realm already made ought to pay or forfeit for
not coming or repairing to any church, chapel, or usual place of
common prayer, or for saying, hearing, or being at any mass;
(7) and shall also be seized and had to and for her Majesty's use
and behoof, as hereafter in this act is mentioned; any pretence,
colour, feigned consideration, or expressing of any use, to the
contrary notwithstanding.

<small>made by recusants shall be void to the Queen. In what courts they shall be convicted. 23 Eliz. c. 1. Moor 523. pl. 691. Lane 60, 91. 1 Roll. 7, 92, 93.</small>

IV. And be it also enacted by the authority aforesaid, That
every such offender, in not repairing to divine service, but forbearing the same contrary to the said statute, as hereafter shall
fortune to be thereof once convicted, shall in such of the terms
of *Easter* or *Michaelmas* as shall be next after such conviction,
pay into the said receipt of the exchequer after the rate of twenty
pounds for every month, which shall be contained in the indictment whereupon such conviction shall be; (2) and shall also for
every month after such conviction, without any other indictment
or conviction, pay into the receipt of the exchequer aforesaid at
two times in the year, that is to say, in every *Easter* term and
Michaelmas term, as much as then shall remain unpaid, after the
rate of twenty pounds for every month after such conviction:
(3) and if default shall be made in any part of any payment

<small>2 Roll. 30.

11 Co. 57.

The Queen may take all the offender's goods, and two parts of his lands and leases, who payeth not twenty pounds a month.</small>

E E

418 CHURCH AND STATE UNDER THE TUDORS

¹ Roll. 04.
² Roll. 25.
12 Co. 2.
Enforced by
1 Jac. 1. c. 4.
s. 5.

aforesaid, contrary to the form herein before limited, That then and so often the Queen's majesty shall and may, by process out of the said exchequer, take, seize and enjoy all the goods, and two parts as well of all the lands, tenements and hereditaments, leases and farms of such offender, as of all other the lands, tenements and hereditaments liable to such seisure or to the penalties aforesaid, by the true meaning of this act, leaving the third part only of the same lands, tenements and hereditaments, leases and farms, to and for the maintenance and relief of the same offender, his wife, children and family.

35 ELIZABETH.

Cap. I.

An act to retain the Queen's majesty's subjects in their due obedience.

Punishment of persons obstinately refusing to come to church, and persuading others to impugn the Queen's authority in ecclesiastical causes.

For the preventing and avoiding of such great inconveniencies and perils as might happen and grow by the wicked and dangerous practices of seditious sectaries and disloyal persons; (2) be it enacted by the Queen's most excellent majesty, and by the lords spiritual and temporal, and the commons, in this present parliament assembled, and by the authority of the same, That if any person or persons above the age of sixteen years, which shall obstinately refuse to repair to some church, chapel or usual place of common prayer, to hear divine service established by her Majesty's laws and statutes in that behalf made, and shall forbear to do the same by the space of a month next after, without any lawful cause, shall at any time after forty days next after the end of this session of parliament, by printing, writing, or express words or speeches, advisedly or purposely practise or go about to move or persuade any of her Majesty's subjects, or any other within her Highness realms or dominions, to deny, withstand and impugn her Majesty's power and authority in cases ecclesiastical, united and annexed to the imperial crown of this realm; (3) or to that end or purpose shall advisedly and maliciously move or persuade any other person whatsoever to forbear or abstain from coming to church to hear divine service, or to receive the communion according to her Majesty's laws and statutes aforesaid, or to come to or be present at any unlawful assemblies, conventicles or meetings, under colour or pretence of any exercise of religion, contrary to her Majesty's said laws and statutes : (4) or if any person or persons which shall obstinately refuse to repair to some

Altered by 1
W. & M. sess.
1. c. 18.

church, chapel or usual place of common prayer, and shall forbear by the space of a month to hear divine service, as is aforesaid, shall after the said forty days, either of him or themselves, or by the motion, persuasion, enticement or allurement of any other, willingly join in, or be present at, any such assemblies, conventicles or meetings, under colour or pretence of any such exercise of religion, contrary to the laws and statutes of this realm, as is aforesaid ; (5) that then every such person so offending as aforesaid, and being thereof lawfully convicted, shall be committed to prison, there to remain without bail or mainprise, until they shall conform and yield themselves to come to some church, chapel or usual place of common prayer, and hear divine service, according to her Majesty's laws and statutes aforesaid, and to make such open submission and declaration of their said conformity, as hereafter in this act is declared and appointed. The penalty for being present at unlawful conventicles for religion.

II. Provided always, and be it further enacted by the authority aforesaid, That if any such person or persons, which shall offend against this act as aforesaid, shall not within three months next after they shall be convicted of their said offence, conform themselves to the obedience of the laws and statutes of this realm, in coming to the church to hear divine service, and in making such publick confession and submission, as hereafter in this act is appointed and expressed, being thereunto required by the bishop of the diocese, or any justice of the peace of the county where the same person shall happen to be, or by the minister or curate of the parish ; that in every such case every such offender, being thereunto warned or required by any justice of the peace of the same county where such offender shall then be, shall upon his and their corporal oath before the justices of the peace in the open quarter-sessions of the same county, or at the assizes and gaol-delivery of the same county, before the justices of the same assizes and gaol-delivery, abjure this realm of *England*, and all other the Queen's majesty's dominions for ever, unless her Majesty shall license the party to return ; (2) and thereupon shall depart out of this realm at such haven or port, and within such time, as shall in that behalf be assigned and appointed by the said justices before whom such abjuration shall be made, unless the same offender be letted or stayed by such lawful and reasonable means or causes, as by the common laws of this realm are permitted and allowed in cases of abjuration for felony ; and in such cases of let or stay, then within such reasonable and convenient time after, as the common law requireth in case of abjuration for felony, as is aforesaid : (3) and that the justices of peace before whom any An offender not conforming himself shall abjure the realm.

such abjuration shall happen to be made, as is aforesaid, shall cause the same presently to be entred of record before them, and shall certify the same to the justices of assizes and gaol-delivery of the said county, at the next assizes or gaol-delivery to be holden in the same county.

The punishment for refusing to abjure, not departing, or returning without licence.

III. And if any such offender, which by the tenor and intent of this act is to be abjured as is aforesaid, shall refuse to make such abjuration as is aforesaid, or after such abjuration made, shall not go to such haven, and within such time as is before appointed, and from thence depart out of this realm, according to this present act, or after such his departure shall return or come again into any her Majesty's realms or dominions, without her Majesty's special licence in that behalf first had and obtained ; that then in every such case the person so offending shall be adjudged a felon, and shall suffer as in case of felony, without benefit of clergy.

An offender shall be discharged upon his open submission. Latch 16.

IV. And furthermore be it enacted by the authority of this present parliament, That if any person or persons that shall at any time hereafter offend against this act, shall before he or they be so warned or required to make abjuration according to the tenor of this act, repair to some parish church on some *Sunday* or other festival day, and then and there hear divine service, and at service-time, before the sermon, or reading of the gospel, make public and open submission and declaration of his and their conformity to her Majesty's laws and statutes, as hereafter in this act is declared and appointed ; that then the same offender shall thereupon be clearly discharged of and from all and every the penalties and punishments inflicted or imposed by this act for any of the offences aforesaid. The same submission to be made as hereafter followeth ; that is to say,

The form of the submission.

V. I *A. B.* do humbly confess and acknowledge, That I have grievously offended God in contemning her Majesty's godly and lawful government and authority, by absenting my self from church, and from hearing divine service, contrary to the godly laws and statutes of this realm, and in using and frequenting disordered and unlawful conventicles and assemblies, under pretence and colour of exercise of religion : (2) and I am heartily sorry for the same, and do acknowledge and testify in my conscience that no other person hath or ought to have any power or authority over her Majesty : (3) and I do promise and protest, without any dissimulation, or any colour or means of any dispensation, That from henceforth I will from time to time obey and perform her Majesty's laws and statutes, in repairing to the church and hearing divine service, and do my uttermost endeavour to maintain and defend the same.

VI. And that every minister or curate of every parish where such submission and declaration of conformity shall hereafter be so made by any such offender as aforesaid, shall presently enter the same into a book to be kept in every parish for that purpose, and within ten days next following shall certify the same in writing to the bishop of the same diocese. *The minister shall enter the submission in a book.*

VII. Provided nevertheless, That if any such offender, after such submission made as is aforesaid, shall afterwards fall into relapse, or eftsoons obstinately refuse to repair to some church, chapel or usual place of common prayer, to hear divine service, and shall forbear the same as aforesaid, or shall come or be present at any such assemblies, conventicles or meetings, under colour or pretence of any exercise of religion, contrary to her Majesty's laws and statutes; that then every such offender shall lose all such benefit as he or she might otherwise by virtue of this act have or enjoy by reason of their said submission, and shall thereupon stand and remain in such plight, condition and degree, to all intents as though such submission had never been made. *The offender submitting, falleth into a relapse.*

VIII. *And for that every person having house and family, is in duty bound to have special regard to the good government and ordering of the same ;* Be it enacted by the authority aforesaid, That if any person or persons shall at any time hereafter relieve, maintain, retain or keep in his or their house or otherwise, any person which shall obstinately refuse to come to some church, chapel or usual place of common prayer, to hear divine service, and shall forbear the same by the space of a month together, contrary to the laws and statutes of this realm ; that then every person which shall so relieve, maintain, retain or keep any such person offending as aforesaid, after notice thereof to him or them given by the ordinary of the diocese, any justice of assizes of the circuit, or any justice of peace of the county, or the minister, curate or church-wardens of the parish where such person shall then be, or by any of them, shall forfeit to the Queen's majesty for every person so relieved, maintained, retained or kept, after such notice as aforesaid, ten pounds for every month that he or they shall so relieve, maintain, retain or keep any such person so offending. *The forfeiture for the keeping a recusant in one's house after notice. Repealed by 3 Jac. 1. c. 4. s. 31. and other provisions relating hereto, s. 32.*

IX. Provided nevertheless, That this act shall not in any wise extend to punish or impeach any person or persons for relieving, maintaining or keeping his or their wife, father, mother, child or children, wards, brother or sister, or his wife's father or mother, *What sort of recusants may be kept, &c. repealed by 3 Jac. 1. c. 4. s. 31.*

not having any certain place of habitation of their own, or the husbands or wives of any of them ; or for relieving, maintaining or keeping any such person as shall be committed by authority to the custody of any by whom they shall be so relieved, maintained or kept ; any thing in this act contained to the contrary notwithstanding.

<small>Popish recusants. Feme covert.</small> XII. Provided also, That no popish recusant, or feme covert, shall be compelled or bound to abjure by virtue of this act.

Cap. II.

An act for restraining popish recusants to some certain places of abode.

<small>Penalty of a convicted popish recusant removing above five miles from his house. Where a recusant having no house shall make his abode. 3 Bulstr. 87. Carthew 291.</small> *For the better discovering and avoiding of such traiterous and most dangerous conspiracies and attempts as are daily devised and practised against our most gracious sovereign lady the Queen's majesty and the happy estate of this common weal, by sundry wicked and seditious persons, who terming themselves catholicks, and being indeed spies and intelligencers, not only for her Majesty's foreign enemies, but also for rebellious and traiterous subjects born within her Highness realms and dominions, and hiding their most detestable and devilish purposes under a false pretext of religion and conscience, do secretly wander and shift from place to place within this realm, to corrupt and seduce her Majesty's subjects, and to stir them to sedition and rebellion:*

II. Be it ordained and enacted by our sovereign lady the Queen's majesty, and the lords spiritual and temporal, and the commons, in this present parliament assembled, and by the authority of the same, That every person above the age of sixteen years, born within any of the Queen's majesty's realms and dominions, or made denizen, being a popish recusant, and before the end of this session of parliament convicted for not repairing to some church, chapel or usual place of common prayer, to hear divine service there, but forbearing the same, contrary to the tenor of the laws and statutes heretofore made and provided in that behalf, and having any certain place of dwelling and abode within this realm, shall within forty days next after the end of this session of parliament (if they be within this realm, and not restrained or stayed either by imprisonment, or by her Majesty's commandment, or by order and direction of some six or more of the privy council, or by such sickness and infirmity of body, as they shall not be able to travel without imminent danger of life, and in such cases of absence out of the realm, restraint or stay, then within twenty days next after they shall return into the realm, and be enlarged of such imprisonment or restraint, and shall be able to travel) repair to their place of dwelling where they usually heretofore made their common abode, and shall not at any time after pass or remove above five miles from thence.

III. And also that every person being above the age of sixteen years, born within any her Majesty's realms or dominions, or made denizen, and having, or which hereafter shall have, any certain place of dwelling and abode within this realm, which being then a popish recusant, shall at any time hereafter be lawfully convicted for not repairing to some church, chapel or usual place of common prayer to hear divine service there, but forbearing the same contrary to the said laws and statutes, and being within this realm at the time that they shall be convicted, shall within forty days next after the same conviction (if they be not restrained or stayed by imprisonment or otherwise, as is aforesaid, and in such cases of restraint and stay, then within twenty days next after they shall be enlarged of such imprisonment or restraint, and shall be able to travel) repair to their place of usual dwelling and abode, and shall not at any time after pass or remove above five miles from thence; (2) upon pain that every person and persons that shall offend against the tenor and intent of this act in any thing before-mentioned, shall lose and forfeit all his and their goods and chattels, and shall also lose and forfeit to the Queen's majesty all the lands, tenements and hereditaments, and all the rents and annuities of every such person so doing or offending, during the life of the same offender. *Recusants that shall be convicted hereafter shall repair to their usual dwelling.* *The penalty of an offender.*

IV. And be it also enacted by the authority aforesaid, That every person above the age of sixteen years, born within any her Majesty's realms or dominions, not having any certain place of dwelling and abode within this realm, and being a popish recusant, not usually repairing to some church, chapel or usual place of common prayer, but forbearing the same contrary to the same laws and statutes in that behalf made, shall within forty days next after the end of this session of parliament (if they be then within this realm, and not imprisoned, restrained or stayed as aforesaid, and in such case of absence out of the realm, imprisonment, restraint or stay, then within twenty days next after they shall return into the realm, and be enlarged of such imprisonment or restraint, and shall be able to travel) repair to the place where such person was born, or where the father or mother of such person shall then be dwelling, and shall not at any time after remove or pass above five miles from thence; (2) upon pain that every person *What a recusant shall do that hath no place of abode.* *The forfeiture of a* and persons which shall offend against the tenor and intent of this act in any thing before mentioned, shall lose and forfeit all his and their goods and chattels, and shall also forfeit to the Queen's majesty all the lands, tenements and hereditaments, and all the rents and annuities of every such person so doing or offending, during the life of the same person.

<small>*recusant removing above five miles from his place of abode.*</small>

V. And be it further enacted by the authority aforesaid, That every such offender as is before mentioned, which hath or shall have any lands, tenements or hereditaments, by copy of court-roll, or by any other customary tenure at the will of the lord, according to the custom of any manor, shall forfeit all and singular his and their said lands, tenements and hereditaments so holden by copy of court-roll or customary tenure, as aforesaid, for and during the life of such offender (if his or her estate so long continue) to the lord or lords of whom the same be immediately holden, if the same lord or lords be not then a popish recusant, and convicted for not coming to church to hear divine service, but forbearing the same contrary to the laws and statutes aforesaid, nor seised or possessed upon trust, to the use or behoof of any such recusant as aforesaid, and in such case the same forfeiture to be to the Queen's majesty.

<small>*A recusant copyholder departing five miles from his place of abode.*</small>

VI. Provided always, and be it further enacted by the authority aforesaid, That all such persons as by the intent and true meaning of this act are to make their repair to their place of dwelling and abode, or to the place where they were born, or where their father or mother shall be dwelling, and not to remove or pass above five miles from thence as is aforesaid, shall within twenty days next after their coming to any of the said places (as the case shall happen) notify their coming thither, and present themselves, and deliver their true names in writing, to the minister or curate of the same parish, and to the constable, headborough or tithingman of the town, and thereupon the said minister or curate shall presently enter the same into a book to be kept in every parish for that purpose.

<small>*Recusants shall notify their living, and deliver their names to the curate.*</small>

VII. And afterward the said minister or curate, and the said constable, headborough or tithingman, shall certify the same in writing to the justices of the peace of the same county at the next general or quarter-sessions to be holden in the same county, and the said justices shall cause the same to be entred by the clerk of the peace in the rolls of the same sessions.

<small>*Recusants names certified to the justices.*</small>

VIII. *And to the end that the realm be not pestered and overcharged with the multitude of such seditious and dangerous people as is aforesaid, who having little or no ability to answer or satisfy any competent penalty for their contempt and disobedience of the said laws and statutes, and being committed to prison for the same, do live for the most part in better case there, than they could if they were abroad at their own liberty;* (2) the lords spiritual and temporal, and the commons, in this present parliament assembled, do most humbly and instantly beseech the Queen's majesty, that it may be further enacted, That if any such person or persons, being a popish recusant (not being a *feme covert*, and not having lands, tenements, rents or annuities, of an absolute estate of inheritance or freehold, of the clear yearly value of twenty marks, above all charges, to their own use and behoof, and not upon any secret trust or confidence for any other, or goods and chattels in their own right, and to their own proper use and behoof, and not upon any such secret trust and confidence for any other, above the value of forty pounds) shall not within the time before in this act in that behalf limited and appointed, repair to their place of usual dwelling and abode, if they have any, or else to the place where they were born, or where their father or mother shall be dwelling, according to the tenor and intent of this present act; and thereupon notify their coming, and present themselves, and deliver their true names in writing to the minister or curate of the parish, and to the constable, headborough or tithingman of the town, within such time, and in such manner and form as is aforesaid; or at any time after such their repairing to any such place as is before appointed, shall pass or remove above five miles from the same; (3) and shall not within three months next after such person shall be apprehended or taken for offending as is aforesaid, conform themselves to the obedience of the laws and statutes of this realm, in coming usually to the church to hear divine service, and in making such publick confession and submission, as hereafter in this act is appointed and expressed, being thereunto required by the bishop of the diocese, or any justice of the peace of the county where the same person shall happen to be, or by the minister or curate of the parish; (4) that in every such case every such offender, being thereunto warned or required by any two justices of the peace or coroner of the same county where such offenders shall then be, shall upon his or their corporal oath before any two justices of the peace, or coroner of the same county, abjure this realm of *England,* and all other the Queen's majesty's dominions for ever; (5) and thereupon shall depart out of this realm at such haven and port, and within such time, as shall in that behalf be assigned and appointed by the said justices of peace or

[marginal notes:] The penalty of a recusant of small ability not repairing to the place appointed, or departing thence.

Recusants abjuring and departing the realm.

coroner, before whom such abjuration shall be made, unless the same offenders be letted or stayed by such lawful and reasonable means or causes, as by the common laws of this realm are permitted and allowed in cases of abjuration for felony; and in such cases of let or stay; then within such reasonable and convenient time after, as the common law requireth in case of abjuration for felony as is aforesaid.

<small>Entering abjuration of record, and certifying the same.</small>

IX. And that every justice of peace or coroner before whom any such abjuration shall happen to be made as is aforesaid, shall cause the same presently to be entred of record before them, and shall certify the same to the justices of assizes or gaol-delivery of the said county, at the next assizes or gaol-delivery to be holden in the same county.

<small>It shall be felony for a recusant not to abjure, not going, or returning without licence.</small>

X. And if any such offender, which by the tenor and intent of this act is to be abjured as is aforesaid, shall refuse to make such abjuration as is aforesaid, or after such abjuration made shall not go to such haven, and within such time as is before appointed, and from thence depart out of this realm, according to this present act, or after such his departure shall return or come again into any her Majesty's realms or dominions, without her Majesty's special licence in that behalf first had and obtained; that then in every such case the person so offending shall be adjudged a felon, and shall suffer and lose as in case of felony without benefit of clergy.

<small>A jesuit or priest refusing to answer shall be imprisoned.
1 Salk. 351.</small>

XI. And be it further enacted and ordained by the authority aforesaid, That if any person which shall be suspected to be a jesuit, seminary or massing priest, being examined by any person having lawful authority in that behalf to examine such person which shall be so suspected, shall refuse to answer directly and truly whether he be a jesuit, or a seminary or massing priest, as is aforesaid, every such person so refusing to answer shall for his disobedience and contempt in that behalf, be committed to prison by such as shall examine him as is aforesaid, and thereupon shall remain and continue in prison without bail or mainprise, until he shall make direct and true answer to the said questions whereupon he shall be so examined.

<small>Licence to travel above five miles.
Repealed by 3 Jac. 1. c. 5, s. 6.</small>

XII. Provided nevertheless, and be it further enacted by the authority aforesaid, That if any of the persons which are hereby limited and appointed to continue and abide within five miles of their usual dwelling-place, or of such place where they were born, or where their father or mother shall be dwelling as is aforesaid, shall have necessary occasion or business to go and travel out of the compass of the said five miles; that then and in every such

APPENDIX 427

case, upon licence in that behalf to be gotten under the hands of two of the justices of the peace of the same county, with the privity and assent in writing of the bishop of the diocese, or of the lieutenant, or of any deputy-lieutenant of the same county, under their hands, it shall and may be lawful for every such person to go and travel about such their necessary business, and for such time only for their travelling, attending and returning, as shall be comprized in the same licence ; any thing before in this act to the contrary notwithstanding.

XIII. Provided also, That if any such person so restrained as is aforesaid, shall be urged by process, without fraud or covin, or be bounden without fraud or covin, to make appearance in any of her Majesty's courts, or shall be sent for, commanded or required by any three or more of her Majesty's privy council, or by any four or more of any commissioners to be in that behalf nominated and assigned by her Majesty, to make appearance before her Majesty's said council or commissioners ; that in every such case, every such person so bounden, urged, commanded or required to make such appearance, shall not incur any pain, forfeiture or loss for travelling to make appearance accordingly, nor for his abode concerning the same, nor for convenient time for his return back again upon the same. Persons urged by process or commandment.

XIV. And be it further provided and enacted by the authority aforesaid, That if any such person or persons so restrained as is aforesaid, shall be bound, or ought to yield and render their bodies to the sheriff of the county where they shall happen to be, upon proclamation in that behalf without fraud or covin to be made ; that then in every such case, every person which shall be so bounden, or ought to yield and render their body as aforesaid, shall not incur any pain, forfeiture or loss for travelling for that intent and purpose only, without any fraud or covin, nor for convenient time taken for the return back again upon the same. Persons which are to yield their bodies to the sheriff.

XV. And furthermore be it enacted by the authority of this present parliament, That if any person or persons that shall at any time hereafter offend against this act, shall before he or they shall be thereof convicted, come to some parish church on some *Sunday* or other festival day, and then and there hear divine service, and at service-time, before the sermon, or reading of the gospel, make publick and open submission and declaration of his and their conformity to her Majesty's laws and statutes, as hereafter in this act is declared and appointed ; that then the same offender shall thereupon be clearly discharged of and from all An offender upon open submission shall be discharged.

and every pains and forfeitures inflicted or imposed by this act for any of the said offences in this act contained : (2) the same submission to be made as hereafter followeth : that is to say,

<small>The form of the submission.</small>

XVI. I *A. B.* do humbly confess and acknowledge, That I have grievously offended God in contemning her Majesty's godly and lawful government and authority, by absenting my self from church, and from hearing divine service, contrary to the godly laws and statutes of this realm : (2) and I am heartily sorry for the same, and do acknowledge and testify in my conscience, that the bishop or see of *Rome* hath not, nor ought to have, any power or authority over her Majesty, or within any her Majesty's realms or dominions : (3) and I do promise and protest, without any dissimulation, or any colour or means of any dispensation, that from henceforth I will from time to time obey and perform her Majesty's laws and statutes, in repairing to the church, and hearing divine service, and do my uttermost endeavour to maintain and defend the same.

<small>The minister shall enter the submission.</small>

XVII. And that every minister or curate of every parish, where such submission and declaration of conformity shall hereafter be so made by any such offender as aforesaid, shall presently enter the same into a book to be kept in every parish for that purpose, and within ten days then next following shall certify the same in writing to the bishop of the same diocese.

<small>A recusant submitting, falleth into a relapse. 1 Bulstr. 133.</small>

XVIII. Provided nevertheless, That if any such offender, after such submission made as is aforesaid, shall afterward fall into relapse, or eftsoons become a recusant, in not repairing to church to hear divine service, but shall forbear the same, contrary to the laws and statutes in that behalf made and provided ; that then every such offender shall lose all such benefit as he or she might otherwise by virtue of this act have or enjoy by reason of their said submission ; and shall thereupon stand and remain in such plight, condition and degree, to all intents, as though such submission had never been made.

<small>Women bound, saving for abjuration. Bridg. 120.</small>

XIX. Provided always, and be it enacted by the authority aforesaid, That all and every woman married, or hereafter to be married, shall be bound by all and every article, branch and matter contained in this statute, other than the branch and article of abjuration before-mentioned : (2) and that no such woman married, or to be married, during marriage, shall be in any wise forced or compelled to abjure, or be abjured, by virtue of this act ; any thing therein contained to the contrary thereof nothwithstanding. 23 *Eliz. c.* 1. 29 *Eliz. c.* 6. 1 *Jac.* 1. *c.* 4. 3 *Jac.* 1. *c.* 4, 5.

39 ELIZABETH.

Cap. VIII.

An act concerning the confirmation and establishment of the deprivations of divers bishops and deans, in the beginning of her Majesty's reign.

Whereas divers and sundry persons exercising the office and function of bishops and deans of divers sees and bishopricks, and deanries within this realm in the reign of our late sovereign lady Queen Mary, were before the tenth day of November in the fourth year of the most happy and blessed government of the Queen's most excellent Majesty that now is, lawfully and justly deprived from such bishopricks and deanries as they severally enjoyed, and took upon them to hold, and in their steads and places sundry excellent and worthy men duly preferred to the same: (2) and whereas the parties so deprived did notwithstanding, as is pretended, make secret appeals, and used other secret means, pretending thereby to support the continuance of their said offices and functions, Be it &c.

www.ingramcontent.com/pod-product-compliance
Lightning Source LLC
Chambersburg PA
CBHW022136300426
44115CB00006B/218